Populism, Demagoguery, and Rhetoric
in Historical Perspective

Populism, Demagoguery, and Rhetoric in Historical Perspective

Edited by
GIUSEPPE BALLACCI
and
ROB GOODMAN

OXFORD
UNIVERSITY PRESS

Oxford University Press is a department of the University of Oxford.
It furthers the University's objective of excellence in research, scholarship,
and education by publishing worldwide. Oxford is a registered trade mark of
Oxford University Press in the UK and certain other countries.

Published in the United States of America by Oxford University Press
198 Madison Avenue, New York, NY 10016, United States of America.

© Oxford University Press 2024

All rights reserved. No part of this publication may be reproduced, stored in
a retrieval system, or transmitted, in any form or by any means, without the
prior permission in writing of Oxford University Press, or as expressly permitted
by law, by license, or under terms agreed with the appropriate reproduction
rights organization. Inquiries concerning reproduction outside the scope of the
above should be sent to the Rights Department, Oxford University Press, at the
address above.

You must not circulate this work in any other form
and you must impose this same condition on any acquirer.

CIP data is on file at the Library of Congress

ISBN 978-0-19-765098-1 (pbk.)
ISBN 978-0-19-765097-4 (hbk.)

DOI: 10.1093/oso/9780197650974.001.0001

Paperback printed by Marquis Book Printing, Canada
Hardback printed by Bridgeport National Bindery, Inc., United States of America

Contents

List of Contributors   vii

    Introduction: Populism, demagoguery, rhetoric and history   1
    Giuseppe Ballacci and Rob Goodman

PART I. ANCIENT AND EARLY MODERN THEMES

1. *Parrhêsia*: The Unbridled Tongue in Ancient Democratic Athens   29
    Arlene W. Saxonhouse

2. Democracy's Shadow: The Problem of Populism in Plato's Political Thought   55
    Tae-Yeoun Keum

3. "Naked" Speech in Late Republican Rome   78
    Rob Goodman

4. Rhetoric and Republicanism in the Thought of Brunetto Latini   103
    Cary J. Nederman

5. Republicanism and Populism in Early Modern Italian Political Thought: The Case of Democracy as the Rule of the Poor   123
    Alessandro Mulieri

6. On the Battlefield of Rhetoric: Eloquence, Virtue, and Political Legitimacy in Italian Humanism   146
    David Ragazzoni

PART II. MODERN AND CONTEMPORARY THEMES

7. Demagoguery, Populism, and Political Culture in Cooper's *The American Democrat*   173
    Daniel Kapust

8. Anti-Parliamentary Politics: Populist Momentum in Historical Perspective   201
    Kari Palonen

CONTENTS

9. Vilfredo Pareto on Rhetoric and Populism 222
   Giovanni Damele

10. Palaces for the People: How and of What Should Public Buildings Persuade Citizens in a Democracy? 241
    Jan-Werner Müller

11. Reconstructing Pluralism and Populism: Not "Opposites" but a More Complex Configuration 268
    Mark Wenman

12. Democracy, Plutocracy, and the Populist Cry of Pain 299
    John P. McCormick

13. Populism, Celebrity Politics, and Politainment 315
    Paula Diehl

14. Rhetorical Resonance: From Everyday Speech to Insurrection 341
    Simon Lambek

    Conclusion 361
    Giuseppe Ballacci and Rob Goodman

    Index 365

Contributors

Giuseppe Ballacci is Research Fellow at the Centre for Ethics, Politics and Society (CEPS) at the University of Minho.

Giovanni Damele is Assistant Professor of Political Philosophy at Universidade Nova de Lisboa.

Paula Diehl is Professor of Political Theory, History of Ideas, and Political Culture at Kiel University.

Rob Goodman is Associate Professor of Politics and Public Administration at Toronto Metropolitan University.

Daniel Kapust is Judith Hicks Stiehm Chair in Political Theory at the University of Wisconsin-Madison.

Tae-Yeoun Keum is Assistant Professor of Political Science at the University of California, Santa Barbara.

Simon Lambek is Assistant Professor of Political Science at the University of the Fraser Valley.

John P. McCormick is Professor of Political Science at the University of Chicago.

Alessandro Mulieri is Global Marie Sklodowska-Curie Fellow at the University of Pennsylvania and Ca' Foscari University, and Research Associate at KU Leuven.

Jan-Werner Müller is Roger Williams Straus Professor of Social Sciences and Professor of Politics at Princeton University.

Cary J. Nederman is Professor of Political Science at Texas A&M University.

Kari Palonen is Professor Emeritus of Political Science at the University of Jyväskylä.

David Ragazzoni is Core Lecturer in Contemporary Civilization at Columbia University.

Arlene W. Saxonhouse is Caroline Robbins Collegiate Professor Emerita of Political Science and Women's Studies at the University of Michigan.

Mark Wenman is Associate Professor in Political Theory at the University of Birmingham.

Introduction

Populism, demagoguery, rhetoric and history

Giuseppe Ballacci and Rob Goodman[1]

Populism is one of the most discussed topics in political theory—to say nothing of political science as a whole. In a relatively short amount of time, populism has developed into one of our discipline's central objects of study. As populist or populist-adjacent figures and movements proliferate, academic conferences, articles, monographs, and edited volumes follow in their wake, hopefully not too far behind.

What is good news for the study of populism as a whole—its growth into a rich and complexly articulated field of inquiry—is, however, equivocal news for any particular new entry into that study. To a degree that was simply not the case ten or even five years ago, a new work or collection of works on populism has to justify its existence, its claim to be heard above the noise of a crowded room. What more is there to say?

We are confident that the works contributed to this volume will speak persuasively for themselves. Individually and collectively, these chapters by leading scholars of populism, rhetoric, and the history of political thought demonstrate that a great deal remains to be said—about the roots of populism in the history of political thought and its divergences from those roots, about the value of rhetoric as a coherent tradition and mode of analysis in political theory, about the historically and theoretically informed assessment of populism's prospects, and more.

To what extent is contemporary populism a distinctively modern phenomenon? To what extent does it have precedents in earlier periods of political history? And how can studying populism in the light of rhetoric and the history of political thought help us answer these questions? As a collection

---

[1] This work is part of the project "Populism, Demagoguery, and Rhetoric in Historical Perspective," funded by the Foundation for Science and Technology of Portugal. https://doi.org/10.54499/2022.05060.PTDC.

of essays, the chapters that follow demonstrate the importance of these questions and offer some provocative answers. They help to clarify the very concept of populism, as well as its relationship to and implications for liberal democracy and representative government. They help to fill one of the most conspicuous gaps in the populism literature—our insufficient understanding of populism in historical context. These contributions draw from a wide range of methodologies and perspectives on populism, and they speak on their own behalf more eloquently than we can speak for them. Nevertheless, taken as a whole, they suggest a distinctive approach to the study of populism, an approach we hope to defend in this Introduction.

This volume is titled *Populism, Demagoguery, and Rhetoric in Historical Perspective*, and we think that the best way to express our idea of its contribution to the field is to consider each of those terms separately. How does the study of rhetoric help us to understand populism? How does the phenomenon of demagoguery help us to understand populism? And how does a deep historical perspective—which, as a look at the table of contents will indicate, extends from democratic Athens to the current century—help us to understand populism?

We can begin with rhetoric. Put simply, we believe that the rhetorical approach can do valuable work in bridging the gap between the theoretical approaches that have heretofore dominated the study of populism—that it can bring a new degree of coherence to the field. To explain this claim, it will help to discuss a number of those theoretical approaches, before turning to the value of rhetoric as a kind of theoretical bridge.[2]

One benefit of the proliferation of populist studies, which we observed at the outset, is an increased opportunity to systematize approaches to the field. The definition of populism remains hotly contested. But at the very least, it is increasingly possible to categorize the range of definitions on offer, and to consider fruitful points of overlap within and between these categories.

Consider two recent classifications of approaches to populism. Benjamin Moffitt proposes four approaches: populism as "ideology," "strategy," "discourse," and "political logic."[3] Cas Mudde proposes three: the "ideational,"

---

[2] : The discussion of rhetoric and populism below draws from arguments we have made in more detail in Giuseppe Ballacci and Rob Goodman, "Populism as Form and Content: Toward a Holistic Approach," *Populism* 6, no. 1 (2023): 1–27.

[3] Benjamin Moffitt, *The Global Rise of Populism: Performance, Political Style, and Representation* (Palo Alto, CA: Stanford University Press, 2016), 17.

the "political-strategic," and the "socio-cultural."[4] It is a promising start that these classifications mostly overlap, with just one difference (Moffitt reserves a category for Ernesto Laclau's conception of populism as "political logic,"[5] to which we return below). But we argue that a further degree of simplification is possible. In our view, the essential fault line in definitions of populism runs between those that stress its ideational aspects and those that stress its formal/stylistic aspects. In other words, the fault line runs between approaches to populism as *content* and approaches to populism as *form*.

The first approach has identified the following features as characteristic of populist ideology: the reduction of the ideological spectrum to a basic opposition between the pure people and the corrupt elite, along with the defense of a homogenous idea of "the people" and of the paramount principle of popular sovereignty.[6] In Mudde's well-known formulation of this view, populism is "an ideology that considers society to be ultimately separated into two homogeneous and antagonistic groups, 'the pure people' versus 'the corrupt elite,' and which argues that politics should be an expression of the *volonté générale* (general will) of the people."[7] In this view, populism is primarily an ideology, rather than a style. But in contrast to "thick-centered" ideologies (such as fascism or socialism) with more comprehensively developed notions about human nature, society, and the political, "thin-centered ideologies such as populism have a restricted morphology, which necessary appears attached to—and sometimes is even assimilated into—other ideologies." As the ideational approach generally has it, left-populism might conceive of politics as a struggle between the plebeians and the moneyed elite, and right-populism might conceive of politics as a struggle between the authentically native people and the cosmopolitan elite, but both are equally populist.

---

[4] Cas Mudde, "Populism: An Ideational Approach," in *The Oxford Handbook of Populism*, ed. Cristóbal Rovira Kaltwasser, Paul Taggart, Paulina Ochoa Espejo, and Pierre Ostiguy (Oxford: Oxford University Press, 2017), 27–47. A sevenfold classification is also offered by Takis S. Pappas: populism as "movement," "style," "ideology," "discourse," "strategy," and "political culture," and as an "omnibus concept." See Pappas, "Modern Populism: Research Advances, Conceptual and Methodological Pitfalls, and the Minimal Definition," in *Oxford Research Encyclopedia of Politics*, ed. William R. Thompson (Oxford: Oxford University Press, 2016). https://doi.org/10.1093/acrefore/9780190228637.013.17.

[5] Ernesto Laclau, *On Populist Reason* (London: Verso, 2005), 67.

[6] E.g., Margaret Canovan, "Taking Politics to the People: Populism as the Ideology of Democracy," in *Democracies and the Populist Challenge*, ed. Yves Mény and Yves Surel (London: Palgrave Macmillan, 2002), 25–44; Cas Mudde, "The Populist Zeitgeist," *Government & Opposition* 39, no. 4 (2004): 541–63; Mudde, "Populism: An Ideational Approach"; Ben Stanley, "The Thin Ideology of Populism," *Journal of Political Ideologies* 13, no. 1 (2008): 95–110; Jan-Werner Müller, *What Is Populism?* (Philadelphia: University of Pennsylvania Press, 2016).

[7] Mudde, "The Populist Zeitgeist," 543. See also Mudde and Rovira Kaltwasser, *Populism: A Very Short Introduction* (Oxford: Oxford University Press, 2017), 6.

The second approach looks to the language, symbols, and aesthetics adopted by populists, as well as the ways in which populists perform their political role: for instance, how they interpellate, mobilize, organize, and represent their constituencies. We consider this a *formal* approach, which emphasizes both the basic underlying form of populist discourse (the division of society into two antagonistic blocs[8]) and the more specific stylistic qualities with which that discourse is manifested: emotive or disruptive rhetoric,[9] spectacle,[10] invocations of imminent crisis,[11] or a tendency to adopt modes of presentation that are self-consciously "of the people."[12] We also consider it reasonable to fold into this category the "strategic" approach to populist movements, which focuses on populism as a means of capturing power through the combination of charismatic leadership, plebiscitarianism, and unmediated bonds between the populist leader and the people.[13] We do so[14] because we follow Laclau and Chantal Mouffe in presuming that discursive practices can be both linguistic and non-linguistic.[15] Disruptive or "unmannerly" speech is an aspect of populist discourse, but so is the populist strategy of promoting unmediated popular identification with the leader. Both are "dimensions of the discourses through which these movements and political identities are constituted."[16]

There is, of course, some overlap between these two sets of approaches. From one perspective, for instance, charismatic leadership is a formal aspect of populism, given the way that charisma seems to transcend ideological categories. But from another perspective, it is part of populism's ideological

---

[8] Yannis Stavrakakis, "Discourse Theory in Populism Research," *Journal of Language and Politics* 16 (2017): 523–34; Giorgos Katsambekis, "Constructing 'the People' of Populism: A Critique of the Ideational Approach from a Discursive Perspective," *Journal of Political Ideologies* 27, no. 1 (2022): 53–74.

[9] Pierre-André Taguieff, *L'illusion populiste. Essai sur les démagogies de l'âge démocratique* (Paris: Flammarion, 2007); Jan Jagers and Stefaan Walgrave, "Populism as Political Communication Style: An Empirical Study of Political Parties' Discourse in Belgium," *European Journal of Political Research* 46, no. 3 (2007): 319–45; Carlos de la Torre, *Populist Seduction in Latin America* (Athens: Ohio University Press, 2010).

[10] Meghan Sutherland, "Populism and Spectacle," *Cultural Studies* 26 (2012): 330–45; Benjamin Moffitt and Simon Tormey, "Rethinking Populism: Politics, Mediatisation and Political Style," *Political Studies* 62, no. 2 (2014): 381–97; Moffitt, *The Global Rise of Populism*, 43–45.

[11] Moffitt, *The Global Rise of Populism*, 38.

[12] Ostiguy, "Populism: A Socio-Cultural Approach," in *The Oxford Handbook of Populism*, 79.

[13] E.g., Torcuato S. Di Tella, "Populism into the Twenty-First Century," *Government and Opposition* 32, no. 2 (1997): 187–200; Taguieff, *L'illusion populiste*; Kurt Weyland, "Populism: A Political-Strategic Approach," in *The Oxford Handbook of Populism*, 48–72.

[14] Contra Christopher J. Bickerton and Carlo Invernizzi Accetti, *Technopopulism: The New Logic of Democratic Politics* (New York: Oxford University Press, 2021), 25–26.

[15] Ernesto Laclau and Chantal Mouffe, *Hegemony and Socialist Strategy* (London: Verso, 2001); Laclau, *On Populist Reason*, 13.

[16] Yannis Stavrakakis, "Religion and Populism in Contemporary Greece," in *Populism and the Mirror of Democracy*, ed. Francisco Panizza (London: Verso, 2005), 233.

content, in that an emphasis on charisma can go hand in hand with particular political positions, such as decisionism or a distrust of representative procedures and institutions. In fact, as we go on to argue, overlaps like these are quite frequent: they suggest that populist form and content are ultimately mutually reinforcing. But for the moment, we simply want to emphasize our judgment that these two broad families of study—populism as content and populism as form—are currently the most influential in the literature, with the content-based or ideational approach generally occupying the leading position. While proponents of the formal/stylistic or discursive approach do not always reject the ideational approach *in toto*, for the most part they assume that the two families of study stand in a relationship that is tense or even antagonistic, rather than complementary.[17]

But where does this assessment leave populism as "political logic," or the view associated with Laclau? From our perspective, Laclau's most important claim is that the main stylistic features of populism—namely, its ideological emptiness, the emotional character of its discourse, and the role it gives to charismatic leaders—play a crucial role in populism's constitution of the political and its division of society into two sharply distinguished blocs. Populism, for Laclau, is an especially pointed attempt to construct these blocs out of the complexity of the social world; to the extent its forms of discourse make such constructions possible, they do important political work.[18] Given that Laclau's theory situates the political importance of populism entirely in its forms, we consider his to be a formal theory of populism.[19] This approach has, in turn, been criticized for its excessive formalism and self-validating generality,[20] as well as for entailing a problematic conception of the people-as-one and a strong decisionism.[21]

---

[17] E.g., Yannis Stavrakakis and Giorgos Katsambekis, "Left-Wing Populism in the European Periphery: The Case of SYRIZA," *Journal of Political Ideologies* 19, no. 2 (2014): 119–42; Paris Aslanidis, "Is Populism an Ideology? A Refutation and a New Perspective," *Political Studies* 64, no. 1 (2016): 88–104; Benjamin Moffitt, *Populism* (Cambridge: Polity Press, 2020), ch. 2; Katsambekis, "Constructing 'the People' of Populism"; Ostiguy, Panizza, and Moffitt, "Introduction," in *Populism in Global Perspective: A Performative and Discursive Approach*, ed. Ostiguy, Panizza, and Moffitt (New York: Routledge, 2021), 1–18.

[18] Laclau, *On Populist Reason*, 67, 161–63.

[19] Ibid., 44.

[20] Benjamin Arditi, *Politics on the Edges of Liberalism: Difference, Populism, Revolution, Agitation* (Edinburgh: Edinburgh University Press, 2007); Cristóbal Rovira Kaltwasser, "The Ambivalence of Populism: Threat and Corrective for Democracy," *Democratization* 9, no. 2 (2012): 184–208; Felipe Carreira da Silva and Mónica Brito Vieira, "Populism and the Politics of Redemption," *Thesis Eleven* 149, no. 1 (2018): 16.

[21] Nadia Urbinati, *Democracy Disfigured: Opinion, Truth, and the People* (Cambridge, MA: Harvard University Press, 2014), 132; Camila Vergara, "Populism as Plebeian Politics: Inequality, Domination, and Popular Empowerment," *Journal of Political Philosophy* 28, no. 2 (2020): 231.

Partly in response to such criticism, "post-Laclaunian" scholars have moved to reintroduce sociology into the study of populism, while retaining Laclau's focus on discursive and articulatory practices. But from our perspective, Laclau's approach and those approaches that descend from his work still fail to unpack the implicit ideological content of populist style and forms.[22] Further, Laclau describes populism as "the political operation par excellence": that is, "the construction of a people."[23] But if this is the case, then the phenomenon of populism is essentially collapsed into the category of politics itself. However accurate that claim may be as a high-level assessment, it leaves us theoretically unable to identify or evaluate a concrete set of populist movements, practices, or rhetorics, and it leaves empirical political scientists with a definition that is quite difficult to operationalize.[24]

We propose, instead, to draw from the important insight that populist content and form entail one another, without going so far as to define populism as the essence of politics. In fact, it is our contention that the two families of approaches that we identified above, populism as content and populism as form, need one another. Each supplies some insights that the other, taken on its own, seems to lack.

For one, we argue that the content-centered approach can benefit from an increased attention to form and style. Proponents of this approach tend to downplay or neglect the role of forms in populism, not enlisting them among its core features and implicitly suggesting that populism can attach to a wide range of forms.[25] By contrast, we would argue that the plausible range of populist forms and styles is more limited, precisely because populism is a thin ideology. Given its relative lack of ideological content, in comparison with thicker ideologies, populism relies heavily on its forms and styles in order to convey its political message. Its content is conveyed not ideationally but performatively, in the ways in which populism engages, acts, and argues in a given political context. The people/elite dichotomy that is stressed in the ideational account also serves to limit populism's plausible forms, because this

---

[22] Nadia Urbinati, *Me the People: How Populism Transforms Democracy* (Cambridge, MA: Harvard University Press, 2019), 206.

[23] Laclau, *On Populist Reason*, 153.

[24] Nevertheless, some scholars have argued that Laclau's theory can in fact be operationalized by focusing on the two criteria of "people-centrism" and "anti-elitism." Stavrakakis, for instance, points out that a host of empirical research has been conducted within the framework of Laclau's discursive approach. See Stavrakakis, "Discourse Theory in Populism Research."

[25] Mudde, "Populism: An Ideational Approach," 30; Mudde and Rovira Kaltwasser, *Populism*, 62.

dichotomy centers populist discourse on questions of representation, and the formal qualities needed to make representation authentic.[26]

On the other hand, some advocates of the formal/stylistic approach, including such post-Laclaunians as Moffitt, acknowledge in principle that populist "style and content are interrelated."[27] Yet downplaying the ideological content of populism makes it difficult for advocates of this approach to explore the details of that interrelation—for instance, to explain why populist styles are adopted by some political actors and not others, or why some democracies harbor a greater tendency to populist politics than others. We contend that understanding key stylistic components of populism, such as "bad manners," requires us to make reference to its ideological dimension: in the case of "bad manners," to the principle of popular sovereignty, the idea that liberal democracy leads to the entrenchment of political elites, and the claim that this entrenchment can and should be disrupted by outsiders. We are required, in other words, to consider the ideological stakes of populist performance—a claim that some post-Laclaunians implicitly concede when they distinguish right-wing from left-wing versions of populism on the basis of their different articulatory practices.[28]

Our claim, then, is that scholars of populism can and should do more to integrate the study of populist content and populist form. Populism's very ideological thinness means that its formal/stylistic dimension takes on a crucial role, in the sense that populism tends to convey its views performatively, through particular styles and forms of action.[29] We propose that populism can be more fruitfully studied as a set of *content-forms*: formal/stylistic aspects that inevitably entail ideological positions, even if they do not always do so explicitly or coherently. Let us take a few examples of these content-forms in order to show how this integration might work in practice.

---

[26] Ostiguy, "Populism: A Socio-Cultural Approach," 92.

[27] Moffitt, *The Global Rise of Populism*, 49.

[28] Yannis Stavrakakis, Alexandros Kioupkiolis, Katsambekis, Nikos Nikisianis, and Thomas Siomos, "Contemporary Left-Wing Populism in Latin America: Leadership, Horizontalism, and Postdemocracy in Chávez's Venezuela," *Latin American Politics and Society* 58, no. 3 (2016): 51–76; Ostiguy and Moffitt, "Who Would Identify with an 'Empty Signifier'? The Relational, Performative Approach to Populism," in *Populism in Global Perspective*, 47–72.

[29] To be sure, form and content are connected in all ideologies. What sets a "thin" ideology like populism apart is the degree to which its form and content are tightly linked. Unlike "thicker" ideologies, such as socialism or liberal democracy, which draw on a more robust set of key texts and intellectual traditions, populist content is conveyed to a proportionally greater extent through its forms—that is, performatively rather than ideationally. See Alan Finlayson, "Ideology and Political Rhetoric," in *The Oxford Handbook of Political Ideologies*, ed. Michael Freeden, Lyman Tower Sargent, and Marc Stears (Oxford: Oxford University Press, 2013), 199.

Consider what many scholars have characterized as the imprecise, elusive, and simplistic qualities of populist discourse.[30] On the one hand, of course, these are stylistic features of populist rhetoric. But on the other hand, they are politically and ideologically meaningful features, because they enable populists to construct "the people" through the inclusion of as many heterogeneous social instances as possible. As Laclau puts it, "the people" is an empty signifier: the very vagueness and imprecision of the concept enable as many demands as possible to accumulate around it, without requiring that the constitutive parts of "the people" significantly change their identities or undergo strong persuasion.[31]

These features of populist rhetoric can be both a strategic and a democratic asset, in that the category of "the people" always remains open to resignification.[32] At the same time, these features also contribute to populist decisionism, as a means of imposing stability and coherence on the inarticulate and multiply-constituted populist subject.[33] And again, decisionism has roots in populism's ideological and discursive elements. Michael Freeden, in fact, argues that the role of decisionism in a given ideology is directly proportional to its level of ideological inarticulation. The less an ideology is articulated, the less it can play the role of "converting the inevitable variety of options into the monolithic certainty which is the unavoidable feature of political decision, and which is the basis of the forging of a political identity."[34] A similar dynamic is at play in the populist conception of sovereignty as inhering in the voice of a unitary people, in contrast to many liberals' less majoritarian and more mediated view of sovereignty.[35]

Anti-intellectualism and the preference for action over theory are other important items in populism's ideological and stylistic repertoire. In contrast to

---

[30] Kirk A. Hawkins, "Is Chávez Populist?: Measuring Populist Discourse in Comparative Perspective," *Comparative Political Studies* 42, no. 8 (2009): 1040–67; Moffitt and Tormey, "Rethinking Populism"; Ramona Kreis, "The 'Tweet Politics' of President Trump," *Journal of Language and Politics* 16, no. 4 (2017): 607–18; Elena Block and Ralph Negrine, "The Populist Communication Style: Toward a Critical Framework," *International Journal of Communication* 11 (2017): 178–97.

[31] Laclau, *On Populist Reason*, 3–4, 17–18, 67–69, 167; Laclau, "Why Constructing a People Is the Main Task of Radical Politics," *Critical Inquiry* 32, no. 4 (2006): 646–80.

[32] Paris Aslanidis, "Populism as a Collective Action Master Frame for Transnational Mobilization," *Sociological Forum* 33, no. 2 (2018): 458.

[33] Urbinati, *Me the People*, 163.

[34] Michael Freeden, *Ideologies and Political Theory: A Conceptual Approach* (Oxford: Oxford University Press, 1996), 76–77.

[35] Urbinati, "Populism and the Principle of Majority," in *The Oxford Handbook of Populism*, 571–89; Alessandro Ferrara, "Can Political Liberalism Help Us Rescue 'the People' from Populism?" *Philosophy & Social Criticism* 44, no. 4 (2018): 463–77.

the liberal emphasis on deliberation and the principle of justification,[36] populist rhetoric stresses urgency, sharp and sometimes Manichean conflicts, the need for immediate and resolute action, and frustration with needlessly complex proceduralism.[37] We can observe populism's resistance to intellectualism in the absence of a "Populist International" and the paucity of widely acknowledged, foundational populist texts of the kind that characterize and shape thicker ideologies. By contrast, the ideological content of populism is generally conveyed performatively rather than textually—but this very skepticism of text, deliberation, and justification is essential to populism's political vision. Stylistically, this vision is reflected in a range of key practices of populist discourse, such as the attitude of "flaunting the low,"[38] or the display of affinity for the demotic or common-sense in opposition to the supposed expertise and sophistication of the elites.[39] These practices serve the strategic aim of constructing opposed popular and elite blocs, but they also grow from populism's ideological content.

They also contribute to populism's strongly emotive content, often centered on the affects of anger, outrage, or indignation.[40] Such affects are a natural outgrowth of populism's ideological orientation: What other response is appropriate if the people have been wronged? But populist affects can also take on more optimistic and even utopian coloring, which Margaret Canovan refers to in her description of the "populist mood": the hopeful and redemptive sense of empowerment conveyed by movements to restore justice and rectify betrayals. In both its negative and positive aspects, populist emotionalism shows the influence of the Schmittian view that politics entails conflict for existential stakes, and thus cannot dispense with the extra-rational. Populist emotionalism also responds to the problem of the empty signifier of "the people," which we noted above, helping to build the solidarity of the populist subject through anti-establishment resentment. Resentment is both a recurrent theme in populist rhetoric[41] and a product of

---

[36] Mudde and Rovira Kaltwasser, *Populism*, 64; Eric Merkley, "Anti-Intellectualism, Populism, and Motivated Resistance to Expert Consensus," *Public Opinion Quarterly* 84, no. 1 (2020): 24–48.

[37] Jagers and Walgrave, "Populism as Political Communication Style"; Müller, *What Is Populism?*, ch. 1; Mudde and Rovira Kaltwasser, *Populism*, 12; Fabio Wolkenstein, "Populism, Liberal Democracy and the Ethics of Peoplehood," *European Journal of Political Theory* 18, no. 3 (2019): 330–48.

[38] Ostiguy, "Populism: A Socio-Cultural Approach."

[39] Moffitt, *The Global Rise of Populism*, 57–62; Colleen J. Shogan, "Anti-Intellectualism in the Modern Presidency: A Republican Populism," *Perspectives on Politics* 5, no. 2 (2007): 295–303.

[40] Paolo Cossarini and Fernando Vallespín, *Populism and Passions: Democratic Legitimacy after Austerity* (New York: Routledge, 2019).

[41] Moffitt, *The Global Rise of Populism*, 45ff; Carreira and Brito Vieira, "Populism and the Politics of Redemption."

its political vision, which centers on the betrayal of the people and a future in which such betrayal will finally be rectified.

Last, populist "bad manners" are another feature with both stylistic and ideological aspects.[42] Disruptive rhetoric and political practices help to legitimize populist movements, demonstrating their authenticity, spontaneity, and courage in questioning the status quo. At the same time, the deliberately ill-mannered stance is part of populism's political content, which Benjamin Arditi captures through the metaphor of "the awkward dinner guest," who disrupts the party but also poses embarrassing questions that the other guests would rather avoid.[43] By adopting bad rhetorical manners, then, populist figures position themselves as outsiders to the cozy political club and imply that the more restrained behavior of the other guests is evasive and self-serving.

On the whole, then, a significant number of populism's key features grow out of the interrelationship of its forms and styles, on the one hand, and its ideological content, on the other. This is why we have argued that it makes sense to conceive of them as neither strictly stylistic nor strictly ideological, but as content-forms.

But to make this claim is also to insist on the value of the *rhetorical* study of populism as a bridge between the theoretical approaches we have canvassed. On a more specific level, as many of the chapters in this volume show, rhetoric is a valuable lens for understanding a wide range of populist phenomena. The tradition of rhetoric has long engaged with such issues as claims to representation, struggle between mass and elite, and the political roles of passion and group dynamics—all of which are also central to an understanding of contemporary populism. If a fondness for emotive, norm-breaking, and "commonsensical" language is one of the hallmarks of the populist leader, then placing that language in the context of the long study of political speech can surely help us understand what is distinctive, and what is familiar, about today's populism. We return to this point in the Conclusion to this volume, expanding on the idea of rhetoric as a methodological bridge for integrating political content and form, and as an essential lens for the study of populism.

Now, however, we turn to the question of demagoguery and demagogic rhetoric. In fact, a focus on demagogic rhetoric may be mutually beneficial for the study of rhetoric and of populism within political theory. Rhetoric

---

[42] Moffitt and Tormey, "Rethinking Populism," 392.
[43] Arditi, *Politics on the Edges of Liberalism*, 78.

has dramatically expanded as an area of study in the discipline (over much the same time frame as the expansion of interest in populism), to the point that the "rhetoric revival"[44] is a widely recognized movement among political theorists. In recent years, rhetoric revivalists have worked to correct what they see as the misguided view of an earlier generation of deliberatively oriented theorists who treat rhetoric as a deficient or inherently suspect form of communication. For rhetoric revivalists, by contrast, rhetoric is a valuable "form of reasoning itself," and a source of ideas "of how to generate trust in ways that preserve an audience's autonomy and accord with the norms of friendship."[45]

These are valuable insights and a much-needed counterbalance to rhetoric-skeptical views in the discipline. But sometimes this advocacy can lead rhetoric revivalists to minimize rhetoric's dangers. To cite one chapter title as an illustration: "Rhetoric: A Good Thing."[46] Our conviction is that rhetoric certainly is a good thing under many circumstances, not least for its democratizing propensity to subject political elites to risk and uncertainty in their efforts to understand and persuade mass publics.[47] At the same time, the rhetorical tradition has comprised not only the study of persuasion, but insights into the identification and prevention of dangerous and demagogic speech. The contributors to this volume combine a deep interest and grounding in rhetoric with a willingness to confront and investigate in detail rhetoric's darker aspects, including the pitfalls associated with demagoguery. As the "rhetoric revival" matures, and as the sources of populist politicians' appeal remain deeply contentious, we hope that this volume will represent a valuable intervention into scholarly and public debate.

But just how applicable is the category of demagoguery to the study of populism? Today, the concept of demagoguery has lost much of its relevance in our academic vocabulary. Once a staple of political thought, it is now often considered both too normatively charged and too imprecise for social-scientific analysis. In its place, political scientists are more likely to draw on such theoretically thick notions as ideology, or on more systemic

---

[44] Bryan Garsten, "The Rhetoric Revival in Political Theory," *Annual Review of Political Science* 14 (2011): 159–80.
[45] Garsten, "The Rhetoric Revival," 160; Danielle S. Allen, *Talking to Strangers: Anxieties of Citizenship since Brown v. Board of Education* (Chicago: University of Chicago Press, 2004), 141.
[46] Allen, *Talking to Strangers*, 140.
[47] Rob Goodman, *Words on Fire: Eloquence and Its Conditions* (Cambridge, UK: Cambridge University Press, 2022).

and impersonal analyses of the conditions of public opinion formation.[48] But one might ask what is lost from a scientific point of view by discarding a term that is still widely used in common parlance—particularly when that term has such a long intellectual history behind it.

In fact, given that "demagogue" continues to have such wide popular currency, we would argue that scholars can do an important service by clarifying the term, its history, and its relationship to populism. Consider some recent examples. In 2016, the *New Yorker* reported on the election of Rodrigo Duterte as president of the Philippines under the headline: "When a Populist Demagogue Takes Power."[49] In 2019, Martin Wolf applied the label to a host of world leaders in the *Financial Times*: "Leading examples are Vladimir Putin in Russia, Recep Tayyip Erdogan in Turkey, Narendra Modi in India, Nicolás Maduro in Venezuela, Rodrigo Duterte in the Philippines, Jair Bolsonaro in Brazil, Benjamin Netanyahu in Israel, Matteo Salvini in Italy and Donald Trump in the US.... To be successful, a populist demagogue has to project belief in himself as a man of destiny."[50] At the end of Trump's presidency, Michael Lind argued that he was best understood not as a would-be fascist dictator, "but rather as an American-style populist demagogue."[51]

In all of these instances, and many more, we could conceivably take "populist" to be modifying "demagogue": a populist demagogue is one kind of demagogue, but perhaps there are other kinds. Or maybe, grammar aside, the modification runs the other way around: because the modern valence of "demagogue" is unambiguously negative in a way that "populist" is not, to call someone a "populist demagogue" is to imply that he or she is a populist of the decidedly bad kind. In practice, however, common usage seems to treat the terms as synonymous: populists simply are demagogues, full stop.

By contrast, our view is that treating the terms as synonymous takes their resemblance too far. But examining them side by side is still a valuable exercise, because it reminds us of the way in which these terms themselves have been sites of political struggle. The normative meaning of "populism" has still not crystallized; perhaps it never will. In this volume alone, some

---

[48] James W. Ceaser, "Demagoguery, Statesmanship, and the American Presidency," *Critical Review* 19, no. 2–3 (2007): 257–98, here 259; Haig Patapan, "On Populists and Demagogues," *Canadian Journal of Political Science/Revue canadienne de science politique* 52, no. 4 (2019): 743–59.

[49] Adrian Chin, "When a Populist Demagogue Takes Power," *The New Yorker*, November 13, 2016, www.newyorker.com/magazine/2016/11/21/when-a-populist-demagogue-takes-power.

[50] Martin Wolf, "The Age of the Elected Despot Is Here," *Financial Times*, April 23, 2019, www.ft.com/content/9198533e-6521-11e9-a79d-04f350474d62.

[51] Michael Lind, "Demagogues vs. Dictators," *Project Syndicate*, February 8, 2021, www.project-syndicate.org/commentary/trump-demagogue-not-fascist-dictator-by-michael-lind-2021-02.

contributors treat it as a praiseworthy or sympathetic concept, some use it as an imprecation, and still others aim to use the term as neutrally as possible. "Demagoguery," on the other hand, has crystallized in a way that "populism" has not—but it is worth recalling that, at its origins, it was a neutral, descriptive term, and that the process by which it took on its negative valence was itself politicized and contestable.

As Melissa Lane has argued, "demagogue" and its cognate terms were, at their origins in democratic Athens, descriptive terms for a popular leader, not evaluative terms for an especially destructive kind of leader. "The Athenians did have variegated concepts of political leadership," writes Lane, "and they did have the idea of a form of political leadership appealing particularly to the common people as opposed to the elite. But the latter was a descriptive category which could apply to good and bad leaders alike."[52] In literal terms, a demagogue is simply a leader of the people (*dēmos* + *ago*)—not necessarily an insult in a government of the *dēmos*.[53] Despite occasional appearances in Aristophanes and Thucydides (again, as Lane shows, in a neutral sense), "demagogue" was one of a group of related terms for a popular leader, but by no means the most common. It owes its prominence, and its conversion into a term of abuse, to Plato, who introduced the distinction between the wise statesman and the manipulative demagogue; to Aristotle, who used the term in a more limited sense, applying it not as an insult to all democratic politicians in the manner of his teacher, but specifically to those whose appeals to the people undermined the rule of law and the stability of democracy; and to Plutarch, who popularized the term and associated it with a fixed cast of "bad" leaders (e.g., Cleon and Alcibiades) who became, in his *Lives*, our demagogic prototypes.[54]

The transition of "demagogue" from descriptive to pejorative, then, represents an important and influential political intervention, one closely associated with criticisms of Athenian democracy itself (whether in radical form, as in Plato, or more moderated form, as in Aristotle). This in itself is an important insight for the study of populism, which today sits somewhere close to the analogous position occupied by "demagogue" before Plato. As

---

[52] Melissa Lane, "The Origins of the Statesman-Demagogue Distinction in and after Ancient Athens," *Journal of the History of Ideas* 73, no. 2 (2012): 180.
[53] Josiah Ober, *Mass and Elite in Democratic Athens* (Princeton, NJ: Princeton University Press, 1989), 106 n.7 (cited in Lane, "The Origins of the Statesman-Demagogue Distinction").
[54] But see also Matthew Simonton, *Classical Greek Oligarchy: A Political History* (Princeton, NJ: Princeton University Press, 2017).

with demagoguery and similarly charged political terms, it is difficult or even impossible to separate definition from political struggle.[55]

The comparison with demagoguery helps to set off populism's historical antecedents, as well as its distinctiveness. The demagogue, in Plato's *Gorgias*, engages in "flattery and a base mob-oratory"[56]—and it is likely that many of today's critics of "populist demagogues" would agree that little has changed. "With members of his audience, he is flattering, teasing, accommodating," read an early review of Trump's campaign rhetoric, before he had captured his party's nomination. "He brings emotional release, even satisfaction."[57] On the other hand, if populism is a thin ideology, demagoguery as redefined by Plato is surely even thinner, or lacking in content altogether. After all, inherent in the idea of the demagogue flattering the whims of the people is the claim that the people are defined by their whims: that they have no stable interests or preferences to speak of. If this is the case, then demagoguery has no content beyond whatever pleases the audience's sweet tooth and wins its acclaim from moment to moment. However, if we move to republican Rome, and the dispute between *populares* and *optimates*, the ideological dimension of demagoguery stands out in somewhat sharper relief: here, it can be associated with the defense of popular rights and power, within the framework of a political vision that understood the republic as characterized by a constant conflict between social orders.

Nonetheless, populist narratives of the authentic people, elite betrayal, and the general will expressed through popular sovereignty seem to have a higher degree of solidity than classical demagoguery. In contrast to demagoguery, populism cannot be understood without reference to the modern principle that sovereignty belongs to the people, the principle that became the new foundation of the state after the modern political revolutions. Without reference to this ideological principle—including, of course, the

---

[55] See Andrea Bocchi, *L'eterno demagogo* (Ascona: Aragno, 2011). On the political use of "populism," see, for instance, the works of those who have critically engaged with the liberal critique of populism, focusing on the phenomenon of anti-populism: Yannis Stavrakakis, "The Return of 'the People': Populism and Anti-Populism in the Shadow of the European Crisis," *Constellations* 21, no. 4 (2014): 505–17; Yannis Stavrakakis, Giorgos Katsambekis, Alexandros Kioupkiolis, Nikos Nikisianis, and Thomas Siomos, "Populism, Anti-Populism and Crisis," *Contemporary Political Theory* 17, no. 1 (2018): 4–27; Thomas Frank, *The People, No: A Brief History of Anti-Populism* (New York: Metropolitan, 2020); Antoine Chollet, *L'antipopulisme ou la nouvelle haine de la démocratie* (Paris: Textuel, 2023).

[56] Plato, *Gorgias*, in *Lysias, Symposium, Gorgias*, trans. W. R. M. Lamb (Cambridge, MA: Harvard University Press, 1925), 502e.

[57] David Denby, "The Plot against America: Donald Trump's Rhetoric," *The New Yorker*, December 15, 2015, www.newyorker.com/culture/cultural-comment/plot-america-donald-trumps-rhetoric.

rhetorical uses to which this principle is put—it would be difficult (despite populism's ideological thinness and inarticulation) to explain the legitimacy that a great deal of the populist styles, performances, and discourses currently have. Populists, however, tend to understand and employ this principle in a distinctive sense—with the more or less implicit suggestion that those who win the elections represent the will of the people as a whole[58]—which is at the heart of their objection to liberal democracy. While liberal democracy mediates popular sovereignty through representation, an emphasis on proceduralism, and deliberation among representatives, populism promises the people a more un-mediated access to political rule, a promise conveyed by such populist forms as personalism, the appeal to the emotions, and "bad manners."

The comparison with demagoguery also casts populism's relationship with political representation into sharper relief. Demagoguery, of course, originated under direct democracy, but we doubt that anyone would argue that representative democracy, by definition, cannot produce demagogues. The case of populism is somewhat different: it is more tightly bound to representative government and embedded in its premises, even though its discourse is quite often a critique of representation—or, more precisely, a critique of representation in the form of a party system that it has taken in contemporary liberal-democratic regimes.

Quite often, populist sentiments are expressed as a critique of liberal democracy's representativeness deficit—a deficit that results from a deep tension in liberal democracy itself.[59] Pierre Rosanvallon has argued that this tension derives from the conflict between the people as a "political principle" and the people as a "sociological principle."[60] The former refers to the people as a whole that exercises sovereignty; the latter, to the concrete complexity of the people in their everyday life. How can such a multifaceted complexity become a political subject capable of exercising sovereignty?

Representation and the party system have been one influential answer to this question: representative procedures transform a multifarious people into a political subject that is nevertheless marked as contingent and permanently subject to revision. In this view, the representative system does not

---

[58] See Axel Mueller, "The Meaning of 'Populism,'" *Philosophy & Social Criticism* 45, no. 9–10 (2019): 1025–57.
[59] See Pierre Rosanvallon, *Le peuple introuvable: Histoire de la représentation démocratique en France* (Paris: Gallimard, 1998), 227.
[60] Pierre Rosanvallon, *Democracy Past and Future* (New York: Columbia University Press, 2006), 37, 469.

compromise democracy—it is essential to democracy.[61] By contrast, the populist stress on the unitary people and on recurring crises of representation in liberal democracies calls this solution into doubt: for populists, liberal representative governments are often an obstacle to popular sovereignty to the extent that they offer only a highly mediated and regulated access to rule and at the same time are prone to be captured by special interests. Populism, in this view, is the most efficient way to reverse this widening gap between the people and the institutions that claim to speak and act on their behalf: it is a "redemptive" force capable of revitalizing democracy when power grows too remote from its ultimate source.[62] Critics of populism, on the other hand, see this stance against the liberal representative system as emblematic of populism's anti-democratic and anti-pluralist nature.

Populism and demagoguery, then, are both appeals to the people; they both carry words for "the people" in their names. But as this brief discussion of representation shows, appeals to the people are stamped by their context: representation is part of the populist context in a way that is not the case for demagoguery. As a result, questions related to the complex dilemmas of representation (such as the tensions between "trustee" or "delegate" models, or the contributions of recent constructivist accounts) play a key role in the study of populism, while they are less relevant to our understanding of demagoguery.

Nevertheless, this point hardly exhausts the connections and resonances between contemporary populism and appeals to the people in other historical contexts. Exploring those resonances is this book's third key contribution.

Despite the burgeoning interest in populism, most recent works on the subject are dedicated to populism as a contemporary phenomenon, paying special attention to its rise in recent global politics. These works are less occupied with populism's historical roots; where they do investigate these roots, they generally trace them to the late nineteenth or early twentieth century at the earliest. The American People's Party and the Russian *narodniki* make up the bulk of appearances as populist antecedents. This focus on contemporary populism is understandable, but we argue that there remains a

---

[61] Nadia Urbinati, *Representative Democracy: Principles and Genealogy* (Chicago: University of Chicago Press, 2006), 4.

[62] Margaret Canovan, "'Trust the People!' Populism and the Two Faces of Democracy," *Political Studies* 47, no. 1 (1999): 2–16; Arditi, *Politics on the Edges of Liberalism*; Vergara, "Populism as Plebeian Politics." Cf. Carreira and Brito Vieira, "Populism and the Politics of Redemption."

great deal to be said about populism's deeper historical background. In fact, a number of the volume's chapters make the case that the political conflicts of previous eras can be productively viewed through a populist lens, which stresses such features as the rejection of pluralism, the strategic construction of membership in "the people," and conflict between supposedly pure masses and corrupt elites. As our discussion of distinctions between populism and demagoguery suggests, overly hasty historical comparisons can obscure populism's distinctive features, rather than illuminate them—but by the same token, careful and context-aware history can help us to see populism in a new light.

At the same time, however, we do not think that the historical analysis of populism should be reduced to a genealogical analysis aimed at discovering some pure, foundational experience from which the definitive meaning of populism could be extracted.[63] Populism, as we have argued, is a phenomenon that brings into play a wide range of issues that have a long tradition in the history of political thought. Indeed, it is difficult to analyze populism without at the same time expressing normative positions on a series of concepts closely interlinked to it, starting with those of democracy, the people, representation, human rights, the nature of the common good, and so on.[64] Instead, in this volume we aim to enrich the theoretical understanding on populism through a historical perspective that escapes the danger of presentism, while still going beyond the most commonly cited cases of populist history (namely, the American People's Party and the Russian *narodniki*) to take in the wide range of phenomena and issues bound up with the question of populism.

We should also note that we do not intend to construe populism as an historically transcendent phenomenon, or to elide the contemporary political conditions that contribute to its success. We do not intend to issue Cleon, Cola di Rienzo, and Jair Bolsonaro membership cards in a trans-historical Populist Party. At the same time, we believe that there remains a great deal to be said about populism's longer history as a concept and mode of politics, and about its historical analogues and predecessors. How can repeated conflicts between "the few" and "the many," or struggles over the proper

---

[63] Federico Tarragoni, "Populism, an Ideology without History? A New Genetic Approach." *Journal of Political Ideologies* 29, no. 1 (2024): 42–63; Chollet, *L'antipopulisme ou la nouvelle haine de la démocratie*.

[64] Cf. Paulina Ochoa Espejo, "Populism and the Idea of the People," in *The Oxford Handbook of Populism*, ed. Cristóbal Rovira Kaltwasser, Paul Taggart, Paulina Ochoa Espejo, and Pierre Ostiguy (Oxford: Oxford University Press, 2017), 607.

meaning of political representation, shed light on contemporary populist politics? Is populism a uniquely modern phenomenon, or can it be seen as a recurring pattern in political life? How can democracies reconcile popular and elitist approaches to rhetorical persuasion, or technical expertise and the judgment of the public?

By raising such questions, we hope that this volume will do two things: first, that it will provide historical depth to conversations on populism that are too often fixed on the immediate present or the recent past; and second, that it will demonstrate the value of populism itself as a new way into some of the long-standing debates and disputes in our field. But rather than make the case in general terms, we turn now to a brief synopsis and preview of the essays that make up this volume, which is divided chronologically into two parts: "Ancient and Early Modern Themes" and "Modern and Contemporary Themes," respectively. As we said by way of introduction, the best argument for the value of this project—for taking the long view of populism—lies in our contributors' detailed exploration of populist themes in the history of political thought.

In Chapter 1, Arlene W. Saxonhouse explores the ambivalent status of *parrhêsia* (literally "saying all," but often translated as "frank speech") in fifth-century Athens. Athenian citizens valued *parrhêsia* as a central practice or ideal for their democratic regime, a centrality they highlighted by naming one of their city's ships *Parrhêsia*. The Athenian commitment to *isêgoria* ensured that every citizen had an equal opportunity to speak in the assembly where the laws and policy decisions of the Athenians were determined, but *parrhêsia* entailed the broader principle of daring to speak openly—without regard for tradition or hierarchy—as to what one truly believed. But two challenges confronted the practice of *parrhêsia* of which the Athenians were so proud. First, there is no assurance that the one speaking freely is boldly saying what he truly believes, rather than trying to control and manipulate others. Second, the uncovering of the truth by saying all—the unbridled tongue free of shame and threats of punishment—may challenge the traditions of a society, destabilizing that society and threatening the regime that has fostered it. After considering the status of *parrhêsia* in several speeches given in the Athenian assemblies presented in Thucydides's *History*, Saxonhouse turns to the practice of *parrhesia* in Plato and in one of Aristophanes's comedies. These two authors suggest an alternative venue for the exercise of *parrhêsia*, removing it from the public life of the deliberative Assembly.

In Chapter 2, Tae-Yeoun Keum considers the problem of populism in Plato's political thought. Strictly speaking, to discuss populism in the context of the age of Plato is an anachronism. Yet efforts to define the notoriously elusive term "populism" have often coalesced around an opposition between populism and constitutional democracy, where the former represents a special, "derivative" kind of subversion of the latter. Such a broadly construed tension between a more orthodox form of democracy and its populist counterpart has an important precedent in ancient Athenian political discourse leading up to the age of Plato. In fact, ancient Athenian political thinkers had developed a comparable concept of a kind of shadow democracy that, while parasitic on democratic institutions and norms, ultimately undermined democratic ends. Keum recasts Plato as a participant in this rich political tradition focused on imagining the tension between democracy and its inversion. In particular, his account of the degeneration of democracy in Book 8 of the *Republic* can be read as both an elaboration of and a critical intervention in this traditional discourse. Plato was critical of the antidemocratic effect of the trope of the demagogue who subjugates the *dēmos* for personal gain. His critique, however, was also bound up in an effort to reimagine alternate possibilities of constructive engagement with collective assemblies.

In Chapter 3, Rob Goodman turns to the work of Cicero and his contemporaries to offer evidence for existence, distinctiveness, and key qualities of populist rhetoric in the late Roman republic. In contrast to claims that the republic was characterized by "ideological monotony," this chapter argues that we can trace the outlines not only of a *popularis* ideology in the late republic, but also of a *popularis* style—a style that, in turn, was grounded in important and contestable assumptions about the relationship between orator and audience, and between the various institutions of republican politics. Cicero consistently characterizes the speech of his *popularis* adversaries as *nudus*, or "naked," casting it as lacking in artifice and control, more a product of nature than of human craft. While these terms are polemical, they also point to a recognizable difference in the rhetorical styles on offer to the Roman public. The chapter argues that Cicero conceived of stylistic diversity and abundance as means by which the orator demonstrated responsiveness and accommodation to the audience—qualities that the *populares* evidently sought to minimize through the pursuit of unaffected speech. For such politicians, refusal to accommodate can itself send a powerful signal: that the speaker's identification with the people is so complete that no accommodation is required. Cicero, by contrast, strove to make visible the sheer difficulty of rhetorical responsiveness, drawing an analogy between "mixed speech" and mixed government.

In Chapter 4, Cary J. Nederman explores the thought and influences of Brunetto Latini, a leading Florentine republican of the thirteenth century. The extent to which Latini should be considered a thoroughgoing populist, or something short thereof, has been a matter of some dispute. But his devotion to Cicero is beyond doubt—and was highly relevant in the political world of medieval Italy. Over the course of the thirteenth century, Italian cities grew in size, economic stature, and political self-confidence. In many cases, the long-held dominance of lords (*seigneurs*) had been challenged and their rulership displaced by populist, self-governing *communes*, some of which styled themselves on the model of the Roman Republic. Congruent with these developments, political theories emerged that centered on the normative as well as practical issues associated with the Italian cities—among which Latini's was one of the most influential. In order to clarify the nature of Latini's republicanism, Nederman distinguishes two strands of Ciceronian thought: "rhetorical republicanism" and "rationalist republicanism." While the former draws on Cicero's account of how social relations and political institutions initially arose from the urgings of a wise orator, the latter denotes Cicero's conception of a constitutional political order based on an idea of justice derived from the ability of reason to apprehend natural law. The chapter places Latini squarely in the rhetorical camp. In other words, constitutional rationalism plays no evident part in his work.

In Chapter 5, Alessandro Mulieri contributes to ongoing debates on the nature of early modern republicanism and its relationship to populist politics. Recent years have seen a "plebeian" or "radical republican" turn within the scholarship on late medieval and early modern Italian political writers, especially Machiavelli. This chapter aims to contribute to those debates on the Italian language of republicanism and its relationship to populism, with a focus on a particular theme that the rediscovery of Aristotle's ethical and political works brought to the political thought of this period: the definition of democracy as the rule of the poor. By comparing Aristotle's thought to that of some late medieval and early modern thinkers, including Machiavelli, Mulieri shows that the latter's support for popular republics marked an important conceptual rupture with the Aristotelian condemnation of democracy as a regime that empowers the poor. However, the chapter also argues that Machiavelli's account of the relationship between democracy and poverty shares important similarities with other contemporary republicans who tackled the same theme. These similarities include the championing of institutions that promote a more inclusive idea of the people (e.g., the Great Council of Florence, or magistrates modeled on the Roman tribunes of the plebs), as well as a common reinterpretation of Aristotle's ideas in order to make them more functional to radical republican agendas. This leads Mulieri to the hypothesis that a crucial feature of the Italian popular/populist republican tradition is its tendency to draw on the most populist ideas of Aristotelianism.

In Chapter 6, David Ragazzoni points out that, although the humanists of the Italian Renaissance breathed new life into the study of ancient rhetoric, their debates on the morality of political rhetoric are often cited but seldom explored by political theorists. By contrast, this chapter offers an account of the *political theories of rhetoric* in the Italian Renaissance. It shows that a new kind of *institutio* was envisioned as the first step in the reform of political institutions. *Eloquentia* turned into an article of faith among a new generation of thinkers who emphasized the need for educated political leaders to address their fellow citizens as equals. Relatedly, the chapter draws renewed attention to the moral connotation acquired by the humanist study of eloquence, as an indispensable tool for political leadership, in contrast to the ways in which rhetoric was studied in law schools as a purely technical skill. The chapter also unpacks two implications of this moral reading of eloquence. First, the constitutional specifics of regime types were much less important than the intellectual (and thus moral) texture of those trained to rule. Second, the humanist rhetorical program was meritocratic and, at least in its driving ambition, profoundly egalitarian. While championing virtuous individuals' right to rule, the humanist rhetoricians made it clear that the virtuous politician was educated, not born, precisely because virtue could be learned and cultivated, particularly through the study and practice of rhetoric.

In Chapter 7, Daniel Kapust explores the theme of demagoguery by engaging with the work of one of America's first great novelists, James Fenimore Cooper. While demagoguery has been relatively neglected in recent political theory, it was a central concern in early American political thought—not only in the founding period, but also in the nineteenth-century period of democratization. Cooper, a leading writer of that period, identified demagoguery as one of the chief problems of American political life while seeking to educate his readers about its dangers and its signs. The 1838 book in which Cooper did so, *The American Democrat*, analyzes the figure of a flattering demagogue who is (though Cooper does not use the term) recognizably populist. Cooper's book is of particularly interest because of its relationship to the history of political thought, which places it in a long tradition of anti-demagogic texts, ultimately traceable to Plutarch. Yet Cooper's account straddles two different ways of approaching the problem of demagoguery: the first is both recognizably Plutarchean and consonant with the decidedly pejorative account common in late-eighteenth- and early-nineteenth-century America; the second focuses less on the character of the demagogue and more on what demagogic speakers do. Kapust argues that the first, moralistic account suffers from structural defects common to *all* moralistic accounts of demagoguery, while Cooper's discourse-centered account points toward ways in which demagogic—and populist—appeals could find less purchase in political discourse, through a process of mass cultural transformation and the elite practice of rhetoric.

In Chapter 8, Kari Palonen situates certain rhetorical *topoi* of contemporary "populist" politics with respect to anti-parliamentary thinking in Western Europe since the mid-nineteenth century. The populist tradition deviates from classical anti-parliamentarism in an important respect: it shows no nostalgia toward monarchy and the order of estates, but considers itself "democratic" in its explicit appeal to "the people." It combines, however, four other anti-parliamentary *topoi*, which are interconnected but still refer to different aspects of politics that are not necessarily linked to each other. In line with older anti-parliamentarism, the contemporary populists reject or denigrate political representation, parliamentarism's "empty talk," political professionalism, and the procedural style of politics. The chapter's aim is to discuss the political significance of the anti-parliamentary *topoi* in a wider historical perspective. The common consequence of these varieties of anti-parliamentary thinking, as opposed to the parliamentary style of politics, lies in their attempt to depoliticize politics. Contemporary populists give this depoliticization some new nuances, while still longing to do away with politics, just as the other anti-parliamentary styles of thinking and acting did.

In Chapter 9, Giovanni Damele considers the historical context and contemporary relevance of Vilfredo Pareto's early-twentieth-century work on democracy, plutocracy, and rhetoric. Pareto, along with Gaetano Mosca and Robert Michels, is often considered one of the "founding fathers" of classical elitism. Drawing on more recent scholarship, however, Damele brings Pareto's democratic sympathies to the fore. Among Pareto's most consistent concerns, in fact, was the distorting effect of economic inequality on democracy: much of his work aimed at checking the power of plutocratic wealth in an era of emerging mass politics. While Pareto is frequently seen as an antidemocratic or even proto-fascist thinker, Damele argues that he should instead be reinterpreted as an opponent of liberal parliamentarism based on an oligarchic system of representation. This reinterpretation, which focuses on Pareto's criticisms of plutocratic oligarchy, gives his arguments an almost populistic nuance. In order to develop Pareto's critique as a resource for contemporary democratic politics, Damele makes two further interventions. First, he emphasizes that the theory of elite circulation plays a crucial, rather than subsidiary, role in Pareto's political thought. Second, he stresses the pivotal function attributed by Pareto to emotions and "sentiments" in the field of politics. Combined, these concepts enable Pareto to demonstrate how demagogic rhetorical practices can emerge from intra-elite competition under plutocratic regimes, and to generalize about the circumstances under which they are most likely to do so.

In Chapter 10, Jan-Werner Müller asks how a commitment to popular rule should express itself in architecture. If the often-monumental buildings housing democratic legislatures are the people's "palaces"—a term used regularly in debates over such architecture—what should a palace for the people look like? How can such a building persuade the people that it is really theirs? Or is that idea a path to the problematic image of a single, homogenous people, and to the "stormings" of parliaments, with "mobs" incited by populist leaders determined to remove supposedly illegitimate elite usurpers of the people's palace? Müller breaks the question of democratic palaces into four elements: first, the relationship of democracy to monumentality; second, the possible associations between democracy and various building styles and materials; third, the question of which iconographic program, if any, best promotes democratic values; and fourth, the spaces provided by buildings devoted to democracy, and the scripts and dramaturgies that they make possible. Müller argues that there is no uniquely democratic style, material, or iconography. But it does not follow that democracy is somehow beyond all representation and embodiment. While democracy does pose special problems for processes of symbolic condensation, partly because of its internally plural character, democracy is not necessarily bereft of visual strategies to persuade citizens of its merits and to inspire them to engage in democratic practices. Much more important than representations are spaces that can facilitate such practices. And because democratic practices are plural, democratic spaces should be, as well.

In Chapter 11, Mark Wenman aims to bring a greater focus to the question of the relationship between populism and pluralism. Drawing on a conceptual and historical reconstruction of "pluralism," and a consideration of populist and pluralist rhetoric style, Wenman argues that pluralism can help address the challenges presented by populism—but that it is misleading to construe the two concepts as "opposites." In support of this argument, Wenman disaggregates the various meanings that have accumulated around the term "pluralism," with a particular focus on differentiating the tradition of American political pluralism from other iterations. The chapter also argues that one iteration in particular, which associates pluralism with liberalism and its anti-political tendencies, is actively harmful to attempts at countering populism. While populism, especially its right-wing versions, presents a danger to individual liberty and the rule of law, Wenman argues that we misstep if we place too much emphasis on upholding liberal values in response to this predicament: we should look elsewhere for a more *political* response to the authoritarian tendency within populism. Thankfully, we find alternative resources in the rather different account of pluralism that emerged in the mid-twentieth-century United States: an account whose key normative commitments are the inhibition of unhealthy concentrations of power and the facilitation of ordinary citizens' control over the policy agenda and the outcome of governmental decisions.

In Chapter 12, John P. McCormick observes that, as contemporary democracies succumb to unremitting plutocratic usurpation, populism has re-emerged as a powerful political force. Populism in its right-wing, xenophobic form, McCormick writes, has done nothing to ameliorate the problem of intensifying economic and political inequality. It remains to be seen whether more inclusive, egalitarian populist movements will gain the momentum necessary to propel a reversal—whether they can achieve the kinds of mass mobilization capable of compelling governing elites to enact, and economic elites to accept, fundamental institutional change. Thus far, progressive movements have proven much less effective in organizing themselves in pursuit of institutional and policy change than have right-wing ones, but McCormick argues that we should not give up on populism as such. Populism, he argues, is the necessary vehicle for realizing the effective reform of contemporary democracy. At the same time, populism potentially endangers precisely the kind of robust democracy that can only be achieved through populist means of mass mobilization. This chapter elaborates the reasons why both plutocracy and populism are phenomena endemic to electoral democracy—and are not in any way peculiar to our own particular era in the history of representative government. McCormick specifies criteria that might be used to distinguish right-wing from progressive forms of populism. Finally, drawing on Machiavelli, he sketches the kinds of institutional reforms that progressive populist movements should pursue in efforts to counteract rampant economic and political inequality.

In Chapter 13, Paula Diehl takes up the phenomena of celebrity politics and "politainment." In recent years, right-wing leaders such as Donald Trump, Matteo Salvini, and Jair Bolsonaro have generated a hybrid form of populism, celebrity, and media entertainment. Diehl's chapter aims to analyze this hybrid into its constitutive elements and to show its continuities with, and innovative departures from, earlier political forms. Diehl argues that transformations in the communications and media environment in the 1990s and the new millennium laid the groundwork for a new relationship between media and populism, giving birth to new hybrid arrangements of populism. The implications of these new arrangements for democracy cannot be overestimated. Diehl shows how the radicalization of celebrity politics and "politainment" blurs the borders between politics and entertainment, private and public, and, even more importantly, between the real and the fictional. At the same time, the traditional logic of populism, and the logics of celebrity politics and "politainment," do not pull in the same direction when it comes to questions of reality and truth. Whereas populism is a political logic claiming to speak the truth about the common will, celebrity politics and "politainment" introduce an element of hyperreality that destabilizes the same notions of truth that populism claims to defend. As a consequence, the new populist arrangement fundamentally alters citizens' and representatives' relationship to politics. In order to grasp the effects of this new phenomenon, its differences from traditional populist rhetoric need to be considered. Keeping in mind populism's hybridization with celebrity culture, entertainment, and new media, we are better situated to answer the question: *What is changing in populism?*

Finally, in Chapter 14, Simon Lambek considers the political impact of "everyday speech." When political theorists consider rhetoric, they are often concerned, by contrast, with exceptional speech—speech that triggers judgment and imaginative thinking or, conversely, affectively charged speech that is strategically manipulative. What is missing, Lambek argues, is a framework that captures the political effects of far more mundane and commonplace forms of rhetoric: speech acts that are received in stride and do not stand out as exceptional, but which nonetheless have significant political consequences. This chapter proposes the concept of "rhetorical resonance" and makes a case for attending to the iterative, constitutive effects of everyday rhetorical encounters. Building from the hermeneutic theory of Hans-Georg Gadamer, Lambek argues that rhetoric that "resonates" with our discursive horizons can nevertheless transform those horizons, ushering in new conditions of political possibility. To illustrate the power of resonant rhetoric, the chapter considers the lead-up to the 2021 storming of the U.S. Capitol. It attends to the resonant effects of repeated claims of election fraud and mismanagement, arguing that the resonant nature of these claims was instrumental both for producing the attempted putsch, and then later for sanctioning the insurrection as "legitimate political discourse."

In the Conclusion, we sum up the general sense of the volume and come back to rhetoric, to explain why, as many of the chapters reveal, it provides a particularly useful perspective to study populism.

PART I
ANCIENT AND EARLY MODERN THEMES

1
Parrhêsia
The Unbridled Tongue in Ancient Democratic Athens

Arlene W. Saxonhouse

Introduction

During the flourishing of Athenian democracy in the mid-fifth-century BCE, the Athenian citizens voted to name one of their state ships *Parrhêsia*.[1] The name means "saying all," and has generally been translated as "free speech" or "frank speech," the readiness to express one's beliefs daringly and openly without fear of the consequences of such openness. As such, the *parrhêsiast*, the one speaking freely, could cast a critical eye on those in power and on the traditions of the regime in which one lived. *Parrhêsia* embodied the freedoms treasured by the Athenians, who enjoyed a regime where deliberating in the popular assemblies or arguing in the courtroom were the central aspects of their public life. Naming a ship *Parrhêsia* celebrated that freedom.

Throughout the fifth century BCE, the playwrights joined in that celebration. Aeschylus in *The Persians*, first performed in 472 BCE, has his Chorus of Persian elders, after learning about the defeat of the Persian tyrant at Salamis, sing:

> Now fear no more shall bridle speech;
> Uncurbed the common tongue shall prate
> Of freedom; for the yoke of State
> Lies broken on the bloody beach.[2]

---

[1] Jeffrey Henderson, "Attic Comedy, Frank Speech, and Democracy," in *Democracy, Empire, and the Arts in Fifth Century Athens*, ed. Deborah Boedeker and Kurt A. Raaflaub (Cambridge, MA: Harvard University Press, 1998), 406 n.16; Mogens Herman Hansen, "The Athenian and the Modern Liberal View of Liberty as a Democratic Ideal," in *Dēmokratia: A Conversation on Democracies, Ancient and Modern*, ed. Josiah Ober and Charles Hedrick (Princeton, NJ: Princeton University Press, 1996), 92, 101 n.19.

[2] Translation by Phillip Vellacott, *Aeschylus: Prometheus Bound, The Suppliants, Seven against Thebes, The Persians* (Harmondsworth, UK: Penguin Books, 1961), 139.

That "common tongue"—unbridled—captures the contrast between the despotism of the East and the freedom of the Greek city. Euripides's *Ion*, performed many decades later, around 411 BCE, has the young hero wonder whether he should move to Athens; if he goes as a citizen, he would have *parrhêsia*, but if he goes as an outsider lacking *parrhêsia* he would have the mouth of a slave (670–75).[3] Polyneices, the son/brother of Oedipus, speaks in Euripides's *Phoenician Women* of his longing to return to Thebes (a stand-in for Athens), telling his mother Jocasta that the greatest evil for him living as an exile is that he lacks *parrhêsia*; Jocasta agrees that it is the life of a slave to be unable to say what one thinks (391–92). And in Euripides's *Hippolytus*, Phaedra determines that only by killing herself will her children "flourishing as men be free to speak freely/frankly" (420–23). Comedy, too, highlights the special status of those enjoying the opportunity to practice *parrhêsia*. In Aristophanes's *Thesmophoriazusae* of 411 BCE, an assembly of women imitate the all-male assemblies in Athens. One of the women attending that all female assembly asks: "Are we not female city dwellers for whom it is permitted to speak having *parrhêsia*?" (540–43).

Yet, even as they celebrated the practice of open and free speech, Athenian authors also acknowledged the problematic aspects of *parrhêsia*, a practice that might not be used to search for the truth or to say what one truly believed, but rather might open the door to the pursuit of power or threaten the civility on which political regimes depend. Exploring the nature and impact of *parrhêsia* as they do, the texts from ancient Athens address many of the same challenges faced by contemporary regimes that treasure free and frank speech but are confronted by the potential misuse of such a freedom to control, manipulate, and deceive one's audience. Below I consider the ambivalent status of the celebrated *parrhêsia* as a practice that frees the tongue from slavery with a view to highlighting the challenges posed by an attachment to the unbridled tongue, whether in ancient Athens or in today's world of democratic politics. The texts from ancient Athens pose the uncomfortable question of whether the practice of free and frank speech in the public arena benefits the polity or fosters a perversion of democratic principles of equal and open deliberation. It is a question that, with the rise of populism emerging in response to the powerful rhetoric of manipulative speakers, continues to vex the long-held pieties of democratic regimes.

---

[3] Throughout I use the standard citations for Greek texts. References to tragedies and comedies are by lines. Unless otherwise noted, translations are my own.

After considering the status of *parrhêsia* in several speeches given in the Athenian assemblies as presented in Thucydides's *History*, I turn briefly to the practice of *parrhesia* in two of Plato's dialogues and one of Aristophanes's comedies. These latter two authors suggest alternative venues for the exercise of *parrhêsia*, removing it from the public life of the deliberative Assembly.[4] These alternative venues may separate *parrhêsia* from its role in fostering a dangerous populism, but as Socrates illustrates in the *Apology*, the frankness it cultivates may entail its own concerns by undermining the civic life of the polity.

First, though, it is necessary to distinguish *parrhêsia* from *isêgoria*, a word often used as a synonym for *parrhêsia* in works about ancient Athens.[5] *Isêgoria* draws on the principle of equality (as the "*iso*" suggests) and on the practice of speaking in public places such as the marketplace (the *agora*) and more specifically the Assembly. *Isêgoria*, in contrast to *parrhêsia*, is closely associated with the institution of the Athenian Assembly where the *dêmos* gathered about forty times a year to deliberate and vote on policy and pass laws. There, at least in principle, every Athenian citizen had an equal opportunity to speak. Three institutions marked Athenian democracy in the fifth and fourth centuries BCE: the *ecclesia* or Assembly, the law courts, and the administrative offices which were filled by a lottery in which all citizens were eligible. Each of these institutions emphasized the equality of those deemed Athenian citizens, affirming an equal capacity among the citizens to fill the administrative offices of the city, to judge court cases, and to deliberate in the Assembly. As an expression of this equality,

---

[4] Michel Foucault, *Fearless Speech* (Los Angeles, CA: Semitoext(e), 2001), relying on different texts, also writes of how the practice of *parrhêsia* as "truth-telling" travels from the Assembly to the multiple venues where Socrates engages with citizens and non-citizens.

[5] The study of *parrhesia*, and its relation to *isêgoria*, within Athenian democracy has become something of a cottage industry. Generally see: Lindsay Mahon Rathan, "The Marketplace of Ideas and the Agora: Herodotus on the Power of Isegoria," *American Political Science Review* 117, no. 1 (2023): 140–52; Matthew Landauer, "'Parrhesia' and the 'Demos Tyrannos': Frank Speech, Flattery and Accountability in Democratic Athens," *History of Political Thought* 33, no. 2 (2012): 105–208; David Konstan, "The Two Faces of *Parrhêsia*: Free Speech and Self-Expression in Ancient Greece," *Antichthon* 46 (2012): 1–13; Arlene W. Saxonhouse, *Free Speech and Democracy in Ancient Athens* (Cambridge, UK: Cambridge University Press, 2004); Kurt Raaflaub, *The Discovery of Freedom in Ancient Greece* (Chicago: University of Chicago Press, 2004); the essays in *Free Speech in Classical Antiquity*, ed. Ineke Sluiter and Ralph M. Rosen (Leiden: Brill, 2004); Foucault, *Fearless Speech*; S. Sara Monoson, *Plato's Democratic Entanglements: Athenian Politics and the Practice of Philosophy* (Princeton, NJ: Princeton University Press, 2000), ch. 2; Robert W. Wallace, "Law, Freedom and the Concept of Citizens' Rights in Democratic Athens," in *Dēmokratia*, 105–19; Arnoldo Momigliano, "Freedom of Speech in Antiquity," in *Dictionary of the History of Ideas: Selected Studies of Pivotal Ideas*, ed. Philip O. Wiener (New York: Scribner, 1973–1974), 252–63.

at the beginning of each session of the Assembly, a herald with a voice sufficiently strong to be heard by the assembled six or seven thousand citizens would rise and, after the proper invocations to the gods, ask: "Who wishes to speak?" Certain guidelines controlled who spoke first and, for sure, not all six thousand availed themselves of the opportunity to speak, but *isêgoria* in a gesture of equality opened the floor to all. As Socrates in Plato's dialogue *Protagoras* remarks, anyone, "carpenter, bronze worker, shoemaker, merchant, shop-owner, rich, poor, noble, lowly born" can rise to speak (319cd). Even in the assembly of women of Aristophanes's *Thesmophoriazusae*, a "heraldess" asks: "Who wishes to speak?" (379). *Isêgoria* asserted that all could speak in the public forum; *parrhêsia* affirmed that all could express without blame what seemed true and best to them. In the literature from and about ancient Athens, the terms *isêgoria* and *parrhêsia* may slide into one another and the practices they denoted are interrelated, but *parrhêsia* went beyond the Assembly to the way of life of the citizens. *Isêgoria* was more directly tied to the institutional and egalitarian structure of Athenian democracy, while *parrhêsia* suggested the boldness entailed in a willingness to articulate unpopular, perhaps offensive, views that challenged the hierarchies and conventions of the times, to display what can be called a certain "shamelessness."[6]

In a brief section in Book II of Homer's *Iliad*, as the Achaean kings debate whether to abandon their siege of Troy, a certain common soldier named Thersites rises to speak. Homer describes him as "disorderly / vain, and without decency, [ready] to quarrel with princes." More than that: "He was the ugliest man who came beneath Ilion . . . / bandy-legged . . . / his skull went up to a point with the wool grown sparsely upon it" (2.213–19).[7] This man of "choice insults," who regularly abused the ruling generals, steps into the circle of deliberating kings to offer his dismissive view of Agamemnon, the leader of the Achaean army. Agamemnon is greedy and fails to appreciate the value of his best warrior, Achilles. These are not the words of a fool;

---

[6] I develop this in Saxonhouse, "A Shameless Socrates on Trial in Democratic Athens," in *Readings of Plato's* Apology of Socrates: *Defending the Philosophical Life*," ed. Vivil Valvik Haraldsen, Olof Pettersson, and Oda E. W. Tvedt. (Lanham, MD: Lexington Books, 2018), 17–36; and Saxonhouse, *Free Speech*, Chapter 5. Ryan K. Balot, *Courage in the Democratic Polis: Ideology and Critique in Classical Athens* (New York: Oxford University Press, 2014), argues that *parrhêsia* was the new form of courage for the democratic citizen, replacing the military virtue that defined the Homeric heroes.

[7] For the translation of the *Iliad* I rely on Richmond Lattimore, *The Iliad of Homer* (Chicago: University of Chicago Press, 1951). Citations are to Book and line.

they are exactly what every reader has observed in the previous lines of the poem, with Thersites repeating almost word for word an earlier speech by Achilles. And yet, for being so outspoken, for entering the deliberate circle of kings, the king Odysseus "swiftly / came beside him and laid a harsh word upon him . . . 'your words are / ill-considered. Stop, nor stand up alone against princes'" (2.243–47). Odysseus follows with lashes on Thersites's back and shoulders so that "a round tear dropped from him," and "a bloody welt stood up between his shoulders" (2.66–67). The other Achaeans laugh at the sight. Thersites did not enjoy the privileges of *isêgoria* or *parrhêsia* in the aristocratically ordered Achaean camp. He was not equal to the kings, and even though the words he spoke were true, they were not welcome. Instead, they provoked Odysseus's harsh words and punishing whip. Thersites's plight stands in contrast to the world of Athenian democracy where the common citizen—however scuzzy and bowlegged he may be—is equal to all other citizens in the opportunity to respond to the herald's call of "Who wishes to speak?" Infusing the political life of the Athenians, *isêgoria* and *parrhêsia* had come to the Pnyx, the spot where the Athenians assembled to deliberate.

The presence of *parrhêsia* in the Assembly, however, is complicated, and whereas along with *isêgoria* it offers the opportunity for all to say all, to daringly uncover what one truly believes without the fear of Odysseus's whip or the scorn of one's fellows, such a freedom also enables, as suggested above, deception and manipulation. As the speeches in Thucydides will illustrate, the speakers with their unbridled tongues for which the Persian Chorus so longed all may (or may not) have spoken what they truly believe in pursuit of political power. At the same time, the unbridled tongue exercised by the philosopher (in particular, Socrates) may lead to the questioning of the traditional beliefs that support the life of the community. Though the writings of the ancient Athenian authors may not provide solutions to the contemporary conundrums surrounding our own practices of free speech and its place in the polity, they force on us an awareness of the dangers of a simplistic attachment to the unbridled tongue in democratic regimes. A political rhetoric of lies and the culture wars permeating our private lives are the modern manifestations of the challenges presented by a celebration of *parrhêsia*. That practice may have been treasured by fifth- and fourth-century Athenian democrats, but the writers of that time recognized that it also threatened the political life of their regime.

Thucydides's *History*: The Mytilenian Debate

During the fourth year of the Peloponnesian War between Athens and Sparta, as recorded in Thucydides's *History*, the Mytilenians living on the island of Lesbos rebel against the Athenians who had subjected Lesbos to their empire.[8] The Athenians suppress the rebellion, put on trial the oligarchs who fomented it, and vote to execute those responsible for the rebellion, kill all the men of Mytilene, and sell the women and children into slavery. After a day of reflection on the enormity of this punishment, however, the Athenians meet to reassess their decision, prompting a debate between Cleon, described by Thucydides as the most forceful of the citizens (3.36), and Diodotus, the son of Eucrates, a character who appears only at this point in the narrative and whose full name means Gift of Zeus, son of Good Power. In this debate, Thucydides has each character reflect implicitly on how the practice of *parrhêsia* in the Assembly impacts decision-making in the popular Assembly of the city.

Cleon

Cleon, this most forceful of Athenians, rises to argue that the Athenians should not revoke their decision to punish severely the Mytilenians; the men must be massacred and the women and children sold into slavery. Cleon does not refrain from harshly criticizing the Athenians assembled before him, as well as the democratic regime on which they pride themselves. Though the Athenians have acquired a huge empire across much of the Mediterranean, Cleon tells them that he has often thought that democracies cannot rule over other cities. Indeed, the mere fact that they now want to reverse their decision is evidence that democracies lack the grit to rule effectively over others. Speaking to committed democrats, he attacks citizens of democracies: They are too trusting; they are too ready to feel pity. As a result of trusting each other, they do not recognize the importance of fear as a ruling principle for a city aspiring to imperial power. He shows no shame in attacking the practices underlying the regime that his audience holds dear. That regime hinders them from being an effective imperial power. The principles that allow him to speak freely open the door to attack those principles. Cleon's *parrhêsia*

---

[8] This section draws in part from Saxonhouse, *Free Speech* (2006), 151–63.

becomes an indictment of *parrhêsia*, indeed a critique not only of free speech but of speech itself, of what lies at the heart of the Athenian political regime, centered as it is on the Assembly and the open deliberation among the citizens who freely and courageously express their views.

As with most of the speeches in Thucydides's *History*, Cleon's speech is filled with such ironies. In Cleon's speech, the speaker attacks speaking, but there he is speaking courageously—and outrageously—before the Athenian Assembly, criticizing them for attending to words more than deeds, relying on listening more than seeing. And in a potent mixed metaphor, he accuses the Athenians of "being spectators of words and listeners of deeds ... trusting sight less than what comes through hearing, giving honor to what comes beautifully from speech" (3.38).[9] The Athenians who gloried in their resistance to the Persian tyrant in the Persian Wars fifty years prior, who celebrated their freedom as what distinguished them from barbarians, are now offensively called "slaves" by Cleon. Their slavishness lies in their subjection not to harsh masters like the Persian tyrant who curbed his subjects' tongues, but to the intangible words they hear as they sit in the Assembly, "overcome by the pleasure of listening and seated as if attending the theater of the Sophists rather than deliberating for the city" (3.38). Availing himself of the Athenian practice of *parrhêsia*, he chastises the Athenians for delighting in listening to the speeches of others who, failing to speak boldly, refuse to acknowledge that Athens is a "tyrant" ruling over an empire. He appeals to popular sentiment by uncovering their limitations as rulers.

Cleon, for sure, demonstrates the courage that goes along with the practice of *parrhêsia*, the willingness to express what may offend by pointing out flaws in what the Athenians treasure about their own political regime. *Parrhêsia* enables him to attack speeches that flatter and entertain. Diodotus, proposing a reversal of the original decision to execute the men of Mytilene and sell the women and children into slavery, does just the opposite; he defends speech as the necessary source of good policy for an imperial power, but he also identifies how *parrhêsia* must be treated as suspect, how Cleon, while deriding flattering and entertaining speeches and openly and offensively expressing what he professes to believe, may himself, under the cover of *parrhesia*, be deceptively manipulating his listeners.

---

[9] Translations from Thucydides come from Jeremy Mynott, *Thucydides, The War of the Peloponnesians and the Athenians* (Cambridge, UK: Cambridge University Press, 2013), unless otherwise noted.

Diodotus, Son of Eucrates

We know nothing of Diodotus apart from the speech that Thucydides assigns him. His speech, though, justifies his name as the Gift of Zeus, son of Good Rule. He articulates a vision of a polis that practices *parrhêsia* at the same time that he recognizes the challenges that such a regime would face. By acknowledging those challenges, his speech becomes a pessimistic warning to political leaders about how *parrhêsia* needs to be a source of subterfuge rather than revealing one's true beliefs.

Cleon had opposed rescinding the original Athenian decree concerning the punishment of the Mytilenians and blamed democratic Athenians for allowing themselves to be enchanted by the speakers who entertain rather than uncover harsh truths. Diodotus, in arguing to rescind the decree, does not attack the free deliberations in the Assembly, as had Cleon. But he suggests that the Assembly—despite the Athenian pride in *parrhêsia*—limits *parrhêsia*, thereby interfering with its capacity to make wise policy decisions. Diodotus does not refrain from attacking Cleon. He calls anyone (namely, Cleon) who might argue that speech is an impediment to good policy "stupid" and accuses such a person of attending to his own self-interest rather than the interest of the city (3.34). Good policy decisions depend on predicting the future, he says, and the only way to foresee the future is through speech. Yet, while speech is necessary for making such assessments about the future, speech—as Cleon understands only too well—can also be a medium of manipulation.

Recognizing this, Diodotus envisions a city in which *parrhêsia* reigns, but does not transform into a tool of manipulation. Instead, in his imagined city the "good citizen" is not perceived as a threat to those with whom he disagrees, but is recognized as "speaking better." He calls such a dream city where *parrhêsia* is properly practiced a "moderate city" (3.42). In such a city there are neither excessive honors for those whose opinions are judged best nor shame for those whose advice is rejected. This is a city in which the free exchange of ideas would predominate. In such a city, words are not necessarily associated with a particular speaker, and speakers would not be concerned with how their words are received by the assembled citizens. Speakers would not seek praise, nor would they worry about shame should they fail to persuade. The speakers in this moderate city would speak freely because the listeners would hear the words without, in a sense, seeing the speaker. In a reversal of Cleon's formulation, they would be listeners of words, not their spectators. Arguments would exist independently of the person expressing them. Such speeches would engender policies that benefit the city rather than the speaker. Cleon had accused the Athenian Assemblymen of craving entertainment, thereby encouraging speakers to say what is pleasing rather than express the harsh truths Cleon insists on. The speakers in Diodtous's moderate city, not saying what they do not think best, nor eager to say what is entertaining (3.42), would fulfill the promise of *parrhêsia*, the practice on which the Athenians pride themselves but do not, both Cleon and Diodotus suggest, in fact enjoy.

This moderate city of wise counsel unfortunately, though, exists only in Diodotus's imagination. Diodotus recognizes the difference between his dreams and the practices governed by a human nature that is suspicious, that does not welcome criticisms, that longs for entertainment. For Cleon, the Athenians were incapable of ruling an empire because they were too trusting; democracy softened them so that they lacked the suspicious nature that would enable them to see the self-interest behind the charming speeches given in the Assembly. For Diodotus, in contrast, the Athenians are *too* suspicious, assuming that speakers are concerned with their private advantages rather than the public welfare, causing Athenians to resist good advice along with the bad. *Parrhêsia* is undermined when both good and bad advice are equally subject to suspicion. For the practice to contribute to the health of the city, citizens must trust one another. Once suspicion enters the democratic polity, deception replaces *parrhêsia*. Advisers, even if they are eager to advise wisely, must do so under cover (3.43). Thus, even Diodotus—that gift of Zeus—must not speak with *parrhêsia*, courageously saying what he believes to be best, but must speak under the pretense of speaking freely.

Are we, then, to accept what Diodotus says as what he really believes—or not? Is he concerned about his reputation before the citizens of Athens— or not? He warns his listeners that given the current situation in Athens where suspicion reigns, speakers will adjust their speeches to suit the audience, just as Cleon accused his audience of encouraging speakers to do when they responded to the theatrical performances of orators in the Assembly. Diodotus had imagined a city of free speech in the utopian vision of a moderate city where neither blame nor praise followed a speaker's willingness to say what he thought to be best, but the Athens in which he lives is not such a utopia. Thus, does the speech he gives come from what he really believes, free from any concern with reputation—or is it one that he fashions to win praise?

After his prefatory remarks about the need for deception in the city that is not moderate, Diodotus launches into his arguments, first flattering his audience: "I have come forward neither to represent the Mytilenians nor to accuse them. The issue for us, if *we are [moderate]* is not about their wrongdoing but about [*our* good counsel]" (3.44).[10] He joins himself with his audience when he uses the phrases "if *we* are moderate" (the same word he used to describe the city of his dreams) and "*our* good counsel." Following his criticism of the suspicious nature of those taking counsel in the Assembly as unable to listen to good advice, he describes the *dêmos*, along with himself, as good deliberators, moderate and of good counsel. As such, they should look not to the guilt or innocence of the Mytilenians, the justice or injustice of their rebellion, but to what serves the interests of the Athenians: "If I showed them to be guilty of great crimes I would not on that account urge you to go on and put them to death unless that were expedient for us" (3.44). He then enumerates the benefits of rescinding the previous day's decision: Harsh punishments only encourage other rebels to fight to the death rather than yield quickly, thereby costing the Athenians more to subdue rebellions. Further, a rebel city will resist longer and their resources will be destroyed in the process of subduing it.

With such reasoning, Diodotus persuades the Athenians to dismiss Cleon's arguments, to rescind the decree, and to dispatch a ship canceling the previously decreed punishment. Only the leaders of the rebellion will be executed; the women and children will not be sold into slavery. Thucydides, in a rare moment of revealing his own thoughts, sighs in relief: "By luck there were no contrary winds, and since the first ship was not hurrying on its unwelcome mission" (3.49); the second ship reaches Mytilene prior to the one carrying the original decree. Diodotus's speech prevented the massacre, but given his prefatory remarks we do not know whether this gift of Zeus was speaking frankly or deceptively, whether his claims not to care about justice, about the consequences of harsh punishments, were what he truly believed or simply devices to lead the Athenians to make a more humane (and just) decision.

Thucydides has with this famous interlude himself uncovered the problematic nature of the practice of *parrhêsia*, a practice essential for a democratic regime and celebrated by those citizens who enjoyed it, but difficult to follow given a human nature that is either (as Cleon suggests) too trusting

---

[10] Mynott's translation modified in the bracketed phrases.

or (as Diodotus suggests) too suspicious. As a practice cherished and celebrated by the free Athenians of the unbridled tongue, it may only function effectively in Diodotus's imagined regime and not in the everyday politics of democratic Athens.

Thucydides's *History*: The Sicilian Expedition, *Parrhêsia*, and Facts

The speakers in the Mytilenian debate reveal the tensions surrounding the exercise of *parrhêsia* and the challenges of applying such a practice in an assembly deliberating about what actions best serve the collective whole. Much later in the *History* and during the war itself, Thucydides records another debate at Athens, this time about whether to respond to a request from Athens's allies, the Egestaeans, to send ships to Sicily to support them in their conflict with Selinuntines. Ultimately, the issue is not whether to support an ally, but whether to expand the empire through an expedition to Sicily against the rising power of Syracuse who threatens Athenian dominance in the Mediterranean. In this set piece Thucydides records three speeches, two by the general Nicias and one by Alcibiades. Discussion about the resources necessary for an expedition to Sicily becomes a reconsideration of the initial decision to embark on such an adventure.

Thucydides introduces the Sicilian expedition by writing that the Athenians were "inexperienced" (6.1) of the nature, the size, and the population of the island of Sicily. He writes this despite reporting in the previous book that in response to frequent requests from the Egestaeans, the Athenians had sent scouts to Egesta to assess that city's resources and consider whether it would serve Athens's interest to have the Egestaeans as allies. Though the scouts reported many attractions that might induce the Athenians to embark on the expedition, the intelligence was misleading or, as Thucydides writes, was "not true" (6.8). Either the scouts had been bribed or misled, but in either case the Athenians (as Cleon had warned) were too trusting. They did not question the motives of their scouts and, relying on misleading reports, the Athenians voted to send sixty ships under the command of Nicias, Alcibiades, and Lamachus to Sicily. The speeches of Nicias and Alcibiades reassessing this decision are plagued by the inadequacy of access to knowledge, raising the issue of how the freedom to speak that which is based on inadequate information or facts harms the city. Speaking freely entails courageously saying what one truly believes—but that does not ensure that what one believes and dares to say is accurate.

Given the uncertainty of knowledge, *parrhêsia*, rather than being act of courage, of speaking truth to power as Thersites does, can become an occasion to use uncertain facts to mislead one's listeners. As Thucydides presents it, speaking freely in the debate about Sicily is not only an *opportunity* to deceive; it becomes a necessity, a necessity that Diodotus had suggested for all cities except his moderate city of *parrhêsiastes*, those who speak freely, a necessity that Nicias fails to understand at first and only exercises too late to save Athens from the disaster that follows. After the Athenians voted to sail to Sicily, they meet four days later to assess how to equip the expedition. At this meeting Nicias urges a reconsideration of their initial decision and Alcibiades responds.

Nicias 1

Thucydides prefaces Nicias's speech by telling us that "Nicias had been elected to the command against his wishes, and he thought that the city had reached the wrong decision and was harboring ambitions for Sicily as a whole, a huge undertaking but one conceived on the basis of slight and specious considerations" (6.8). Thucydides indicates that the speech Nicias gives matches his understanding of the situation. Nicias speaks here without deception and tells the Athenians directly that he does not think that they conducted an adequate investigation prior to voting to go to Sicily. A more careful and slower consideration would be necessary before trusting the foreign ambassadors (6.9). To emphasize that his words express what he truly believes, he acknowledges that should he serve as a general on this expedition, he would earn the Athenians' esteem (i.e., he would benefit from the expedition he urges the Athenians to reconsider). By opposing it, he must be looking to the city's, not his own, advantage. He continues: "I have never in the past sought preferment by speaking contrary to my real beliefs, nor do I do so now" (6.9). He presents himself as entirely transparent. He recognizes, though, the difficulties in persuading them; the Athenian character is too active, too driven to resist expanding its rule. He simply wants to persuade them to delay until a more propitious time, and so he identifies the pressures the Athenians still face in Greece: the Spartan forces ready to attack, the rebellious Chalcedonians in Thrace, the potential rebellions in other subject cities. He does not flatter the Athenians by noting their successes; he highlights their vulnerabilities. Rather than praise their daring, he says that their earlier victories against Sparta were not the result of great skill or their unique character, but "contrary to reason" (6.11). They simply were lucky, not the great military power they imagine themselves to be. No flattery here. Such is Nicias's venture into the realm of *parrhêsia*, speaking truth to the locus of power in the city, the *dêmos* listening to him as they sit in their Assembly. It does him and the city little good.

While Nicias affirms his willingness to speak truthfully without fearing the consequences, he recognizes well that others may not speak truthfully. The Egestaeans may have "lied beautifully" (61.2), he says, but he is even more concerned about Alcibiades, who is about to speak enthusiastically in favor of the expedition. Nicias's honest expression of his views, his warnings that others may lie, that the facts about conditions in Sicily may be difficult to discern, have little effect. Most of those who spoke following his speech argue in favor of the decision to fund the expedition. But Nicias was not only worried that an absence of careful consideration of the facts enabled by the possibly lying Egestaeans; he worried as well that Alcibiades who, he anticipated, taking advantage of the uncertainty about the facts of the situation, would defend the expedition out of a concern for his own aggrandizement. Alcibiades's speech does not disappoint.

Alcibiades

Alcibiades is brazen and daring, unrestrained, freely revealing himself to the eager audience. Immediately he tells the Athenians, whose democratic regime is built on the equality of all citizens who share rule in the city, of his own preeminence: "It more fitting for me to rule than others" (6.16). He deserves such stature, he says, because of the honor he has brought to his ancestors and the benefits he has given the fatherland. Neither modesty nor shame marks Alcibiades's self-presentation. He alone, he says, rescued Athens from its low reputation among other cities through his victories in the Olympic games. His success accrues to the success of Athens, he asserts, as he defends his superiority before those living in a regime that embraces equality: "It is not unjust that the one who is great think of himself as not equal ... let others endure the arrogance of those who flourish" (6.16).[11] Fearlessly, arrogantly,

[11] My translation.

shamelessly, Alcibiades speaks of his stature. He acknowledges that such superiority may arouse envy in others, those inferior to himself, but they must overcome their envy. They must abandon their egalitarian principles, and he asks the Athenians outright whether they can identify anyone more competent than he to handle the city's affairs (6.16). Alcibiades feels no need to deceive the Athenians about himself, about his suitability for leading the expedition. He speaks with *parrhêsia*, as he suggests in language all too familiar in the modern world of populist leaders that he alone can serve as the hero to whom Athens must turn to save them and expand their greatness.

To lead the expedition, though, the Athenians must confirm their decision to pursue the expedition and defend it against Nicias's warnings about the dangers it poses. Though Alcibiades has no more evidence about the situation in Sicily than does Nicias, he simply asserts that he "has heard reports" ("people tell me") about the fragility of the Sicilian forces (6.17). He does not mention who provided these reports. He could be making them up—or not. Those who brought the reports could have been lying. Nevertheless, Alcibiades shows no hesitation in asserting the certainty of what he wants those reports to say. We do not know if he deceives. Whether he lies or offers inadequate information, though, is irrelevant. The Athenians are enthralled by his boldness in speaking freely of his ambitions and his own excellence, abandoning their own commitment to equality. Satisfied by his assurances of the Syracusans' weakness and their own strength, they become even more eager to pursue the expedition. Dismissive of Nicias's warnings and under the spell of Alcibiades, the Athenians accept Alcibiades's claims that the Peloponnesians are no longer a threat, and they remain eager for the Sicilian expedition.

Nicias 2

Nicias's second speech in this meeting of the Assembly is perhaps the most curious speech in all of Thucydides's *History*. Nicias reverses himself. Recognizing that the Athenians had become more enthusiastic about the expedition and that nothing he could say along the lines of his previous arguments would persuade them to abandon the expedition, he tries to discourage them by detailing the enormity of the preparations required for such an adventure, to show how challenging it would be to send forces to Sicily. The Athenians would need to leave nothing to chance, requiring a huge commitment of resources. As with the introductory remarks before Nicias's first speech, Thucydides writes of Nicias's intentions: "Nicias said all this, thinking that he would thereby deter the Athenians by the magnitude of the task he was presenting or, if he were forced to undertake the expedition, they would... be sailing out with the maximum security" (6.24).

In his first speech Nicias had spoken what he truly believed, but he discovered that doing so did not foster good judgment among the Athenians. In this second try at dissuading the Athenians from the expedition, he hopes to be more effective, speaking manipulatively rather than saying what he really believes, exaggerating and appearing to condone the expedition that he opposes. In this second speech he tries to follow the Diodotus's lesson: Athens is not the moderate city where everyone speaking what they believed—indifferent to the praise or blame that might follow their speeches, indifferent to what serves their own interests—would foster careful deliberation and good policy decisions. Instead, the successful speaker must avoid speaking openly of what he truly believes; he must structure his words with a view to the frailties of the audience. Diodotus speaking in that fashion, as he argued against the harsh punishment for the Mytilenians, claiming to be indifferent to questions of justice, ensured that justice would be done. Nicias, in exaggerating the resources necessary for the expedition, is not so successful. The Athenians become even more enthusiastic after his speech, a speech Nicias had intended to dampen their enthusiasm. They vote to supply all the resources Nicias enumerated—and more. Nicias was not as successful as Diodotus was in manipulating the people to make the right decisions. But then again, Nicias was a historical character active in fifth-century Athens; Diodotus, otherwise unknown, was the "gift of Zeus."

When Nicias is killed by the Syracusans, Thucydides offers a sympathetic obituary notice, describing Nicias as one whose "life had been regulated by virtuous practices" (7.86). He tried to exercise the Athenian practice of *parrhêsia*,[12] but his fortunes were caught up in the ambiguity of how *parrhêsia*'s effects played out in the political world of democratic Athens. Diodotus explained that unabashedly speaking what one considered best in the Assembly, however valued by the Athenians as a central element of their free democratic regime, did not necessarily benefit the city—nor the individuals who did so. The unbridled tongue may have differentiated

---

[12] See also the letter he writes to the Athenian Assembly in which he depicts without restraint the suffering of the Athenians in Sicily (7.11–15).

tyranny from the free regime, but when put into practice in a political setting before a people—whether too trusting or too suspicious—it did not always benefit the city. It may take that gift of Zeus to persuade a people to act both justly and for the welfare of the city as a whole.

What happens when *parrhêsia* leaves the Assembly and infuses the speeches of Socrates and the comic stage of Aristophanes?

Plato

Turning briefly to Plato, we see the civic virtue of *parrhêsia* functioning in the private realm, where its multifaceted nature surfaces once again. Plato's dialogues bring *parrhêsia* from the public world where speakers respond to the call "Who wishes to speak?" to the private lives of an array of the Athenian citizens and others with whom Socrates engages.[13] There, Socrates's *parrhêsia* marks the behavior of the private individual, the one who is or has the potential to be the Socratic philosopher who brashly investigates the city's beliefs, boldly striving to uncover the truths often hidden behind the city's opinions, however uncomfortable those truths may be for his interlocutors.

Socrates's execution in democratic Athens has led many to question the degree to which Athens *was* a democracy with freedom of speech. The story of his execution is complicated and the subject of a variety of competing theories, from amazement that he survived as long as he did, to the theory that the Athenians were responding to his aggressive criticism of democracy, to the notion that his execution was provoked by his ties to the members of the recently expelled Thirty Tyrants who had been installed by Sparta after Athens's defeat in the Peloponnesian War—and more.[14] All these theories build on the expectation that a democratic regime that celebrates the freedoms of its citizens would not execute someone for speaking freely, for pursuing the truth and fostering the good life through dialogue. The paradox of Socrates's execution haunts defenders of democracy and of free speech. Yet, the practice of *parrhêsia* itself calls forth the paradox, for free speech as a treasured privilege can both allow one to express one's views, as with Cleon and Nicias's first speech, and it can also be deceptive and

---

[13] For a full discussion of *parrhêsia*'s significance for Plato's dialogues and philosophy, see Monoson, *Plato's Democratic Entanglements*, chapter 2.

[14] For a review of the many theories considering why Socrates was executed, see Saxonhouse, *Free Speech*, 100–12.

manipulative, as with Diodotus. In addition, in the case of the Socratic adventure, by uncovering the tensions and inconsistencies in the norms and practices of a society, *parrhêsia* can reveal painful truths and can threaten the stability of the community. Socrates's most famous words may be "The unexamined life is not worth living," but examining one's life may painfully expose the paradoxes that constitute the assumed certainties on which one's city is constructed.

The Apology of Socrates

At the beginning of the *Apology of Socrates*, Plato's rendition of Socrates's speech at his trial for impiety and the corruption of the young, Socrates claims that he is "not a clever speaker" and that those who have spoken of him as such will immediately be refuted when he begins to speak—that is, "unless of course they call a clever speaker the one who speaks the truth" (17b).[15] Of course, Socrates's speech is exceedingly "clever," employing a multitude of rhetorical devices, not least of which is the false modesty apparent in his opening statement. He may take a self-deprecating stance, but he speaks without any concern for shame for himself or respect for Athens.[16] Like Cleon and Nicias in his first speech, Socrates refuses to flatter the Athenians. His speech becomes an opening up, an uncovering of himself and his own flaws, as well as the flaws of the Athenians, those who are listening to the speech and who will judge him. He neither preserves a realm of privacy for himself, nor does he allow the Athenians to retreat self-contentedly into their conventions and their traditional religious beliefs. His *parrhêsia*, guided by a refusal to flatter and an eagerness to reveal himself, challenges the city. Rather than understand the Socrates of the *Apology* as a martyr for free speech, as so many have done,[17] I propose that we read this speech in the context of Athenian democracy and the role of *parrhêsia* as the shameless uncovering of oneself and a disregard for the limiting effects of respect.[18] For Socrates, this entailed the unrestrained search for

---

[15] I use the translation by Thomas G. West and Grace Starry West, *Four Texts on Socrates* (Ithaca, NY: Cornell University Press, 1984), with Stephanus pagination.
[16] Eva Brann entitles an article on the *Apology* "The Offense of Socrates: A Re-reading of Plato's *Apology*," *Interpretation* 7, no. 2 (1978): 1–21.
[17] Most famously, perhaps, John Stuart Mill in *On Liberty*, edited by Elizabeth Rapaport (Indianapolis, IN: Hackett, 1978), 23.
[18] For a fuller discussion, see Saxonhouse, "A Shameless Socrates."

"truth," *alêthê*, a word repeated over and over and over in the *Apology*. Yet uncovering the truth about himself before the Athenians, revealing who he is, describing the peculiar life he has lived for seventy years and that he refuses to abandon, also reveals the truth about the Athenians, leading him to offend his listeners even as he mocks himself. Several times he must ask them to restrain their cries of anger so that he can continue to speak (20e, 30c).

The *Apology* begins with Socrates acknowledging the power of speech to deceive, telling the jurors that the clever rhetoric of his accusers has almost made him forget who he is. He, in contrast, will present himself unadorned by deceptive "cosmetics." He will disabuse them of the fabrications circulating about him, namely that he is "a wise man, a thinker on the things aloft, who has investigated all things under the earth, who makes the weaker speech appear the stronger" (18bc) and one who teaches the young. These slanders prevent his accusers and the city from seeing who he truly is. He finds the source of these slanders in his "wisdom," what he calls "perhaps a human wisdom" (20d). This "human wisdom" derives from the story of his friend Chaerephon's visit to the oracle at Delphi, where the oracle told Chaerephon that there is no one wiser than Socrates. Ready to disprove the oracle (openly admitting that he does not hesitate to challenge even the gods, to suggest that the oracle may be false), Socrates questions the politicians, poets, and artisans, only to discover that the wisdom the oracle attributes to him rests in his willingness to acknowledge that he does not know. Unlike the others who present themselves as wise, Socrates without shame makes no pretense to wisdom. By uncovering the ignorance of those who pretend to be wise, he earns their contempt and hatred.

Though Socrates had claimed that his wisdom came from knowing that he did not know, during his speech he communicates the principles that have guided his life. They are, however, also principles that undermine the traditions that govern the political and cultural world of the Athenians. Emphasizing his disdain for what they honor, he does not soften the grounds for the Athenians' animus toward him. Responding to an imagined "someone" who might question whether he is not ashamed to put his life in danger, he likens himself to the Homeric demi-god Achilles. There he is, short, stooped, bug-eyed, a snub-nosed old man resembling a satyr or crawfish, a Thersites-like character, suggesting that they should view him as the Athenian version of the great warrior of the Homeric epics. The arrogance of such a comparison does not inhibit Socrates, but it does arouse the resentment of the crowd listening to his speech. This, though, is only the preface to even more outrageous statements. From telling the jury that he is wise because he knows that he does not know (and neither do the jurors to whom he is speaking), Socrates reminds the Athenians of how he "go[es] around and do[es] nothing but persuade you, both younger and older, not to care for bodies and money before, nor as vehemently as, how your soul will be best possible" (30b). He has tried to topple their warrior hero and now he demeans what the Athenians esteem; the visible signs of success are to be replaced by the qualities of an invisible soul, impervious to human judgment or punishment. So much for the value of a jury of citizens assembled to judge him.

As Socrates, on trial for impiety and corruption of the young, continues to expose himself to the Athenians, he next suggests that they should welcome him as a gift from the gods to the city. What sort of gift? A gadfly, a contemptable little bug that bites the sleeping horse that is Athens. Athens, glorious Athens, in Socrates's defense speech before the city, is a lazy beast. The *parrhêsia* he enjoys as an Athenian citizen allows him to insult the city even as he mocks himself. As the crowd responds to his offensive suggestion, Socrates admonishes them: "Do not be angered at me speaking true things" (31e). He is simply engaging in the practice in which the democrats before whom he speaks take such pride.

At the core of Socrates's *Apology* is the indictment of the Athenians who do not follow their own principles of *parrhesia*, lacking the courage to speak openly, relying on speech to provide "cosmetics" that hide the truth. Consequently, Socrates retreats from the political realm. "Do you suppose," he rhetorically asks his judges, "that I would have survived so many years if I had been publicly active?" (32e). Instead, Socrates must take *parrhêsia* as the opportunity to examine all without hesitation, away from the public realm of the democratic city with its deliberative Assembly and its law courts, to the private world of the gymnasia, the homes of the wealthy, the woods outside the city where the Platonic dialogues take place. Given that in "public I do not dare to go up before your multitude to counsel the city," he becomes what he calls a "busybody in private" (31c). Had he been politically active, he explains, "I would long ago have perished and I would have benefited neither you nor myself" (31d). The philosopher with his unbridled tongue must practice *parrhêsia* in private, eschewing the deceptive speeches that Diodotus indicated were necessary in the non-utopian democratic city of Athens.

Democracy in the *Republic*

In the eighth book of Plato's *Republic*, as Socrates describes the descent from the regime he has portrayed as just, a regime in which there is no freedom of speech, where poetry is censored and Homer's stories are drastically altered lest they seem to condone cowardice, excessive grief, and self-indulgences, Socrates turns to a portrayal of the democratic regime. He ignores the institutions that define Athenian democracy, the Assembly, the law courts, the offices, and focuses instead on what we might today refer to as the culture of the regime, what is the "character" of the regime (8.557a). He phrases his initial description of democracy as a series of questions: "In the first place, then, aren't they free? And isn't the city full of freedom and free speech (*parrhêsia*)? And isn't there license in it to do whatever one wants?" He continues: "And where there's license, it's plain that each man would organize his life in it privately just as it pleases him" (557b).[19] The portrait he offers of life in this regime, filled with *parrhêsia*, shows a city "unbridled," completely unrestrained, where "purchased slaves, male and female, are no less free than those who have bought them." He continues: "And we almost forgot to mention the extent of the law of equality and of freedom in the relations of women with men and men with women." This comment provokes his interlocutor Adeimantus to ask: "Won't we with Aeschylus say whatever just came to our lips?" (563bc), alerting the readers of the dialogue to the potential for blasphemy in this democracy, the regime filled with *parrhêsia*.

While there is a certain horror at how far this freedom can go—even the horses and asses refuse to step aside for citizens—with the regime ultimately becoming a tyranny as a result of its excesses of freedom, Socrates initially suggests an ambiguity. He describes democracy as "the fairest (*kallistê*, most beautiful) of regimes . . . just like a many-colored cloak . . . decorated with all dispositions." As such, it would look "most beautiful" (*kallistê*, again)," and "many . . . like boys and women looking at many-colored things, would judge this to be the fairest (*kallistê*, yet again)" (557c). In this brief comment, Socrates uses "most beautiful" three times. It is beautiful because it is many colored and "contains all species of regimes"; and because of that "it is probably necessary for the man who wishes to organize a city, as we were just doing, to go to a city under a democracy" (557d). The freedom of the

---

[19] I use the translation of *Republic* by Allan Bloom, *The Republic of Plato* (New York: Basic Books, 1968), with Stephanus pagination. All references are to Book 8.

democracy described in the *Republic*, filled as it is with *parrhêsia*, opens the space for philosophers such as Socrates to philosophize, to engage in just the sort of discourses that fill the Platonic dialogues—whether they be about the nature of justice, the meaning of friendship, the source of knowledge, or the multitude of other issues about which Socrates questions his companions.

Immediately after the passage on the beauty of democracy, Socrates notes that in this democratic city no one is compelled to rule or to make war when the city is at war. In Athens, citizens were expected to fill the various offices; citizens went to war when the city did.[20] As Pericles remarks in his Funeral Oration: "We alone regard the person who fails to participate in public affairs not just as harmless but as positively useless" (2.40). Not so in Socrates's democracy, where there is "the absence of any compulsion to rule ... even if you are competent to rule" (557e). In this regime of *parrhêsia* the philosopher can be the philosopher.

In this dialogue, where Socrates imagines the sort of democratic regime of *parrhêsia* where he could converse with others to explore the nature of justice and found a just city in speech, he nevertheless acknowledges that the freedom to engage in such conversations can lead to a regime of indiscriminate desires and disorder, laying the groundwork for the unbounded force of the tyrannical regime. The license that allows everyone to say whatever "comes to one's lips," the failure to distinguish between good and bad speech, the blasphemy to which Adeimantus alludes, culminates in tyranny. Yet, that license in Athens itself had enabled Socrates to philosophize for seventy years. *Parrhêsia* benefits and harms. In Socrates's telling, what may harm the public world with its license to misrepresent and blaspheme, to ignore useful restraints, is essential for the philosopher to be free to examine all, one's own life, ancient beliefs, and contemporary values.[21]

In Socrates's telling, the freedom to say whatever one thinks or wants to say—true or not true, blasphemous or pious—leads directly to tyranny. The refusal to discriminate good speech from bad speech allows for the emergence of the tyrant as the democracy full of freedom is replaced by a regime of maximal restraint.

---

[20] In the next section on Aristophanes's *Acharnians* we will meet a citizen who tries to avoid the compulsion to go to war when the city does.
[21] Other Platonic dialogues examine the place of *parrhêsia* in the philosophic life. See especially the *Laches* and *Gorgias* and the discussions in Monoson, *Plato's Democratic Entanglements* and Foucault, *Fearless Speech*.

Aristophanes

When Adeimantus imagines the blasphemy that accompanies the freedom to say whatever one pleases, he could easily be thinking of Aristophanes's fifth-century comedies. Aristophanes did not hold back in his comedies—mocking the gods with abandon, imagining a timid Dionysus or an impotent Zeus. Nor did he refrain from making fun of political leaders, the Athenian *dêmos*, renowned tragic playwrights. Nothing and no one were beyond Aristophanes's satirical pen; all were ripe for ridicule before the Athenian audiences. Space does not allow a full exploration of the many comedies in which Aristophanes openly exercises his willingness and freedom to uncover the vanities and frailties of those around him; I consider here only his first comedy, the *Acharnians*, where the exercise of *parrhêsia* explicitly enters the action of the play.

In this comedy the protagonist is a man named Dikaiopolis (Just City) who, tired of the deprivations imposed by the war with Sparta, decides to make a private peace with Sparta by buying a thirty-year treaty from a "treaty-seller." He does this after initially appearing on stage, waiting impatiently for the Athenian citizens to arrive for a meeting of the Assembly. He has been frustrated in his previous efforts to argue for peace before the *dêmos*. When the citizens finally arrive, the question (per practice) is posed: "Who wishes to speak (45)?"[22] Dikaiopolis rises, but contrary to the practice of *isêgoria*, he is repeatedly told to sit down and be quiet (59, 64, 123). The Assemblymen instead spend their time criticizing current political leaders and considering possible alliances with Persia and Thracian mercenaries, before adjourning (much to Dikaiopolis's consternation) without discussing peace. Indeed, throughout the comedy Dikaiopolis is denied the opportunity to speak. "Won't you listen to me, isn't it necessary that you listen to me?" he asks (321) the Chorus of Acharnians, who threaten to stone him to death for entering into a private treaty, only to be told "We won't listen.... May I die if I listen to you" (323–24). Consistent with the inconsistency of comedy, the Chorus nevertheless insists on being persuaded by Dikaiopolis that he is not a traitor to the city—at the same time that they also refuse to listen to him. After telling him that he must persuade them that they should not stone him to death, they continue to refuse to listen, chanting: "You shall die now" (324).

---

[22] Translations from the *Acharnians* are my own.

But this is a comedy, and Dikaiopolis is not stoned to death. He has taken hostage a basket of coal, a commodity dear to the economic heart of the Chorus of men from the coal-producing area of Acharnia, and he threatens to "kill" the coal (whatever that may mean). Under this pressure, the Chorus now asks him to speak "what seems best to you" (338); terrified about the fate of their beloved coal, they listen. Freed to speak what he thinks, Dikaiopolis initially chastises the Chorus for refusing to hear him, for being unwilling to listen "equal to equal" (354). Though they claim to be devoted patriots who love Athens, they reject the central principles of Athens's democratic regime: *parrhêsia* and *isêgoria*. Neither those who came to the Assembly at the beginning of the comedy nor the Chorus that threatens Dikaiopolis with stoning had allowed Dikaiopolis to speak. The Chorus claims to act on behalf of their city, a city that they say does no wrong, one that could not be responsible even in part for the destructive war with Sparta, but these supposed defenders of Athens do not value what makes Athens worthy of defense. The Chorus was not willing to hear how its sense of what is in its and the city's interest might be mistaken. Loath to engage in the deliberations that are supposed to characterize the democratic regime at Athens, the Acharnians resisted considering why the city might want to seek out the treaty-seller, as had Dikaiolpolis. Dikaiopolis, holding that hostage basket of coal, though, can now explain why the city should pursue peace and not war.

As happens often in Aristophanic comedy, mid-comedy the Chorus abandons its role as a character in the action of the play and speaks directly to the audience in defense of and in the voice of Aristophanes. In the persona of the Chorus, Aristophanes defends himself and criticizes the *dêmos* for failing to acknowledge the benefits that would be theirs were they to listen to what Aristophanes (as Dikaiopolis) advises. Dikaiopolis had been threatened with stoning on stage; analogously, Aristophanes had been slandered by Cleon. To defend himself against Cleon, he does not rise in response to heralds' question in the Assembly; rather, he speaks freely from the comic stage, giving voice to criticisms he is prepared to make about Athenian politics and policies. They, his audience, he tells them, are too quick to make judgments; they are arrogant and hubristic toward the comic poet. They are like the Chorus of his comedy, ready to throw stones at those whose speeches they dislike, unwilling to listen to them when they speak of what seems best to serve the welfare of themselves and of the city. For this unreflective *dêmos*, he tells them, he—the comic poet—has brought about many good things. In particular, he has protected them from being deceived by the contrived and novel speeches they hear in the Assembly; he has taught them to resist the orators' flattery. Further, he protects them from being deceived by the shiny offerings and flattering words of ambassadors from abroad. It is he, Aristophanes himself, who can save the city from itself, who can prevent the crowd of citizens from becoming the crazed stone-throwing Acharnians he has portrayed on stage. Were they to become such stone-throwers, they too might become the ridiculous objects of the city's laughter. As Dikaiopolis had said moments before, while pouring disdain on the old, flustered coal-loving men, the comic poet teaches just things (500–1, 661–62).

Aristophanes goes so far as to say that he has educated "the *dêmos* within cities as to how to be governed democratically" (642). Having portrayed on stage an Assembly of Athenian citizens that rejected honest deliberation when they initially denied Dikaiopolis the opportunity to speak at the beginning of the play, Aristophanes, speaking through the transformed Chorus, courageously claims that the democratic citizenry of Athens, lacking the guidance of the poet, is simply a fickle crowd subject to the cunning and flattery of manipulative speakers. They do not know what is best, what is just, refusing to listen to those who speak honestly. They do not see the truths that are hidden by what seems to be; they are fooled by the disguises with which clever speakers can readily attire themselves. Celebrating *parrhesia* as a special Athenian attribute, they nevertheless subject themselves to deceitful speech. Both Cleon's and Diodotus's shadows hang heavily over the citizens of Aristophanes's jeremiad.

This part of the Chorus's song, with Aristophanes defending himself from the slanders of Cleon, concludes by reiterating the importance of the poet for the city. Aristophanes again insists that it is the poet writing his comedies who teaches just things (655) and thereby ensures the city's flourishing. He does so, the Chorus says, "Not by flattery nor bribery nor deception nor evil doing, but by teaching what is best" (657–58) when he reveals the Athenians to themselves on stage. The comedian, through his admirable courage, protects the *dêmos* from itself, draining from them the anger that drove them to attack the peace-loving Dikaiopolis. The comic poet, the Chorus suggests, molds the *dêmos* by fearlessly exposing its faults. Socrates's efforts in the *Apology* did not ultimately deter the jury from condemning him to death. Aristophanes's efforts through comedy allow him to remain a writer of comedy for many more decades.

The *Acharnians* is unabashedly an anti-war piece. When Aristophanes speaks to his audience, he does not voice a platitudinous love of the fatherland, as had the stone-throwing Chorus ready to kill the peace-loving "Just City." He acknowledges, as had Dikaiopolis, Athens's culpability in the starting the war. Aristophanes's comedies build on his recognition of and sympathy for the bodily longings that drive humans—their sexual, gustatory, even excretory desires. This makes his characters fit for the comic stage, and though he may mock them, he does not disdain those longings. Instead, he is eager to show that satisfying them depends on wise policies directed toward peace. He uses what ties the human to the animal world, what makes them fit for the comic stage, to raise them up. Revenge and martial glory hinder human happiness, as well as the pursuit of what is right and just. The just city and the character named "Just City" are peaceful and happy. The city at war is not. The stone-throwing, angry, vengeful Chorus of Acharnians, blaming the Spartans and not themselves for suffering the ravages of war, forfeit and hinder the enjoyment that the body and soul desire. This is the message that the Athenian practice of *parrhêsia* allows Aristophanes to present—but it is a message, Aristophanes suggests, better communicated on the comic stage than in the deliberative Assembly of deceptive speeches, where (as shown in the comedy's beginning) Assemblymen shout down the one saying what they do not want to hear.

In the *Acharnians*, the Chorus speaking in the voice of Aristophanes persuades the Chorus as an actor in his comedy to change from thoughtless patriots to more reflective citizens recognizing the faults of their city. After Aristophanes's speech, the Chorus decries the city that has allowed young, skillful orators with their verbal tricks to make the feeble graybeards who comprise the Chorus suffer. In particular, the Chorus bewails the abuse they endure from the young who scorn the glory they earned at Marathon. Military fame, they come to understand, is transient. Dikaiopolis had wanted peace because he wanted to enjoy life's pleasures—food and young girls—and not to live on an ephemeral reputation for military successes. The Chorus, through the comedy, comes to recognize that as well.

The *Acharnians* concludes with the contrast between Dikaiopolis, enjoying his stuffed fig leaves, thrushes, and pigeon meat, and the Athenian general Lamachus, still engaged in battle, who is reduced to eating onions and rotten fish. Happiness depends on learning from the poet who practices *parrhêsia* on the comic stage—not in the Assembly in response to the Herald asking: "Who wishes to speak?" As the debates in Thucydides's *History* suggest, the public speeches were given to manipulate and bring fame to oneself, not to use the privileges of *parrhêsia* to engage in serious deliberation about the welfare of the city. Athens is not the utopia Diodotus longs for. For Aristophanes the comic stage provides the venue for *parrhêsia*, speaking truth to power, telling the *dêmos* truths it may not want to hear.

Conclusion

For Aristophanes, *parrhêsia* is not a practice to be exercised in the political world of the Assembly; it belongs to the comic stage where the comic poet, in order to teach "just things," can freely mock those with power. Like Socrates, he eschews the political realm that has been corrupted by its orators who take advantage of the principles of *parrhêsia* to manipulate, rather than search for or state what is true. Diodotus's perceptive analysis of human nature recognized the necessity of deception in the speeches in the Assembly, but apart from Diodotus's perhaps almost surreal perceptiveness of how the opportunity to speak freely might benefit the city, neither wisdom nor justice necessarily emerged from those highly compromised "deliberations" portrayed by Thucydides in his *History*.

The contemporary obsession with freedom of speech often fails to address the ambivalent and ambiguous role of this practice as illustrated in the ancient texts. Socrates's description of democracy as a regime filled with freedom and *parrhêsia* saw that freedom as leading to a beautiful regime, but also recognized how that freedom could foster the demagogue-turned tyrant. And while his *Apology* exalts the life of the philosopher, it also captures the potential for introducing instability into life of the city as the philosopher's search for the truth leads its citizens to question the fundamental principles and moral beliefs that govern that life. When the Athenians named their ship *Parrhêsia*, they celebrated their commitment to the unbridled tongue that marked their distinctiveness from other regimes. Thucydides, Plato, and Aristophanes capture for us the nuanced consequences that follow from that celebration. This is not to diminish what the Athenians found worthy in their enjoyment of the freedom to say all; it is to recognize how the writers of that time addressed the challenging political consequences of that freedom.

2
Democracy's Shadow

The Problem of Populism in Plato's Political Thought

Tae-Yeoun Keum

Introduction

Strictly speaking, to talk about populism in conjunction with Plato is an anachronism. The concept of populism as such did not arise until the nineteenth century in the context of the growth and spread of representative democracy, just as its twenty-first-century resurgence is inextricably bound up in the conditions particular to the contemporary geopolitical landscape.[1] Efforts to define this notoriously elusive term, however, have often coalesced around an opposition that commentators tend to draw between populism and constitutional democracy, where the former represents a special, "derivative" kind of subversion of the latter.[2] Such a broadly construed tension between a more orthodox form of democracy and its populist counterpart has an important precedent in ancient Athenian political discourse leading up to the age of Plato.

The ancient Athenian version of this tension manifested in the form of an anxiety over the possibility that democratic norms and institutions in the established constitutional order could be misappropriated to serve antidemocratic ends—such as a net loss in the overall freedom of the *dēmos*, or people. In particular, ancient Athenian expressions of this fear regularly fixated on elements now commonly associated with contemporary populist movements. These included the rise in political discourse of

---

[1] Nadia Urbinati, "Political Theory of Populism," *Annual Review of Political Science* 22 (2019): 112, 114.
[2] Urbinati, "Political Theory of Populism," 113; see also Jan-Werner Müller, *What Is Populism?* (Philadelphia: University of Pennsylvania Press, 2016); and the discussions in Koen Abts and Stefan Rummens, "Populism versus Democracy," *Political Studies* 55, no. 2 (2007): 405–24; Paula Diehl, "For a Complex Concept of Populism," *Polity* 54, no. 3 (July 2022): 511; Ernesto Laclau, *On Populist Reason* (London: Verso, 2005), 175–78 and also 74, 125–28.

anti-establishment rhetoric and appeals to an authentic "people," usually equated with the non-elite majority of the population. Athenians also repeatedly voiced concerns over the potential for this same demographic to overidentify with a demagogic leader, and for the potential, in turn, for its support of demagogues or certain popular policies to bring about self-undermining effects.

The specter of a dark mirror image of democracy incubating in democracy's own weaknesses is a prominent political concern in a body of Athenian literature that flourished from the fifth through fourth centuries BCE. This was a body of critical discourse intensely focused on the nature and limits of democracy at large, which Josiah Ober has famously attributed to a community of elite, intellectual critics of democracy writing in dialogue with actual contemporaneous democratic practice, and which reached a special high-water mark during the democratic renewal that followed the shock of the rule of the Thirty Tyrants in 404 BCE.[3] Students of ancient Greek political thought sometimes disagree on the extent to which this group of authors could be understood as a coherent critical community, whether the political positions of particular authors were in fact opposed to democracy, and, relatedly, the degree to which the non-democratic alternatives they envisioned were indebted to a preexisting, traditional framework for conceptualizing democratic norms and practices.[4]

A broad point of agreement, however, is that critical discourse on democracy's pathologies flourished in dynamic conversation with the democratic ideology of the times, resulting in a sharper articulation of both the Athenian democratic ideal and its shortcomings. This body of literature in turn supplied what would go on to become some of the most iconic points of reference in a much longer tradition of skepticism regarding the idea of popular rule: Thucydides's and Aristophanes's portraits of demagogic leaders like Cleon and Alcibiades; their diagnoses of the vulnerability of deliberative democratic institutions to the sway of mere rhetoric; and the suspicion, stretching from the Old Oligarch to Aristotle, that the rule of the people amounted in fact to the rule of just the poor, uneducated masses.

---

[3] Josiah Ober, *Political Dissent in Democratic Athens: Intellectual Critics of Popular Rule* (Princeton, NJ: Princeton University Press, 1998).

[4] See, e.g., S. Sara Monoson, *Plato's Democratic Entanglements: Athenian Politics and the Practice of Philosophy* (Princeton, NJ: Princeton University Press, 2000); J. Peter Euben, *Corrupting Youth: Political Education, Democratic Culture, and Political Theory* (Princeton, NJ: Princeton University Press, 1997).

One aim of this chapter is to suggest that this familiar catalogue of the potential weaknesses of democracy often consolidated around a concrete, detailed portrait in the Athenian political imagination of a kind of shadow democracy that, while parasitic on democratic institutions and norms, ultimately undermined democratic ideals. The other is to recast Plato as a participant in that particular body of discourse, and not just the tradition of Athenian intellectuals critical of democracy at large.

Of all authors writing in antiquity, if not in the history of political thought, Plato is often caricatured as the prototypical and most influential enemy of democracy.[5] In recent years, his account in Book 8 of the *Republic* of the inevitable descent of democracy to tyranny has re-emerged as a touchstone in contemporary commentaries on the rise of global populism, where Plato is recruited as the first, prescient alarm-ringer for the susceptibility of democracies to populist capture.[6] These portraits can sometimes suggest a Plato who was quick to equate democracy with a kind of mob rule that provides an ancient antecedent to present-day populism. But it is arguably more accurate to read Plato as a theorist who both inherited and developed the opposition in Athenian political thought between a democratic ideal and a counter-ideal that shares recognizable affinities with contemporary populism.

The argument develops in three parts. In the first, I suggest that Athenian political discourse leading up to Plato's time developed a detailed account of a shadow democracy that was parasitic on democracy, which manifested in a series of tensions between central democratic ideals and their inversions. The second and third parts revisit Plato's famous account of the degeneration of democracy to tyranny in Book 8 of the *Republic*, and show how it can be read as both an elaboration of and a critical intervention in this traditional discourse. Expounding on this intervention, the final section explores, with reference to two particular passages in the *Laws* and the *Gorgias*, Plato's

---

[5] Karl Popper, *The Open Society and Its Enemies*, Vol. 1: *The Spell of Plato* (Princeton, NJ: Princeton University Press, 1966); R. C. Cross and A.D. Woozley, *Plato's Republic: A Philosophical Commentary* (London: Macmillan, 1964); Jennifer Tolbert Roberts, *Athens on Trial: The Antidemocratic Tradition in Western Thought* (Princeton, NJ: Princeton University Press, 1994), 71–86; John Dunn, *Setting the People Free: The Story of Democracy* (Princeton, NJ: Princeton University Press, 2019), 44–45; see also the discussions in Malcolm Schofield, *Plato: Political Philosophy* (Oxford: Oxford University Press, 2006), 51–135; Ober, *Political Dissent*, 156–248.

[6] Andrew Sullivan, "America Has Never Been So Ripe for Tyranny," *New York Magazine*, May 2, 2016, http://nymag.com/daily/intelligencer/2016/04/america-tyranny-donald-trump.html; "Madison's Nightmare: Political Theorists Have Been Worrying about Mob Rule for 2,000 Years," *The Economist*, January 16, 2021, https://www.economist.com/international/2021/01/16/political-theorists-have-been-worrying-about-mob-rule-for-2000-years.

preoccupation with the possibility of constructive engagement with collective assemblies.

Democracy and Its Shadow in Athenian Political Discourse before Plato

Athenian democracy in the time of Plato was largely a product of the reforms of Cleisthenes—about eighty years old by the time Plato was born—to the ancient, sixth-century constitution attributed to Solon. Democracy was practiced in a number of celebrated formal institutions of popular rule like the citizen Assembly (*ekklēsia*), the Council of Five Hundred (*boulē*), and the law courts (*dikastēria*), in which participation was open to all adult male citizens who met a relatively minimal set of requirements. But democracy as a broader practice was also manifested in a constellation of less formal institutions and norms, which coalesced around a roughly coherent set of ideological principles.

The traditional Athenian conception of democracy placed special emphasis on the ideal of a unified citizenry governing as political equals, regardless of differences among its members in wealth or family ties, and the belief that this form of rule granted citizens a kind of freedom seen nowhere else in the ancient world. Democracy, as Pericles defined it in Thucydides's rendering of his Funeral Oration of 431/430 BCE, required that "power is in the hands not of a minority but of the whole people," and that contestations both private and public be guided by the attendant principle that "everyone is equal before the law."[7] According to this iconic account of Athenian exceptionalism, political culture in democratic Athens had achieved an equilibrium between a "deep respect" of the laws and a tolerance of diversity that could be felt in all aspects of life—from education, foreign policy, civic and religious festivals, to how citizens spend their leisure time.[8] In particular, the faith that Athens placed in the autonomy, judgment, and public spirit of its citizens went hand in hand with the formation of a democratic identity that could guide individual action "without afterthought, relying on our free liberality."[9]

---

[7] Thucydides, *History of the Peloponnesian War*, trans. Rex Warner (New York: Penguin, 1986), 145 [II.37.1].
[8] Thucydides, *History*, trans. Warner, 145 [II.37.3–II.39.4].
[9] Thucydides, *History*, trans. Warner, 147 [II.40.2–II.41.1].

But even those texts that provide the clearest extant articulations of Athenian democratic ideology consistently acknowledge that this ideal was a fragile one. Much ink has been spilled, for instance, on Thucydides's choice to follow Pericles's triumphalist oration with an account of the anarchy into which the city descended during the Plague of Athens—a pointed reminder, for many commentators, of the instability of that deep-rooted respect for the rule of law so touted in Pericles's speech. A less commonly cited but more explicit example of the tendency of Athenian authors to pair celebratory representations of democracy with acknowledgments of its fragility can be found in Aeschylus's *Eumenides*, an earlier specimen of democratic commentary from before the Peloponnesian War.

Performed at the City Dionysia in 458 BCE as the third of the tragedies comprising the *Oresteia*, the *Eumenides* was written in part in the shadow of the democratic expansion brought about by the reforms of Ephialtes just four years prior.[10] The play's famous ending, in which Athena establishes Athens's first citizen court, appeals to the epistemic and ethical ideal that a judgment reached collectively by democratic citizens should be anchored in truth and justice, and that certain matters call for such collective judgments over those of any one mortal man or even the goddess herself.[11] But the celebratory image of democracy that the goddess draws out of this act of founding is qualified from the very first by a warning about its precarity:

> Here the reverence
> of citizens, their fear and kindred do-no-wrong
> shall hold by the day and in the blessing of night alike
> all while the people do not muddy their own laws
> with foul infusions. But if bright water you stain
> with mud, you nevermore will find it fit to drink.
> No anarchy, no rule of a single master. Thus
> I advise my citizens to govern and to grace,
> and not to cast fear utterly from your city.[12]

---

[10] J. Peter Euben, *The Tragedy of Political Theory: The Road Not Taken* (Princeton, NJ: Princeton University Press, 1990), 51–52; Se-Hyoung Yi, "Democratic Inclusion and 'Suffering Together' in 'The Eumenides': Duality of Immigrants," *Political Theory* 43, no. 1 (2015): 30–53, 37. Aeschylus's personal position on this and other major developments in contemporaneous Athenian politics is a topic of wide debate.
[11] Aeschylus, *Eumenides*, ll. 469–489.
[12] Aeschylus, *Eumenides*, in *Oresteia*, ed. David Grene and Richard Lattimore, trans. Richard Lattimore (Chicago: University of Chicago Press, 1953), 159–60 [ll. 690–98].

Democracy, here conceived with an explicit focus on citizens and their capacity to govern, is perfectly balanced between the extreme poles of "anarchy" and the "rule of a single master." Crucial to maintaining this balance, in turn, is an element of fear and the citizens' awareness of their own capacity for self-sabotage. For Aeschylus, the possibility that these same citizens could "muddy their own laws with foul infusions" was never far away. Rather, the "bright water" of democracy depended on the people's vigilance in ensuring that they did not themselves corrupt the political frameworks that structured their lives—and, if Athena's drinking-water metaphor is to be taken seriously, on which their survival depended.[13]

Traditional to Athenian discourse about democracy, then, was a built-in awareness of the fragility of popular government. It also contained highly specific ideas about just what happens to democracy when it does go wrong. Democracy, according to this body of discourse, had a particular way of dissolving into an inverted version of itself, which undermined democratic principles, and yet was sustained through failings that were specifically parasitic on democratic institutions, structures and norms. This hypothesis presented itself as a series of richly imagined tensions between a foundational set of democratic ideals and their corresponding counter-ideals.

If a pillar of democratic ideology was faith in its popular institutions, especially the Assembly and courts, Athenian authors voiced a countervailing anxiety that these same institutions could be abused by enterprising individuals for personal gain. So Thucydides's depictions of certain especially consequential meetings of the Assembly give a scathing diagnosis of the vulnerability of Athens's deliberative bodies to demagogues like Cleon and Alcibiades, whose motivations for continuing the doomed war are frankly attributed to private interest.[14]

The idea that democratic institutions nominally serving the public good can be usurped by private interests was in turn related to two overlapping concerns about the soundness of the epistemic ideal underlying the principle of popular rule. One was the fear that the people, often from being duped by bad advisors, would make bad judgments.[15] The other was that the people

---

[13] See also Aeschylus, *Eumenides*, ll. 700–1.

[14] Thucydides speculates that Cleon was opposed to peace because his warmongering allowed him to distract attention from his personal crimes and critics. Thucydides is likewise blunt about Alcibiades's greed for honor and wealth to support his expensive hobbies, which is taken to be the true motivation behind his speech in the Assembly in support of the Sicilian expedition. Thucydides, *History*, V.16.1; VI.15.2–3; see also II.65.7–10.

[15] See Matthew Landauer, *Dangerous Counsel: Accountability and Advice in Ancient Greece* (Chicago: University of Chicago Press, 2019), e.g., 5–10, 14–16.

would do so in a way that undermined their own interest. This, for instance, was certainly Thucydides's interpretation of the course of events that resulted in the disaster of the Sicilian expedition, and it was also Aristophanes's diagnosis of popular support for Cleon's move in 425 BCE to increase jury pay—a nominally democratic policy that enabled a wider reach of the citizen population to participate in jury service. For the character Bdelycleon in the *Wasps*, however, the demagogues who appeased the people through such policies were in fact entrenching their own power at the citizens' expense:

> They want you to be poor, and I'll tell you why: they're training you to know the hand that feeds you. Then, when the time comes, they can let you loose on some enemy or other: "Go on! Good dog! Bite him! That's the way!" If they really wanted to give the people a decent standard of living, they could do it easily.... Instead of which you have to queue up for your pay like a lot of olive-pickers.[16]

Bdelycleon's portrait of a democracy run by self-interested demagogues shines a light on the extent to which democracy can fall short on its promise to guarantee freedom and prosperity for its citizens. In fact, citizens who find themselves in this particular corrupted form of democracy can expect nothing less than the exact opposite of those ideals: for Bdelycleon, being made to "sit back and croon with delight if you're given three obols," while the demagogues and their accomplices enrich themselves, is effectively a condition of "slavery."[17]

Finally, a perennial target of democracy's ancient critics was its idealization of a unified citizenry that can be collectively thought of as the *dēmos*.[18] In the Athenian political imagination, this figurative ideal brought with it the fear that those speaking, judging, and acting in the name of the *dēmos* as a whole consistently represented just a part of the citizenry—and almost always, the poor, uneducated demographic that made up the majority of the citizen population. This familiar line of argument can be found in numerous critiques of democracy, ranging from the Old Oligarch's verdict that democracies by nature "assign more to the worst persons, to the poor, and to

---

[16] Aristophanes, *Wasps*, in *Frogs and Other Plays*, trans. David Barrett (London: Penguin, 2007), 63 [ll. 698–712].
[17] Aristophanes, *Wasps*, trans. Barrett, 62 [ll. 682–84].
[18] Ober, *Political Dissent*, 39–40, 69; Josiah Ober, *The Athenian Revolution: Essays on Ancient Greek Democracy and Political Theory* (Princeton, NJ: Princeton University Press, 1996), 117–20.

the popular types than to the good men," to Aristotle's much later definition of democracy as government by the poor majority.[19] But critical reflections on who precisely is meant by the *dēmos*—all of the citizenry, or just a poor, uneducated subset of it—also fed into a vivid, concrete vision of how political entrepreneurs might exploit this particular ambiguity in the concept in their rhetoric. Any individual or party that has captured the favor of the poor—and, according to the same critical tradition, more suggestible and manipulable—majority of the citizenry would then be empowered to appeal to the authority of the collective *dēmos* to antagonize sources of political opposition, reinforce preexisting class divisions, and alienate minorities.

By the time Plato was writing, then, Athenians had been for decades imagining a corrupted, shadow form of democracy that can only come into being through the exploitation of some of democracy's most foundational features. What they imagined, as we have seen, repeatedly placed special emphasis on a number of possible scenarios:

(1) that democratic institutions could be usurped by demagogues to serve private rather than public interests;
(2) that popular judgment could err, or be misled, into undermining the people's own interest rather than advancing it; and
(3) that deceptive appeals to the ideal of the collective *dēmos* could foment division rather than unity.

The Shadow Democracy of *Republic* 8

Plato was a direct inheritor of the rich tradition of Athenian political discourse that developed a portrait of a shadow democracy that grew out of democratic institutions and practices and yet undermined democratic values. In fact, his writings perhaps offer the most detailed and sophisticated elaboration in this tradition of the process by which democracy's own features can be turned against itself to result in the kinds of self-undermining outcomes envisaged by his predecessors. Precisely because his diagnoses of democracy's weaknesses are so vivid, Plato has often been read

---

[19] Ps-Xenophon, *The Constitution of the Athenians*, ed. and trans. G. W. Bowersock, in *Xenophon VII. Scripta Minora*, ed. E. C. Marchant and G. W. Bowersock, Loeb Classical Library (Cambridge, MA: Harvard University Press, 1968). I.4; Aristotle, *Politics*, 1290b.

as an opponent of democracy—one whose influence, at least according to some, launched an enduring antidemocratic tradition in Western political thought.[20]

In recent decades, scholars like Sara Monoson have begun to challenge this long-standing portrait, arguing instead for reading Plato as an "immanent" rather than a direct critic of democracy, who operated within and in critical dialogue with the dominant democratic ideology of his time.[21] Building on their work, it is possible to locate Plato within a body of political and cultural discourse that contained, not just an idealized image of democracy, but an especially specific account of how it might be corrupted. When we read Plato as a participant in this latter discourse, a more nuanced portrait emerges than that of an antidemocrat who simply collapsed democracy into its worst possible version. In particular, Plato's iconic representation of democracy's decline in Book 8 of the *Republic* ought not to be taken hastily as his final word on democracy per se, but rather as his extension of an inherited, imaginative discourse devoted to envisioning one specific form of a corrupted democracy.

For Socrates in these passages of the *Republic*, the inevitable degeneration of democracy into tyranny is something like a law of nature governing "seasons, plants, bodies," but also "constitutions." This is because the driving force of this extreme transition results directly from the very essence of democracy: the premium it places on freedom is an "excessive action in one direction" that "usually sets up a reaction in the opposite direction" (*Rep.* 563e).[22] It is the democratic aversion to "having any master all" that sets up the regime for the inevitable pendulum-swing to the exact opposite state of extreme slavery under a tyrant (563e; see 569b–c). This process has several components that rehearse familiar Athenian tropes about the potential for democracy to turn into an inversion of itself.

---

[20] Popper, *Open Society and Its Enemies*; Roberts, *Athens on Trial*, 71–86.
[21] S. Sara Monoson, *Plato's Democratic Entanglements: Athenian Politics and the Practice of Philosophy* (Princeton, NJ: Princeton University Press, 2000); see also Arlene Saxonhouse, "Democracy, Equality and Eidê: A Radical View from Book 8 of Plato's Republic," *American Political Science Review* 92, no. 2 (1998): 273–83; Arlene Saxonhouse, "The Socratic Narrative: A Democratic Reading of Plato's Dialogues," *Political Theory* 37, no. 6 (2009): 728–53; Arlene Saxonhouse, *Athenian Democracy: Modern Mythmakers and Ancient Theorists* (Notre Dame: University of Notre Dame Press, 1996); J. Peter Euben, *Corrupting Youth: Political Education, Democratic Culture, and Political Theory* (Princeton, NJ: Princeton University Press, 1997); Anders Dahl Sørensen, *Plato on Democracy and Political Technē* (Leiden: Brill, 2016).
[22] References to English translations of passages from Plato are to the translations in Plato, *Complete Works*, ed. John M. Cooper and D. S. Hutchinson (Indianapolis: Hackett, 1997).

First, on Socrates's analysis, the deliberative institutions of democracies, and the political cultures formed around them, allow for the emergence and deepening of factions in the city. Democratic constitutions, he believes, empower a class of politically enterprising but otherwise idle "drones" who organize themselves around speaking roles in such venues—either as speakers themselves or as supporters that "buzz" near the speaker's platform (564d). Socrates blames this class of drones for provoking enmity between the other two—otherwise politically neutral—classes of the money-makers and "the people [*dēmos*] . . . who work with their own hands" (564e). The money-makers, for their part, turn to the same deliberative institutions to "defend themselves by speaking before the people and doing whatever else they can" (565b), so that there are "impeachments, judgments, and trials on both sides" (565c).

Second, Socrates depicts these same institutions—and especially the courts—being usurped by a demagogue who uses them to pave his own rise to power. Spurred into political engagement by the class of drones, the *dēmos* end up aiding the rise of a demagogic "leader of the people," whose primary and most characteristic political pursuit during this phase of his career consists in the persecution of political scapegoats and enemies, which he accomplishes by bringing false charges against them in the popular courts (565e). Socrates presents this abuse of the courts as a distinctively heinous moral crime that seals the transformation of the demagogic leader into a tyrant. The moment "his impious tongue and lips taste kindred citizen blood" through his litigious activity marks an irreversible turning point—an act that Socrates compares to the myth of Lycaon, who becomes a wolf after tasting human flesh (565d-e).[23]

Finally, for Socrates, the progressive exclusion of the economic elite under a corrupted democracy is driven through rhetoric and policies that are at once in the *dēmos*'s name but not to their benefit. The class of drones mobilizes the *dēmos* against the money-making class through redistributive efforts that give the people "a share of the honey," but largely enrich the drones themselves (565a). The demagogic would-be tyrant, too, pits the *dēmos* against the money-makers, often through redistributive policies that promise to benefit the people but in fact favor private interests. He seduces the people through "the cancellation of debts and the redistribution of land"

---

[23] Pausanias viii.2; Ovid, *Metamorphoses*, ll. 216–239. On the significance of Plato's allusion to the Lycaon myth, see Cinzia Arruzza, *A Wolf in the City: Tyranny and the Tyrant in Plato's Republic* (Oxford: Oxford University Press, 2018), 200, 205–13.

(565e–566a, 566d). These economic reforms, however, are realized through the stirring of "civil wars against the rich" (566a), which are in turn a prelude to external wars, paid for by the people themselves, and waged by the would-be tyrant to cultivate the people's dependency on him (566e–567a). For both the drones and the would-be tyrant, appeals to democracy and to the idea of the *dēmos* are important instruments in their vilification of the money-making class—as when the drones accuse the wealthy of "plotting against the people and of being oligarchs" (565b), or when the demagogic leader accuses a wealthy man of being "an enemy of the people" (566c).

In the *Republic*, the corruption of democracy still leads to a tyranny. But the path of decline by which one degrades into the other is a trajectory that systematically rearticulates and develops the central features of a shadow form of democracy, intensely theorized by Plato's forebears in a traditional body of discourse reflecting on the nature of democracy.[24] If the degeneration of democracy into tyranny, as Socrates envisions it in the *Republic*, is the natural process by which the cultural freedom endemic to democracy inevitably swings to the opposite political extreme, his account of the mechanics of this transition can also be read as a series of inversions of the same democratic ideals that had long exercised the imaginations of Athenian political thinkers. In this account:

(1) the faith that democrats placed in their popular institutions had a sinister counterpart in the capacity of these same institutions to be manipulated by a class of enterprising "drones" and, later, demagogic leaders to serve their private interests;
(2) the democratic ideal that popular judgment might yield outcomes that serve the public good had to be balanced against the other, extreme possibility that the *dēmos* can be tricked into their own impoverishment and effective enslavement; and

[24] In her elegant study, Zena Hitz also characterizes all the degenerate regimes in *Republic* 8–9, including democracy, as being defined by a distinct set of "shadow-virtues," and she likewise understands Plato to be in conversation with a discourse on "real-life Athenian ideals." But whereas a shadow-virtue, for Hitz, is a weak version of virtue without wisdom that nonetheless acts as a check on each deficient regime, I use similar language to denote a particular image of democratic corruption already in existence in the Athenian political imaginary. Zena Hitz, "Degenerate Regimes in Plato's *Republic*," in *Plato's Republic: A Critical Guide*, ed. Mark L. McPherran (Cambridge, UK: Cambridge University Press, 2010), esp. 121–22. For the idea that each degenerate regime, including democracy, is defined in some way by a distinct inversion of classically recognized virtues or political ideals, see also Mark J. Boone, "The Unity of the Virtues and the Degeneration of *Kallipolis*," *Apeiron* 44, no. 2 (2011): 131–46; Bruce Rosenstock, "Athena's Cloak: Plato's Critique of the Democratic City in the *Republic*," *Political Theory* 22, no. 3 (1994), esp. 369.

(3) the ideological fiction of a unified *dēmos* could be misappropriated to aggravate existing class divisions in the citizen population.

Demagogic Fantasies

If Plato can be recast as a participant in a traditional Athenian discourse focused on filling out such a portrait of democratic perversion, he was also a distinctively complex interlocutor. One way of appreciating his intervention in this tradition is to consider the possibility that the construct of the shadow democracy may have served a cautionary role in Athenian society, where it presented a warning to democrats about the weaknesses of a regime that required their vigilance and protection. It has been suggested, for instance, that political rhetoric and culture in democratic Athens were unusually preoccupied with the specter of tyranny even through periods in which it was in no way a serious threat.[25] Imagining such phantoms was arguably a way for Athenian democrats to keep the city watchful of antidemocratic threats before they materialized, and to affirm democratic principles for the wider citizenry.[26]

A recurring theme in Plato's work, however, is that this strand of the Athenian political imaginary—however cautionary—can itself have a distinctly antidemocratic effect. Among the central motifs of the inverted form of democracy imagined and elaborated in civic discourse, the figure of the demagogue, in particular, occupies an especially prominent place in Plato's political writings. For Plato, the Athenian fixation on the possibility of the capture of democratic institutions by demagogues was not just a call for vigilance. It also provided, to some degree, a playbook for the politically ambitious seeking to game the system. Plato takes up this concern head-on in the *Gorgias* and, I believe, also in those very passages in Book 8 of the *Republic* detailing the decline of democracy. On this reading, Book 8 of the *Republic* is not only a contribution to traditional discourse about the fragility of democracy, but also a critical intervention grappling with the potentially harmful effect of this same discourse.[27]

---

[25] Kurt A. Raaflaub, "Stick and Glue: The Function of Tyranny in Fifth-Century Athenian Democracy," in *Popular Tyranny: Sovereignty and Its Discontents in Ancient Greece*, ed. Kathryn A. Morgan (Austin: University of Texas Press, 2003), 62–63.
[26] Raaflaub, "Stick and Glue," 70–71.
[27] The argument of this section partly draws on a reading of *Republic* 8 I have advanced in Tae-Yeoun Keum, "Crowds and Crowd-Pleasing in Plato," *The Review of Politics* 85, no. 2 (2023), 199.

As we have seen, a crucial inflection point in Socrates's account of the transition of democracy to tyranny in the *Republic* is the rise of a demagogic figure who secures his power by manipulating the *dēmos* in the city's deliberative institutions. The potential for individuals to use these institutions to their personal advantage, in particular by winning over the microcosmic representations of the *dēmos* in attendance, is heavily thematized in the *Gorgias*. Gaining political power through the skillful manipulation of audiences in democratic venues is precisely what rhetoric—the subject of the *Gorgias*—is meant to be good *for*. Gorgias, a rhetorician, promises to teach a skill that will enable individuals to "persuade with speeches either judges in a law court, councillors in a council meeting, and assemblymen in an assembly or in any other political gathering that might take place" (*Gorg.* 452e). This is an especially attractive prospect that draws ambitious youths to seek to study with Gorgias, and they in turn come to understand rhetoric as an essentially tyrannical power operating through democratic institutions. Capturing the *dēmos* in these settings allows rhetoricians, "like tyrants," to "put to death anyone they want, and confiscate the property and banish from their cities anyone they see fit" (466b–c).

On the one hand, the fate of democracy in Book 8 of the *Republic* reads as the nightmarish fulfillment of those very fantasies of power cultivated by the admirers of rhetoric in the *Gorgias*. The political trajectory of the demagogic figure in the *Republic* appears to closely track the account given by Gorgias's supporters of the promise of rhetoric to empower individuals to exploit democracy's weaknesses for personal political gain. Just as Polus in the *Gorgias* fantasizes about the tyrannical power of the rhetorician to ruin any number of arbitrary victims in the Assembly and courts, the demagogic figure in Book 8 of the *Republic* easily subjugates a "docile mob" into prosecuting his enemies, real or imagined, in the court systems (*Rep.* 565e).

On the other hand, Socrates insists, consistently and emphatically throughout the *Gorgias*, that the admirers of rhetoric are wrong to imagine that the *dēmos* can in fact be taken over this way. Indeed, he contends that it is in fact the *dēmos* that ultimately controls the rhetorician, and not the other way around. Punning on the name of his interlocutor's love interest, Socrates casts Callicles as a lover "of the *dēmos* [people] of Athens, and the Demos who's the son of Pyrilampes":

> I notice that in each case you're unable to contradict your beloved, clever though you are, no matter what he says or what he claims is so. You keep

shifting back and forth. If you say anything in the Assembly and the Athenian demos denies it, you shift your ground and say what it wants to hear." (*Gorg.* 481d–e)

Those who fantasize about seizing political power through the *dēmos*, Socrates suggests, are in reality akin to lovers rendered helpless by those whose affection they are so desperate to win and to maintain.[28]

The account of democracy's degeneration in the *Republic* can likewise be read as a continuation of Socrates's effort in the *Gorgias* to disarm the cultural trope of the demagogue who has gamed the system of democracy. Although the demagogic figure in Book 8 of the *Republic* does successfully manipulate the *dēmos* to win power, Socrates also emphasizes the instability of this undertaking. In much the same way a hapless lover might struggle to keep his beloved interested, basing one's power on the *dēmos* entails constantly having to come up with new popular policies to appease the people and sustain their dependency on him. In coming to power, the demagogic leader had to "drop hints to the people" about debt cancellation and land redistribution (*Rep.* 565e–566a). Once he has made good on this promise, however, he then has to "stir up a war, so that the people will continue to feel the need of a leader," and also so that "they'll become poor through having to pay war taxes, for that way they'll have to concern themselves with their daily needs and be less likely to plot against him" (566e–567a). His approach, Socrates suggests, is ultimately unsustainable: a leader who has to "be always stirring up a war" can only be "all the more readily hated by the citizens" (567b). The demagogue-turned-tyrant may once have won over the "docile mob," but he must now either "live with the inferior majority, even though they hate him, or not... live at all" (567d).

Plato's depiction of the corruption of democracy in the *Republic*, then, both continues and challenges the tradition he inherited. It riffs on a long-standing trope within this tradition about democracy's vulnerability to demagoguery. But it does so while simultaneously refuting a persistent antidemocratic fantasy stemming from the very same trope: the idea that individual politicians can secure genuine power through the manipulation of democratic institutions.

---

[28] See also *Rep.* 493a; Aristophanes, *Knights*.

Managing the Multitude: Alternative Visions

One way of understanding Plato's critical intervention in the discourse on democracy and demagogues is as part of a larger preoccupation with the bedrock democratic principle that collective assemblies will yield productive outcomes. Plato's extensive reflections on the nature of collective gatherings are well known—from the iconic image of the ship of state besieged by a crowd of squabbling sailors (488a–e), to his comparison of the whims of the multitude to the "moods and appetites of a huge, strong beast" (493a), and the accompanying verdict that "the majority [*plēthos*] cannot be philosophic" (494a). These reflections, in turn, consistently betray a conviction that the dynamics that govern collectives are categorically different from those of individuals. A dominant theme of Socrates's position in the *Gorgias* and Book 8 of the *Republic* had been that fantasies of usurping the *dēmos* as a pathway to personal power were an illusion: the nature and extent of a demagogue's control over the *dēmos* were in fact much more tenuous. Rather, those who subscribed to such fantasies were not stopping to question their assumption that the *dēmos* and its institutional incarnations could be controlled in the first place. For Plato, this was the prior, and more difficult, question that was not being asked in democratic discourse: whether collective gatherings could be constructively engaged at all.

The orthodox view is that Plato's answer to this question was unequivocally in the negative. Famously in the *Gorgias*, the kind of politically useful rhetoric that Gorgias teaches is defended as an art particularly suited to "crowds" and "any other political gathering" (*Gorg.* 452e), whereas Socrates claims that his own method of philosophical cross-examination is catered to the individual (474a–b). Speaking to crowds means speaking "among those who don't have knowledge" (459a), whereas speaking to individuals offers the best hope for drawing out the quiet voice of reason that so often gets drowned out by the clamoring of the many. Socrates's deep suspicion of collective dynamics, and the contrast he draws between the respective audiences of rhetoric and philosophy, have often led Plato's readers to understand him as a proponent of a reclusive philosophy removed from the hubbub of ordinary politics—or, just as often, as an authoritarian who resorts to brutal suppression to do away with the problem of having to contend with the general populace. But two passages, one in the *Laws* and another in the *Gorgias*, complicate that picture. Considered against the background of Plato's engagement with an extant political discourse on the shadow democracy lurking within democratic frameworks, we might take such passages to offer a more positive alternative to the cultural trope of the demagogue who captures the *dēmos*.

Laws 700a–701b

Plato, as we have seen, was critical of the Athenians' doubled-edged fascination with demagogues, arguing that they could not in fact exercise any true control over the collective audiences they claimed to command. In Book 3 of the *Laws*, however, in a strange, complex passage that ostensibly presents a critique of such audiences and collective behavior, an alternative vision emerges of what managing them constructively might entail.

Identifying a particular genre of song, *nomes*, as the etymological root of *nomos*, law,[29] the Athenian Stranger sketches a genealogy of the origins and decline of law in Athens, as told through the history of Athenian music. According to this account, the idea of *nomos* emerged during a time when there were strict norms governing musical genres—like *nomes*—as well as the corresponding behavior of audiences. In this orderly age, musicians did not mix genres in their songs, just as "people of taste and education" set an expectation that the audience would listen in silence, so keeping "children, their attendants, and the general public [*tōi plestōi ochlōi*]" in check (*Laws* 700c–d). The rule of law started breaking down as bold composers began to mix musical styles in innovative combinations. The resulting confusion of expectations gave the general public "a taste for breaking the laws of music"—and, crucially, the impression that what makes any piece of music good or bad was a matter of their own judgment rather than any objective criteria (700e). This combination paved the path for the catcalls, shouting, and applause that have since become commonplace in performances. More importantly, it also marked the advent of a "theatocracy" that the Athenian Stranger equates with democracy (701a).

On the surface, the Athenian Stranger pins the blame for the decline of the rule of law in Athens squarely on the pathologies particular to collective behavior. As he suggests earlier in the *Laws*, "the general public [*ho ge polus ochlos*]" is, contrary to their understanding of their own authority, an unqualified judge of musical merit, let alone of political policy: "they have long been

---

[29] These are the same word in Greek.

drilled into singing to the pipes and marching in step, and they never stop to think that they do all this without the smallest understanding of it" (670b). The *Laws* is hardly the only dialogue in which Plato draws out the political ramifications of the culture of groupthink bred in musical venues.[30] If, for the Athenian Stranger, the erosion of public judgment in musical matters spreads like an infection into political culture, Socrates in the *Gorgias* reduces rhetoric to "what is left" when "melody, rhythm, and meter" are stripped off from music, insofar as the primary aim of rhetoricians speaking in political venues is no different from that of musicians seeking to "gratify the crowd of spectators" (*Gorg.* 502a–c). As Kathryn Morgan points out in her discussion of these passages, "in all instances, it is the mass nature of the audience that causes problems."[31] In Book 6 of the *Republic*—in one of Plato's most vivid condemnations of collective behavior—Socrates runs together the political, military, and musical venues in which such problematic audiences gather:

> Whenever the multitude [*polloi*] are sitting together in assemblies, courts, theaters, army camps, or in some other public gathering of the crowd, they object very loudly and excessively to some of the things that are said or done and approve others in the same way, shouting and clapping, so that the very rocks and surroundings echo the din of their praise or blame and double it. In circumstances like that, what is the effect, as they say, on a young person's heart? What private training can hold out and not be swept away by that kind of praise or blame and be carried by the flood wherever it goes . . . ? (*Rep.* 492b–c)[32]

It is tempting to read the Athenian Stranger's genealogy of Athenian theatocracy as a continuation of these other pejorative depictions in the Platonic corpus of collective audiences in musical settings. But the *Laws* passage offers a somewhat different take on the merits of collective assemblies. In contrast, for instance, to the decisive opposition drawn in Book 6 of the *Republic* between "private training" and the corrupting effect of the multitude, the Athenian

---

[30] Kathryn A. Morgan, "The Tyranny of the Audience in Plato and Isocrates," in *Popular Tyranny: Sovereignty and Its Discontents in Ancient Greece*, ed. Kathryn A. Morgan (Austin: University of Texas Press, 2003), 203–4, citing Robert W. Wallace, "Poet, Public, and 'Theatocracy': Audience Performance in Classical Athens," in *Poet, Public, and Performance in Ancient Greece*, ed. Lowell Edmunds and Robert W. Wallace (Baltimore, MD: Johns Hopkins University Press, 1997), 97–99 and n.3.
[31] Morgan, "Tyranny of the Audience," 203.
[32] Translation modified for *hotan ... polloi* at 492b.

Stranger makes no prescriptions about shielding individuals from the influence of collective culture. In her gloss on the same passage in the *Laws*, Sara Monoson even suggests that Plato takes the noisy behavior of the audience as a "signal" of "the masses' claim to a measure of intellectual capability."[33] But there's more: at stake in the Athenian Stranger's account is not so much a concern about the capacity of people in collective settings to formulate and understand intellectual content, but a more fundamental preoccupation with taste and ingrained habits of judgment. According to these passages, judging well, be it in aesthetic or political contexts, is not a feat that individuals perform in isolated instances. Rather, it is the product of a broader habit of intuitions and inclinations, which develops over time, and which takes its cues from expectations embedded into cultures of collective judgment-making.[34] Practicing good judgment, then, cannot simply result from insulating individuals from the crowd and teaching them instead to listen to their own reason. It must instead be attuned to shared public norms around good taste.

More pressingly, the point of the Athenian Stranger's story is not that the general collective should be ignored, but that it be kept under a harmonious discipline—an ideal for which music provides a helpful model. The Athenian Stranger concludes that "music proved to be the starting point of everyone's conviction that he was an authority on everything, and of a general disregard for the law" (*Laws* 701a). But, if his etymological claim linking *nomes* to *nomos* is to be taken seriously, it would be more accurate to think of music as the starting point of the idea of the law instead. What is at fault, rather, is bad music—and the anarchic model of collectivity corresponding to it. In the Athenian Stranger's story, the undifferentiated crowds thrown together in theater audiences—and under the general heading of the *dēmos* in democracies—are akin to disorderly music, in which all sorts of genre conventions are mixed up together. If Plato's ideas about good music place a premium on harmony and hierarchical differentiation,[35] the general crowd is, by his standards, unmusical. In any context where norms—musical or otherwise—are jumbled up in an undisciplined manner, engagement with the audience cannot but appeal to the lowest common denominator (669e–670a).

---

[33] Monoson, *Plato's Democratic Entanglements*, 105.

[34] On the continuity of music and critical judgment in the *Republic*, see the excellent Nina Valiquette Moreau, "Musical Mimesis and Political Ethos in Plato's *Republic*," *Political Theory* 45, no. 2 (2017): 192–215.

[35] Moreau, "Musical Mimesis."

The Athenian Stranger's account, moreover, arises in the context of a comparison of two extremes: the Persians' absolute obedience to their tyrant, on the one hand, and the absolute licentiousness of contemporary democratic Athens, on the other. Although he is critical of the licentiousness into which Athenian society has devolved, he is just as wary of its polar opposite. It is in this sense that he concludes that the experience of the Athenians under democracy was "the same experience" as that of the Persians under tyranny: where successions of Persian tyrants "reduced the people to a state of complete subjection," Athens swung to the "opposite extreme" by "encourag[ing] the masses to . . . unfettered liberty" (699e). In contrast to both these radical outcomes, the Athenian Stranger's story romanticizes a time when the general populace was under some, but not excessive, measure of control. For Plato, then, managing the collective audiences that take center stage in democracy was a worthy political ideal, but it was one defined by moderation, steered toward a kind of freedom situated at a happy medium between anarchy and tyranny. Like good music, this management would carve out differentiated venues and outlets appropriate to different subsets of the citizenry, so that the parts together form a harmonious whole, and it would in turn cultivate good taste as a shared value, a precondition for good collective judgment.

Gorgias 482c–e

If the Athenian Stranger's story in the *Laws* about unruly musical audiences suggests a Platonic vision of what constructive engagement with collective assemblies may look like, a striking moment in the *Gorgias* provides a window into an equivalent possibility in his understanding of philosophic practice.[36]

About two-thirds of the way through the dialogue, Callicles begins to insult Socrates by accusing him of "acting like a true crowd-pleaser [*dēmēgoros*]," of "playing to the crowd [*dēmēgoreis*]," and of bringing the discussion to "crowd-pleasing vulgarities [*dēmēgorika*]" (*Gorg*. 482c–e), repeating the insult a little later by calling him a "regular crowd-pleaser [*dēmēgoros*]"

---

[36] I have explored the passage in question more fully in previous work, and my reading of it here draws extensively on arguments I have made in Tae-Yeoun Keum, "Why Did Socrates Conduct his Dialogues before an Audience?" *History of Political Thought* 37, no. 3 (2016): 411–37; and Keum, "Crowds and Crowd-Pleasing in Plato."

(494d). This family of words—cognate with the English *demagogue*—is relatively uncommon in Greek use and overtly political, typically applied to popular oratory in the Assembly.[37] Both Callicles and Socrates use these terms pejoratively throughout the *Gorgias*.[38] (For instance, "popular harangue [*dēmēgoria*]" is the term Socrates uses when he dismisses rhetoric as a stripped-down form of music that does little more than flatter the audience [502c–d].) But Socrates never explicitly rejects Callicles's complaint, even admitting at a later point in the dialogue to having himself lapsed into "a real popular harangue [*dēmēgorein*]" (519d).

Why does Callicles—repeatedly and emphatically—choose to describe Socrates using this unusual set of words? What truth is there to the claim that Socrates is a *dēmēgoros*—a term whose political valences conjure those very antidemocratic fantasies he sets out to critique? Commentators have tended to read this passage as an effort on Callicles's part to deflect Socrates's unflattering insinuations about his love life—the charge that he is simultaneously besotted with the Athenian *dēmos* and a youth named Demos[39]—and as a more general critique of popular morality.[40] But Callicles's pointed language is also a comment on Socrates's conduct and dynamic with the literal crowd that has gathered to witness the discussion.[41]

Throughout the *Gorgias*, Socrates insists on upholding a strict distinction between speech directed at "the multitude" and speech directed at individuals. Whereas he sees rhetoricians as dealing in the pleasing of crowds and of the general *dēmos*, he squarely places his own method of philosophical cross-examination in the latter camp, alleging that he speaks exclusively to the individual he is engaging in conversation while ignoring the

---

[37] *Dēmagōgos* and Plato's preferred *dēmēgoros* are both traditionally translated as "demagogue." Melissa Lane, "The Origins of the Statesman-Demagogue Distinction in and after Ancient Athens," *Journal of the History of Ideas* 73, no. 2 (2012): 179–200. See also Henry George Liddell, Robert Scott, and Henry Stuart Jones, *A Greek-English Lexicon* (Oxford: Clarendon Press, 1996), s.v. *dēmēgoros* and *dēmēgoreō*; Josiah Ober, *Mass and Elite in Democratic Athens* (Princeton, NJ: Princeton University Press, 1989), 106n7.

[38] Melissa Lane attributes the pejorative meaning of the word to Plato. Lane, "Origins of the Statesman-Demagogue Distinction"; Liddell, Scott, and Jones, *A Greek-English Lexicon*, s.v. *dēmēgoros*.

[39] Ober, *Political Dissent*, 205–6; Victoria Wohl, *Love among the Ruins: The Erotics of Democracy in Classical Athens* (Princeton, NJ: Princeton University Press, 2002), 82. Wohl suggests that Callicles takes Socrates's characterization of his relationship with *dēmos* in stride. See also Kenneth J. Dover, *Greek Homosexuality* (Cambridge, MA: Harvard University Press, 1989), 103.

[40] James H. Nichols, trans., *Gorgias and Phaedrus* (Ithaca, NY: Cornell University Press, 1998), 142; see also Ober, *Political Dissent*, 198–202. On Callicles's influence on Nietzsche, see E. R. Dodds, ed., *Gorgias* (Oxford: Clarendon, 1959), 386–91.

[41] E. R. Dodds reads Callicles's description of Socrates as a *dēmēgoros* as an accusation of "talking for effect." Dodds ed., *Gorgias*, 264.

rest (474a–b).[42] Callicles's characterization of Socrates as a *dēmēgoros* or crowd-pleaser has to be read in part as an effort to expose the hypocrisy of the philosopher's presentation of his method and allegiances: Socrates may not be entirely convincing in his claims to give the crowd no attention. Whether he is making titillating remarks about love lives, appeals to familiar tenets of popular morality, or—as in the occasion that triggers Callicles's final repetition of his accusation—graphic, off-the-wall comments about itches that require endless scratching, Socrates can reasonably be faulted for offering the sort of provocations that tend to excite and to entertain a crowd.[43]

More concretely, Callicles's remarks also draw attention to the incongruous effect of Socrates's tendency to stage his philosophical discussions in settings that attract audiences.[44] With some notable exceptions, Socrates's conversations often take place in public or semi-public settings where groups of listeners can gather. His activity is most prominently associated with the agora (see *Ap.* 17c) and other public spaces in the vicinity of the Athenian city center (*Menexenus*; *Euthyphro, Theages*). But his philosophical encounters also take place in gymnasia (*Theaetetus*; *Sophist*; *Statesman*), schools of wrestling (*Charmides*; *Lysis*) and grammar (*Lesser Hippias*; *Rival Lovers*), the Lyceum (*Euthydemus*), unnamed exhibition spaces (*Laches*; *Gorgias*; *Greater Hippias*; *Meno*; *Ion*), as well as well-attended gatherings in private homes (*Parmenides*; *Protagoras*), including parties held during particular public festivals in the Athenian calendar (*Symposium*; *Republic*; *Timaeus*; *Critias*).[45] In some dialogues, Socrates inherits at least part of an audience from an exhibition that took place prior to his arrival (*Gorgias*; *Laches*; *Hippias Minor*), or he brings along his own companions (*Parm.* 127c; *Euthyd.* 274b; see *Clitoph.* 409a, 409d, 410a). If his practice is really meant to engage just the individual, as he claims, this sits oddly, for instance, with Crito's report in the *Euthydemus* that "[t]here was such a crowd standing around" that he "couldn't hear anything" (*Euthyd.* 271a; see also

---

[42] See Christina H. Tarnopolsky, *Prudes, Perverts, and Tyrants: Plato's Gorgias and the Politics of Shame* (Princeton, NJ: Princeton University Press, 2010), 42.

[43] Similarly, Socrates's opponents, and to some extent Socrates himself, have noted his tendency to embarrass his interlocutors for the entertainment of the bystanders. See *Ap.* 22b–c, 23a; *Gorg.* 461b, 482d. See also Elizabeth Markovits, *The Politics of Sincerity: Plato, Frank Speech, and Democratic Judgment* (University Park: Pennsylvania State University Press, 2008), 99, 105; Seth Benardete, *The Rhetoric of Morality and Philosophy: Plato's Gorgias and Phaedrus* (Chicago: University of Chicago Press, 1991), 9; Devin Stauffer, *The Unity of Plato's Gorgias: Rhetoric, Justice, and the Philosophic Life* (Cambridge: Cambridge University Press, 2006), 85–6.

[44] See Keum, "Why Did Socrates Conduct his Dialogues before an Audience?"

[45] For a helpful catalogue of the settings of the dialogues see Debra Nails, *The People of Plato: A Prosopography of Plato and Other Socratics* (Indianapolis, IN: Hackett, 2002), Appendix I.

304d)—or with Socrates's own account of examining individual experts before groups of "bystanders" who practically proved more adept at answering his questions (*Ap.* 22b–c; see also 23a, 21c–d). Indeed, collective audiences feature explicitly in Socrates's reflections about his method: in the *Protagoras* and *Euthydemus*, the question of whether to converse "alone or in the presence of others" is a live and prominent issue (*Prot.* 316b–c; see *Euthyd.* 305b).[46]

Undoubtedly, there are significant aspects in which it would be unfair to characterize Socrates's activity and motives as crowd-pleasing. Socrates sets his own practice apart from the rhetoric of "flattery ... and shameful public harangue [*aischra dēmēgoria*]" by claiming allegiance to philosophy (482a–b) and later to a higher, ideal form of rhetoric aimed at what truly benefits his audience (502a–503c). And in contrast to those admirers of rhetoric who view the manipulation of the *dēmos* as a pathway to power, Socrates decisively distances himself from such aspirations to "slight the common good for the sake of [one's] own private good" (502e). Finally, Socrates's conduct with his audiences may be immune to some of the political, and specifically demagogic, connotations of the word *dēmēgoros*. As varied as Socrates's audiences are across the Platonic dialogues, it would be a stretch to conceive of them in association with the ordinary *dēmos*; there are few farmers to be found at the gymnasium.

In a limited sense, however, Callicles is right. Socrates does often appear to address the collective audience beyond just his immediate individual interlocutor, he is often exceptionally savvy in interacting with the crowds that have gathered to watch his conversations, and his practice regularly incorporates such audience engagement. While these encounters may be a far cry from the posturing of speakers in the Assembly and popular courts, they are not entirely apolitical either. Socrates's account of his activities in the *Apology*—examining not only the politicians and poets but also the craftsmen—suggests a broader and more diverse range of both interlocutors and informal bystanders than those depicted in the greater part of Plato's work, which likely skews toward portraying dialogues with Socrates's more prominent interlocutors. As several commentators have suggested, the indiscriminate openness with which Socrates claims to invite different swaths of Athenian society to conversation can even be seen as an especially

---

[46] In both dialogues, the question of whether to converse before an audience is bound up with considerations about the potential dangers of doing so, with the *Euthydemus* concluding that being "willing to argue ... in front of a large crowd" is inadvisable (*Euthyd.* 305).

democratic practice.[47] In turn, the ambiguous role played by the audiences that Socrates involves in these exchanges is often thematized using vocabulary borrowed from the idioms of democratic politics. Just as Plato's readers would have been sensitive, for instance, to the valences of Callicles's charge that Socrates was acting the *dēmēgoros* with the assembled crowd, they would have also appreciated Plato's choice of words when the same audience is depicted erupting into *thoruboi*—the collective crowd noises that were an endemic feature of the Assembly and courts (*Gorg.* 458c; see *Prot.* 339d).[48]

Socrates's practice of incorporating his audiences into his philosophical investigations—and in turn, Plato's choice to dramatize this tendency— betrays a more ambivalent stance toward collective gatherings than his more famous assertions on the matter suggest. On the question at the heart of democratic ideology and institutional design, of whether they can be mobilized toward positive ends, Plato might have been skeptical but not pessimistic. His answer to the question may not look like democracy, but it also does not leave collective assemblies, or even necessarily the *dēmos*, out of the picture. Notwithstanding his reservations about the way demagogic fantasies have come to fester in political discourse—on both democracy and its shadowy counterpart trailing closely behind—Plato was arguably committed to imagining alternative approaches to working with the multitude. We might understand Socrates's practice as a small-scale, experimental effort to explore new ways of managing the dynamics of collectives.

---

[47] E.g., Saxonhouse, *Athenian Democracy*, 89.

[48] Victor Bers, "Dikastic Thorubos," in *Crux: Essays Presented to G. E. M. de Ste. Croix on His 75th Birthday*, ed. Paul Cartledge and F. D. Harvey (London: Duckworth, 1985), 1–15; Landauer, *Dangerous Counsel*, 172; Ober, *Mass and Elite*, 104, 138, 147; Adriaan M. Lanni, "Spectator Sport or Serious Politics? Oi Periesthkotes and the Athenian Lawcourts," *Journal of Hellenic Studies* 117 (1997): 183–89, 187.

3
"Naked" Speech in Late Republican Rome

Rob Goodman

Introduction

Can populist rhetoric be identified by a stable set of features, tropes, or stylistic qualities? The question is more fraught than it might appear at first glance. As intuitive as it may be to posit a coherent set of characteristics for populist speech, it has also been plausibly argued that "populist rhetoric" is a redundant phrase.[1] That is, virtually all democratic politicians claim to speak in the name of "the people," to embody the authentic will of the majority, to stand against an elite of one kind or another. If their oratory is not exactly Ciceronian, that is because they meet the people where they are—but, on the level of style, a Silvio Berlusconi, Jair Bolsonaro, or Donald Trump is different from the ordinary run of politicians in degree, not in kind.

This chapter is not about any of those contemporary figures, but I hope that the historical investigation it undertakes can contribute to a better understanding of the populist style in our own more recent history. That is not because I believe that Populism is a transhistorical, capital-letter essence, but simply because I believe that we still have a great deal to learn about the strategies with which political actors in various times and places have constructed and appealed to "the people" as against "the elite." The deflationary account of "populist rhetoric" relies on an implicitly historical claim—that the search for public support reliably drives politicians into certain rhetorical channels—and so must any attempt to challenge it. A full history of populist rhetoric has yet to be written.

---

[1] For instance, Nadia Urbinati argues that "manipulation by means of speech is part of the art of rhetoric in open democratic competition. There is nothing scandalous in the rhetoric of demagoguery or populism per se; as a matter of fact, all modern political parties tend to adopt the populist strategy of exalting emotions against their adversaries in electoral competition. In a government based on *doxa*, populist style is ubiquitous; it is difficult to distinguish between populist rhetoric and party rhetoric." Nadia Urbinati, *Me the People: How Populism Transforms Democracy* (Cambridge, MA: Harvard University Press, 2019), 103.

This chapter's contribution toward that history comes from the late Roman republic. Drawing on the work of Cicero and his contemporaries, I offer evidence for the existence and distinctiveness of populist rhetoric, at least in the Roman context, and discuss its key qualities.[2] Republican Rome rewards rhetorical study not just because its political actors were so conscious of the implications of their rhetorical personae, but also because of its suggestive parallels with contemporary political life—for instance, its combination of institutional complexity and deep polarization. But another intriguing parallel is historiographic. Much of the recent scholarship on Roman rhetoric is marked by its own deflationary account, which denies the existence of a specifically populist[3] rhetoric, and it is that account with which I take issue here.

In the Roman context, the deflationary account holds that the late republic's popular rhetoric was characterized by "ideological monotony."[4] In the influential version of this argument advanced by Robert Morstein-Marx, among others, populist rhetoric was everywhere in Rome, and therefore nowhere: when addressing the Roman people, *populares* and *optimates* alike gestured toward popular sovereignty and presented themselves as the

---

[2] It would be anachronistic to characterize the Roman *populares* as a stable political party or movement. Nevertheless, as Antonio Duplá points out, there are a number of recurring themes in *popularis* politics from the time of the Gracchi to Caesar's civil war. These themes are both substantive (especially emphasizing land reform and the urban grain supply) and procedural (emphasizing popular assemblies and the tribunes in their struggle with the senate over these substantive concerns). While M. A. Robb and Amy Russell caution us that a simple *populares/optimates* model is misleading—for instance, because ostensible political divisions distract from the reality of elite consensus, and because individual *populares* strove to distinguish themselves rather than pursuing a unified "party line"—I am interested here in the broad features of Roman populism as a political tendency, and in the way that tendency shaped rhetorical strategies and styles. Antonio Duplá, "*Consules populares,*" in *Consuls and Res Publica: Holding High Office in the Roman Republic*, ed. Hans Beck, Duplá, Martin Jehne, and Francisco Pina Polo (Cambridge, UK: Cambridge University Press, 2011), 279; M. A. Robb, *Beyond Populares and Optimates: Political Language in the Late Republic* (Stuttgart: Franz Steiner Verlag, 2010); Amy Russell, "Speech, Competition, and Collaboration: Tribunician Politics and the Development of Popular Ideology," in *Community and Communication: Oratory and Politics in Republican Rome*, ed. Catherine Steel and Henriette van der Blom (Oxford: Oxford University Press, 2013), 101–16.

[3] Just as it would be anachronistic to describe the *populares* as a "political party," it would also be mistaken to posit any direct connection between Roman *populares* and contemporary populists. These political tendencies do seem to share some important characteristics, such as a politics of anti-elitist majoritarianism and popular sovereignty, led by charismatic figures who are themselves often opportunistic members of the elite; nevertheless, I do not attempt to draw that connection here. I do, however, take the liberty of using the term "populist" with specific reference to Roman politics. On people/elite dichotomies in classical political thought, see David E. Hahm, "The Mixed Constitution in Greek Thought," in *A Companion to Greek and Roman Political Thought*, ed. Ryan K. Balot (Oxford; Malden, MA: Wiley-Blackwell, 2009), 180–96. On the *populares* and modern populists, see Tim Elliott, "Reinterpreting *Populares*: Modern Populism and the Roman Republic" (forthcoming).

[4] Robert Morstein-Marx, *Mass Oratory and Political Power in the Late Roman Republic* (Cambridge, UK: Cambridge University Press, 2004).

people's champions.[5] The result was an impoverished public discourse, in which elites and oligarchs so effectively cloaked themselves in the language of populism that their audiences were denied meaningful political choices. On the other hand, recent scholarship has pushed back on the "ideological monotony" thesis: J. A. Rosenblitt, for instance, has argued that the instances of *popularis* rhetoric recorded by Sallust reflect a distinctively populist ideology of conflict between social orders.[6] This dispute is itself part of a long-running argument over the extent of popular power in republican Rome.[7]

I argue that it is possible to identify populist rhetoric in the late Roman republic, and in particular, that we can trace the outlines not only of a populist ideology, but of a populist style—a style that, in turn, is grounded in important and contestable assumptions about the relationship between orator and audience, and between the various institutions of republican politics. Of course, any attempt to reconstruct this style must confront a set of well-known problems with the available sources. For one, the only Roman political orations that survive in anything other than fragmentary form are Cicero's. While the works of Cicero himself—his surviving orations, as well as his rhetorical theory—are a valuable source of reflections on the rhetoric of his contemporaries, his accounts of the rhetorical practices of such figures as Catiline, Clodius, and Marcus Antonius are so distorted by animosity that it is difficult to extract the details of their speech from the swells of invective in which they float.

But it is not impossible. In this chapter, I attempt to reconstruct Roman populist rhetoric through a method of triangulation. If the relatively

---

[5] Karl-J. Hölkeskamp, "The Roman Republic: Government of the People, by the People, for the People?," *Scripta Classica Israelica* 19 (2000): 203–23; Karl-J. Hölkeskamp, "Friends, Romans, Countrymen: Addressing the Roman People and the Rhetoric of Inclusion," in *Community and Communication*, ed. Catherine Steel and Henriette van der Blom (Oxford: Oxford Academic, 2013), 11–28.

[6] J. A. Rosenblitt, "Hostile Politics: Sallust and the Rhetoric of Popular Champions in the Late Republic," *American Journal of Philology* 137, no. 4 (2016): 655–88.

[7] Important entries in this debate include J. A. North, "Democratic Politics in Republican Rome," *Past and Present* 126, no. 1 (1990): 3–21; Fergus Millar, *The Crowd in Rome in the Late Republic* (Ann Arbor: University of Michigan Press, 1998); Andrew Lintott, *The Constitution of the Roman Republic* (Oxford: Oxford University Press, 1999); T. P. Wiseman, *Remembering the Roman People: Essays on Late-Republican Politics* (Oxford: Oxford University Press, 2009); Allan M. Ward, "How Democratic Was the Roman Republic?," *New England Classical Journal* 31, no. 2 (2004): 101–19; Alexander Yakobson, "Traditional Political Culture and the People's Role in the Roman Republic," *Historia* 59, no. 3 (2010): 282–302; Michael Crawford, "Reconstructing What Roman Republic," *Bulletin of the Institute of Classical Studies* 54, no. 2 (2011): 105–14; Frédéric Hurlet, "Démocratie a Rome. Quelle démocratie? En relisant Millar (et Hölkeskamp)," in *Rome, a City and Its Empire in Perspective: The Impact of the Roman World through Fergus Millar's Research*, ed. Stéphane Benoist (Leiden: Brill, 2012), 19–44. For an overview, see Cristina Rosillo-López, *Public Opinion and Politics in the Late Roman Republic* (Cambridge, UK: Cambridge University Press, 2017), 12–16.

unknown variable is the populist speech of Cicero's enemies, the better-known variables are the rhetorical practices of Cicero's somewhat friendlier rivals—in particular, the "Atticist" orators and Caesar.[8] While Cicero is critical of these latter practices, he also describes them in enough detail to be helpful to the modern scholar. Cicero does not describe *popularis* rhetoric in any such detail—but he does offer us a critical piece of evidence in his use of the same word to characterize the language of both Caesar and Antonius: it is *nudus*, or "naked." In fact, Cicero consistently describes populist speech in such terms, casting it as lacking in artifice and control, more a product of nature than of human craft, missing what Burke would call "the decent drapery of life." Though Cicero does not repeat the term *nudus* in his discussions of the Atticists, he nevertheless applies a similar conceptual vocabulary to their rhetoric.[9]

What does this recurring vocabulary tell us? For one, it tells us that Cicero consistently distinguished between his own speech—dressed up with *copia* and *ornatus*—and the comparatively artless speech of a range of his opponents.[10] This claim, if true, tells us something important about populist style in the late republic: while it was not an absolute outlier, Cicero had at least some reason to claim that it was distinct from his own practice. What was at stake in this distinction was more than Cicero's allegedly superior

---

[8] Caesar stands out in this context for the way in which he bridges these categories: he is arguably both an Atticist and a *popularis*. Nevertheless, I discuss him separately in this chapter because of the way in which Cicero treats him separately from either group. Cicero's generally less contemptuous attitude toward Caesar's rhetoric seems to stem from a combination of genuine admiration and political caution. But as I argue in the first section below, the parallels in Cicero's treatment of Caesar and the Atticists raise the political stakes of his rhetorical critique of the latter. On Caesar as an Atticist, see A. E. Douglas, "M. Calidius and the Atticists," *Classical Quarterly* 5, no. 3–4 (1955): 241–47; Jakob Wisse, "Greeks, Romans, and the Rise of Atticism," in *Greek Literary Theory after Aristotle*, ed. Jelle G. J. Abbenes, S. R. Slings, and Ineke Sluiter (Amsterdam: VU University Press, 1995), 65–82; Brian Krostenko, *Cicero, Catullus, and the Language of Social Performance* (Chicago: University of Chicago Press, 2001), 228–29; Alessandro Garcea, *Caesar's De Analogia* (Oxford: Oxford University Press, 2012), 119–24; and Giuseppe Pezzini, "Caesar the Linguist: The Debate about the Latin Language," in *The Cambridge Companion to the Writings of Julius Caesar*, ed. Luca Grillo and Christopher B. Krebs (Cambridge, UK: Cambridge University Press, 2018), 188.

[9] John Dugan, "Preventing Ciceronianism: C. Licinius Calvus' Regimens for Sexual and Oratorical Self-Mastery," *Classical Philology* 96 (2001): 400–28.

[10] It is important to note that Cicero did not always criticize the speech of his opponents in these terms—which indicates that they were considered judgments rather than automatic terms of abuse. For instance, Cicero's forensic rival Hortensius was considered to have excessively ornate tendencies, and Cicero describes the Gracchi as combining impeccable style with *popularis* politics (which would seem to make them outliers in comparison with the other *populares* Cicero discusses—perhaps because they were safely dead). It should also be noted that Cicero's published speeches likely differed from their spoken versions, which raises the possibility that some of the *ornatus* was added after the fact of public performance. On Hortensius, see Cicero, *Brutus*, 325; on the Gracchi, see Cicero, *De oratore* III, 226.

command of language—it was the purpose of oratory itself. Studying Cicero's response to the Atticists and Caesar shows that he did not simply conceive of stylistic diversity and abundance as effective tools of persuasion, but as means by which the orator demonstrated responsiveness and accommodation to the audience, using a range of spoken registers to track listeners' shifting responses.[11] By these lights, the choice of an artless style is a choice against adapting to the audience. So if I am correct that Cicero perceived the same lack of artifice in the *populares* as he did in the Atticists and Caesar, this in turn suggests that the *populares*, by pursuing their own kind of "naked" speech, minimized their pursuit of rhetorical responsiveness.

Why would a politician intent on securing popular support want to *minimize* his responsiveness to the audience? In the populist case, a refusal to accommodate can itself send a powerful signal: that the speaker's identification with the audience is so complete that no accommodation is required. In the hands of a populist orator such as Clodius, then, "naked" speech can "deactivate the boundary between [the orator] and his listeners."[12] Cicero's approach, by contrast, strove to make visible the sheer difficulty of rhetorical responsiveness—not only as a display of talent and ingenuity, but because he pursued a different kind of identification. Cicero tends to identify himself not with "the people" or with any given audience, but with *res publica* as a whole, in all its institutional complexity. The republic with which Cicero strives to identify himself is a complex of "component parts" that must be accommodated through a complex of spoken styles and registers.[13] The contrast between populist and Ciceronian styles is thus more than an aesthetic clash. It is an ideological clash—an audible dispute about responsiveness to the audience and the locus of authority in the republic, the existence of which casts doubt on the thesis of "ideological monotony."

In what follows, I assemble evidence for this claim. I begin with Cicero's assessment of the Atticists and Caesar, showing how it forms the groundwork of his stress on rhetorical responsiveness. I then turn to Cicero's

---

[11] See Rob Goodman, *Words on Fire: Eloquence and Its Conditions* (Cambridge, UK: Cambridge University Press, 2021), ch. 2.

[12] James Tan, "Publius Clodius and the Boundaries of the Contio," in *Community and Communication: Oratory and Politics in Republican Rome*, ed. Catherine Steel and Henriette van der Blom (Oxford: Oxford University Press, 2013), 118. See also Catherine Steel, "Tribunician Sacrosanctity and Oratorical Performance in the Late Republic," in *Form and Function in Roman Oratory*, ed. D. H. Berry and Andrew Erskine (Cambridge, UK: Cambridge University Press, 2010), 37–50.

[13] Cicero, *Pro Sestio*, 46. In *The Orations of Marcus Tullius Cicero*, trans. C. D. Yonge, vol. 3 (London: George Bell & Sons, 1891).

various discussions of *popularis* rhetoric—supplemented with accounts of the rhetoric of Clodius and of several earlier *populares* discussed by Sallust—exploring how rhetorical "nakedness" and populist identification with the audience go hand in hand. In the final section, I draw out the political stakes of the contrast between Ciceronian and *popularis* rhetoric, focusing on the analogy between mixed government and "mixed speech" that underlies Cicero's performance of identification with the republic. I concede at the outset that the Ciceronian bias of the sources means that recovering Roman populist rhetoric will have to be a task of inference rather than direct observation. But this work of inference can nonetheless lead us to valuable conclusions—not least, the conclusion that a distinct populist tendency in rhetoric was plausibly real enough for Cicero to refer to it across a wide span of his career. And I believe that we can do our best to correct for Ciceronian bias through the time-honored art of rhetorical re-description. Whereas Cicero casts the rhetorical contest as one between the republic and its undertakers, we can treat it in more disinterested terms, stressing the way in which Cicero and his enemies pursue competing representative claims.[14] These claims, in turn, each rely on a kind of selective concealment: Cicero makes visible the difficulties and uncertainties of persuasion, but he conceals the deep antagonisms of the republic beneath an image of concord; the *populares* make those social antagonisms sharply visible, but their "naked" speech conceals their persuasive work by presenting themselves as indissolubly bound to the Roman people.

Cicero on the Atticists and Caesar

Cicero's two most substantial works of rhetorical criticism, the dialogue *Brutus* and the treatise *Orator*, were both likely written in 46 BCE, a year that saw the consolidation of Caesar's dictatorship and Cicero's withdrawal from active politics. *Brutus* is a chronicle of Roman rhetorical history, and the *Orator* is an essay on prose style and the aesthetics of oratory. But while these are ostensibly apolitical subjects—a safe choice of material in a time of civil war and political crisis—the political subtext is never far from the surface. *Brutus* paints a memorable picture of the empty and silent Forum; the rhetorical history it narrates turns out to be an abruptly truncated one.[15] A pivotal

---

[14] Michael Saward, *The Representative Claim* (Oxford: Oxford University Press, 2010).
[15] Cicero, *Brutus*, 6.

argument in the *Orator* turns on the example of Demosthenes—not only the most eloquent Athenian orator, but a famous enemy of tyranny, whom Cicero would self-consciously imitate by delivering his own series of "Philippics" less than two years later. So while Cicero's critiques of his opponents in these texts are carefully couched in literary terms, it is hardly a stretch to consider the political dimensions of these critiques—which, I argue, ultimately lie in the orator's relationship with those he seeks to persuade.

Let me begin with Cicero's dispute with the "Atticist" orators, who, of the figures considered in this chapter, stand highest in the scale of his political sympathies. The Atticists were not members of an organized movement, but rather a collection of orators who claimed the mantle of "Attic" speech—at least as it existed in the Roman imagination. Atticism, in the Latin literary context, connoted simplicity, plainness, and directness of style, qualities that Roman Atticists associated with such Greek writers and orators as Lysias and (more controversially) Demosthenes.[16] Politically, Cicero and many of the leading Atticists, including Gaius Licinius Calvus and Marcus Junius Brutus, seem to have shared a traditionalist republicanism. But Cicero also apparently perceived Atticism as a generational threat, a reaction against his relatively more elaborate style from a rising cohort of public figures.[17] In any case, what is left of their mutual polemics suggests an occasionally embittered rivalry, one often centered, as John Dugan has observed, on metaphors of manhood and the male body. If the rhetorical body of the average Atticist is, according to Cicero, *attenuata* ("thinned"), *inopia* ("sparse"), and *aridus* ("dry"), Cicero's own body is, according to the Atticists, *fractum atque elumbem* ("broken and loinless"; *fractus* has the additional meaning of "effeminate"), as well as *enervis* ("sinewless," or more evocatively, "neutered").[18]

Beyond this gendered invective, Cicero's *Orator* attacks the Atticists for selectively misreading the Greek past. Demosthenes, the argument goes, is commonly agreed to be the greatest of the original Attic orators and the

---

[16] On the Atticists, in addition to the works cited in note 8 above, see Alan Edward Douglas, "The Intellectual Background of Cicero's Rhetorica: A Study in Method," *Aufstieg und Niedergang der römischen Welt* 1, no. 3 (1973): 95–138; Thomas Gelzer, "Klassizismus, Attizismus und Asianismus," in *Le classicisme à Rome*, ed. Hellmut Flashar (Vandoeuvres-Geneva: Fondation Hardt, 1979), 1–41; and Emanuele Narducci, *Cicerone e l'eloquenza romana* (Rome: Laterza, 1997), 130; all cited in Craig, "A Survey of Recent Work," 314–15. See also James May, "Cicero as Rhetorician," in *A Companion to Roman Rhetoric*, ed. William J. Dominik and Jon Hall (Oxford: Blackwell, 2007), 256–57.

[17] John Dugan, *Making a New Man: Ciceronian Self-Fashioning in the Rhetorical Works* (Oxford: Oxford University Press, 2005), 279.

[18] Dugan, "Preventing Ciceronianism," 412–13.

accepted model for imitation; his iconic status among aristocratic Romans is confirmed by the bust of Demosthenes in Brutus's own home. So, as Cicero writes, "We should advise those whose ignorant chatter has spread abroad—who either long to be called 'Attic' or actually claim to speak in the Attic manner—to admire this man above all: I doubt that Athens itself was more Attic than he. They should learn from him what the Attic manner is and gauge eloquence by his strength, not their own weakness."[19] The question, then, is whether the historical Demosthenes more resembled the stylistically plain Atticists or the stylistically promiscuous Cicero—and naturally, for Cicero, the answer is the latter.

To press home this point, Cicero draws on the "doctrine of the three styles," the idea, originating in Greek rhetorical theory, that speech can be categorized into low, middle, and high styles or registers, depending on such factors as diction, density of figures, complexity of rhythm, and subject matter.[20] Some orators "deploy an abundance of weighty thoughts and majestic diction," others speak "lucidly, without amplification, using precise, succinct, and refined speech," others fall in between those extremes—and the greatest of all can speak across the entire breadth of registers.[21] Demosthenes is introduced as one of the few instances of the latter: "There has never appeared any speaker more impressive nor craftier nor more balanced."[22] He "is able . . . to speak in whatever manner the case demands"; he outdoes Lysias in the plain style and Aeschines in the high.[23] Demosthenes's most famous speech, "On the Crown," is praised specifically for its stylistic range and versatility: "He adopts the middle style whenever he wishes, generally gliding to that level from his grandest style."[24] In *Brutus*, Cicero makes the same point: Demosthenes's plain style is as plain as possible, and his high style is maximally grand.[25]

It is important to note, then, that the bulk of Cicero's response to the Atticists is centered on stylistic diversity, rather than stylistic grandiosity.

---

[19] Cicero, *Orator*. This and all subsequent quotations from *Brutus* and *Orator* are from *Brutus and Orator*, trans. Robert A. Kaster (Oxford: Oxford University Press, 2020), 23.

[20] George Kennedy, *The Art of Persuasion in Greece* (Princeton, NJ: Princeton University Press, 1963), 279; Elaine Fantham, "Theophrastus and the Theory of Style," in *Theophrastus of Eresus: On His Life and Work*, ed. William Wall Fortenbaugh, Pamela M. Huby, and Anthony A. Long (New Brunswick, NJ: Transaction Books, 1985), 251–69; and Elaine Fantham, *The Roman World of Cicero's De oratore* (New York: Oxford University Press, 2004), 242.

[21] Cicero, *Orator*, 20–21.

[22] Ibid., 23.

[23] Ibid., 105, 110.

[24] Ibid, 111.

[25] Cicero, *Brutus*, 35.

Demosthenes is the appropriate model for Roman rhetorical practice not because his speech is ornate while the Atticists' is plain, but because his speech is polyvocal while the Atticists' is confined to a single register. Demosthenes, in Cicero's self-flattering argument, is clearly a stand-in for Cicero. But what matters for our purposes is not the accuracy of the comparison, but rather the terms in which Cicero cast his oratorical ideal—flexibility and adaptability, in opposition to purity and consistency.

The political import of this opposition comes into focus when we observe that Cicero wrote about the dictator Caesar in provocatively similar terms. Caesar's status as an Atticist remains in dispute. But what is difficult to dispute is the fact that Cicero discusses Caesar as if he *were* one. In fact, Cicero's harsh treatment of the Atticists is arguably a displaced polemic on Caesar: by abusing the Atticists, and then painting Caesar as an Atticist-by-association in otherwise respectful passages, Cicero is in effect able to moot criticisms of the dictator that would have been unsafe to voice explicitly.[26]

In *Brutus*, Cicero frames his discussion of Caesar around a quotation from the latter's own work on language, *De analogia*. That work, now lost, evidently focused on clarity of speech and the development of proper *Latinitas* in diction and grammar. Cicero's own rhetorical theory minimized these qualities: any successful orator would already have internalized good Latin usage as a function of his social class, before proceeding on to the more difficult pursuit of eloquence.[27] But Caesar took a different view. In the quotation preserved in *Brutus*, he addresses these words to Cicero:

> If some succeeded, through application and practice, in expressing their thoughts with distinction, we ought to judge that you—practically the inventor of abundantly resourceful speech and its foremost exponent—have well served the name and dignity of the Roman people: are we now to regard as abandoned the knowledge of this ready and colloquial way of speaking?[28]

In other words, Caesar appears to claim for himself the mantle of "ready and colloquial" speech rather than "abundantly resourceful speech."

---

[26] Frederick Ahl, "The Art of Safe Criticism in Greece and Rome," *American Journal of Philology* 105, no. 2 (1984): 174–208.

[27] Debra L. Nousek, "Genres and Generic Contaminations: The *Comentarii*," in *The Cambridge Companion to the Writings of Julius Caesar*, ed. Luca Grillo and Christopher Krebs (Cambridge, UK: Cambridge University Press, 2017), 105.

[28] Cicero, *Brutus*, 253.

Cicero, in turn, accepts and expands on this self-description. Caesar "uses common language that's pure and unspoiled to correct the sort that's flawed and corrupt. When he joins to this refined [*elegantia*] Latin diction—something indispensable even if you're a freeborn Roman citizen, not an orator—the elaboration appropriate to oratory, it's as though he's displaying well-painted pictures in good light."[29] Moreover, Caesar's prose is "bare [*nudus*], straightforward, alluring, with all rhetorical elaboration stripped away."[30]

The first thing to observe here is the equivocal nature of Cicero's approval. Congratulating a rival for speaking correctly and grammatically would seem to be the definition of damning with faint praise. In fact, Caesar's good diction, to which he dedicated an entire book, is attainable by any "freeborn Roman citizen." Even the allowance that Caesar sometimes attains "the elaboration appropriate to oratory" is couched in conditional terms.

But what elevates the importance of this discussion beyond that of a series of cleverly insulting compliments is the consistent association of Caesar with the low or plain style, and therefore with Atticism. Purity, common language, refinement/elegance, and bareness/nakedness were all terms synonymous with the plain style, and all terms that the Atticists applied to themselves. These terms were not necessarily pejorative. Caesar used them favorably in *De analogia*, and Aulus Hirtius, a subordinate of Caesar who added a book to *De bello Gallico* after the dictator's assassination, praised his style in words that echoed Cicero's, including *elegantia* and *emendate* ("correct").[31] But what makes these terms effectively pejorative in Cicero's use is his consistent contrast between mere correctness and true eloquence, not to mention the series of links between Caesar and the Atticists, who come in for such sharp Ciceronian criticism.

In Cicero's view, the Atticists and Caesar represent a flattening of Roman rhetorical possibilities, the former operating through the force of generational change, and the latter employing the resources of political power to enforce new, restrictive speech norms. Biographically, it is all too easy to read in this response Cicero's fear of cultural and political displacement. But on the level of rhetorical theory, we should also do justice to the stakes of these

---

[29] Ibid., 261.
[30] Ibid., 262; A. D. Leeman, "Julius Caesar, the Orator of Paradox," in *The Orator in Action and Theory in Greece and Rome: Essays in Honor of George A. Kennedy*, ed. Cecil W. Wooten (Leiden: Brill, 2001), 102.
[31] Aulus Hirtius, *Comentarii de Bello Gallico*, 8, praef.

developments as Cicero described them—to the moral and political value of stylistic abundance, and the costs of its erosion.

Cicero identifies the orator's adaptability to the audience as an exercise in *decorum*, which is, tellingly, both a normative and a rhetorical value. Normatively, *decorum* describes the appropriateness of an action to a given situation; rhetorically, it describes the fit between words and occasion. In the *Orator*, Cicero describes *decorum* in terms of navigation across stylistic levels:

> The man who controls and blends these three kinds of style will need great judgment and superior facility, since he will gauge what each case requires and be able to speak however the case demands. But eloquence, like all else, is founded on wisdom. And as in life so in oratory the greatest challenge lies in seeing what is appropriate: the Greeks call it *prepon*, we of course call it "decorum."[32]

For Cicero, stylistic versatility requires "judgment" and "wisdom" in a way that stylistic consistency does not. In pursuing *decorum*, the orator hones and demonstrates his ability to read situations and audiences—so that Cicero's stylistic ideal is as much a question of attentiveness to the audience as of verbal dexterity. In the same way, Cicero describes eloquence as a difficult, painful, and fearful endeavor, largely because tracking the needs of an unpredictable audience is such an uncertain undertaking.[33] Conversely, it is precisely the quality of attentiveness that the practitioners of the exclusively plain style lack: what the Atticists describe as a principled purity of speech is, for Cicero, a deliberate refusal of *decorum*, an imposition of themselves on an audience that they seek to render passive. In his moral writings, Cicero describes the pursuit of *decorum* as conformity "with duty and nature," a sign of regard for others and their claims on us.[34] The public figure's stylistic versatility is the political manifestation of this regard, just as the rhetoric of the Atticists and Caesar represents its negation.

Of course, as I observed above, our ability to reconstruct the latter figures' own understanding of their stylistic choices is limited by the Ciceronian bias

---

[32] Cicero, *Orator*, 70.

[33] Rob Goodman, "'I Tremble with My Whole Heart': Cicero on the Anxieties of Eloquence," *European Journal of Political Theory* 20, no. 4 (2019): 698–718.

[34] Cicero, *De officiis*, 1.146. In *Ethical Writings of Cicero*, trans. Andrew W. Peabody (Boston: Little, Brown, 1887), 1–146; Daniel Kapust, "Cicero on Decorum and the Morality of Rhetoric," *European Journal of Political Theory* 10, no. 1 (2011): 92–112.

of the sources. Given the rhetorical education of the Roman elite, and given in particular Caesar's reputation for rhetorical brilliance,[35] it seems clear that we are dealing with a refusal of, rather than an incapacity for, the demands of *decorum* as Cicero understood it. In the Atticists' case, we might speculate that the plain style was associated with an idealized Greek past, as well as with a kind of aristocratic frankness, in which Cicero's "great judgment" of the audience would have been re-described as a kind of servility. In Caesar's case, as I have argued elsewhere, a shift toward more straightforward speech norms not only would have comported with his military persona, but also would have hedged against a range of rhetorically powerful challenges to his political authority.[36] But whatever the specific motivations behind the stylistic choices that Cicero decried, it seems plausible that different motives can result in quite similar stylistic outcomes. With this in mind, in the next section I consider the evidence for the "nakedness" of *popularis* speech. And I argue that many Roman populists would have their own distinctive reasons for rejecting the kind of visible accommodation to the audience envisioned by Cicero.

Popularis Style: Performing Identification with the People

In the years after Caesar's assassination, Cicero's rivalry with Marcus Antonius led him to deliver a series of fourteen "Philippics," the last major speeches of a prolific career. As I noted above, Cicero's choice of title aims to associate himself with Demosthenes and his enemy with Philip of Macedon, the prototypical tyrant. Just as important, however, is the way in which Cicero's rhetorical criticism of Antonius places him on a continuum with Caesar and the Atticists.

Cicero's lengthiest attack on Antonius comes in the Second Philippic, written in the fall of 44; though it purports to be a speech to the Senate, Cicero opted to publish it rather than deliver it in person. While its insults are sexual, political, financial, and sartorial, as well as rhetorical, its treatment of Antonius as orator is an important thread in its own right, and worth singling out. The dominant theme in this criticism is nakedness. "Oh how splendid was that eloquence of yours," Cicero sarcastically declares, "when

---

[35] Plutarch, "The Life of Caesar," 3.2.
[36] Goodman, *Words on Fire*, ch. 1.

you harangued the people stark naked!" He returns to the theme in the peroration, where, building on the fiction that Antonius is present and able to respond, asks:

> What will you now reply to these arguments? For I am waiting to witness your eloquence; I knew your grandfather, who was a most eloquent man, but I know you to be a more undisguised speaker than he was; he never harangued the people naked; but we have seen your breast, man, without disguise as you are.

Nor is this the only claim that Antonius has failed to live up to his famous grandfather (also named Marcus Antonius): "Just see now what a difference there is between you and your grandfather. He used with great deliberation to bring forth arguments advantageous to the cause he was advocating; you pour forth in a hurry the sentiments which you have been taught by another."[37]

So, on the one hand, we have the artifice, deliberateness, and clothed rhetorical body of Marcus Antonius senior—set against the spontaneity, effusions, and stark nakedness of Marcus Antonius junior. Given a pointed contrast between two public figures, one of whom is emphatically "without disguise," and the other of whom is disguised by implication, a modern audience would almost certainly expect the contrast to favor the first figure. But for Cicero, the opposite is the case: Marcus Antonius senior is decorously covered, while Marcus Antonius junior is obscenely naked.[38] Of course, the polemical nature of this comparison means that we ought to take it with a grain of salt—but it nevertheless tells us something important about what Cicero and his audience considered praiseworthy and blameworthy in public performance.[39]

What does it mean, in rhetorical terms, for Antonius to be "naked" and "undisguised"? One clue, as we have seen, comes from Cicero's use of a similar complex of ideas with reference to Caesar. Caesar's prose is "naked,

---

[37] Cicero, Second Philippic, 34, 43, 17. In *Orations*, trans. C. D. Yonge, vol. 4.

[38] These were fraught issues in classical oratory. Cf. Aeschines, *Against Timarchus* 1.26, where he compares the old orators who modestly kept both hands inside the cloak to an opponent who gesticulates "like an athlete in the pankration."

[39] In fact, Antonius seems to have been a much more effective orator than Cicero's attacks would lead us to believe. See Trevor Mahy, "Antonius, Triumvir and Orator: Career, Style, and Effectiveness," in *Community and Communication: Oratory and Politics in Republican Rome*, ed. Catherine Steel and Henriette van der Blom (Oxford: Oxford University Press, 2013), 329–44.

straightforward, alluring"; and while these are terms of guarded praise, they also go hand in hand with the implication that Caesar imposes himself on, rather than accommodates himself to, the audience. Rhetorical ornamentation, like clothing, is both a kind of disguise and a kind of self-expression, one that can be calibrated to others in a way that nakedness cannot be. The rhetorical nakedness of Antonius is at the far end of this spectrum, in that it is entirely uncalculated and offensive. Borrowing terms from art criticism, we could consider the implied contrast between Caesar and Antonius as one between "nude" and "naked," in which only the latter term connotes obscenity.[40] Cicero adds to this impression when, in an infamous passage, he claims that a hungover Antonius vomited on the tribunal at a public assembly, "in the sight of the Roman people."[41] Cicero evidently wants his audience to perceive Antonius's speech from that tribunal in the same way, as a shameful public exposure of that which ought to be private.[42]

So far, then, we have seen that Cicero links the Atticists to Caesar, and Caesar to Antonius. But this need not imply (through some sort of transitive property of rhetorical criticism) that Cicero perceives Antonius as an Atticist. In fact, there is some evidence that Antonius's rhetoric was regarded as "Asianist," a pejorative term for unrestrained speech used as the counterpart to Atticism (though this evidence deserves some skepticism, given that it comes from Plutarch and Suetonius, who wrote at a considerable historical remove from Antonius).[43] Calvus and Antonius may have cut very different figures on the tribunal—but Cicero evidently claimed that they, along with Caesar, shared an important underlying trait: the absence of the artful accommodation or responsiveness that he associated with the practice of *decorum*. This absence can be demonstrated in a consistently florid style as much as in a consistently plain one: what matters for Cicero is their consistency against his flexibility.

---

[40] Kenneth Clark, *The Nude: A Study in Ideal Form* (New York: Pantheon, 1956).
[41] Cicero, Second Philippic, 25.
[42] Valentina Arena, "Roman Oratorical Invective," in *A Companion to Roman Rhetoric*, ed. William Dominik and Jon Hall (Malden, MA: Blackwell, 2007), 154; Isak Hammar, *Making Enemies: The Logic of Immorality in Ciceronian Oratory* (Lund: Lund University Press, 2013), 311; and Ian Goh, "It All Comes Out: Vomit as a Source of Comedy in Roman Moralizing Texts," *Illinois Classical Studies* 43, no. 2 (2018): 438–58.
[43] Plutarch, "Life of Antonius," 2.4–5; Suetonius, "Life of Augustus," 86.2–3. For reasons to treat these sources skeptically, see C. B. R. Pelling, *Plutarch: Life of Antony* (Cambridge: Cambridge University Press, 1988), 119–20; Brigette Ford Russell, "The Emasculation of Antony: The Construction of Gender in Plutarch's *Life of Antony*," *Helios* 25 (1998): 134; and Mahy, "Antonius," 342–43 and n.80.

There is also another telling clue to the Ciceronian meaning of *nudus* in the repeated contrast between Antonius and his grandfather—who, as luck and the closed nature of the Roman oligarchy would have it, was one of Cicero's own oratorical role models. In fact, Antonius senior is one of the two leading figures in the dialogue *De oratore* (55 BCE), Cicero's most substantial work of rhetorical theory. Remarkably, Cicero also associates Antonius senior with nakedness, but with a key difference. In an important passage on *actio*, Cicero has Antonius senior explain how, "prompted ... by deep grief and passion," he won the jury's sympathies in a corruption trial by ripping off his client's tunic and exposing his battle scars.[44] So Cicero's ideal orator, while remaining clothed, strategically exposes the nakedness of others: nakedness is something that he deliberately uses for his purposes, not a state that he inhabits. He exposes himself only with "great deliberation," in a series of stylized and conventional gestures, such as the display of the client's scars. Genuine as his passions may be, they are also the *correct* passions, deployed in the right way and at the right time: his use of his emotions contrasts with his grandson's emotional incontinence. And his sense for the situational aptness of these gestures and passions is the result of intense psychological study of the public. As Cicero has Antonius argue elsewhere in the dialogue, the ideal orator is someone "who with keen scent can track down the thoughts, the feelings, the opinions, and the hopes of his fellow citizens and of those people whom he wants to persuade with his oratory. He must have his finger on the pulse of every class, every age group, every social rank."[45] Antonius senior's own speech, while it appears artful, stylized, and "clothed," is credited to his care and consideration for his audience. Cicero's contrast between grandfather and grandson could not be more stark.

The Second Philippic places Antonius in a long line of *popularis* or allegedly *popularis* figures. In the text's first lines, he is cast as "more audacious than Catiline, more frantic than Clodius." Later, reflecting on Antonius's growing power, Cicero asks, "Was it for this ... that Spurius Cassius, and Spurius Maelius, and Marcus Manlius were slain?"[46] Given that Catiline was killed in battle with the Roman army and the latter four figures assassinated as would-be tyrants by members of the senatorial elite (Clodius in recent memory, and the remaining three in the earlier republic), the threat of violence against Antonius is clear. His insertion into this populist lineage is,

---

[44] Cicero, *De or.*, 2.195.
[45] Ibid., 1.223.
[46] Cicero, Second Philippic, 1, 34.

again, an act of polemical aggression, rather than a dispassionate rendering of Roman history. Cicero's strategy arguably elides his own earlier flirtations with *popularis* politics,[47] as well as the extent to which his enmity to such figures as Clodius and Marcus Antonius is ultimately personal rather than ideological. But for our purposes, the salient fact is that Cicero is constructing a lineage not only of populist politics, but of populist speech.

And, in fact, the tropes with which Cicero degrades the rhetoric of Antonius also appear in his earlier treatments of populist or populist-adjacent rhetoric. Catiline's rhetoric, for instance, queasily confounds public and private: "You remember how often the speech of that vile gladiator, which, it was said, he delivered in an oration conducted in his own house, was reported."[48] Catiline is described as speaking in a private *contio*—that is, a public assembly held in his own home. As W. Jeffrey Tatum adds, "*Contio domestica* is a striking oxymoron, unparalleled so far as I am aware"; the phrase appeals to the same kind of disquiet provoked by Antonius's metaphorically unclothed appearance on the tribunal.[49] Similarly, the set of binaries that shape Cicero's contrast between Antonius senior and junior—decorous self-control against uncontrolled spontaneity—also shape his contrasts between *optimates* and *populares* writ large. In the speech *pro Sestio* (56 BCE), which introduced the (tendentious) *optimates/populares* distinction, Cicero casts the "frantic voice" of Clodius and his "turbulent" assemblies in opposition to the *contiones* convened by Cicero's allies, in which "the greatest fluency of language" was received "amid such silent attention and such visible approbation."[50] Again, in the speech *pro Plancio* (54 BCE), popular assemblies are figured as forces of nature—"a deep and wide sea"—to be tamed by the orator's artifice and cultured skill:

> It is our duty—ours, I say, who are driven about by the winds and waves of this people—to hear the whims of the people with moderation, to strive to win over their affections when alienated from us, to retain them when we have won them, to tranquilize them when in a state of agitation.[51]

---

[47] E.g., in his speeches *in Verrem* (70 BCE) and *de imperio Gn. Pompei* (66 BCE).
[48] Cicero, *Pro Murena*, trans. W. Jeffrey Tatum, 50.
[49] W. Jeffrey Tatum, "Campaign Rhetoric," in *Community and Communication: Oratory and Politics in Republican Rome*, ed. Catherine Steel and Henriette van der Blom (Oxford: Oxford University Press, 2013), 146.
[50] Cicero, *Pro Sestio*, 50.
[51] Cicero, *Pro Plancio*, 4. In *Orations*, trans. C. D. Yonge, vol. 3.

The metaphor of winds and waves is a particularly apt one for Cicero's theory of orator-audience interaction: sailors cannot control the wind, and sometimes it causes them to capsize, but they can generally shape their sails so that the wind collaborates in their journey.

If these are all familiar and even clichéd tropes of anti-populist rhetoric, it was in part because Cicero made them so.[52] But corroborating evidence also suggests that Cicero's accounts of populist rhetoric, while far from objective reporting, were founded on a plausible basis. Some of that corroborating evidence comes from Cicero's more straightforward treatments of his opponents' conduct—cases in which we can more easily separate fact from fulmination. For instance, we know from a letter to Atticus in the spring of 60 BCE that Clodius discussed in a *contio* such un-political topics as the speed of his travel from Sicily to Rome when a private citizen.[53] We also know that, on another occasion, Clodius read from the tribunal a private letter from Caesar, in which Caesar informally referred to himself and Clodius by *cognomen* only (which put them on the equivalent of a "first-name basis").[54]

James Tan offers a convincing reading of these incidents as part of Clodius's efforts to cultivate an air of frankness and informality with his audience. Tan describes the mundane narration of travel as the speaker's attempt to "personalize his presence on the *rostra*." Compared to more traditional oratory, this was "more personal and casual, perhaps more at home in the epistolographical conventions of acquaintances." Similarly, his choice to share a private letter "gave his *contio* a sense of frankness, as if he were stripping away the cover of politics and inviting his audience to join in life behind the aristocracy's veil. 'Why be formal,' he was essentially asking, 'when we're all friends here?'"[55] Here again, we see something of the blurred public–private distinction that was integral to Cicero's critique of populist rhetoric. We also see what appears to be Clodius's deliberate departure from the conventional and stylized behavior that rendered oratory property "clothed."

---

[52] Roughly twenty-five years later, the image of winds and waves would make a famous appearance in Book 1 of the *Aeneid*, where Vergil compares Neptune calming the sea to an orator calming the crowd. The notable difference is that, for Cicero, the orator sometimes sails on the winds of public emotion, as well: "As often, when rebellion breaks out in a great nation, and the common rabble rage with passion, and soon stones and fiery torches fly (frenzy supplying weapons), if they then see a man of great virtue, and weighty service, they are silent, and stand there listening attentively: he sways their passions with his words and soothes their hearts: so all the uproar of the ocean died." Vergil, *Aeneid*, 1.148–54, trans. A. S. Kline, 2002.

[53] Cicero, *Att.* 2.1.5.

[54] Cicero, *De domo sua*, 22; this and the above cited in Tan, "Publius Clodius."

[55] Tan, "Publius Clodius," 121–22.

Additional evidence comes from Sallust, a contemporary of Cicero, Clodius, and Caesar with *popularis* sympathies, who depicts a series of earlier *populares* in his histories. Sallust, in conventional fashion, composed speeches for a number of these historical figures. But while these speeches are not transcriptions, Rosenblitt argues that they are a roughly accurate guide to the themes of populist rhetoric in the prior generation, filtered through Sallust's own experience in the waning years of the republic. For Rosenblitt, the rhetoric of Sallust's popular champions constructs a "hostile politics," in which the elite are not the fellow citizens of the plebs, but rather an enemy power that has "conquered, despoiled, and enslaved" them.[56] I want to highlight a key rhetorical move in this populist discourse: one in which the republic's institutions are performatively stripped of their conventional names, and renamed in uglier, more "disillusioned" terms. For Memmius, tribune in 111 BCE, priesthoods and consulships are *praeda* ("booty"). For Lepidus, consul in 78 BCE, the plebs are captives rather than citizens, and the property of the elite is *spolia* ("spoils"). For Macer, tribune in 73 BCE, the *otium* of civil concord (incidentally, a favorite term of Cicero's) is in fact *servitium*.[57]

Elsewhere, Sallust attributes to Marius—the *popularis* leader who won his first of seven consulships in 104 BCE —the boast that "he had wrested the consulship from [the nobles] as the spoils of victory." Sallust's Marius, much like Cicero, associates plain speech with the populist cause and *copia* with the elite: "I am of course well aware that if they should deign to reply to me, their language would be abundantly eloquent and elaborate.... My words are not well chosen; I care little for that."[58] Of course, characterizing political offices as spoils or plunder *is* a choice.[59] But by describing it as an inept choice, the speaker effectively makes the new name of the office ("spoils") into a brute fact of nature and the old name of the office ("the consulship") into a clever artifice that disguises the truth. Cicero aimed to shock his audience's sense of propriety by describing the *popularis* cause as "undisguised"; Sallust's *populares* accept this characterization but reverse its valence, claiming their

---

[56] Rosenblitt, "Hostile Politics," 661.
[57] Sallust, *Bellum Iugurthinum*, 31.10; Sallust, *Historiae*, 1.55M, 7; 3.48M, 13; trans. Rosenblitt.
[58] Sallust, *Bellum Iugurthinum*, trans. John C. Rolfe (Cambridge, MA: Harvard University Press, 1921), 84.1, 85.26, 31.
[59] It is, in fact, a choice to use the figure of paradiastolic re-description, which was often employed to excuse vices by re-describing them as related virtues ("cowardice" to "caution," for instance), but could also be used in the opposite direction—in this case, by re-describing a supposedly honorable and freely given office as plunder. Quentin Skinner, *Reason and Rhetoric in the Philosophy of Hobbes* (Cambridge, UK: Cambridge University Press, 1997), 166.

undisguised and *non composita* words as a mark of truthfulness and the exposure of political reality under conditions of oligarchy.

At this point, I think it is fair to conclude that politics in the late Roman republic did include a distinctive *popularis* rhetoric. The common thread of this rhetoric is not necessarily vehemence or anger—qualities that could be displayed by the elite as well as their opponents[60]—but rather a deliberately artless, unaffected, and informal style, at least in relative terms, which Cicero summed up in the metaphor of nakedness. There is also reason to believe that this style was consistent with a kind of rhetorical "realism," in which political institutions were re-described in depreciatory and purportedly more accurate terms. Stylistic choices are often political choices—certainly when they are choices displayed in public speech. What, then, can Roman populist style tell us about Roman populist politics and ideology?

I would argue that the variety of Roman populist speech considered here pursues a kind of identification with the audience that Ciceronian speech does not. That is not the case because speech in a "low" register was necessarily received as sociologically low. We have already seen that figures with sterling elitist credentials, such as Calvus, could speak in the low style; further, while the low style reads as relatively unaffected in the Roman context, it was still a literary language at some distance from colloquial speech.[61] Rather, I think we can understand the kind of identification pursued by the orator—the way his speech "deactivates the boundary," in Tan's terms—by contrasting it with Cicero's ideal of rhetorical accommodation and responsiveness. For Cicero, the ideal orator pursues and shapes himself to the audience: he "tracks down the thoughts, the feelings, the opinions, and the hopes of his fellow citizens," he trims his sails in response to their wind, he "tranquilizes" them when they are agitated, and above all he demonstrates *decorum* by adapting his style to the needs of the moment. All of this can be rhetorically effective in the right hands—but it all presumes the *separateness* of orator and audience. The audience is the external force that the orator reacts to, and tries to react on; the greater the distance between the two is imagined to be, the more admirable the successful orator's accomplishment.

---

[60] Jakob Wisse, "The Bad Orator: Between Clumsy Delivery and Political Danger," in *Community and Communication: Oratory and Politics in Republican Rome*, ed. Catherine Steel and Henriette van der Blom (Oxford: Oxford University Press, 2013), 177.

[61] Rolando Ferri and Philomen Probert, "Roman Authors on Colloquial Language," in *Colloquial and Literary Latin*, ed. Eleanor Dickey and Anna Chahoud (Cambridge, UK: Cambridge University Press, 2010), 18–28; Rosillo-López, *Public Opinion*, 19.

The populist style is grounded on the opposite set of assumptions. If the pursuit of *decorum* and stylistic diversity is a way of tracking the audience, the pursuit of a consistent and unaffected style is a denial that the audience needs to be tracked at all. It is a conspicuous removal of the *difficulty* of oratory that Cicero did so much to stress. In effect, the populist orator's self-consciously artless style suggests that accommodating the people is easy when one is authentically *of* the people; conversely, Cicero's rather sweaty invocations of the "judgment," "facility," and "deliberation" that shape his every utterance amount to a confession that he is constitutionally at odds with the people. We can see the *populares*' strategy of identification with the audience in any number of small gestures, such as Clodius's use of call-and-response, or the references to the crowd as "us" (as opposed to the usual "you") in Sallust's Marius.[62] But more than these discrete moments, the populists' strategy of identification is a general rhetorical posture, a style that consistently denies the separateness of orator and audience on which Cicero relies. The degree of separation between orator and audience is not, of course, a sociological fact—Cicero was famously a "new man," while Clodius descended from a long line of consuls. Rather, it is a political construct: when the *populares* speak in a style that is ostentatiously *non composita*, we should understand them as performing identification with the people.

The gap between "naked" and "clothed" speech seems to result, then, from a serious dispute over the nature and value of rhetorical responsiveness, and over the appropriate relationship between the orator and the audience. This conclusion, on its own, weighs against the "ideological monotony" thesis: the stylistic difference here is itself an ideological difference. Moreover, this difference was grounded not only in rhetorical theory, but in a deeper dispute on the source of legitimate authority in the republic.

Cicero against *Popularis* Style: Mixed Government and Mixed Speech

Cicero's rhetoric, just as much as the *populares*', pursues its own strategy of identification. The difference is that Cicero seeks to identify himself with the republic as a whole. In fact, he quite explicitly claims that "Cicero" and "*res publica*" ought to be taken as synonymous terms. In the speech *pro Sestio*, he

---

[62] Cicero, *Ad Quintum fratrem*, 2.3.1–2; Sallust, *Bellum Iugurthinum*, 85.41.

concludes an attack on one opponent in these terms: "I have been carried away by indignation on my own account and on that of the republic (and I do not know which of us two he hates most)." And that identification with the republic repeats itself in the very first line of the Second Philippic: "To what destiny of mine ... shall I say it is owing, that none for the last twenty years has been an enemy to the republic without at the same time declaring war against me?"[63] At least as far as the senatorial audience is concerned, Antonius's hostility to Cicero is itself proof of his enmity to the republican constitution.

What is at stake in these competing strategies of identification? Arguably the most significant distinction is that, for Cicero, the republic is institutionally variegated. Mixed government is a central theme of his political philosophy, particularly *De re publica* (ca. 51 BCE), but also of his oratory. In the speech *pro Sestio*, the republic is specifically defined as a complex of institutions:

> These are the component parts, which ought to be upheld by the chief men, and to be defended even at the hazard of their lives: religious observances, the auspices, the civil power of magistrates, the authority of the senate, the laws, the usages of one's ancestors, the courts of justice, the jurisdiction of the judges, good faith, the provinces, the allies, the glory of the empire, the whole affairs of the army, the treasury.[64]

Provocatively enough, the "popular" elements of the constitution are minimized in this litany, though one can read "magistrates" to include the tribunes, and "the laws" to imply the people's assemblies that held formal law-making power. In any case, the theory seems to be that the authority of the republic inheres in these institutions collectively, and not solely in the assemblies that were emphasized by the *populares*.

This is the light in which we should read Cicero's frequent invocations of public opinion from the days of Catiline to those of Antonius, of the "incredible unanimous will of the whole Roman people," in which "all men were of one and the same opinion."[65] The will of the whole Roman people emerges from the complex of mixed institutions, not from any crowd or assembly that

---

[63] Cicero, *Pro Sestio*, 52; Second Philippic, 1.
[64] Cicero, *Pro Sestio*, 46.
[65] Cicero, First Philippic, 36; Fourth Catilinarian, 14; trans. Cristina Rosillo-López.

purports to be the people. Again, in the speech *pro Sestio*, Cicero is explicit on this point:

> Do you not see, then, what a great difference there is between the Roman people and an assembly [*inter populum Romanum et contionem*]? Do you not see that the masters of the assemblies are the object of the hatred of the Roman people? and that those who are not permitted to appear without insult in the assembly of artisans, are honoured by every possible mark of respect by the Roman people?[66]

On one level, as Cicero claims, the *contiones* convened by Clodius are illegitimate representations of the people—while the *contiones* convened by Cicero's allies *are* legitimate—because the attendees of the first were bribed, or because they are exclusively assemblies "of artisans." But this passage should also be read in light of the earlier discussion of the republic's "component parts." No *contio* can speak for the Roman people, because the *contio* is only one institution among many (and an informal one at that), and the will of the people is generated by the institutional complex as a whole.[67] Conversely, we can infer that Clodius claimed that public assemblies (or at least his own *contiones*) *did* constitute the people.

It should not be surprising to find populists and anti-populists at odds over the true nature of "the people." Nor should we be surprised to see the crisis of the late republic, in part, as a dispute over the locus of political authority—the dispute that emerged, for instance, in several unsuccessful attempts to pass popular agrarian laws in the face of senatorial opposition.[68] But what I want to emphasize in conclusion is the way in which these disputes manifested themselves rhetorically—and therefore, the way in which they would have been publicly *perceptible* in the republic's political life.

For Cicero, there is an important linkage between mixed government and mixed speech. In other words, Cicero's rhetorical model calls for the

---

[66] Cicero, *Pro Sestio*, 59.

[67] There is a similar criticism of government centered on popular assemblies (in this case, for leading to the decline of the Greek city-states) in *Pro Flacco*, 7. On the contested role of *contiones* in republican politics, see Egon Flaig, *Ritualisierte Politik: Zeichen, Gesten und Herrschaft im Alten Rom* (Göttingen: Vandenhoeck & Ruprecht, 2003); Claudia Tiersch, "Politische Öffentlichkeit statt Mitbestimmung? Zur Bedeutung der *contiones* in der mittleren und späten römischen Republik," *Klio* 9 (2009): 58; and Yakobson, "Traditional Political Culture."

[68] See Jed W. Atkins, *Roman Political Thought* (Cambridge, UK: Cambridge University Press, 2018), 25.

cultivation of a wide stylistic range not only because the moods of any given audience can be expected to shift from moment to moment, but because the ideal orator will have to argue across institutional settings and social classes in order to be truly successful. In *De oratore*, for instance, Cicero draws a stylistic contrast between speeches to the senate and to the people.[69] And in the passage on the "component parts" above, consider how the various institutions listed—religious observances, the senate, the courts, alliance diplomacy, the army, and so on—could each be expected to have their own distinctive sets of speech norms. It is of more than numerological significance that Cicero praises the Roman constitution as a mixture of three forms of government (democracy, aristocracy, and monarch) and the speech of the ideal Roman orator as a mixture of three styles (low, middle, and high).[70] In each case, the idea of mixture connotes balance, flexibility, and resilience. On the other hand, an idea of legitimate authority that centered largely on popular assemblies, rather than on what I have called the institutional complex, would most likely privilege the cultivation of speech norms best suited to winning over those assemblies. The artlessness and inadaptability that Cicero perceives in populist speech ultimately derives, I would argue, from the populist definition of the people as the assemblies.

As a result, Ciceronian and populist rhetoric are, at the same time, competing styles and the embodiment of competing representative claims—practices that offer linked answers to the questions "who speaks for the people?" and "how should the people be spoken to?" In the view developed by contemporary political theorists, including Michael Saward and Lisa Disch, representation is not simply an institutional matter of elections won and offices held. "Prior to that," in Saward's words, "it is a multi-sided process of claim-making and the reception and judgment of claims." Representation, in this view, "invokes—consists of—claims that one stands for others by virtue of roles one can play."[71] The Roman rhetorical strategies that I have

---

[69] Cicero, *De or.*, 2.334.

[70] Cicero, *De re publica*, 2.42, 66. See Jed William Atkins, "Cicero on the Mixed Regime," American Political Science Association Annual Meeting paper, 2011, papers.ssrn.com/sol3/papers.cfm?abstract_id = 1902886. The anonymous *Rhetorica ad Herennium*, written in Cicero's early years, proposes that there are healthy and degenerate versions of the low, middle, and high styles (4.8–10), a suggestive parallel to Aristotle's categorization of political regimes.

[71] Michael Saward, *The Representative Claim* (Oxford: Oxford University Press, 2010), 2, 42. See also Lisa Disch, "Toward a Mobilization Conception of Democratic Representation," *American Political Science Review* 105, no. 1 (2011): 100–14.

considered here are forms of claim-making in action: they depend on assertions about the nature of the object that is represented; they enable the speaker to perform identification with the represented object through his choice of style and language; and they are submitted to the judgment of various rhetorical audiences. Understanding these rhetorical strategies as representative claims turns our attention away from the question of who in fact represented the Roman people—a question that construes representation in far too rigid terms—and toward the ways in which each competing claim strategically obscures some aspects of the late-republican political situation and brings other aspects into clearer focus.

When Cicero identifies himself with the republic's institutional complexity, and at the same time asserts that he speaks for the Roman people's "incredible unanimous will," these are, of course, efforts to construct a favorable political terrain rather than statements of fact. But these statements should also be read alongside Cicero's frequent emphasis on the difficulty of oratory, especially the difficulty of oratory across the range of styles. What Cicero brings to light, I think, is the sheer contingency and uncertainty of representative claims in the Roman context (or perhaps in any context). Whatever the degree of confidence with which his claims are voiced, Cicero's rhetorical theory tells us that they are fragile and entropic things, held together by a constant input of oratorical energy, and capable of falling apart at a moment's notice. But Cicero's images of concord, consensus, and unanimity obscure deep and real divisions—and ultimately proved incapable of papering them over.

Conversely, we can look to the *populares* for a far more accurate account of the social antagonisms of the late republic. A politics in which one man's fairly acquired office is another's "spoils," in which institutions are competing centers of legitimacy rather than cooperative cogs in the constitutional machine, in which the "us" of an assembly stands in implicit tension with the "them" outside of it—all of this strikes a note of reality in contrast to a cardboard-cutout struggle between "every good man" and the wicked.[72] What the *populares* obscure, on the other hand, is the irreducible gap between orator and audience, or between representative and represented, in any system in which representative claims are made. Roman populist rhetoric really does seem to aspire to a state in which the orator and the audience

[72] Cicero, *Pro Sestio*, 45.

are an indissoluble "us." The *populares'* rhetoric appears naked because it evidently performs the kind of unself-consciousness we assume with ourselves when no one is watching. But Clodius is, in fact, being watched. And no amount of effortlessness can change where he stands in relation to the crowd: he is on the *rostra*, and they are not.

4
Rhetoric and Republicanism in the Thought of Brunetto Latini

Cary J. Nederman

Introduction

Interest in republican political thought, from both philosophical and historical perspectives, has burgeoned during the last quarter century or so, especially, but not exclusively, in the English-speaking world.[1] Sitting in the midst of the theory and history of republicanism is the great Roman statesman and philosopher Marcus Tullius Cicero.[2] One problem immediately poses itself, however: *Which* Cicero is relevant to the study and application of republican principles? This question is not as odd as it might seem *prima facie*. As I pointed out a number of years ago, at least two distinct foundations for republican principles may be located in Cicero's large body of writings, one of which I labeled "rhetorical republicanism" and the other "rationalist republicanism."[3] By the former phrase, I meant to convey emphasis on his account of how social relations and political institutions initially arose from the urgings of a wise orator, who later becomes the model for the republican statesman (such as Cicero himself), a view that appears mainly in Ciceronian texts such as *De inventione* and *De oratore*, and some of his speeches, especially *Pro*

---

[1] The literature has simply become too large to survey and summarize in brief compass here. Two excellent overviews are Luca Baccelli, "Republicanism: Political Language and/or Political Paradigm" and Debora Spini, "The Price of Liberty: On Democracy, Republicanism, and Non-Domination," both contained in *Republicanism: A Theoretical and Historical Perspective*, ed. Fabrizio Ricciardelli and Marcello Fantoni (Rome: Viella, 2020), 21–44 and 45–60, respectively.

[2] From the side of political philosophy, for instance, see Philip Pettit, *Republicanism: A Theory of Freedom and Government* (Oxford: Oxford University Press, 1997), 5, 19; of a more historical bent is Joy Connolly, *The Life of Roman Republicanism* (Princeton, NJ: Princeton University Press, 2015), 23–64.

[3] Cary J. Nederman, "Rhetoric, Reason and Republic: Republicanisms—Ancient, Medieval, and Modern," in *Renaissance Civic Humanism: Reappraisals and Reflections*, ed. James Hankins (Cambridge, UK: Cambridge University Press, 2000), 249–59.

Cary J. Nederman, *Rhetoric and Republicanism in the Thought of Brunetto Latini* In: *Populism, Demagoguery, and Rhetoric in Historical Perspective*. Edited by: Giuseppe Ballacci and Rob Goodman, Oxford University Press.
© Oxford University Press 2024. DOI: 10.1093/oso/9780197650974.003.0005

Sestio. The latter term denoted Cicero's conception of constitutional political order based on an idea of justice derived from the ability of reason to apprehend natural law, a position articulated, for instance, in *De republica, De legibus,* and *De officiis.*

Another aspect of the recent revival of attention to republicanism has been a growing examination of how republican ideas re-emerged and were re-energized in Europe. Scholars have devoted considerable attention to the contribution of so-called Renaissance civic humanism.[4] But the Latin Middle Ages has received close scrutiny as well, with particular focus on authors such as Ptolemy of Lucca and Marsiglio of Padua.[5] Another figure has also become a darling of scholars in search of the roots of European republicanism: Brunetto Latini. His best-known work is *Li livres dou tresor* (*The Books of Treasure*), a philosophical encyclopedia compiled and composed in French during the early 1260s.[6] As his name suggests, Latini was not himself of French heritage, but a Florentine who was trained as a professional rhetorician and mainly worked as a civil servant in his native city, serving as chancellor of its populist government (the so-called *primo popolo*) aligned with the Guelf party during the 1250s. When the regime was overthrown in 1260 and an "elite" faction associated with the Ghibellines grabbed power, he was forced into exile for more than half a decade and took employment as a notary in several cities in France.[7] In addition to the *Tresor*, he produced during the period of his banishment a partial translation into the Tuscan variant of Italian, together with an exposition, of Cicero's *De inventione* (under the title *La rettorica*), as well as vernacular versions of several Ciceronian

---

[4] See the contributions to Hankins, ed., *Renaissance Civic Humanism.*

[5] A useful overview of the ideas of Ptolemy and Marsiglio, among other figures, is offered by James Blythe, "'Civic Humanism' and Medieval Political Thought," in *Renaissance Civic Humanism: Reappraisals and Reflections*, ed. James Hankins (Cambridge, UK: Cambridge University Press, 2000), 30–74. Recently, however, the association of both figures with republicanism has been challenged. See Bee Yun, "Ptolemy of Lucca—A Pioneer of Civic Republicanism: A Reassessment," *History of Political Thought* 29, no. 3 (2008): 417–39; Cary J. Nederman, "Post-Republicanism and Quasi-Cosmopolitanism in Marsiglio of Padua's *Defensor pacis*," in *Al di là del repubblicanesimo: Modernità politica e origini dello Stato*, ed. Guido Cappelli (Naples: UniorPress, 2020), 131–46.

[6] Paul Barnette and Spurgeon Baldwin produced both an edition of the *Tresor* (Tempe: Arizona Center for Medieval and Renaissance Studies, 2003) and an English translation of it (New York: Garland, 1993). Still useful, especially for its critical apparatus, is the earlier edition of the *Tresor* edited by F. J. Carmody (Berkeley: University of California Press, 1948). I shall generally follow the Barnette and Baldwin translation, with occasional modifications. I henceforth refer to this work as *Tresor.*

[7] An overview of the complexities of Florentine politics, including some reference to Latini's place in it, during the period may be found in John Najemy, *A History of Florence, 1200–1575* (Oxford: Blackwell, 2006), 63–95. A further discussion of Latini's specific political circumstances is offered by David Napolitano, "Brunetto Latini's *Politica*: A Political Rewriting of Giovanni da Viterbo's *De Regimine Civitatum*," *Reti Medievali Rivista* 19, no. 1 (2018): 189–209.

orations (*Orazioni*) and a didactic dream poem entitled the *Tesoretto* (*Little Treasure*).[8]

The *Tresor* is not a work of political theory per se. Rather, it takes the form of a survey of all human knowledge. It is divided into three books: the first treats the fields of theology, history, geography, and natural philosophy; the second examines ethics; and the third addresses *de bone parleure*, under which heading Latini includes rhetoric and politics. When attention has been paid to the *Tresor*, interest has generally been directed toward the latter book, commonly referred to as the *Politica*,[9] which discusses forms of government and the characteristics necessary for officials (especially the administrative heads of urban communities), of which rhetorical skill is the single most important. For many scholars, Latini has become the very epitome of medieval republicanism, and especially of the Roman kind. In his influential *Foundations of Modern Political Thought*, Quentin Skinner proclaimed, "The most unequivocal expression of a preference for Republican liberty over any other form of government is pronounced by Latini."[10] Styling him "Brunetto the republican," Charles Til Davis maintained that "patriotism was one of the strongest influences in his life. He attempted to place it in the context of the cultural rhetoric of Rome.... His study of Cicero and other classical authors furnished him with a civic and moral ideal."[11] Alexander Lee connects Latini's praise of his home city of Florence in a manner that "recalled its Roman origins in *Li livres dou Trésor*."[12] In Francis Oakley's widely praised three-volume study, *The Emergence of Western Political Thought in the Latin Middle Ages*, Latini is lauded for having "mounted the first full-scale defense of the characteristic political values of the old city republics. Thus Latini himself bluntly declared that the republican government of peoples surpassed both monarchic and aristocratic forms in its ability to promote the

---

[8] Brunetto Latini, *La Rettorica*, ed. Francesco Maggini (Florence: Felice le Monnier, 1968). An English translation of *La Rettorica* by Stefania D'Agata D'Ottavi has lately been published (Kalamazoo: Medieval Institute Publications, 2016). For an especially useful overview of Latini's reliance on Cicero, see Gian Carlo Alessio, "Brunetto Latini e Cicerone (e i dettatori)," *Italia Medioevale e Umanistica* 22 (1979): 123–69. See also Carole Mabboux, *Cicéron et la Commune: Le rhéteur comme modèle civiqque (Italie, XIIIe-XIVe s)* (Rome: École française de Rome, 2022).

[9] John Najemy, "Brunetto Latini's 'Politica,'" *Dante Studies*, no. 112 (1994): 33–51.

[10] Quentin Skinner, *The Foundations of Modern Political Thought*, 2 vols. (Cambridge, UK: Cambridge University Press, 1978), I, 40. Latini's republicanism is also foregrounded in "Ambrogio Lorenzetti and the Portrayal of Virtuous Government," in Quentin Skinner, *Visions of Politics*, 3 vols. (Cambridge, UK: Cambridge University Press, 2002), II, 39–92.

[11] Charles T. Davis, *Dante's Italy and Other Essays* (Philadelphia: University of Pennsylvania Press, 1984), 179–80.

[12] Alexander Lee, *Humanism and Empire: The Imperial Ideal in Fourteenth-Century Italy* (Oxford: Oxford University Press, 2018), 33.

common good and political virtue."[13] Perhaps the most forceful statement of this position was Ronald Witt's proclamation that "Latini emphasized the parallel between the modern commune and republican Rome, drew on Cicero to glorify republicanism as a form of government, and addressed his fellow Florentines primarily as citizens of the commune. Latini's primary goal was to adapt the political experience of the ancient Romans in order to create a civic consciousness in his native Florence."[14] The extent to which Latini should be considered a thoroughgoing populist or something short thereof has been a matter of some dispute.[15] Among the factors favoring the former view are his repeated insistence that the civic administrator must be elected by the citizens on an annual basis (3.76.1, 3.102.1); his emphasis on "common consent" or "common assent of the people" as necessary to legitimize the acts of magistrates (3.77.2; 3.87.2; 3.99.1); and his rejection of hereditary nobility as a valid standard for the selection of the city's governor (3.75.3, 2.114.2).[16] Whether or not these elements found in the *Tresor* are sufficient to qualify him as a populist, Latini's devotion to Cicero and concomitantly to some vision of republicanism is beyond doubt.

Latini and Romanism

That the Roman Republic constituted the apotheosis of self-government during the later Middle Ages and Renaissance is incontrovertible. From Ptolemy of Lucca to Machiavelli, prominent political theorists of a republican persuasion considered Rome's institutional order and constitutional structures to be the very embodiment of their own preferred system of government.[17] Not that they agreed on the specifics—considerable distance separates Ptolemy circa 1300 from Machiavelli a couple of centuries later.[18]

---

[13] Francis Oakley, *The Emergence of Western Political Thought in the Latin Middle Ages*, Vol. 3: *The Watershed of Modern Politics: Law, Virtue, Kingship, and Consent (1300–1650)* (New Haven, CT: Yale University Press, 2015), 63.

[14] Ronald G. Witt, *The Two Latin Cultures and the Foundation of Renaissance Humanism in Medieval Italy* (Cambridge, UK: Cambridge University Press, 2012), 455.

[15] Whether or not Latini was some sort of "populist" has been a matter of considerable contention. For a summary, see Napolitano, "Brunetto Latini's *Politica*," 201 and n.108.

[16] On the latter, see Davis, *Dante's Italy*, 180–84.

[17] For extended reflection on this complex topic, see James Hankins, *Virtue Politics* (Cambridge, MA: Harvard University Press, 2019), 63–102.

[18] Cary J. Nederman and Mary Elizabeth Sullivan, "The Polybian Moment: The Transformation of Republican Thought from Ptolemy of Lucca to Machiavelli," *The European Legacy: Toward New Paradigms* 17, no. 7 (2012): 867–81.

But I wonder whether, as the generally held view has it, an inherent connection actually exists between the Roman exemplar and its preeminent theorist Cicero, or at least in the specific case of Latini. Certainly, Gianluca Briguglia thinks so. In his recent survey, *Il pensiero politico medievale*, Briguglia holds Latini worthy of substantial attention, indeed devoting to him an entire chapter of twenty pages in length.[19] (By contrast, Briguglia accords Thomas Aquinas half that number—quite properly, in my view.) Briguglia bases his view primarily on Latini's effusive praise of Cicero,[20] as well as copious references in the *Tresor* to Cato's speeches in defense of the Republic in the face of Catiline's conspiracy to overthrow it.[21] I do not doubt the sympathy (even empathy) Latini felt for their cause, especially when one considers the threat posed by Julius Caesar. But Briguglia takes this one step further by making the claim that the often heard association between Rome and Florence leads to a cultural, political, and personal identification between Cicero and Latini himself (at least in the imagination of the latter).[22] While Briguglia is perhaps the most forceful advocate for such an interpretation, he is not alone. Carole Mabboux, Catherine Keen, and Johannes Bartuschat have all suggested similar versions of the same thesis.[23]

It should be noted, however, that at least one scholar, namely, John Pocock, has attempted to detach Latini from any connection to republican Rome whatsoever, on account of his Guelfist proclivities. Pocock draws attention to a long passage in the *Tresor* that recapitulates the narrative of *translatio imperii* which pervaded pro-papal, anti-imperial treatises.[24] He observes that its "context seems to connect both monarchy and empire with the coming of Christ; it may be worth recalling that this was a providential decision and that providence may choose unhallowed instruments."[25] As a consequence, Pocock concludes, Latini has no interest in Roman history

---

[19] Gianluca Briguglia, *Il pensiero politico medievale* (Turin: Einaudi, 2018), 34–54.
[20] Ibid., 38–39.
[21] Ibid., 40–41.
[22] Ibid., 39–40.
[23] Carole Mabboux, "Entre auteur aux côtés de l'*auctoritas*: Brunet Latin, Cicéron et la Commune," *Bullettino dell'Istituto Storico Italiano per il Medio Evo* 115 (2013): 287–325; Catherine M. Keen, "A Florentine *Tullio*: Dual Authorship and the Politics of Translation in Brunetto Latini's *Rettorica*," in *The Afterlife of Cicero*, ed. Gesine Manuwald (London: Institute of Classical Studies, 2016), 1–16; Johannes Bartuschat, "Sur la mémoire de la Rome Républicaine dans la Toscane du XIIIe Siècle," in *La Mémoire en pièces*, ed. Anne Raffarin and Giuseppe Marcellino (Paris: Garnier Classiques, 2020), 443–63.
[24] J. G. A. Pocock, *Barbarism and Religion*, III, *The First Decline and Fall* (Cambridge, UK: Cambridge University Press, 2003), 139–41.
[25] Ibid., 140.

or even constitutional arrangements per se: "From history he turns to civil philosophy, which significantly focusses on the rule of a *podestà* over free men."[26] Someone unfamiliar with the *Tresor* would not realize the extent of Pocock's distortion of the substance of the book; more than one hundred pages separate the *translatio imperii* section from the beginning of its discussion of political theory. Of greater concern is the reductionist reading that arbitrarily equates Latini with his Guelfism—and nothing more—on the basis of a single passage contained in a quite lengthy treatise. Logically speaking, there is no reason why Guelf convictions required Latini to set aside republican sympathies. After all, Ptolemy of Lucca subscribed to the pro-papal position—to the extent that he penned multiple treatises appealing to *translatio imperii* in order to endorse the pope's superiority over the emperor.[27] It seems unproblematic, then, to investigate Latini's republicanism without concern for his concomitant belief that the bishop of Rome, by virtue of the Donation of Constantine, enjoyed the authority to assign (or to deny) the imperial office to whomever he selected. The latter involved no necessary implications for the former.[28]

Without going so far as Pocock, I argue in the present chapter that Skinner and others have overplayed their hand by conflating rationalist with rhetorical versions of republicanism. To be clear, I do not claim that these Ciceronian versions of republicanism are mutually exclusive. But leading scholars today recognize the primacy of one or the other tendency in Cicero's own thought. On the one hand, according to Joy Connolly, "Thinking about the republic sculpts the ideological imperatives of Cicero's rhetorical discourse, with rhetoric in turn leaving its own stamp on his theories of republican civic identity. His conceptions of citizenship and public speech take shape together."[29] On the other hand, Benjamin Straumann insists that "it is the state and its institutions, especially the courts, which are called upon to guarantee and enforce the norms of natural law. The very purpose of the state lies in upholding *ius*, and *ius*, understood as valid qua natural law, provides the body of higher order norms that governs and constrains politics and legislation. This ... is the key ingredient

---

[26] Ibid., 141.
[27] James M. Blythe, *The Worldview and Thought of Tolomeo Fiadoni (Ptolemy of Lucca)* (Turnout: Brepols, 2003), 73–124.
[28] Indeed, this is the overarching theme of Lee, *Humanism and Empire*.
[29] Joy Connolly, *The State of Speech: Rhetoric and Political Thought in Ancient Rome* (Princeton, NJ: Princeton University Press, 2007), 18.

in Cicero's contribution to constitutional thought."[30] While these scholarly advocates of rhetorical and rationalistic readings of Cicero's republicanism each pay lip service to one another's interpretations, their basic positions overwhelmingly predominate in their respective presentations of his political ideas. Not so with many current readers of Latini's republicanism, who seem determined to find the entirety of the ingredients of the Ciceronian framework, regardless of their trajectories, in his theory. This chapter seeks to disaggregate them in a manner that follows modern scholarship on Cicero himself and to place Latini squarely in the rhetorical camp. In other words, constitutional rationalism of the sort that favors Rome plays no evident part in his work.

Rhetoric and Politics

Without question, Latini foregrounds the association between eloquent speech and public affairs in Ciceronian fashion. Throughout the *Tresor*, he treats rhetoric as the defining feature of what is best and most noble about humanity. This is most evident in Book 3. With *De inventione* I.6 apparently in mind, Latini commences the book with the claim that "Tully says that the highest science of governing the city is rhetoric, that is to say, the science of speaking; for without speaking, there were not and would not have been either cities or the institution of justice or human companionship" (3.1.2) Although the chapters immediately following this statement read like a brief commentary on *De inventione*, surely cribbed from the *Rettorica*, Latini's purpose is to introduce the study of rhetoric as a subject which the prospective ruler of a city must master. After examining the elements of rhetoric, he immediately moves on to discuss the duties connected with civic government. And among the primary requirements elucidated by Latini for appointment to public office is that one must be "a very good speaker" (3.75.8), as well as be knowledgeable in "everything concerning matters of truth" (3.75.5), presumably including the contents of Books 1 and 2 of the *Tresor*. These attributes indicate that a necessary precondition for competence as a governor is the attainment of qualifications as a Ciceronian orator, who must be wise as well as skillful.

---

[30] Benjamin Straumann, *Crisis and Constitutionalism: Roman Political Thought from the Fall of the Republic to the Ages of Revolution* (Oxford: Oxford University Press, 2016), 168.

The *Tresor* signals recognition, however, that there are potential problems with the centrality of rhetoric to governance (as had Cicero himself). In particular, as Latini admits, a potential danger to the community arises when persuasive speech is not accompanied by a well-formed intellect. Adopting a view essentially aligned with Cicero's, he remarks that "just as it is the case that speech is given to all men, ... wisdom (*sapience*) is given to a few" (3.1.2). Latini then enumerates four different types of relationship which are possible between eloquence and wisdom: when reason and good speech are present together, "it is the flower of the world"; when neither are present, it is a "great disaster"; when one speaks well but lacks reason, there is "very great peril"; and when one possesses reason, yet eloquence is absent, instruction and aid are required (3.1.2). Latini says nothing more about the second and fourth categories.[31] Instead, he concentrates on promoting the union of wisdom and eloquence, and hence on averting the threat to communal amity posed by their disjunction. In particular, he points to Julius Caesar's speech in defense of the Catilinarian conspirators as a paradigmatic instance of how the use of brilliant rhetorical technique may be employed for duplicitous ("concealed" and "dishonest") purposes detrimental to the common good (3.36), as will be discussed in greater detail below.

Thus, Latini adopts the Ciceronian position that oratory, as the union of wisdom and eloquence, is of the greatest benefit to the entire community: "And when wisdom is joined to speech, who will say that it cannot give rise to goodness?" (3.1.6). His evidence for the usefulness of oratory rests, in turn, on Cicero's claim that society itself would be impossible in the absence of speech:

> Tully says that, in the beginning, men lived according to the law of beasts, without their own houses and without knowledge of God, in the forests and in rural retreats, without regard for marriage or cognizance of parents or children. Then there appeared a wise and well spoken man, who counseled the others and pointed out the greatness of the soul and the dignity of reason and of discretion, so that he recalled them from their savagery and

---

[31] Although interestingly in the *Rettorica*, when commenting on *De inventione* 1.6, Latini remarks that a "wise man could have achieved the same results by wisdom alone, but not as quickly and in such short a time as he did by means of both wisdom and eloquence" (p. 35). In other words, this seemingly reflects the fourth category.

urged them to come together as one and to protect reason and justice. And by the use of good speech which was accompanied by reason, this man was almost like a second God, who created the world for the sake of the arrangement of human companionship. (3.1.7)

Latini's appreciation of the contribution of the primitive orator, and especially his comparison of the activity of the wise and eloquent speaker to the creative power of God, is striking in its force. The orator is placed in the *Tresor* at the very center of the communal affairs of his city: his words are the fount of civic life.

That Latini regards this oratorical role as a continuing feature of the community is made clear by the idea of "counsel" which runs throughout the third part of the *Tresor*. At times, he seems to mean by "counsel" or "giving counsel" simply one of the three technical divisions of rhetoric (namely, *deliberativa*) enumerated by Cicero in *De inventione*.[32] But in the suggestion that the primitive orator "counseled," and that the man who merely speaks well does not "give counsel," there is an indication that the discipline of rhetoric teaches counsel in a normative sense. "Counsel" seems to connote wise speech for the purpose of achieving public welfare or rectitude. This impression is reinforced by Latini when he turns directly to the governance of the city: citizens should seek "wise counsel" when deciding whom to appoint as their ruler (3.75.1); they are charged with giving their governor "counsel and aid for maintaining his office" (3.74.4); and one of the primary duties of rulers is to assemble the chief and wise men of the city in order to request and consider their "counsel" regarding important matters, such as the conduct of diplomatic affairs (3.87–89; 3.95). Oratory appears to form the basis for such counseling functions: the properly trained orator may be taken to speak on behalf of the interests of the community because his eloquence is coupled with the wisdom to recognize the public good. Thus, not only the ruler, but the body of the citizens (or at least its leading segments) as well, ought to be trained in the field of rhetoric. These claims comport well with the rhetorical republicanism that I discussed previously.

---

[32] Compare also Latini, *Tresor*, 3.2.20 and 3.52.11, with Cicero, *De oratore*, ed. E. W. Sutton and H. Rackham (Cambridge, MA: Harvard University Press, 1943), I.5.7.

Latini's Rome

Yet Latini draws no overt connections between the Ciceronian theory of the rhetorical foundations of social and political life and the Roman Republican constitutional order. So, what did Latini actually think about the Rome itself in Cicero's time? To be sure—and here Pocock is correct—he was "not a sophisticated historian," if we apply the standards of modern historical method.[33] Whatever historical knowledge he possessed was derived mainly from a French vernacular *florilegium* containing excerpts from Sallust, among other historians of Rome.[34] The suggestion has been made that in some instances Latini referred directly to Sallust's own writings.[35] Whether or not this was the case, however, is irrelevant in the present context, since my primary interest concerns how Latini himself explicitly conceived of the Roman system of government, not the accuracy of his history. The discussion of Rome is located almost entirely in first book of the *Tresor*, where we first encounter the city in the tale of its founding by Romulus, about which more will be said later (1.35.3–1.36.2). Following a quick nod to the kings who ruled thereafter, Latini moves on to the story of the rape of Lucretia by Tarquin the Proud. And thus we arrive at the foundation of the Republic: "Because of this crime [of rape] Tarquin was expelled from the kingdom, and the Romans decreed that they would never have a king, but that the city and its territory should be governed by senators, consuls, patricians, tribunes, dictators and other officials in matters appropriate to their position, both inside and outside the city" (1.36.4). Latini immediately jumps from the founding of Rome to the events surrounding the Catilinarian conspiracy, a topic to which he returns in the book time and again in a manner that can only be described as bordering on obsession. Given all that he says, one must conclude that the conspiracy represented to him the end of the Republic—a view that he expresses more explicitly later in the *Tresor*.

Reference to the conspiracy permits Latini to introduce his favorite Roman figure, "the very wise Marcus Tullius Cicero, the finest orator in the world and the master of rhetoric" (1.36.5). In this context, Cicero the theorist is matched by the political Cicero, the man of action, for whom Latini expresses great admiration. More specifically, his idolization of Cicero stemmed from how, "because of his great wisdom he triumphed over the conspirators, took

---

[33] Pocock, *The First Decline and Fall*, 140.
[34] Bartuschat, "Sur la mémoire de la Rome Républicaine dans la Toscane du XIIIe Siècle," 446–47.
[35] Francesco Maggini, *I primi volgarizzamenti die classici latini* (Florence: Monnier, 1952), 35–39.

vengeance on them, and had many of the guilty killed" (1.36.5). The same passage also allows Latini to introduce two other characters who prove important to him: "good Cato," on whose counsel Cicero supposedly relied, and Julius Caesar, who is presented as deceitful and certainly power-hungry, as I have already noted. The *Tresor* carefully analyzes Caesar's speech before the Senate opposing the execution of the conspirators, an oration made all the more audacious, given that many Romans were suspicious that "he was an accomplice in the conspiracy. The truth of the matter is that he [Caesar] had no love for the senators, nor they for him" (1.36.6). Yet "Julius Caesar, who wanted to defend the prisoners, spoke masterfully in a concealed fashion," knowing "very well that the listeners' hearts were turned against what he had in mind" (3.34.3, 3.36.1). As a consequence, he effectively confused his audience to the extent that "the listeners were somewhat inclined to believe what he said" (3.38.2). Caesar thus provides the quintessential example of "speaking without wisdom, for when a man has a good tongue outside and no counsel inside his speaking he is terribly dangerous to the city" (3.1.9). In other words, although there is no direct Latin equivalent for the word, Caesar behaved as a demagogue. The *Tresor* also describes Caesar's rise to power and his status as "the first emperor of the Romans," a title he devised to circumvent the fact that "the Romans could not have kings, according to the laws made at the time of Tarquin" (1.38.1). This underscores Caesar's clever but duplicitous ability to manipulate language to serve his own purposes. In the case of the conspirators, only Cato's eloquent rebuttal "on behalf of the common good and [to] defend the well-being of Rome and destroy all traitors" swayed the Senate against Caesar (3.38.2). No better exemplification of the difference between demagoguery and wise speech might be adduced.

But does all of this amount to a *theory* of Roman republicanism? I am disinclined to suppose so. There are several reasons for my skepticism. First, so far as I can see, he never uses the word "liberty" or any of its cognates anywhere in his discussions of the Roman Republic. Indeed, in a careful search through the *Tresor* as well as the rest of his corpus, I have been unable to identify a single instance at all in which he refers to *liberté* or *libertà*. The closest I can locate is his remark about "la franchise que natura dona premierement" followed by his insistence that "nature fust soumise a joistice & que francise obiest jugement" (3.77.1). This constitutes his justification of lordship, inasmuch as its function is to punish the evil and reward the good, a standard trope of medieval political thought. And "franchise" is clearly regarded to be a gift to humanity from nature, which is to say God.[36] But this is not the same as the civil liberty conceived by Cicero and Romans generally, the maintenance of which was considered to be the fundamental value and purpose of the Republic. Thirteenth- and fourteenth-century authors associated with republicanism or communal self-rule, such as John of Viterbo and Ptolemy of Lucca, also quite openly defended *libertas* as an (perhaps *the*) essential quality of good government. The absence of reference to liberty in the *Tresor* is especially startling in light of Latini's undoubted familiarity with John's *Re regimine civitatum*, which provided one of text's primary sources.[37] In the first sentence of Chapter II of John's treatise (entitled "De interpretatione civitatis"), he declares that "a city is said to exist for the liberty of its citizens, or the immunity of its inhabitants," which he then explains as the absence of force on account of the presence of a governor who protects their freedom.[38] I have detected no echoes of a similar conception of liberty in the writings of Latini, certainly not in his discussions of the nature of the city.

Also worthy of note is Latini's account of the origin of Rome itself. As we have already observed, Book 3 of the *Tresor* follows closely Cicero's rhetorical account of the formation of social relations and political institutions. Likewise, the *Rettorica* presents an extensive expansion of this position in its commentary on De inventione 1–6, describing in detail the processes by which men are brought together into an organized system of justice and law enforced in the context of "the Communes," that is, republican regimes. Indeed, it would be unjust to compel men to obey a superior force without their rational recognition of their communal natures and of all of the advantages that their association yields.[39] Latini's account, in other words, captures the essence of rhetorical republicanism as the result of a voluntary agreement. Yet he presents the origination of Rome in terms of violence, namely, by means of warfare between lawless kings that eventually led to the victory of Romulus, who "founded Rome.... He alone was king over all, and ruled all of Rome," to which he lent his name (1.36.2). It may be that Latini simply takes for granted that the founding of Rome occurred after a more

---

[36] Latini, *Tesoretto*, ll. 289–94.

[37] Napolitano, "Brunetto Latini's *Politics*," 189–209.

[38] John of Viterbo, *Liber regimine civitatum*, ed. Gaietano Salavemini (Bologna: Monte, 1901), 218–19.

[39] In fact, Latini goes much further than Cicero in depicting the material benefits of human assembly to men, commenting that "the best of reasons and the prospective advantages" include provision of "good food, fine dinners, excellent suppers and so many other pleasures, that they were persuaded to come together" (*Rettorica*, p. 34).

primordial time in which primitive and scattered men were first drawn into society. If so, however, there is no evidence for this in any of his writings. In that case, he evidently undermines the basis for his own version of how republics came into being.

Constitutional Diversity

As noted above, some scholars laud Latini's declared preference for the "communal" system of government, as when he says in the *Tresor* that "there are three types of lordship: one of kings, the second of men and the third of communes, which is the best of all. Each type has its opposite" (2.44.1). But they don't necessarily read the text very carefully. Latini then identifies the opposite of kingship, that is, tyranny, but does not in fact name the others, leaving his reader to designate them simply as the anonymous converse of "men" and the "communes." He appears to believe that there is a naturalistic logic of transformation from one constitutional system to the next via corruption, at least if we piece together remarks from a couple of different sections of the *Tresor*. Kingship turns into tyranny (as in the case of Tarquinus Superbus); tyranny is transformed into the rule of "good and great men"; but eventually these, too, "cease to do what is good, with the intent of not letting their lordship leave their family, and do not consider their honor, merit and dignity," as a consequence of which "their lordship changes into the lordship of the commune." Finally, "lordship of the commune is corrupted when good customs and good and praiseworthy laws are abandoned" (2.44.1). In the passage in question, Latini never addresses explicitly what happens following the collapse of communes. But when talking about the emergence of kings, he alludes to their primary role as enforcers of divine law and human law, from which they are assigned the function of restoring the laws that had been corrupted in the "opposite" of communes. "Because commanding or establishing law is of little value," he says, "unless there is someone who can make them obey the law, in order to promote justice and punish wrongdoing, kings and lords of many kinds were established" (1.18.4). Even if my reconstruction of Latini's view about constitutional change is somewhat fanciful, it is clear that elements of it find expression in 2.44.1. Should my interpretation have any merit, however, Latini's conception of how one type of constitution transmutes into its opposite must have been of his own devising.

What has this to do with Rome? Latini evidently regards the Roman Republic to be a variety of commune (see 3.6.3 and 3.36.1). It is difficult to understand how his claim that the commune is preferable squares with his praise of the initial virtue of kingship and the "government of [elite] men." After all, they are presumably equal in their service to the promotion of the common welfare. Logically, communal popular rule is in principle no better than those other forms of good government. In other parts of the *Tresor*, Latini admits as much. A common feature of later medieval political thought is the doctrine that no one constitutional system suits all peoples and nations.[40] In reality (as distinguished from pure theory), there is no "best" form of rule, only one that meets the needs of the society it serves. In their enthusiasm for his relatively few statements about the superiority of a popular regime, readers of Latini apparently pass over his endorsement of quasi-relativism. In the opening pages of the *Tresor*, Latini defines the study of politics as "the highest wisdom and the most noble profession there is among men, for it teaches us to govern others, *in a kingdom or a city or a group of people* or a commune, in peace and war, according to reason and justice" (1.4.5; italics mine). Or consider this remark: "Although there are lordships of all sorts, the worthiest of all is *that of kings* and governing cities and peoples ... according to what is required by the customs of the country and *Roman law*" (2.119.1; italics mine). Adopting a common trope, Latini regards self-government to be appropriate for the Italian cities, whereas kingship coincides better with the conditions of territorial nations such as France.

The warrant for this view derives from an unlikely source: Cicero himself. In *De re publica*, he offered the following definition: "Res publica res populi, populus autem non omnis hominum coetus quoquo modo congregatus, sed coetus multitudinis iuris consensu et utilitatis communione societus" ("A republic is the affair of the people; a people is not any assemblage of human beings congregated in any way, but a multitude that consents to right and to the utility of a common society").[41] Although, as has been said, the full text of *De re publica* was unavailable during the Middle Ages, Cicero's idea of a republic enjoyed wide dissemination via St. Augustine's quarrel with it in the *City of God*.[42] In *La rettorica*, Latini reproduced a somewhat modified

---

[40] Antony Black, *Political Thought in Europe, 1250–1450* (Cambridge, UK: Cambridge University Press, 1992), 111–13.

[41] Cicero, *De re publica*, ed. W. Keyes (Cambridge, MA: Harvard University Press, 1928), I.39.

[42] As is well documented by Matthew Kempshall, "*De re publica* I.39 in Medieval and Renaissance Political Thought," in *Cicero's Republic*, ed. J. G. F Powell and J. A. North (London: Institute of Classical Studies, 2001), 99–135.

version of the Ciceronian definition of a republic.[43] But in the *Tresor*, he adapted it to justify the diversity of legitimate constitutions according to circumstance: "Cicero says that the city [NB, *not* commune, that is, *res publica*] is an assembly of people living in one place and under one law, and just as people and dwellings are different and customs and rights are different throughout the world, so too do they have different types of rulers... it was necessary for men to have different sorts of lords" (3.73.3). The implication here is quite striking. Cicero held that *ius* was invariant; the natural law connoted by *ius* pertained to all people at all times. Thus, his conception of the republic is applicable universally, which is why in *De re publica* he also confidently asserted that the Roman mixed constitution in its heyday fully realized the ideal system of government.[44] Latini turns the Ciceronian position on its head, moving it in an entirely new (if perhaps unwarranted) direction by folding it into a defense of the diversity of constitutional orders. Latini might personally have preferred communal government, but his own arguments militate against the intellectual weight of that conclusion. Although he doesn't directly discuss Latini, James Hankins has pointed out that this was not an uncommon position to stake out by the fourteenth century.[45]

Did Latini even comprehend the fundamental mechanisms of the ancient Roman constitution? As previously indicated, he knew some titles of various offices and social stations in republican Rome. But one searches his corpus in vain for evidence that he understood the actual functioning of Rome's constitution. Indeed, someone with even passing familiarity with the world of the Roman Republic would not have elided "consuls," "senators," and "patricians" as though they designated comparable positions. Elected magistrates, members of an elite assembly, and those endowed with superior class status are mixed together, which suggests to me relative ignorance of or disinterest in how Roman politics and society were organized. The only evidence to the contrary stems from his repeated reports of the trial of the Catilinarian conspirators before the Roman Senate. He thus implicitly recognized that one of the Senate's legitimate functions was judicial. Yet most of what Latini says about the proceeding is presented in the context of elucidating aspects of rhetorical method that Cicero expounded in *De inventione*. In other words, recounting historical events is beside the point

---

[43] Latini, *Le rettorica*, 30.
[44] E.g., Cicero, *De re publica*, II.65–66.
[45] Hankins, *Virtue Politics*, 129–32.

for Latini. The entire trial, as he repurposes it, affords illustrations of how one successfully deploys various technical aspects of effective rhetoric.

The Road Away from Rome

Although Latini may not have fully grasped specifics, we may wonder whether he was at all conscious that his own account of civil government stood at considerable remove from the constitutional order and arrangements of ancient Rome. Let us be generous and grant to him greater knowledge than he displays in his writings. Why would he (or we) ever suppose that the commune as he conceptualized it was on par with the Roman *res publica*? In the third book of the *Tresor*, Latini specifies in almost excruciating detail the features of the properly constituted commune. It is to be governed by a "lord" (in essence, the Italian *podestà*) who is selected after close scrutiny by "the wise men of the city" to serve an annual (preferably non-renewable) term (3.76.1). Latini then does something worthy of our special attention. In describing the methods by which a potential new lord ought to be evaluated, selected, and invited, he constructs an idealized procedure and he drafts the related documents as though they were framed and authorized by the commune of Rome and addressed to the king of Naples, Charles I of Anjou. The position of Roman "lord" (in Latini's language), which was actually titled "Senator and Governor of Rome," had indeed been offered to Charles in 1258, who accepted it, but who did not appear until early 1265 and then almost immediately withdrew to confront dynastic claims elsewhere (3.77.1–2). In the meantime, Rome was left pretty much to its own devices, which meant the intractable conflicts between various major factions—contending noble families of the city, the enervated papacy, and the vain hopes of its ordinary citizens for the restoration of former republican glory. In short, a steaming mess.

Latini surely possessed quite intimate knowledge of these events. He reconstructs in the *Tresor* (albeit in highly stylized form) the deliberations to invite Charles to serve as Rome's *podestà* and what the letter extending the offer of that position at least *ought* to have looked like. His doubtless fanciful instructions reflect a vision of the functions and responsibilities of a professional administrator/ruler in an Italian commune. But what qualifies an individual to serve in the capacity of a civic lord? Latini's answer sounds very much like that found in the "mirror of princes" literature that was in the process of becoming a staple of medieval political writing.[46] First and foremost, the lord must be a man of demonstrated virtue, especially justice, as well as piety. "All lordships and all high positions are given to us by the Sovereign Father," Latini says, "who among the holy establishments of the world wanted the government of cities to be founded on three pillars, that is, of justice, of reverence and of love" (3.74.1). Justice is defined in conventional terms as giving to each his due (3.74.2). Reverence denotes the respect among "his burghers and in his subjects" (*en ses borjois & en ses subjés*) that they feel for their lord (3.74.3). Love constitutes the binding relationship between "lord and subject, for the lord must love his subjects with all his heart and a clear faith," qualities which ensure that he will always serve the common welfare.[47] Likewise, men "must love their lords with a just heart"—and here we get a nod toward communal government in the Italian cities—since they give "counsel and aid" in order that rulers may successfully perform the tasks required of their office. Latini observes that because the lord "is one single person among them, he could not do anything without them" (3.74.4).

Latini then enumerates twelve characteristics that must be considered carefully by those who select their lord: age, personal honor, justice, wisdom, courage, absence of avarice, eloquence (*trés bons parleor*), care with expenditures, calm, independent wealth, lack of holding another office, and faith (3.75.2–13). The qualifications that he stipulates to serve as a lord pertain mainly to personal "habits and virtues" in the same manner as advice-books to monarchs (3.75.14).[48] The lord of a city "should not behave with an excess of pride or humility, but rather pursue the common good in peace and decency, so that he does not fall into the sin (*peché*) of Catiline" (2.74.14). In other words, Latini emphasizes the virtues of persons without concern for the virtues of institutions. This strikes me

---

[46] *Princely Virtues in the Middle Ages, 1200–1500*, ed. Istvàn Bejczy and Cary J. Nederman (Turnhout: Brepols, 2007). The significant similarities have been examined by David Napolitano, "From Royal Court to City Hall: The *Podestà* Literature. A Republican Variant on the Mirror for Princes?" in *Concepts of Ideal Rulership from Antiquity to the Renaissance*, ed. Geert Roskam and Stefan Schorn (Turnhout: Brepols, 2018), 383–416.

[47] I find Latini's repeated use of "subject" quite interesting because it seems more appropriate to kingship than rule over free citizens, but I will happily set that observation to the side. On this distinction, see Cary J. Nederman, "From Moral Virtue to Material Benefit: Dominium and Citizenship in Late Medieval Europe," in *Cultivating Citizens*, ed. Dwight D. Allman and Michael D. Beaty (Lanham, MD: Lexington Books, 2002), 43–60.

[48] Compare these with John of Salisbury, *Policraticus I–IV*, ed. K. S. B. Keats-Rohan (Turnhout: Brepols, 1993), 4.3.

as incommensurable with a core tenet of the rationalistic version of republicanism to prefer constitutional arrangements rather than individual human traits. To state it somewhat bluntly, according to the institutional form of republicanism, the office makes the man, not the man the office. The contrast between this position and Latini's emphasis on the character of leaders is quite revealing.

Latini's interest in the entire story about Catiline's attempt to overthrow the Republic, as I have suggested, amounts to an obsession. How might we explain this? A repeated theme of Latini's writings is the deep fear and loathing of factionalism and the resulting self-destruction of a city. In the *Rettorica*, for example, he speaks autobiographically: "This book owes its existence to the fact that Brunetto Latini, because of the war between the two Florentine factions, was exiled from his city when the Guelph faction ... was expelled and banished from the land."[49] Likewise, he opens the *Tesoretto* with a narration of how he, while returning from a diplomatic mission to the royal court of Spain, learned from a passerby about the Guelph defeat:

> And, becoming sorrowful, / I returned to the nature / That I heard is possessed / By every man coming into the world: / First he is born to parents and relations, and then to his commune [this is adapted from Cicero's *De officiis* I.22] / So that I know none / Whom I would wish to see / Have my city / Entirely in his control, / Or that it be divided; / But all in common / Should pull together on a rope / Of peace and of welfare, / Because a land torn apart / Cannot survive. / Truly my heart broke / With so much sorrow, / Thinking of the great honor / And rich power / That Florence is used to having / Almost through the whole world.[50]

In the *Tresor*, we are told that a lord's possession of the requisite virtues entails the prudent use of the powers that he has been granted to avoid becoming entrapped in sectarian conflicts: "because war and hatred have increased so much among Italians nowadays ... there is division in all cities and enmity between the two factions of citizens." The civic governor must avoid acquiring the love of one party, since he will only provoke the hatred of the other; and if he is truly incompetent, he will incur "the scorn and the bad graces of the very ones who elected him, so that to the extent that each person

---

[49] Latini, *La rettorica*, 27.
[50] Latini, *Tesoretto*, ll. 163–85.

expected to see good things in him, he now sees his harm" (3.75.15). Latini returns to the challenge posed to the lord by partisan strife repeatedly in the closing chapters of the *Tresor*. The lord's eloquence ought to be turned toward reminding the denizens of the commune that they "should live in harmony, and if they do not, then he must redirect them" with reminders of both the blessings that peace brings and the many ills that flow from civil discord, citing the cases of "Rome and other good cities which fell because of internal war" (3.82.9). If it proves impossible to eliminate the hatred between groups of citizens, the lord must at least remain as impartial as possible, resisting all monetary and sexual enticements, and ensuring that the job for which he has been retained is accomplished promptly and properly, in sum, to enforce the laws equitably and maintain the infrastructure efficiently (3.97.4). Such conduct is in the best interests of the commune, as well as the safest strategy for the lord.

Conclusion

It should by now be amply evident that the major features of Latini's depiction of communal self-government simply do not correspond in a recognizable fashion to the constitutional system of the Roman Republic. Of course, Latini never actually *claims* to be reproducing or applying the Roman political model in the context of thirteenth-century Italy. The view that he did so rather reflects the fervent wishes of some modern scholarship that seeks to identify an ur-republican pre-humanist from whom emanated the Romanized Italian humanist republicanism of the fifteenth century. Latini's fascination with Cicero, the Catilinarian conspiracy, and the role of Julius Caesar in facilitating the transformation of Rome from a republican to an imperial form of government does not mean that his theory supports a facsimile of an ancient antecedent. It hardly seems fair to hold him to standards that he did not himself invoke. Should Latini be counted among the many political thinkers of the Middle Ages for whom Cicero was a paragon? Without doubt. Should he be acknowledged for occupying an important place in the development of republican political theory in medieval Europe? By all means. Is Briguglia correct that Latini considered himself to be a new Cicero? That seems reasonable enough. But ought we to infer that Latini's profound admiration for Cicero translates into Romanophilia? I do not feel confident in offering an affirmative answer, for the reasons I have stipulated in the present chapter. To the contrary, I must dissent from scholars who insist that Latini's rhetoric-based theory supports the Roman version of republicanism *en tout*. It *might* do so, but I see no reason why it *must*, to the exclusion of other forms of republican government with which Latini was more directly familiar.

5
Republicanism and Populism in Early Modern Italian Political Thought
The Case of Democracy as the Rule of the Poor

Alessandro Mulieri

Introduction

Studies of early modern republicanism have long been dominated by Hans Baron's ideas of civic humanism and by the Cambridge School's interpretation of classical republicanism.[1] Baron's and Skinner's interpretations of republicanism share two important ideas. The first is that there is continuity between classical political thought and Italian late medieval and early modern republican thought. According to the genealogies of Skinner and of other authors who embrace this continuity thesis, such differing authors as Brunetto Latini, Ptolemy of Lucca, Marsilius of Padua, Coluccio Salutati, Leonardo Bruni, Poggio Bracciolini, Niccolò Machiavelli, among others, all belong to a similar tradition that, influenced by either Aristotelian or neo-Roman sources, proceeded without interruption from the eleventh to the sixteenth century. The second idea is that when Italian late medieval and early modern thinkers spoke about "republics," they were never referring to princely regimes, but rather primarily to non-monarchical self-governed polities. Thus, an "exclusivist" idea of republican regimes very often figures in their thoughts.

Both of these ideas have come under increasing scrutiny in recent scholarly debates. The first idea, of the continuity between the political language of ancient political thought and late medieval and early modern political

---

[1] Hans Baron, *In Search of Florentine Civic Humanism*, 2 vols. (Princeton, NJ: Princeton University Press, 1988). For Cambridge School studies, see, among others, Quentin Skinner, *The Foundations of Modern Political Thought* (Cambridge, UK: Cambridge University Press, 1978); and Maurizio Viroli, *From Politics to Reason of State* (Cambridge: Cambridge University Press, 1992).

theory, has been challenged with respect to both scholastic and humanist authors. Some studies have questioned the extent to which a unified notion such as "classical republicanism" can help make sense of so many different authors across so many centuries.[2] Indeed, scholars have suggested that the idea of classical republicanism does not fully encompass the variety of languages and contexts that account for specific modes of thinking in late medieval and early modern Italian political thought, especially in the case of Machiavelli.

Second, the very idea that late medieval and early modern republicanism was non-monarchical has been subject to strident critique. Several scholars have pointed out that the word *respublica*, which plays such a crucial role in late medieval and early modern republicanism, actually refers to a broad variety of different regimes, which also include princely and monarchical rule in this period.[3] Rather, the exclusivist usage of the notion of *respublica* to refer only to non-monarchical regimes is a pattern that would only become crucial after the Renaissance period, from the seventeenth to eighteenth century. Therefore, the exclusivist interpretation of republican regimes, so often invoked by advocates of the Cambridge School republican thesis, does not accurately portray the complex institutional and political arrangements that can be found in late medieval and early modern Italian political thought.

These critiques suggest the need to provide an alternative conceptualization of republicanism, which can also renew the way we conceptualize the thought of late medieval and early modern Italian political writers. Recent years have seen a "plebeian" or "radical republican" turn within the scholarship on this period, which aims to renew the debate on republicanism, especially in the studies of Machiavelli. Drawing on the works of

---

[2] From very different perspectives, see, among others, Cary Nederman, "Rhetoric, Reason and Republic: Republicanisms: Ancient, Medieval and Modern," in *Renaissance Civic Humanism: Reappraisals and Reflections*, ed. James Hankins (Cambridge, UK: Cambridge University Press, 2000), 247–69; James Hankins, *Virtue Politics: Soulcraft and Statecraft in Renaissance Italy* (Cambridge, MA: Harvard University Press, 2019); John McCormick, *Machiavellian Democracy* (Cambridge, UK: Cambridge University Press, 2011); Paul Rahe, "Situating Machiavelli," in *Renaissance Civic Humanism*, ed. James Hankins (Cambridge, UK: Cambridge University Press, 2004), 270–308; Guido Cappelli (ed.), *Al di là del Repubblicanesimo Modernità politica e origini dello Stato* (Napoli: UniorPress, 2020).

[3] James Hankins, "Exclusivist Republicanism and the Non-Monarchical Republic," *Political Theory* 38, no.4 (2010): 452–82; Gabriele Pedullà, "Humanist Republicanism: Towards a New Paradigm," *History of Political Thought* 41, no. 1 (2020): 43–95; Janet Coleman, *A History of Political Thought: From the Middle Ages to the Renaissance* (Oxford: Blackwell, 2000).

John McCormick, Filippo del Lucchese, Miguel Vatter, Gabriele Pedullà, and others,[4] many scholars now interpret Machiavelli as the theorist of a radical republican, or democratic, thought that strongly challenged the oligarchic political views of classical republicanism.[5] With the aim of contributing to these debates on the renewal of the language of republicanism and its relationship to populism more specifically, this chapter aims to investigate a particular theme that the rediscovery and influence of Aristotle's ethical and political works brought to late medieval and early modern political thought: the definition of democracy as the rule of the poor.

By comparing Aristotle's perspective to those of some late medieval and early modern thinkers, as well as to Machiavelli, the chapter shows that the latter's support for popular republics marked an important conceptual rupture with the Aristotelian condemnation of democracy as a regime that empowers the poor. However, the chapter also shows that Machiavelli's popular republican account of the relationship between democracy and poverty shares some similarities with other popular republican authors who drew on Aristotelianism in the late medieval and early modern period in order to tackle this same theme. Machiavelli and other early modern theorists of popular/populist republicanism shared the goal of championing institutions that promoted a more inclusive idea of the people, for example the Great Council or magistrates shaped after the Roman institution of the tribune of the plebs. Second, a lot of them shared a common reinterpretation of Aristotle's ideas that make the latter functional to radical republican agendas. This might lead to the hypothesis that a crucial feature of the Italian popular/populist republican tradition is also its tendency to draw on the most populist ideas of Aristotelianism.

---

[4] John P. McCormick, *Machiavellian Democracy* (Chicago: Cambridge University Press, 2012); John P. McCormick, *Reading Machiavelli* (Princeton, NJ: Princeton University Press, 2018).

[5] The literature on the radical Machiavelli is vast and is growing more and more. Among notable studies, see Gabriele Pedullà, *Machiavelli in Tumult: The Discourses on Livy and the Origins of Political Conflictualism* (Cambridge, UK: Cambridge University Press, 2018); Filippo Del Lucchese, *Conflict, Power and Multitude in Machiavelli and Spinoza* (London: Bloomsbury, 2009); Miguel Vatter, *Between Form and Event: Machiavelli's Theory of Political Freedom* (Berlin: Springer, 2000); Filippo Del Lucchese, Fabio Frosini and Vittorio Morfino (eds.), *The Radical Machiavelli: Politics, Philosophy, and Language* (Leiden-Boston: Brill, 2015); Jérémie Barthas, *L'argent n'est pas le nerf de la guerre: essai sur une prétendue erreur de Machiavel* (Rome: École française de Rome, 2011); Marie Gaille, *Machiavel et la tradition philosophique* (Paris: Presses universitaires de France, 2014).

Democracy as the Rule of the Poor in Aristotle's *Politics*

As in most cases when we talk about late medieval and early modern republicanism, Aristotle's *Politics*, which was first translated into Latin in the 1260s[6], is a crucial reference point. Aristotle's treatment of democracy spans across several books of the *Politics*, featuring especially in Books 3, 4, 5, and 7. As with most other topics in the Aristotelian text, the analysis of democracy is rather unsystematic, reflecting the unstructured nature of the work.[7] Broadly speaking, in Aristotle's view, democracy is one constitution among the famous sixfold schema of classifying regimes provided in Book 3.[8] Here, as it is well-known, Aristotle lists six different constitutions: three (monarchy, aristocracy, and *politeia* or "constitutional regime") in which the rulers govern for the common good; and three (tyranny, oligarchy, and democracy) that are corrupted forms of the former and in which the rulers govern solely for the sake of their own personal interest and against the common good. In democracy, as we will explore further in a bit, one component of the city, that is, the poor, rule for their own interest against the wealthy and all the other components of the city.

Aristotle shows a much more favorable attitude toward democracy as compared to most other Greek authors who were critical of this regime. First, the very idea of the "constitutional regime" is an attempt to preserve a moderate version of popular government in which the people (and the poor) are presented as a co-ruler with the few, to allow for a sharing of power. This could be read as Aristotle's attempt to avoid the strong condemnation of Athenian democracy that we can find in many of his contemporary authors, especially philosophers, and safeguard some aspects of the ideal type of popular government. In fact, in the same Book 3 in which he presents democracy as a corrupt regime, Aristotle also repeatedly qualifies the multitude (*plethos*) as more prudent and virtuous than each of its members taken separately, at least under certain circumstances.[9]

---

[6] On William of Moerbeke's translation(s) of the *Politics* see Christoph Flüeler, *Rezeption und Interpretation der Aristotelischen Politica im späten Mittelalter*, 2 vols. (Amsterdam: John Benjamins Publishing, 1992).

[7] On the structure and different moments of the composition of the *Politics*, see Jean Aubonnet, *Introduction* in Aristotle, *Politique*, ed. Jean Aubonnet (Paris: les belles lettres, 1960), vii–ccvi.

[8] Aristotle, *Politics*, III.7–8, esp. 1279a22–I280a2.

[9] *Politics*, III.11, 1282 a14–17. In *Politics*, III.11, 1282a 5–23, Aristotle says that the multitude can be sovereign in their choice of magistrates but not in law-making. On some later reinstatements of this Aristotelian theme see Alessandro Mulieri, "Theorizing the Multitude before Machiavelli: Marsilius of Padua between Aristotle and Ibn Rushd," *European Journal of Political Theory* 22, no. 4

Unsurprisingly, in other books of the *Politics*, Aristotle appears to complement, or perhaps revise, the sixfold constitutional scheme that he presents in Book 3. In fact, in Books 4 and 5, Aristotle actually claims that the two most important regimes in any constitutional scheme are democracy and oligarchy.[10] Based on this claim, he goes on to present more specific characterizations of different typologies of democracies and oligarchies, listing five models of each of these two types of constitutions (and in these revised schemas, the constitutions that he elsewhere considered to be good versions of these two regimes, aristocracy and *politeia*, now become two models of their own[11]). This complex classification shows that whenever we speak about democracy in Aristotle, we always have to qualify this term, because different models of democracy might reflect different democratic regimes that existed in his own time and that also feature in the *Politics*.

Within these five models of democracy that he presents in Book 4, Aristotle appears to have a certain preference for a moderate idea of democracy in which income and census matter for citizens' political participation. Scholars disagree about the extent to which this moderate model of democracy corresponds to his idea of the "constitutional regime."[12] However, it is plausible to think that this form of democracy would have corresponded to the Solonian regime established in Athens at the beginning of the sixth century, and in which (1) access to citizenship was based on census and income, and (2) the Areopagus had a central role. In fact, one possible confirmation that Aristotle's preference for this kind of democracy is an endorsement of Solon's first Athenian democracy can be found in Book 2 of the *Politics*, where Aristotle expresses a clear preference for this legislator vis-à-vis Pericles, whom he takes to be the symbol of the Athenian democracy of his own time.[13] Aristotle's preference is based on the fact that, unlike Pericles, Solon excluded the poor from office. This judgment reflects an idea which

---

(2022): 542–64 and Id., "Da Machiavelli a Aristotele. Donato Giannotti sul governo misto e il regime popolare nella Repubblica fiorentina," *Storia e politica* XIII, no. 2 (2022): 421–49.

[10] *Politics*, IV.2, 1290a13–20.
[11] *Politics* IV.4, 1291b30–I292a28.
[12] Among others, see Andrew Lintott, "Aristotle and Democracy," *The Classical Quarterly* 42, no. 1 (1992): 114–28 and Mortimer Chambers, "Aristotle's Forms of Democracy," *Transactions and Proceedings of the American Philological Association* 92, no. 61 (1961): 20–36; Domenico Musti, *Demokratía. Origini di un'idea* (Roma-Bari: Laterza, 2013).
[13] *Politics*, II.2, 1273b–1274a.

was common in Greek thought on Athenian democracy, namely, that under Pericles's regime, the poor received special treatment.[14]

Insofar as we can consider democracy as a general ideal type in the *Politics*, Aristotle characterizes this regime in institutional, political, and social ways. The institutional and the political descriptions of democracy are closely linked herein. Aristotle says that the underlying political principle of democracy is liberty (*eleutheria*) and, like in the *Rhetoric*, he defines democracy as a regime in which the people rule and have a share in everything.[15] In order to give an institutional dimension to this definition of freedom as power-sharing, Aristotle associates democracy with the principle of rotating offices for the main magistracies. As he explains, in a democracy, the idea of liberty is "in the interchange between ruling and being ruled,"[16] and the best way to guarantee rotation in office is by sortition, a procedure that he explicitly labels as "democratic," in contrast to elections, which he sees as an aristocratic procedure.[17] This has led scholars to stress that Aristotle's association of democracy to lots marks an important difference between ancient and modern democracy.[18] While in the latter, legitimacy is based on the principle of consent, which is better guaranteed by elections, in the former, it is based on rotation in office, and casting lots is the best way to guarantee it.

For the present analysis, it is important to emphasize that Aristotle also attaches a social dimension to democracy as a constitution and defines it not simply as a government of the people, but also as empowering a very specific section of the *demos*: the poor. In Books 3, 4, and 5 of the *Politics*, the statements that characterize democracy as the rule of the poor are numerous. Aristotle says that democracy "is directed to the interest of the poor,"[19] "exists where the sovereign authority is composed of the poorer classes, who are without much property,"[20] and calls it "a constitution under which the poor, being also many in number, are in control."[21] Given the

---

[14] In fact, in his famous often-quoted funerary speech in Thucydides, Pericles says that one important characteristic of the Athenian democracy of his own time was that the selection of magistracies was done according to poverty (*kata penia*); see Josiah Ober, *Mass and Elite in Democratic Athens. Rhetoric, Ideology and the Power of the People* (Princeton, NJ: Princeton University Press, 1989), 194.
[15] *Politics*, IV.4, 1291b34–36; VII.2, 1317a40–43.
[16] *Politics*, VII.2, 1317b1–5.
[17] *Politics*, VI.2, 1317b31–1318a3.
[18] Mogens Herman Hansen, *The Athenian Democracy in the Age of Demosthenes: Structures, Principles and Ideology* (Norman: University of Oklahoma Press, 1999); Bernard Manin, *The Principles of Representative Government* (Cambridge, UK: Cambridge University Press, 1997).
[19] *Politics*, III, 7. Eng. trans. Aristotle, *Politics*, trans. Ernest Barker (New York: Oxford, 1995), 100 (henceforth, I will refer to this translation with the page number in brackets).
[20] *Politics*, III.8, I279b16 (101).
[21] *Politics*, III.8, 12791b31 (102).

limited number of people who could be considered rich in a Greek polity and in Athens as well, Aristotle's definition of democracy as the rule of the poor has an immediate quantitative aspect because the non-rich, or the poor, definitely represented the most numerous part of the city. Therefore, the poor automatically constitute both the multitude and the majority. Aristotle's definition of democracy as the rule of the poor, in fact, also plays on the double meaning of the word *demos* that, in Ancient Greek, means "the people," but can also mean "the poor." It is thereby somehow implicit in this double meaning of the very word *demos*, which the Greeks used to refer to the people, that insofar as democracy could be seen as the *kratos* of the people, it was also the *kratos* of the poor.[22] Because democracy is the rule of the people who exercise their power through sortition, democracy is also immediately the rule of the poor. Therefore, to claim that the poor are the rulers automatically amounts to saying that the majority of the people are the rulers.

When Aristotle characterizes democracy as the rule of the poor, he uses several different words to identify the latter term. These include the very word *demos*, as we observed, along with others such as *penetes* and *aporoi*, two Greek words that more literally mean "poor" but in different ways. *Aporoi* especially indicates those who lack any material goods, whereas the former word, *penetes*, is quite standard in Greek to refer to the poor. Aristotle's semantic characterization of the poor who rule in a democracy as *demos*, *penetes*, or *aporoi*, however, hardly helps us to clearly delineate precisely who these poor are. In the *Rhetoric*, when discussing the means necessary for exercising rhetoric, he defines the rich as those who have found "fine means" of self-support.[23] As Ober highlights, one could perhaps argue based on this that the poor are those who do not have "fine means" of self-support.[24] However, the problem is that Aristotle does not specify what "fine means" actually are and thus does not clearly establish a threshold according to which we can define someone as being wealthy or poor. In the absence of a clear characterization of who the poor are, we can simply assume that the defining feature of the poor is what opposes them to the wealthy of the city, that is, the fact that, as Aristotle says in the *Rhetoric*, the poor rely on their work in order to sustain themselves but lack considerable means of self-support.

---

[22] Hansen, *The Athenian Democracy*, 154; Musti, *Demokratìa*, 12–13; Luciano Canfora, *Democracy in Europe: A History of an Ideology* (New York: John Wiley & Sons, 2008).
[23] Aristotle, *Rhetoric*, 1361a12–16.
[24] Ober, *Mass and Elite*, 194–96.

Democracy is that regime that empowers the former, however they are defined, against the wealthy.

Aristotle's definition of democracy as the rule of the poor also has a qualitative aspect. In this sense, his claim that the poor are the rulers does not always amount to saying that the majority rules. As Aristotle writes, "it ought not to be assumed, as some people are nowadays in the habit of doing, that democracy can be defined, without any qualification, as a form of constitution in which the greater number are sovereign."[25] Therefore, defining democracy as the rule of the poor is not so much about emphasizing the people as a majoritarian force as it is really about stressing the fact that democracy empowers the poor. Aristotle makes this very clear in a passage from Book 4 of the *Politics* where he writes that if a city had a total population of 1,300 of which 1,000 of the 1,300 were wealthy, and assigned "no share in office to the remaining 300 poor,"[26] nobody would call such a regime a democracy. Rather, this would be an oligarchy. The same could be said of the opposite situation, in which there are only a few poor men who are in charge of rich men who form a majority. However, nobody would qualify this regime as an oligarchy. In other words, the real criterion by which regimes are defined as either oligarchies or democracies is not the number of people who rule, a majority or the multitude as opposed to a minority or the few, but the social condition of the people who are in charge. This is what Aristotle means when he says that "the real ground of the difference between oligarchy and democracy is poverty and riches."[27]

Aristotle's dislike of democracy lies exactly in the fact that it empowers the poor against the wealthy and the other components of the polity, regardless of their number in the polity. In fact, it is this definition of democracy as the rule of the poor that allows him to characterize democracy as a corrupt regime. Based on the logic of his sixfold constitutional scheme, we saw that there are two different types of popular constitutions: the *politeia* or "constitutional regime" and democracy. The former corresponds to the mixed constitution, which Aristotle characterizes as a combination of oligarchy and democracy and as a good constitution. For Aristotle, there is a binary scheme in the mixed regime between rich and poor, but the stabilization of the mixed regime can take place through either reaching a balance between these two components or through empowering a third class in the polity, that is, the

---

[25] *Politics*, IV.4, I290a30–33 (140).
[26] Aristotle, *Politics*, IV.4, 1290a30 (140).
[27] Aristotle, *Politics*, III.8, 1279b26 (102).

middle class or the *mesoi*.[28] On the contrary, democracy is a degeneration of the *politeia* or "constitutional regime." In the *politeia*, the people rule along with the few, while in democracy, the people, or the poor, alone are in charge. This is what makes stability among the different components of a democracy impossible and what causes this regime to produce chaos and anarchy.[29]

The Late Medieval and Early Modern Condemnation of Democracy

It is rather remarkable that despite all the complex subcategories of democracy that Aristotle provides in his *Politics*, most late medieval and early modern thinkers who drew on Aristotle's text mainly highlighted his definition of democracy as the rule of the poor for critical purposes. In the medieval period, we see this approach in the works of Albert the Great,[30] John of Paris, Marsilius of Padua, Peter of Auvergne,[31] Ptolemy of Lucca,[32] John of Jandun,[33] Bartolus of Saxoferrato,[34] Nicole Oresme,[35] Giles of Rome,[36] and Thomas Aquinas.[37] This same characterization can be found in early

---

[28] Lintott, "Aristotle and Democracy," 126–27. For more on the importance of this Aristotelian theory for late medieval and early modern political thought, see Pedullà, *Machiavelli in Tumult*, esp. ch. 4.

[29] If Aristotle follows the Greek *topos* on the condemnation of democracy, though with a more positive idea of democracy vis-à-vis others, he also provides some reasons for explaining why democracy as the rule of the poor is the best among all the corrupt regimes. In fact, he also says that democracy as the rule of the poor is more stable than oligarchy because the former is only characterized by a fight between the wealthy and the poor, whereas the latter is characterized by a fight between the wealthy and the poor and between different factions of the wealthy who will compete for money. See Aristotle, *Politics*, V, 1, 1302a 10. In addition, democracy is more secure than oligarchy because in a democracy, the domination of the poor makes the regime more stable as the poor are likely to be the majority.

[30] Anthony Black, *Guild and State: European Political Thought from the Twelfth Century to the Present* (London: Routledge, 2017), 83.

[31] For John and Peter, see James Blythe, *Ideal Government and the Mixed Constitution in the Middle Ages* (Princeton, NJ: Princeton University Press, 2014), 146, 89, respectively; Marsilius of Padua, *The Defender of Peace*, trans. Annabel Brett (Cambridge: Cambridge University Press, 2006), 41.

[32] Blythe, *Ideal*, 112.

[33] Roberto Lambertini, "Jandun's Question-Commentary on Aristotle's *Metaphysics*," in *A Companion to the Latin Medieval Commentaries on Aristotle's Metaphysics*, eds. Gabriele Galluzzo and Fabrizio Amerini (Leiden; Boston: Brill, 2014), 392.

[34] Bartolus de Saxoferrato, *Tractatus de regimine civitatis*, in *Politica e diritto nel trecento italiano, il de tyranno di Bartolo da Sassoferrato*, ed. Diego Quaglioni (Florence: Leo Olshki, 1983), 150.

[35] Both in Blythe, *Ideal Government*, 212.

[36] Blythe, *Ideal Government*, 67.

[37] In his commentary on the *Ethics*, he refers to democracy as a *principatus multitudinis*. In his commentary on the *Ethics* (In *librum* 8, *lectio* 10), Thomas gives the more correct translation of *principatus multitudinis*. See Hankins, *Virtue Politics*, 599, n.17. In his *De regimine principum*, however, he calls democracy a *potentatus populi*. See Hankins, *Virtue Politics*, 308.

modern political thought, in the works of, among others, Leonardo Bruni (who expresses this idea in Greek),[38] Lauro Quirini,[39] Francesco Patrizi,[40] Aurelio Lippo Brandolini,[41] Donato Acciaiuoli,[42] and Piero Vettori.[43] When reinstating Aristotle's idea that democracy is the rule of the poor, they all follow the Greek philosopher and use this claim to condemn democracy as a degenerated regime in which one component of the polity (i.e., the poor) rule for their own advantage against the other components, especially the rich.[44]

Naturally, all of these authors who reinstated Aristotle's definition of democracy as the rule of the poor chose different terms for doing so[45]. Moreover, to this we have to add that when late medieval and early modern authors define democracy as the rule of the poor, they obviously have a different idea of poverty in mind than that proposed by Aristotle. For Aristotle, as we saw, the category of poverty is very broad, to the extent that it can encompass all of the people, either those who have to rely on their work in order to subsist, or those who do not own many fine properties like the members of the leisure class.[46] For late medieval and early modern commentators, the poor are often those who absolutely have no means and hold no or little property.[47]

In addition to this, in the early modern period after the rediscovery of Greek and the translation of many texts from Greek into Latin (leading

---

[38] Leonardo Bruni, "Peri tēs politeias tōn Phlōrentinōn. Sulla costituzione fiorentina," in *Opere letterarie e politiche*, ed. Paolo Viti (Turin: UTET, 2013), 514.

[39] Lauro Quirini, *De re publica*, in *Lauro Quirini Umanista*, ed. Vittore Branca and Konrad Krautter (Florence: Leo Olshly, 1977), 137–42.

[40] Hankins, *Virtue Politics*, 370–71.

[41] Aurelio Lippo Brandolini, *Republics and Kingdoms Compared*, ed. and trans. James Hankins (Cambridge, MA: Harvard University Press, 2009), 240–41.

[42] Donati Acciaioli, *In Aristotelis libros octo Politicorum commentarii* (Venice: apud Vincentium Valgrisium, 1566), fol. 202v.

[43] Petri Vettori, *In VIII libros Aristotelis de optimo statu civitatis* (Florence: Bernardi filiorum, 1576), fol. 218–19.

[44] For more on the extent to which the category of the *mediotes* was important for late medieval and early modern theorists, see Marco Toste, "Tantum pauper quantum diues, tantum ydiota quantum studiosus: How Medieval Authors Made Sense of Democracy," in *Von Natur und Herrschaft. «Natura» und «Dominium» in der politischen Theories des 13. Und 14. Jahrhunderts*, ed. Delphine Carron, Matthias Lutz-Bachmann, and Anselm Spindler (Campus Verlag Gmbh, 2018), 293, for a discussion of the late Middle Ages, and Pedullà, *Macchiavelli in Tumult*, esp. 127–44, for a discussion of early modernity and for Machiavelli.

[45] On this see Alessandro Mulieri, "The Language of Democracy between Aristotle and Machiavelli," *History of Political Thought* XLII, no. 3 (2021): 389–413.

[46] Ober, *Mass and Elite*, 194–95.

[47] Marco Toste, "Tantum pauper", esp. 293, n.23. For humanist thought in which the poor are, as Pedullà, *Machiavelli in Tumult*, says, "the poorest members of the urban proletariat," 51–52. For more on the notion of poverty in the late medieval and early modern period in general, see Michel Mollat, *The Poor in the Middle Ages* (New Haven, CT: Yale University Press, 1986).

to texts by Plutarch, Thucydides, Demosthenes, and others to be read),[48] some humanists proved to be aware of the characteristic distinctions between the different phases of Athenian democracy. This reinforced their condemnations of democracy as the rule of the poor, as they opposed a favorable judgment of the census-like democracy of Solon to the more egalitarian democratic regime of Pericles. As Pedullà has shown, while late medieval authors could not historicize and distinguish the different phases of Athenian democracy and especially the census-based Solonian reform and Pericles's more egalitarian democracy, some early modern humanists did.[49] Therefore, the humanist readers of Aristotle's *Politics* also reinstated Aristotle's opposition between Solonian democracy and Periclean democracy and his explicit preference for the former. For example, Leonardo Bruni makes a clear distinction between the two and notably prefers Solon's more restricted conception of democracy that is based on (1) praise of the Aeropaghus, and (2) appreciation of the class-census distinction of Solon's democracy and exclusion of the poor. Most of the later humanists of the early modern period stick to these views, while reinstating Aristotle's critique of democracy as the rule of the poor.[50]

Of course, this does not mean that all late medieval and early modern authors did not want the poor to have any shared power or ability to hold public office. To begin with, in general, those who endorsed Aristotle's mixed regime also agreed with Aristotle's implicit inclusion of the poor in the shared power of this regime. Some are even quite explicit in granting the poor the right to a certain degree of participation in the rule of the polity. In the late medieval period, the positions of Ptolemy of Lucca and Marsilius of Padua are especially important in this regard. In his continuation of Thomas Aquinas's *De regimine principum*, Ptolemy reinstates Aristotle's condemnation of democracy as the rule of the poor. In so doing, he uses Aristotle's typical argument of the poor exercising power for their own advantage against the wealthy and the other components of the city. However, perhaps influenced by his Roman readings, he also adds that those "who live according to virtue" can be rulers, regardless of whether

---

[48] See Gabriele Pedullà's chapters "Athenian Democracy in Late Middle Ages and Early Humanism" and "Athenian Democracy in the Italian Renaissance," in *Brill's Companion to the Reception of Athenian Democracy: From the Middle Ages to the Contemporary Era*, ed. Dino Piovani and Giovanni Giorgini (Leiden; Boston: Brill, 2021), respectively 57–104 and 105–152.
[49] Pedullà, *Athenian Democracy in Late Middle Ages*, 86–89.
[50] Ibid., 86.

they are rich or poor, even though there is less danger in the polity when the rich govern.[51]

In his *Defender of Peace*, Marsilius articulates a similar position. In his very radical definition of the legislator as the multitude (more precisely, the people or the whole body of citizens), Marsilius extensively draws on Aristotle's ideas on the wisdom of the multitude in Book 3 of the *Politics*. He radicalizes the position of some previous commentators on the *Politics*, especially Peter of Auvergne, who had proposed a distinction between a prudent and a vile multitude. For him, the multitude is always prudent and wise and is in charge of the most important legislative and executive functions in the polity.[52] Interestingly, Marsilius also includes workers such as farmers and craftsmen in the multitude. A French translation of Marsilius's *Defender of Peace*[53] was also translated into Florentine vernacular in 1363. This translation was most likely commissioned by some urban tradesmen in a particular *milieu*, namely, the Florence of the end of the fourteenth century in which the "popular" components of the city (e.g., the *popolo minuto*) were gaining increasing importance.[54]

Positions favorable to the idea of a certain degree of a political role for the poor in the polity, such as those of Ptolemy and Marsilius, can also be found in the works of later thinkers and humanists. For instance, Francesco Patrizi argues that a small portion of the urban working poor can participate in public affairs.[55] However, the importance of Ptolemy's text on the question of the relationship between democracy and poverty must be noted, especially for its relevance to Machiavelli's immediate context. In 1494, after Pietro de' Medici had to flee Florence due to his poor handling of negotiations with King Charles VIII of France, who had just invaded Italy, an alliance between Savonarola and some components of the Florentine establishment realized what has been described as the most extreme popular republican regime in the entire history of early modern Italian political thought. This regime, for which Machiavelli worked until 1512 as secretary of the second Chancellery,

---

[51] Ptolemy of Lucca, *On the Government of the Rulers. De Regimine Principum*, trans. James Blythe (Philadelphia: University of Pennsylvania Press, 1997), 267 (IV.20.3).

[52] Marsilius of Padua, *The Defender of Peace*, trans. Annabel Brett (Cambridge, UK: Cambridge University Press, 2005), 65–80 (I.12-13).

[53] Marsilio da Padova, *Defensor Pacis nella traduzione in volgare fiorentino del 1363*, ed. Carlo Pincin (Torino: fondazione Luigi Einaudi, 1966).

[54] For more on this, see Lorenza Tromboni, "Filosofia politica e cultura cittadina a Firenze tra XIV e XV secolo: i volgarizzamenti del 'Defensor pacis' e della 'Monarchia,'" *Studi danteschi* 75 (2010): 79–114, esp. 89–90.

[55] Pedullà, *Machiavelli in Tumult*, 52.

re-established the symbol par excellence of popular republicanism, the Great Council. As several authors have pointed out, this regime was immensely important for the renewal of the language of early modern Italian republicanism.[56] In fact, the institution of the new radical republic triggered an important and lively debate on how to adapt the political and institutional language of the Communal tradition of Florence to the experiment of Savonarola and, later, Soderini's republic.

Savonarola, who drew heavily from Aristotelian and scholastic philosophy, was among the strongest advocates of the popular republican option and among the strongest critics of the idea that Florence could again become an oligarchic republican regime.[57] For this reason, he advocated the idea that Florence should become a popular republic in several sermons and speeches that he delivered, along with his treatise on the Florentine government in 1496. In addition to this claim, Savonarola supported opening what was to be considered the main political and symbolic representation of the popular republican option in Renaissance Florence, the Great Council.

Ptolemy, or Aquinas for those living in the late fifteenth century (because at that time, people generally thought that the author of Ptolemy's *de regimine principum* was Thomas Aquinas), was widely read in this context, and some important proponents of the republics knew his text quite well. As I have shown elsewhere, in this context, the language of the popular state came to overlap with Aristotle's democracy, but the critique that most authors had leveled at democracy, reinstating Aristotle's idea of democracy as the rule of the poor, disappeared in these circumstances. For example, even if both Savonarola and Scala borrowed extensively from Ptolemy's[58] characterization of the civil regime (i.e., as the popular regime) as opposed to democracy, neither condemned any form of popular government for empowering the poor against the rich. As the idea that democracy was the rule of the poor served as a classical argument against democracy, these authors most likely

---

[56] Jean-Louis Fournel and Jean-Claude Zancarini, *La politique de l'expérience: Savonarole, Guicciardini et le républicanisme florentin* (Alessandria: Edizioni dell'Orso, 2002); David Wootton, "The True Origins of Republicanism," in *Il Repubblicanesimo moderno: L'idea di repubblica nella riflessione storica di Franco Venturi*, ed. Manuella Antonietta Albertone (Naples: Bibliopolis, 2006), 271–304.

[57] Even after the Medici were ousted, there were of course those who still supported their power in the city. Aside from supporters of the Medici, there were two main positions in this debate. One tended to privilege the idea of old fourteenth-century popular governments, which also empowered the members of the *Arti Minori* and the lowest strata of the social groups who were living in Florence. The other was the idea of an oligarchic and moderate republican government, which would gather support from the old aristocratic families in the city of Florence and empower them again.

[58] Blythe, *The Worldview of Ptolemy*, 232.

perceived the reinstatement of Aristotle's critique of democracy as the rule of the poor to be damaging to their attempts to legitimize the new Florentine popular republic as a democracy in the Aristotelian sense.

Machiavelli and the Radical Early Modern Republicans

Machiavelli knew Savonarola's ideas well, and his reflection must be placed in the context of the Dominican preacher's time, as well as within the subsequent controversy between oligarchic and populist republicanism that characterized Florentine political thought in the first half of the sixteenth century. Machiavelli's reflection on the relationship between popular republics (*stati popolari*) and poverty spans across several works and, more specifically, in the *Discourses* and in the *Florentine Histories*. Here, I will focus mainly on the *Discourses* because Machiavelli's engagement with classical authorities, especially Aristotle and Polybius, is most evident in this work. As mentioned above, in the most recent scholarly literature, a growing number of scholars interpret Machiavelli's political thought in the *Discourses* to be a form of radical republicanism that is in stark contrast with the oligarchic nature of fifteenth-century humanist republicanism.[59] One way to prove the radical republican nature of Machiavelli's political message in this work is by examining the debt that his language of popular republicanism owes to Aristotle's and the Aristotelian reflection on democracy. As I have already started to deal with this topic elsewhere,[60] I will briefly sum up my thoughts on this, and then will turn to the most important question at stake in this chapter, that is, the relationship between democracy and poverty.

In *Discourses* II. 2, Machiavelli presents a sixfold classification of three good and three corrupt regimes. As countless interpreters have noted, Machiavelli's scheme in the *Discourses* reappropriates Polybius's sixfold constitutional model from Book 6 of his *Histories*, a text that Machiavelli appears to have been among the first to use in the early modern period.[61] Through this appropriation of Polybius's constitutional scheme, however, Machiavelli

---

[59] See note 5.
[60] Alessandro Mulieri, "The Language of Democracy from Aristotle to Machiavelli."
[61] Arnaldo Momigliano, "Polybius' Reappearance in Western Europe," in *Essays in Ancient and Modern Historiography*, ed. F. W. Walbank (Middletown, CT: Wesleyan University Press, 1977), 79–98; Carlo Dionisotti, *Machiavellerie* (Turin: Einaudi, 1980), 138–40. For the relationship between Machiavelli and Polybius, see Gennaro Sasso, "Polibio e Machiavelli: costituzione, potenza, Conquista," in *Studi su Machiavelli* (Naples: Morano editore, 1967), 223–80.

also revises Aristotle's sixfold constitutional scheme[62] presented above into a more complex scheme of typologies of governments. It is worth highlighting two aspects, among others, in the Machiavellian revision of Aristotle's scheme through Polybius that are relevant for the present analysis.

First, Machiavelli's concept of the mixed regime is more Polybian than Aristotelian because, unlike the Aristotelian mix between the two regimes of oligarchy and democracy, it includes three different types of simple regimes, as in Polybius (monarchy, aristocracy, and democracy). At the same time, however, Machiavelli is far from just reinstating the Polybian notion of the mixed regime because he diversifies the mixed regime internally as well. For him, in the *Discourses*,[63] there is a distinction between aristocratic and popular mixed regimes, and this difference depends on whether the guard of freedom, a concept that he introduces in *Discourses*, I.3, lies in the aristocrats or in the people. The best mixed regime is that of Rome, which is a popular mixed regime (meaning that the guard of freedom lies in the hands of the plebs).

The second element of Machiavelli's revision of Aristotle's scheme on constitutional regimes worth noting is his view of popular republics. Machiavelli's defense of mixed republics that are popular does not simply consist of a positive indirect rehabilitation of what people perceived to be Aristotle's conception of democracy[64] at the time. Rather, it also consists of a clear choice of empowering the main actor of any democratic regime and popular republic; the people being understood here as a synonym for the plebs. In this sense, Machiavelli does not at all reinstate the negative Aristotelian view of democracy as a regime that empowers the poor. This is an important breaking point between Machiavelli and most previous authors who had expressed their judgment of Aristotle's conception of democracy. Using Aristotelian language, Machiavelli expresses an uncompromising and unprecedented positive view of popular republics based on a positive view of the people. He also goes beyond the Aristotelian idea that to stabilize the mixed regime, it is necessary either to rely on the *mediani* or to find a balance between the different

---

[62] There is little doubt that Machiavelli was familiar with Aristotle's sixfold constitutional scheme given the importance of this authority for anyone who would have written on political and institutional schemes in his own time.

[63] As known, things become more complex on the role of the mixed regime in Machiavelli's political thought in his later works, and especially in the *Discourse on the Florentine Affairs*, the *Sommario delle cose di Lucca*, and the *Minuta*. On this, see Jérémie Barthas, "Il pensiero costituzionale di Machiavelli e la funzione tribunizia nella Firenze del Rinascimento," in *Il Laboratorio del Rinascimento. Studi di storia e cultura per Riccardo Fubini*, ed. Lorenzo Tanzini (Florence: Le Lettere, 2016), 239–55.

[64] Mulieri, "The Language."

components of the city. For Machiavelli, the stability of the popular mixed regime can only be upheld by perpetuating the conflict between the wealthy and the poor.[65]

We saw that despite relying on Ptolemy of Lucca (who followed Aristotle closely in his characterization of democracy), both Savonarola and Scala—two authors who are essential for understanding the intellectual roots of the Florentine popular republic of the end of the fifteenth century—omit Ptolemy's condemnation of democracy as the rule of the poor, perhaps for fear of weakening their defenses of popular republicanism. Machiavelli does not simply omit this critique. More radically, his political thought on the relation between mixed popular republics and poverty is at odds with the choir of ancient, late medieval, and early modern authors who reinforced their critiques of democracies and popular governments based on Aristotle's characterization of democracy as the rule of the poor. Machiavelli holds that a well-ordered republic (i.e., a popular mixed republic) is a regime in which, as he writes in I.37 of the *Discourses*, one has "to keep the public rich and their citizens poor."[66] In this sentence, Machiavelli refers to the public by the term *stato*, or the institutional and political architecture of a regime, but claims that the people who should be in charge of the *stato* (i.e., the citizens) should all be poor.[67]

Scholars disagree about how to interpret this claim and the relationship between poverty and popular government in Machiavelli's thought. Republican scholars have interpreted it as an attitude that citizens must have toward poverty and wealth in a republic in the sense of celebrating poverty as a civic value of virtue.[68] Others have pushed Machiavelli's claim toward a Marxist or classist view, claiming that with these words, Machiavelli praises material equality among all the citizens of a republic and advances

---

[65] This is the core thesis of Pedullà, *Machiavelli in Tumult*. To my knowledge this is one of the best studies of conflict in Machiavelli and political Aristotelianism.

[66] I quote from the following English translations of Machiavelli's works: Niccolò Machiavelli, *Discourses on Livy*, trans. Harvey Mansfield and Nathan Tarcov (Chicago: Chicago University Press, 1996) (henceforth referred to as *Discourses*). This passage is from *Discourses*, 79.

[67] That this is the right way to interpret Machiavelli's claim that the citizens must be kept poor is clear if we do not want to think that, when Machiavelli says that the citizens should be poor, he is talking about subjects rather than citizens. In a republic, and, more particularly in the kind of popular republic which Machiavelli defends, citizens are those who are in power and could easily become part of the ruling class because there is quite a large degree of social mobility.

[68] Hans Baron, "Franciscan Poverty and Civic Wealth as Factors in the Rise of Humanistic Thought," *Speculum* 13 (1938): 1–37; Maurizio Viroli, *Republicanism* (New York: Hill & Wang, 2002); Julie L. Rose, "'Keep the Citizens Poor': Machiavelli's Prescription for Republican Poverty," *Political Studies* 64, no. 3 (2016): 734–47.

an anti-oligarchic sentiment.[69] There is little doubt that Machiavelli has a form of material equality in mind when he makes this claim about keeping citizens poor. Machiavelli includes a clearly classist dimension to his critique of wealth in republics, and he does so from the perspective of the people understood as the lowest class. In fact, Machiavelli very often identifies the two legal categories of patricians and plebeians with the two social categories of rich and poor.[70] More fundamentally, however, with the expression "keep their citizens poor," Machiavelli might also mean that all the citizens of a republic should be kept poor, perhaps especially when the plebs take power along with the patricians, and above all when in exercising this power, the plebs check or curb the power of the patricians. Thus, Machiavelli's notion of tumults must be read in light of his idea that the citizens of a republic should be kept poor.

In that famous chapter of the *Discourses* wherein he claims that the conflicts between the plebs and the aristocrats in Rome "were the first cause of keeping Rome free,"[71] Machiavelli links his definition of the plebs with the theory of the humors. The difference between the *plebs* and the *grandi* is that the former want to avoid being oppressed, and the latter want to oppress and dominate. Machiavelli frames the humors as desires or perceptions about one's desires. This is an important point. Machiavelli believes that men's desires never change and always remain the same throughout human history. He also thinks that desires are always unlimited and are never fully compatible with the perfection of the Aristotelian middle way. Therefore, the desires of the two humors—that is, that the *grandi* want to dominate, and the plebs want to avoid being dominated—also remain unlimited and there is no credible hope that they will self-regulate. However, Machiavelli shows a normative preference for the humors of the people, as he claims that "the desires of free peoples are rarely pernicious to freedom because they arise either from being oppressed or from suspicion that they may be oppressed."[72] The plebs are motivated by a desire not to be oppressed in their clash with the *grandi*. We could add that this same desire leads Machiavelli to claim that the citizens of well-maintained republics must be kept poor.

---

[69] Filippo Del Lucchese, "Crisis and Power: Economics, Politics and Conflict in Machiavelli's Political Thought," *History of Political Thought* 30, no. 1 (2009): 75–96; John McCormick, "'Keep the Public Rich, But the Citizens Poor': Economic and Political Inequality in Constitutions, Ancient and Modern," *Cardozo Law Review* 34 (2013): 879–92.
[70] Pedullà, *Machiavelli in Tumult*, 255.
[71] *Discourses*, 16 (I. 4).
[72] *Discourses*, I. 4 (17).

For Machiavelli, there are both normative and practical reasons for supporting the idea that the citizens (including those who have to be in power) of popular republics should be poor. On a pragmatic level, Machiavelli appears to be convinced that maintaining the private poor and the public rich is, among other things, the true and best "way to make a republic great and to acquire empire."[73] In terms of his normative and ideological preferences, Machiavelli also thinks that it is useful and effective to keep the citizens poor as a "way of life."[74]

Unlike Aristotle and the Aristotelian tradition, Machiavelli does not look at poverty as a static social characterization of one component of the city, but as a dynamic factor that can shape forms of political agencies within the republic. His idea of the plebs allows him to adopt two different strategies for linking poverty and democracy. First, the fight between the nobles and the plebs is characterized by a factual and spectacular violence. As he writes, these tumults might lead to the "people together crying out against the Senate," or "running tumultuously through the streets, dosing shops."[75] Machiavelli mentions the sense of fear that all of these violent actions might provoke in anyone who witnesses them. The clashes between the plebs and the nobles are harsh and acute. However, and this is the second aspect worth noting, Machiavelli also presents them as a way to stabilize a popular republic. In fact, as he writes, the tumults "have engendered not any exile or violence unfavorable to the common good but laws and orders in benefit of public freedom."[76] For Machiavelli, the rule of the poor and its conflict with the nobles does not lead to chaos, as Aristotle believed. The conflict between the plebs and the nobles and the corresponding idea that the citizens of a republic must be poor are aimed at the common good and at good laws that are, in turn, the causes of education and good examples. Machiavelli's concern with the common good should then not be interpreted as an example of his adherence to classical republicanism. Rather, it is linked to his idea that despite all the difficulties and troubles that a state must go through, it must aim to be stable.

Therefore, Machiavelli's position is as much concerned with a popular democratic agenda that values the plebs, understood as the poor, as he is with a realist perspective on the stability of the state. In fact, the two aspects

---

[73] *Discourses*, II.19 (173).
[74] *Discourses*, III.25 (271).
[75] *Discourses*, I. 4 (16).
[76] *Discourses*, I. 4 (16).

of realism and democratism go together for Machiavelli. In the chapter in which he opposes popular to aristocratic republics, Machiavelli explains that Rome is better than Sparta and Venice if one wants a republic that expands and becomes an empire[77]. This is the purpose of the conflict between the nobles and the plebs because it can guarantee that the republic will have an army to expand and will remain stable while proceeding with expansion. One could claim that in a popular republic, the citizens (including those who can hold positions of power) must be poor also because this favors stability and allows for the expansion of the polity. These aspects of Machiavelli's realist thought (i.e., stability and expansion) show that when he defines a popular republic as a polity in which the citizens are poor, he thinks of this as a mix of both popular democratic ideas and strong political realism.

The idea that the poor should rule in a republic was of course not exclusive to Machiavelli. In addition to the isolated, more favorable ideas of the poor as holding public offices in Ptolemy and Marsilius noted above, James Hankins has shown that there was a lively debate in late medieval and early modern Italian political thought on the relationship between poverty and power or public life. Two main views can be distinguished within this debate. On the one hand, Boccaccio and several later humanists, including Francesco Filelfo, Guarino of Verona, Biondo Flavio, and Paolo Vergerio, endorsed a view that Hankins defines as "political poverty."[78] This was the idea that wealth was bad for republics because it corrupted political life. This view is also partly reflected in Savonarola's critique of wealth and luxury in Florentine political life. In Filelfo's case, the example of Sparta in which the few citizens-warriors devoted their entire lives to fighting for their cities and were kept poor to fulfill this supreme duty could be a source of inspiration for his idea that republics must be poor. On the other hand, there were humanists such as Leonardo Bruni, Poggio Bracciolini, Diomede Carafa, and Donato Giannotti (but, in fact, most humanists) who claimed that private wealth was acceptable in a republic and that citizens could be rich. According to these thinkers, wealth was not necessarily a factor of instability and corruption in the republic, but a factor of growth and the increase of power.[79]

By saying that the citizens must be kept poor, Machiavelli follows Boccaccio and, in his more immediate context, Filelfo, who, as we observed,

---

[77] *Discourses*, I. 6.
[78] Hankins, *Virtue Politics*, 354–63.
[79] Ibid., 206–15.

used Sparta as a model for his idea that wealth could be dangerous to political life. Yet for Machiavelli, Sparta was an aristocratic republic. Even if he exhibited positive views toward Spartan legislators such as Lycurgus and Cleomenes, Machiavelli did not consider Sparta to be the ideal republic because it failed to expand its empire and was an example of a *governo stretto*.[80] Very often, when ancient and contemporary sources of Machiavelli claimed that good republics were also poor republics, they were referring to the examples of Sparta or Rome as mixed republics. Machiavelli's originality lies in his upholding the idea that the citizens of a republic must be poor, by referring to the examples of Athens and Rome, two regimes that for him are popular republics or democracies. In this sense, Machiavelli broke with the classical idea that poverty should be attached to any republic, including *governi stretti*, and instead goes against the negative assessment of Athens as a popular regime in which the poor were in charge, thereby turning this into a positive element. This is why he appropriates Aristotle's idea of democracy as the rule of the poor and turns it into something positive.

Machiavelli's ideas in which poverty and *governi larghi* went hand in hand also had an important echo in the subsequent tradition of early modern Italian radical republicanism. Several popular republicans who were active in early sixteenth-century Florence followed Savonarola in defending a social idea of popular government in which the two themes of poverty and popular republican government (and a strong critique of luxury and wealth) were linked, and Aristotelian thought was used in order to legitimize anti-oligarchic republican ideas.[81] One important laboratory for popular republican ideas in Florentine political thought was the republican experiment that took place in Florence between 1527 and 1530. Several popular republican authors contributed to this event. Among them, we find Pier Filippo Pandolfini, who praised Savonarola's ideas on popular government and reused several Aristotelian ideas to advance an extreme form of popular republicanism based on anti-oligarchic ideas. Pandolfini polarized the distance between the aristocrats and the people (which are very often thought of as

---

[80] For more on the importance of the figure of Cleomenes and other Spartan examples for Machiavelli's "populism," see John McCormick, "Machiavelli's Agathocles: From Criminal Example to Princely Exemplum," in *Exemplarity and Singularity*, ed. Michele Lowrie and Susanne Lüdemann (London: Routledge, 2015), 123–39.

[81] As Rudolf von Albertini explains in *Firenze dalla repubblica al principato* (Turin: Einaudi, 1970), 75, in the *Rucellai Gardens*, the philosophical *milieu* was far more heavily influenced by Aristotle than by Plato. For more on the influence of Savonarola's thought on subsequent popular republican political thought, see Lorenzo Polizzotto, *The Elect Nation: The Savonarolan Movement in Florence, 1494–1545* (Oxford: Clarendon Press, 1994).

to a certain extent overlapping with the poor) to the extreme and presented strong ideas of equality and freedom that radicalized the Aristotelian concept of the middle class.[82]

Coming from a similar *milieu*, Donato Giannotti, who explicitly mentions Aristotle as his main influence, systematically adapted Aristotelian ideas to his own popular republican agenda. In his late republican thought, wherein he defended the idea of a mixed government, he afforded it a very strongly popular sense, by advocating for reopening the Great Council and for a strong role for the people and the plebs in the polity. If his main preference was for the Aristotelian stabilization of a republic through the empowerment and expansion of the middle class,[83] Giannotti proved to be aware of the inevitability of the importance of the plebs and the people for the general balance of actual, not ideal, republics. Sometimes, he identified the people with the plebs, giving the former a strong social characterization and describing them as those people who have no property and are just busy with the essential economic activity of the city.[84] In other instances, Giannotti appears to suggest that the people are actually a different category from the plebs in that the latter are the lowest and most disadvantaged strata of the population.[85] However, in either case, he claims that a good mixed government must have a popular dimension and must include some form of participation from the people and/or the plebs, as separate categories from the middle class. To reach this goal, Giannotti does not hesitate to draw on the Aristotelian idea that a crowd can reach a common decision much better than each of its parts taken separately.[86] It is of little surprise that Giannotti's ideas and those of other popular republicans who wrote in the first half of the sixteenth century were strongly influenced by Machiavelli. In fact, the Florentine secretary participated in the same *Rucellai Gardens* in which many subsequent Aristotelian popular republicans were present (among them, certainly Donato Giannotti and probably Pier Filippo Pandolfini).[87]

---

[82] Pier Filippo Pandolfini, "Discorso alla milizia," *Archivio storico italiano*, I 15 (1851): 350–376. For more on Pandolfini, see Von Albertini, *Firenze dalla repubblica*, 124–25, and Jérèmie Barthas, "Machiavelli e i libertini fiorentini" (1522–1531). Una pagina dimenticata nella storia del libertinismo. Col Sermone sopra l'elezione del gonfaloniere del libertino Pierfilippo Pandolfini," *Rivista storica italiana* 120, no. 2 (2008): 569–603.

[83] Donato Giannotti, *Della repubblica fiorentina*, in *Opere politiche e letterarie di Donato Giannotti collazionate sui manoscritti, precedute da un discorso di Aldo Vannucci*, 2 vol., ed. Filippo Luigi Polidori (Florence: Le Monnier, 1850), I.4 (79). See Mulieri, "Donato Giannotti sul governo misto".

[84] Giannotti, *Della repubblica fiorentina*, I.3 (76).

[85] Giannotti, *Della repubblica fiorentina*, I.5 (97–98).

[86] Giannotti, *Della repubblica fiorentina*, III.5 (177–179).

[87] Von Albertini, *Firenze dalla repubblica*, 125, n.3.

Conclusion

If the traditional category of republicanism cannot fully grasp the conceptual richness of early modern republicanism, we have to be open to speaking about different varieties of republicanism in the early modern period, depending on the context and the specific circumstances in which we study them. Within this renewed overview of the problem of republicanism, the difference between an oligarchic and a popular stream of republicanism takes center stage. In contrast to classical republicanism, plebeian or popular republicanism is not to be thought of as a continuous tradition, but more as an episodic "ideology" that appears in specific circumstances of crises of consolidated power. It is a tradition that has scattered moments of emergence as an intellectual wave in pre-modern Italy, especially in the beginning of the fourteenth century and in the period between the end of the fifteenth century and the beginning of the sixteenth century.

The condemnation of democracy as the rule of the poor is one of those themes in which it is possible to display the important difference between oligarchic and popular ideas of republicanism in all its clarity. By examining the complex relationship that Aristotle established between democracy and poverty in his *Politics*, the chapter has provided a limited survey of how this association evolved in the works of several late medieval and early modern republican thinkers who were influenced by his political thought, and in Machiavelli. Most late medieval and early modern political Italian writers followed Aristotle in criticizing democracy for empowering the poor against the wealthy and the other components of the political community. In pre-modern republican thought, the association between democracy and poverty was then mainly seen as a negative feature that condemned this regime to corruption.

As we saw, however, there were some late medieval and early modern authors, including some popular republicans, who were critical of Aristotle's normative condemnation of democracy for being a regime that empowers the poor. Among them, Machiavelli upholds the association between what he calls mixed popular republics and poverty because he claims that in a well-maintained republic, the public must be rich while the citizens who can hold important public offices must be poor. However, the Florentine Secretary overturned Aristotle's negative idea that the poor must be in charge in popular republics. The idea itself that citizens who hold power in republics must be kept poor was not new. But Machiavelli's handling of this idea was new, in that he linked the idea of the poverty of citizens, the functioning of popular republics, and *governi larghi* by seeing them together through a positive interpretive lens. If, for Aristotle, "poverty produces [...] factional disputes and wrongdoing,"[88] Machiavelli attaches a positive role to poverty, not only as a value in itself in popular republics, but also as a crucial factor for political stability.

[88] *Politics*, II.6 (54).

6
On the Battlefield of Rhetoric
Eloquence, Virtue, and Political Legitimacy in Italian Humanism

David Ragazzoni

Introduction

The importance and practical implications of rhetoric was a signature theme and concern throughout the Renaissance, both intellectually and politically.

Early "civic humanists" played a vital role in breathing new life into the study of ancient rhetoric: a pillar of the broader arsenal of *studia humanitatis*, it provided the tools for harmoniously merging eloquence and reason (the *ratio-oratio* principle) through the five-stage procedure (*quinque partes artis*) governing the crafting and delivering of effective speeches (*inventio-dispositio-elocutio-memoria-pronuntiatio/actio*). Ever since the fourteenth century, in fact, Florentine humanists contributed firsthand to the rediscovery of key Latin manuscripts in the firmament of classic oratory—from Cicero's speeches and epistolary by Petrarch and Coluccio Salutati to Quintilian's *Institutio Oratoria* by Poggio Bracciolini. The unearthing, and later printing, of some of these texts significantly remolded the medieval reputation of Cicero as a rhetorician (largely based on *De inventione* and the spurious *Rhetorica ad Herennium*), shedding unprecedented light on his lifetime project of combining the theory and the practice of rhetoric as both an intellectual (*vita contemplativa*) and a lawyer/statesman (*vita activa*). George of Trebizond's translation of Aristotle's *Rhetoric* from Greek to Latin (the official language of the Renaissance learned community),[1] together with the erudite habit of dissecting texts via glosses and commentaries, further

---

[1] See J. Cornelia Linde, "Translating Aristotle in Fifteenth-Century Italy: George of Trebizond and Leonardo Bruni," in *Et Amicorum: Essays on Renaissance Humanism and Philosophy*, ed. Anthony Ossa-Richardson and Margarete Meserve (Leiden: Brill, 2018), 47–68.

enhanced the rebirth of ancient rhetoric, sometimes paving the way for tentatively new theorizations of speech-crafting beyond the reception and transmission of previous paradigms (e.g., Trebizond's *Rhetoricum libri quinque*, 1433).

At the same time, the rhetorical revival of the classics was intensely political. Cicero himself had made the study and practice of rhetoric a quintessentially public act, at once a gladiatorial confrontation among clashing options (warfare by other means) and an instrument of debate of vital importance for the values and thriving of the Roman Republic. It was not by chance, as many humanists noted, that the manifesto of Ciceronian rhetoric—*De Oratore*—largely privileged forensic (i.e., legal) and deliberative (i.e., political) speeches over epideictic (i.e., ceremonial) ones, implying that politics and law were the domains where oratory could have a visible and lasting impact. In the Renaissance—the "age of Cicero" (*aetas Ciceroniana*) in the words of French historian of eloquence Marc Fumaroli[2]—this aspect could not go unnoticed. The manuals inspired by Cicero's teachings often illustrated the art of speech-crafting and -delivering through political metaphors and lenses, emphasizing the same ideological ambivalence—republican and monarchical—that Cicero himself had pointed out in *De Oratore*, describing eloquence as both "kingly" (*regium*) and "worthy of the free" (*liberale*) and, most strikingly, as a "soul-bending queen" for its power over the audience it rules (*flexanima atque omnium regina rerum oratio*).

The connection between the intellectual and political sides of the "rhetoric" coin—a most valuable currency in the Renaissance—has been recently emphasized and extensively demonstrated by James Hankins.[3] Early Renaissance *literati* across the political and ideological spectrum made the study of rhetoric a key ingredient in their recipe for ideal political leadership, based on the axiomatic belief that soulcraft was essential to statecraft. The Italian "civic humanists" that lived and wrote in the century and a half (the "long Quattrocento") spanning from Petrarch—the forerunner of the Renaissance—to Machiavelli believed, in fact, in the regenerative potential of education as the "doorway" (a metaphor they loved to use) to good character and, in turn, to an enlightened exercise of political power. On their account, intellectual distinction and moral excellence were the prerequisites

---

[2] Marc Fumaroli, *L'âge de l'éloquence: rhétorique et "res literaria" de la Renaissance au seuil de l'époque classique* (Genève: Droz, 1980).
[3] James Hankins, *Virtue Politics: Soulcraft and Statecraft in Renaissance Italy* (Cambridge, MA: Harvard University Press, 2019).

for legitimate political authority; any ruler who lacked both was doomed to be a tyrant. Resonating through their writings and letters was the firm belief that virtue—that is, love of justice and the common good, respect of the laws, self-restraint, and the capacity to look past the allure of personal and partisan interests—was the staple of true political legitimacy in a world of waning or crumbled legitimacies (above all, those of the Catholic Church and the Holy Roman Empire). Humanist intellectuals unanimously blamed current university curricula for the poor ethics of ruling elites. Medieval Scholasticism had turned into a pre-professional training in law, medicine, and the *ars nummaria* (the art of money-making), forging future leaders who would venally obsess over questions of status and wealth and grow completely oblivious of the qualities that good rulership ultimately required. To this end, they envisioned an ambitious and long-term program of educational, moral, and political renewal. In lieu of the unimaginative memorization of legal technicalities, degrading the study of the law to a *loquax ignorantia* ("talkative ignorance") for Petrarch and a *scientia oscitans* ("yawning science") for Leonardo Bruni, the Italian humanists—almost all law school dropouts—rethought from scratch the *artes liberals* (Trivium and Quadrivium). In doing so, they forged a new paradigm (*studia humanitatis*), revolving around the study of grammar and rhetoric as well as poetry, history, and moral philosophy, to make rulers-to-be finally capable of speaking eloquently, imitating the ancients, and crafting their own life and community according to virtue.

Despite the extensive and consistently growing literature on early modern rhetoric among scholars of political thought and intellectual history,[4] the

---

[4] E.g., Jerrold Seigel, *Rhetoric and Philosophy in Renaissance Humanism: The Union of Eloquence and Wisdom, Petrarch to Valla* (Princeton, NJ: Princeton University Press, 1968); Victoria Kahn, *Rhetoric, Prudence, and Skepticism in the Renaissance* (Ithaca, NY: Cornell University Press, 1985); John Monfasani, "Humanism and Rhetoric," in *Renaissance Humanism. Foundations, Forms, and Legacy*, vol. 3, ed. Albert Rabil, Jr. (Philadelphia: University of Pennsylvania Press, 1988), 171–235; Victoria Kahn, *Machiavellian Rhetoric: From the Counter-Reformation to Milton* (Princeton, NJ: Princeton University Press, 1994); *The Cambridge Companion to Renaissance Humanism*, ed. Jill Kraye (Cambridge: Cambridge University Press, 1996), especially the chapters by Peter Mack, "Humanist Rhetoric and Dialectic," 82–99, and James Hankins, "Humanism and the Origins of Modern Political Thought," 118–41); Quentin Skinner, *The Foundations of Modern Political Thought*, Vol. 1: *The Renaissance* (Cambridge, UK: Cambridge University Press, 1997), esp. chapter 2; the chapter by James Hankins, "Rhetoric, History, and Ideology: The Civic Panegyrics of Leonardo Bruni" (143–78); Cary Nederman, "Rhetoric, Reason, and Republic: Republicanism: Ancient, Medieval, and Modern," in *Renaissance Civic Humanism: Reappraisals and Reflections*, ed. James Hankins (Cambridge, UK: Cambridge University Press, 2000), 247–69; and, more recently, three important volumes: Markku Peltonen, *Rhetoric, Politics, and Popularity in Pre-Revolutionary England* (Cambridge, UK: Cambridge University Press, 2013); Skinner, *From Humanism to Hobbes: Studies in Rhetoric and Politics* (Cambridge, UK: Cambridge University Press, 2018); and Stuart McManus, *Empire of Eloquence: The Classical Rhetorical Tradition in Colonial Latin America and the Iberian World* (Cambridge, UK: Cambridge University Press, 2021).

protagonists of the "rhetoric revival"[5] that has animated Anglophone political theory over the past two decades have predominantly neglected the contribution of the Renaissance.[6] One of key texts in this wave of literature—Bryan Garsten's *Saving Persuasion*[7]—has drawn powerfully on the history of political thought to dissipate the conceptual fogginess around notions such as rhetoric, persuasion, and judgment and to distinguish between critics (Hobbes, Rousseau, and Kant) and advocates (Aristotle and Cicero) of persuasive rhetoric. However, beside a few erratic mentions, the book does not consider the Renaissance case for a politics of persuasion, despite the widespread Ciceronian belief, among Renaissance writers, that championing rhetoric ultimately entailed appealing to citizens' capacity for practical judgment. The most comprehensive edited volume on the history of rhetorical politics[8] similarly bypasses the contribution of humanism and the Renaissance. And outside the boundaries of specialized scholarship on the cultural and intellectual history of rhetoric in the Renaissance and/or in the *longue durée*,[9] Renaissance debates on the ethics, potential, and misuse of

---

[5] Bryan Garsten, "The Rhetoric Revival in Political Theory," *Annual Review of Political Science* 14 (2011): 159–80.

[6] Besides several chapters in the encyclopedic *Oxford Handbook of Rhetorical Studies*, ed. Michael J. MacDonald (Oxford: Oxford University Press, 2017), significant and recent contributions to the revived study of rhetoric in historical political theory and/or contemporary democratic theory include Rob Goodman, *Words on Fire: Eloquence and Its Conditions* (Cambridge, UK: Cambridge University Press, 2022); Rob Goodman and Samuel Bagg, "Preaching to the Choir? Rhetoric and Identity in a Polarized Age," *Journal of Politics* 84, no. 1 (2022): 511–24; and *The Oxford Handbook of Rhetoric and Political Theory*, ed. Keith Topper and Dilip Gaonkar (Oxford: Oxford University Press, 2022).

[7] Bryan Garsten, *Saving Persuasion: A Defense of Rhetoric and Judgment* (Cambridge, MA: Harvard University Press, 2009).

[8] *Talking Democracy: Historical Perspectives on Rhetoric and Democracy*, ed. Benedetto Fontana, Cary Nederman, and Gary Remer (State College: Pennsylvania State University Press, 2004).

[9] *Encyclopedia of Rhetoric*, ed. Thomas O. Sloane (Oxford: Oxford University Press, 2001); *The Rhetoric of Cicero in Its Medieval and Early Renaissance Commentary Tradition*, ed. Virginia Cox and John Ward (Leiden: Brill, 2006); Peter Mack, *A History of Renaissance Rhetoric 1380–1620* (Oxford: Oxford University Press, 2011); *The Oxford Handbook of Rhetorical Studies*, 2014. Spanning across more than two decades, the work of Virginia Cox certainly stands among the most substantial and extensive contributions to the scholarship on rhetoric in early and late Renaissance Italy: e.g., "Machiavelli and the *Rhetorica ad Herennium*: Deliberative Rhetoric in *The Prince*," *Sixteenth Century Journal* 28, no. 4 (1997): 1109–41; "Ciceronian Rhetoric in Italy, 1250–1360," *Rhetorica* 17, no. 3 (1999): 239–88; "Ciceronian Rhetorical Theory in the *Volgare*: A Fourteenth-Century Text and Its Fifteenth-Century Readers," in *Rhetoric and Renewal in the Latin West: Essays in Honour of John O. Ward*, ed. Constant J. Mews, Cary Nederman, and Rodney M. Thompson (Turnhout, Belgium: Brepols, 2003), 201–25; "Rhetoric and Humanism in Quattrocento Venice," *Renaissance Quarterly* 56, no. 3 (2003): 652–94; "Leonardo Bruni on Women and Rhetoric: *De studiis et litteris* Revisited," *Rhetorica* 27, no. 1 (2009): 47–75; "Rhetoric and Ethics in Machiavelli," in *The Cambridge Companion to Machiavelli*, ed. John Najemy (Cambridge, UK: Cambridge University Press, 2010), 173–89; "Rhetoric and Medieval Politics," in *The Oxford Handbook of Rhetorical Studies*, 329–40. Most recently, she has been coediting, with Jennifer Richards, *The Cambridge History of Rhetoric*, Vol. 3: *Rhetoric in the Renaissance* (Cambridge, UK: Cambridge University Press, 2023).

political rhetoric are often cited but seldom explored. They were, and still largely are, the darlings of intellectual historians and the orphans of political theorists.

My chapter deliberately goes in a different direction. It draws on the vast bibliographical landscape that I have briefly mapped above to bring together bodies of literature that are usually compartmentalized, in the attempt to offer a nuanced account of the *political theories of rhetoric* in the Italian Renaissance. It shows that a new kind of *institutio* (the civic humanists' Latin equivalent of the Greek *paideia*, "education") was envisioned as the first step in the reform of political institutions. Clarity of speech became a consistent aspiration in a political and social context where the chances to address the public through formal speeches had multiplied. *Eloquentia*—a term that meant both "to speak out" and "to speak bravely and persuasively"—turned into an article of faith among a new generation of thinkers who emphasized the need for *educated* political leaders to address their fellow citizens as equals. Consequently, *orator*—a term that in Renaissance Latin carried the twofold meaning of "spokesperson" and "ambassador"—was anyone who could use their rhetorical training for sound political purposes, unveiling the machinations of the polity's enemies. Eloquence, in the iconic definition by Francesco Patrizi in one of the manifestos of humanist political theory (*De institutione reipublicae*, ca. 1465), was a medicine for both the soul (i.e., an antidote to vice) and public affairs (i.e., a remedy to political corruption) (*ex omnibus disciplinis nulla magis congruat civitati quam oratoria*: "of all disciplines, none is more beneficial to the state than the oratorical one").

Relatedly, the chapter draws renewed attention to the *moral* connotation acquired by the humanist study of eloquence, as an indispensable tool for political leadership, vis-à-vis the ways in which rhetoric was studied in law schools as a purely technical skill for writing letters (*ars dictaminis*) and arguing (*ars aregandi*). In the words of Leonardo Bruni (the leading humanist and historian in the first half of the fifteenth century, apostolic secretary to four popes, and later chancellor of Florence), only the humanities, and the proper study of rhetoric above all, could make a young man a better man. Yet, the humanists' resort to epideictic rhetoric went well beyond the education of future generations of leaders. Having what it takes to speak one's mind powerfully and beautifully was, at once, what enabled someone to achieve their full potential as a human (a distinctively Aristotelian theme) and contribute to the pursuit of the common good by means of persuasion rather than coercion (a clear echo of Cicero). Common in the early Renaissance was, in fact, the belief that a multitude of laws was the staple of irredeemably corrupted polities. As an analysis of both official speeches and familiar letters reveals, public and private rhetoric aimed to make rulers and ruled alike *want* to be virtuous, incentivizing good behavior via praise and blame (rather than via procedural and institutional safeguards).

The chapter also unpacks two crucial and practical implications of this moral reading of eloquence. First, following from the principle that soulcraft represented the precondition for statecraft was the corollary persuasion that constitutional specifics of regime types were much less important than the intellectual (and thus moral) texture of those trained to rule. Governors, rather than governments, were the focus of the educational revolution of the Italian humanists. Second, the program they advocated was meritocratic and, at least in its driving ambition, profoundly egalitarian. While championing virtuous individuals' right to rule, they made it clear that the virtuous politician was educated, not born, precisely because virtue could be learned and cultivated (particularly through the study and practice of rhetoric). Anyone, if properly trained, could develop it; similarly, those born into the ruling elite, and thus blindly privileged by the lottery of life, could eventually fail the test of virtue, if they were reluctant to pursue intellectual—and thus moral—excellence. The fact that the civic humanists of Renaissance Italy cut widely across the political spectrum further confirms the egalitarian, non-elitist tenor of their common pursuit of an empowered meritocracy. Any study of this wide-ranging and ambitious project must begin with the political vision of its intellectual godfather: Petrarch.

Between Cicero's Recipe and Cola's Populism: Petrarch on Virtuous Rulership

Profusely celebrated as a forerunner of Quattrocento humanism, Francesco Petrarca (1304–1374) has protractedly been neglected as a political thinker in his own right (with the partial exception of Skinner). Pervasive across his writings were—so the conventional narrative goes—a mindset and an account of the relationship between *otium* and *negotium*, between the life of the mind and the life of public affairs, that made him the last child of a crumbling world at the dawn of a new era. Testament to his ultimately medieval rather than robustly humanist credentials were, according to most interpreters, his mild commitment to republican liberty, his reluctance to challenge the competing ambitions of the pope and the emperor, his love for the life of seclusion that literary studies enabled, and his hesitancy to reject monarchical regimes as the antimony of free political life. However, over the past fifteen years, this reductionist reading of Petrarch has been increasingly questioned. He never entered the battlefield of political practice, nor did he develop a distinctive political philosophy. Yet, as Peter Stacey and, most recently, James Hankins have emphasized, his "private politics" was synonymous with neither political quietism nor a disdain for the nature and challenges of political rule. Rather, he firmly believed that the education of rulers had far-reaching implications for the quality of their leadership and that the ancient world provided timeless standards for virtuous political action.

Though he never held institutional roles (unlike many Quattrocento humanists who served as chancellors), Petrarch tasked himself with the promotion of a politics of virtue both in his role on several diplomatic missions and in his advising to princely patrons—through speeches on their behalf or through epistles and literary writings addressed to his powerful interlocutors. In ways that foreshadowed the creed of later humanist intellectuals, he vigorously emphasized the importance of moral qualities for the legitimacy of political leadership, subscribing to the notion that laws are necessary but not sufficient to guarantee truly legitimate regimes and that, accordingly, offices and institutions can be handled in different ways based on the character of those in power. True legitimacy, for Petrarch as well as for the following generations of Italian humanists, rests on a genuine commitment to the public good, which entails the ability to rise above the quick-temperedness of one's own passions and to let go of the vanities that adorn the superficiality, rather than the substance, of politics. To be worthy of political authority, rulers must first prove that they know how to rule their souls, as Petrarch made clear in a famous letter praising Robert of Naples, the Guelph monarch who had bestowed upon him the crown as poet laureate (Easter Sunday of 1341):

> I would call him truly a king who rules and reins in not only his subjects but himself, who wields authority over his passions which rebel from the spirit and would overwhelm it if it yielded. Just as there is no more glorious victory than to be victor over oneself, so there is no loftier rule than to rule over oneself.[10]

[10] Quoted from Hankins, *Virtue Politics*, 157–58.

As he put it in the same letter, "[t]rue kings carry within them what makes them worthy of reverence" and "[i]t is great to be a king, but insignificant to be called a king"; or, as he wrote in an earlier letter (*Epistulae Familiares*), "[o]nly justice distinguishes the king from the tyrant."[11]

One decade later, in a treaty drafted as a letter to Niccola Acciaiuoli (a Florentine banker charged with the education of the young king of Naples, Louis I), Petrarch reiterates the structural connection between justice and political rule. Hereditary succession means nothing if the monarch lacks virtue, for titles are empty shells when they are not sustained by virtuous behavior. Those who happen to be predestinated to a position of power must demonstrate that they deserve what random luck has generously gifted them with. "Being a prince," as he writes in 1352, "does not make a man but exposes him," as much as "honors do not change our behavior and spirit but display it." Accordingly, in the language of a mirror for princes, Petrarch urges Acciaiuoli to show King Louis I "the steps by which he has been carried to this summit of fortune and the arts he must use to stay there." He should teach his young advisee that "it is less important to be born a king than to become a king by men's judgment; the first is a gift of fortune, the other of merit."[12]

Virtuous ruling is key also for a long-lasting relationship between the subjects and their ruler, working as a magnet that strongly and enduringly binds the former to the latter, as Petrarch illustrates in a 1358 speech to celebrate the restoration of the Visconti lordship over Novara after the city's brief experience under the Marquis of Monferrato (1356–1358). Upon his military success, Galeazzo II Visconti had refrained from punishing the citizens of Novara. In a public speech delivered before an assembly of the entire citizenry, Petrarch (who had previously served the Visconti rulers of Milan in the early 1350s), celebrates the magnanimity of Galeazzo as paradigmatic of his ability to forgive and forget—a quality typical of the heroes of Roman antiquity and of the merciful God of Christians. Likewise, he extolls the dignity of the peoples that have decided to willingly obey his authority out of respect for his virtues.

The influence of Cicero's *De Officis* and Livy's *Histories* looms large in the way in which Petrarch revisits their prescriptions for virtuous rulership and celebration of distinguished examples, such as the Roman general Camillus

---

[11] Ibid., 155.
[12] Ibid., 159.

taking over the Falerii "justly" and "by virtue," abstaining from violence and honoring the principles of the *jus gentium* that cement all peoples into one *societas*. As Hankins has pointed out, Petrarch skillfully draws on the concept of *iustus metus* or *iustus timor* (well-founded fear), introduced by Bartolus of Sassoferrato in his influential treaty *De tyranno*, to mark the difference between Monferrato and Galeazzo. The former has terrified the citizens of Novara into accepting his rule, while the latter, just like Camillus, has refrained from cruelty and oppression, thus managing to be obeyed without compulsion and to restore justice without violence. At the same time, Petrarch follows closely in the footsteps of Aristotle's *Nicomachean Ethics* and *Politics*, as well as of Sallust's *War against Jugurtha*, when he posits that "not armies nor treasures [. . .] but friends" provide the most solid ground for monarchical government. Friendship is a highly desirable ingredient for virtuous rulership, but—as Petrarch reminds his readers, echoing Seneca's *Moral Letters*—must be handled judiciously. A king "should reflect over everything with his friend," yet he should "first deliberate about his friend," detecting the malice of blandishment and distinguishing a friend from "a flattering enemy."[13]

The emphasis on the importance for political leaders to carefully select their friends was a powerful legacy of Cicero, whose treaty *On Friendship* had warned rulers about the contribution that disinterested men of letters can provide to their patron and his direction of public affairs. Guiding these exceptional individuals, in fact, is a nuanced understanding of human nature, an unshakable sense of right, an in-depth familiarity with law and the liberal arts, and the fearless willingness to advise the ruler in the pursuit of prudence and justice. These qualities make a ruler and his friends intellectual equals, eroding initial differences in socioeconomic conditions and thus providing meaningful chances for men of true virtue to meritocratically rise to the top of society. As Petrarch alerts, "[n]o man should feel shame at a plebeian friendship when intellect and learning make it noble."[14]

Poetry provides a most compelling and effective venue for such "men worthy of friendship" to distill their wisdom for the benefit of the ruler and his subjects. In his public speech on Easter Sunday 1341, when he was crowned poet laureate on the Capitoline in Rome, Petrarch turned to Cicero's

[13] Ibid., 161.
[14] Ibid., 162.

Pro Archia (the manuscript of which he had discovered in Liège in 1333 and would be referenced extensively by later humanists such as Boccaccio and Salutati) as his template for theorizing the nature and scope of a poet's service to the *res publica*. Cicero's argument—namely, that those charging Archias of illegally claiming the status of Roman citizen were baseless since his contribution to the cultural life of the community had already made him worthy of Roman citizenship—provided Petrarch with an authoritative framework to champion and connect—almost symbiotically—the politics of virtue (i.e., the well-deserved place of distinction of virtuous humanists in the public arena) and the virtue of politics (i.e., the importance of honorable rulers properly advised by men of letters). Great poetry—he claimed—arouses noble emotions that are crucial for the pursuit of noble political endeavors. By doing so, it starts a virtuous cycle that fruitfully draws on three psychological drives, ranging from the individual to the collective, and thus benefits the community as a whole: the will to service and honor the city, the ambition to achieve intellectual distinction, and the attempt to spur emulation in words and deeds. When properly steered, the human longing for personal glory—the second *affectus animi* that Petrarch mentions precisely after the desire to contribute to communal well-being—fuels virtuous behavior and propels others on the same path.

However, friendship with wise advisors is necessary, but not sufficient, to forge a virtuous ruler. The autonomous, daily, and tireless practice of humanistic studies—especially rhetoric and history—is equally quintessential for pursuing excellence in the related domains of soulcraft and statecraft. As Petrarch put it vividly, gesturing at Suetonius and his praise of Augustus's painstaking dedication to classical studies in his spare time, "continued and diligent reading" of the ancients provides the best compass to navigate the perilous waters of politics. The following passage from the preface to *Remedies for Fortune Fair and Foul*, filled with rhetorical tropes and reminiscent of classical sources, paradigmatically captures Petrarch's goal of sealing the interplay between a ruler's human flourishing and his capacity for humane ruling:

> Amidst the perpetual turmoil of our minds, like so many bright stars fixed on the firmament of truth, like so many pleasant and favorable breezes, like so many eager and skilled sailors, they [the brilliant and famous authors hundreds of years before our time] point us to the port of rest and guide the drooping sails of our hopes and the helm of our wavering thoughts until

such time as our own judgment, battered by so many storms, shall find firm ground and government.[15]

In the late 1340s Petrarch believed he had found in the arena of political practice the very embodiment of his hopes for a virtuous ruler capable of shepherding Italy out of the quicksand of power strives and toxic factionalism and into a future of justice, virtue, and peace. Cola di Rienzo (a nickname literally standing for "Nicola, son of Lorenzo") was a native of Rome who had managed, through diligent studies and a meticulous cultivation of his natural gift for eloquence, to rise above his humble origins, serve as the spokesperson for the city's government pleading the case of the Roman popular party in front of Pope Clement VI in Avignon, and eventually be appointed notary of the Roman civic treasury by the pope himself. In 1347 Cola started a revolution with the ambitious goal of bringing Rome back to its pristine greatness. On May 20, on top of the Capitoline Hill where Petrarch had been coronated with the laurel six years prior, the visionary leader announced a series of edicts chastising the aristocratic families of Rome and was acclaimed, by popular acclamation, ruler of the city with dictatorial powers.

A few days later, his populist agenda became even more evident: he bestowed upon himself the ancient title of "tribune," which he deliberately chose over that of "consul" (more conventional in the medieval communes of Italy), as well as that of "deliverer of the Holy Roman Republic." Promising to bring politics back to the plebs and the plebs back into politics, he started a bold project of civic education, wherein the city would be adorned with painted murals as a source of literacy for the many, a powerful source for a shared collective memory, and a constant reminder of Rome's glorious past.

Further expressing Cola's scorn for the aristocracy was his denunciation of the gap between their claims to power and distinction and the arrogance of its behaviors, the emptiness of its titles, the superficiality of its historical knowledge, the lack of respect for the city's monuments. As someone who had discovered the inscription recording the original text of the Roman imperial constitution (*Lex de imperio Vespasiani*)—that is, the *lex regia* mentioned in the Digest by which the Roman people authorized the emperor to exercise his power—Cola had an unequaled reverence for Rome's antiquity. Both Cola and Petrarch believed that the past glory of the city had been disfigured by the delusions of greatness and the rapacious appetites of its aristocratic

---

[15] Ibid., 164.

families, fraudulently claiming purely Roman ancestry while practicing violence to preserve their power. In June 1347, soon after Cola became the leader of the Roman Republic, Petrarch wrote him a letter that is best described as a panegyric, calling him "Princeps Romanorum," celebrating him as the new Scipio and Camillus and offering to become the official poet of the restored Roman liberty at the dawn of a new age for Rome and mankind alike.

Unfortunately, Petrarch's enthusiasm for Cola as the embodiment of his virtue politics was destined to be short-lived. Within a few months—no later than the end of the summer of 1347—Cola showed his true colors. He challenged the authority of the Church, entered an alliance with the Hungarians, received and accepted a knighthood from the emperor, started coining his own money (just like a prince), and began to grant Roman citizenship to all Italians (after learning of the *Lex Julia* of 90 BCE, probably from Cicero's *Pro Archia*). Despite writing a disheartened letter to Cola (who would become increasingly isolated and eventually would be forced to flee), Petrarch had no other choice than to acknowledge the end of his dream and move past his disillusionment with the actual possibility of virtuous rulers. However, his bold attempt to rethink the relationship between intellectual education, private and public virtue, and public affairs, and thus reconceptualize the nature and foundations of political legitimacy, invented a new way of thinking about politics that would resonate extensively in fifteenth-century Italy.

Florence on Trial: The Rhetorical Battle of Loschi and Salutati

Leonardo Bruni's *Laudatio Florentinae Urbis* offers a compelling example of the artful connection between politics and rhetoric driving the work of Italian humanists following Petrarch. Its antecedent—the vibrant defense of the Florentine Republic by Bruni's mentor and predecessor as chancellor of Florence, Coluccio Salutati—provides the intellectual and political background to fully capture the arguments as well as the novelty of the *Laudatio*.

At the core of the political life of the Italian peninsula was, in the early 1400s, the rivalry between Florence and Giangaleazzo Visconti. First duke of Milan, he dreamed of recreating the Lombard empire and establishing himself as the signore of all Northern Italy. A major obstacle to his voracious territorial ambitions was—besides Bologna—the republic of Florence. Humanist and rhetorician Antonio Loschi—a member of Visconti's Chancellery since

1391—penned in the first few months of 1401 a "vitriolic"[16] piece titled *Invective against the Florentines* (*Invectiva in Florentinos*) which drew extensively, and skillfully, on Cicero's rhetoric—itself a reference point and template for virtually all Italian humanists between the late fourteenth and the early fifteenth centuries. Two years later, in the very aftermath of the war, Salutati responded to the challenge, at once political and rhetorical, set by Loschi. Interestingly, the two humanists knew each other personally, and the respect and the admiration were mutual. In his early years, Loschi had even left his native Vicenza and moved to Florence in an attempt to make the acquaintance of the most distinguished Florentine humanist and interact closely with his circle (he indeed trained as a rhetorician under the supervision of Salutati's colleague Pasquino Capelli). On his end, Salutati often praised Loschi and his intellectual qualities in the personal correspondence with his own interlocutors. In the opening of his reply to Loschi's *Invective* (written in early 1403), he emphasized the latter's talent and his firsthand familiarity with Florence precisely to question Loschi's paternity of the text. And even in the months that followed, his consideration for Loschi never vanished, urging him, "like a son," to pursue fame through his intellectual abilities, not through mendacities in the service of power. Therefore, as the title explicitly indicates, he decided to address his counter-invective to an anonymous "slanderous detractor" rather than to Loschi himself, giving him the benefit of the doubt and questioning the authenticity of a text filled with "dishonest insults" and "grammatical faults" "unworthy of a man of his erudition." What makes their dispute over the merits and demerits of Florence worth revisiting in the context of this chapter is the fact that both draw on the same source—Cicero's rhetorical writings—to favor their respective agendas and, overall, support their vision of the ideal regime. In other words, Salutati flips the Ciceronian script of Loschi, turning their political and ideological quarrel into a masterful rhetorical challenge.

Loschi's text opens *in medias res*, urging both God and mankind to rightfully punish the citizens of Florence for their multiple disruptions of peace across Italy. Four examples support his portrayal of the Florentine republic as treacherous, ill-willed, and destined to ruin: the baseless claim of its Roman ancestry; the repeated attempts to establish its hegemony over the peninsula; its tyranny over the Florentine subjects; and its estrangement from its former allies.

---

[16] Stefano U. Baldassarri, "Hard Times, Great Expectations, and Our Mutual Friend Cicero: The Loschi-Salutati Controversy," in *City, Court, Academy: Language Choice in Early Modern Italy*, ed. Eva Del Soldato and Andrea Rizzi (New York: Routledge 2018), 67–79.

Building on an illustrious precedent—that is, the beginning of Cicero's speeches on the Catilinarian conspiracy—Loschi asks when the "most evil citizens" of Florence, who are "enemies" of their own republic and undermine the conditions for peaceful political life across the peninsula, will "pay the penalty" for their "crimes." Their behaviors and the punishments that they deserve should work as a powerful reminder of the destructive consequences of "deceptions," in case anyone might ever consider emulating their deeds. The emphasis on the Florentines' "stubborn hostility to peace" and the critique of their "blind" handling of Italian public affairs resonate powerfully also throughout the last pages of Loschi's *Invective*. Honoring the rules of ring compositions, the humanist rhetorician pens a conclusion that rephrases themes outlined in the opening of his text, thus crafting a perfectly circular argumentative structure, adorned with several Ciceronian tributes (either explicit or indirect). These references are not surprising, considering that Loschi had recently published an extensive commentary to eleven speeches by Cicero (*Inquisitio artis in orationibus Ciceronis*, 1392–1396) that soon gained prominence in the rhetoric revival animating Italian humanism.

Relatedly, the *Invective* is the first openly political text by Loschi, who draws on his mastery of the classics to sharpen his arguments in the service of Milanese propaganda. As impeccably demonstrated by Baldassarri,[17] Loschi tacitly quotes from Cicero's *Philippics* and *De Domo Sua* when, toward the end, he labels the Florentines as "cruel and wicked"—two adjectives ("crudele et nefarium") that, together, closely evoke similar lines in those two earlier texts (in particular, *Philippics*, III.1.3: "Quo enim usque tantum bellum—*tam crudele, tam nefarium*—privatis consiliis propulsabitur?": my emphasis). Analogous reverberations of *De Domo Sua* can be detected in section 4 of the *Invective*, where Loschi describes the citizens of Florence as victims of their leaders, longing for someone to liberate them from a government that is pernicious both for the city and for the rest of Italy. By doing so, he rephrases Cicero's description of the Romans wishing to be saved by Pompey.[18] Other significant examples of borrowings from (or tributes to) Cicero include the passage where Loschi, echoing *In Verrem* (I.14), draws

---

[17] Stefano U. Baldassarri, *La vipera e il giglio: lo scontro tra Milano e Firenze nelle invettive di Antonio Loschi e Coluccio Salutati* (Roma: Aracne, 2012) 144–49.

[18] Cf. Cicero, *De Domo Sua*, 25: "[Pompeius] subvenit subito rei publicae civitatemqye fractam malis, mutatam ac debilitatam, abiectam metu ad aliquam *spem libertatis et pristinae dignitatis* erexit"; *Invectiva*: "Sperant equidem hoc uno assertore *suae libertatis* exercitu, vobis prolapsis in servitutem, *dignitatem pristinam*, quam sibi per vos ereptam lugent, tandem esse recuperaturos" (my emphasis).

attention to the devastating consequences of the tyrannical government of Florence for the family life of its citizens.

The challenge posed by Loschi was ingeniously twofold. On the one hand, he created a work at the crossroads of history and ideology, drawing on historical antecedents to suggest analogies with the present situation of Italy, to chastise the expansionistic ambitions of the Florentine Republic, and to call for the political salvation of the peninsula by the Visconti family. On the other, he tacitly meant to compete with his fellow humanists—especially those from Florence and those serving its regime—over the rhetorical ability to employ the same intellectual repertoire (specifically, the influential speeches of Cicero) in the service of competing ideological agendas.

As the chancellor of Florence and the foremost Florentine humanist, Coluccio Salutati participated in this war by means of words with his own *Reply to a Slanderous Detractor Who Has Written Many Wounding Things against the Renowned City of Florence*. Probably patterned after Petrarch's invectives (especially *Contra medicum* [*Against physicians*]), the extensive title of the response (*Contra maledicum et obiurgatorem qui multa pungenter adversus inclitam civitatem Florentiae scripsit*) is noteworthy for the medical terminology that it embraces, comparing the anonymous detractor to someone who has deliberately wounded the reputation of Florence.

Just like Loschi's, Salutati's work begins *in medias res*, rejecting unconditionally all accusations against the Florentine republic as fabricated and presented within a syntactical and rhetorical framework that is consistently flawed. The decision to address the arguments of his opponent as if Loschi was neither the mind behind them nor the author who put them on paper should be read, in turn, as a strategic move. Salutati anticipates that he will articulate his reply as a private citizen willing to do whatever he can to safeguard the honor of his own city, just as he did during his chancellorship serving the Florentine republic. Likewise, he intends to recall at once all the slanders by the anonymous enemy of Florence to later examine them one by one, as he would do in front of the members of a jury. These preliminary notes by Salutati allow his most erudite readers to understand the nuanced nature of the text, skillfully combining epideictic and judicial rhetoric to dismantle the Milanese propaganda of Loschi.

As Baldassarri has pointed out, the two humanists compete through the same sources—Cicero and the Bible—in terms of both content and language. The presence of Cicero looms large already in the letter to Pietro Turchi that Salutati wrote to introduce his *Contra maledicum*: "I was compelled to act by the offense given to my country and by my sense of duty toward our mystic mother—to whom we must feel eternally in debt, whatever the sacrifice."[19] This passage would certainly sound familiar to Quattrocento humanists, reviving their memory of similar formulas in Cicero's writings. More specifically, Salutati's "licet patriae moveret iniuria debitumque quo tenemur huic mysticae genitrici" is modeled after Cicero's "patria, quae communis est parens omnium nostrum" (*Cat.* I.17) and echoes analogues phrases in *De Officiis* (I.17.58) and *De legibus* (II.5). Relatedly, Salutati draws on the pseudo-Ciceronian *Rhetorica ad Herennium* (III.3.4–5) to warn his audience of his intention: throughout the text, he will focus on the arguments of justice ("partes iustitiae") and those of fortitude ("partes fortitudinis") to restore the dignity and standing of Florence.

The rhetorical competition between Salutati and Loschi is palpable also at the level of their respective textual repertoires—that is, of the various texts by Cicero that each decides to revisit. While Loschi, as noted, started his *Invective* with echoes from the first speech against Catiline, Salutati's opening letter to Toschi mimics a passage from the preliminary speech in the oration against Verres (i.e., *In Quintum Caecilium divinatio*, section 1): he imagines a dialogue with himself (Lino di Coluccio), asking whether it would be appropriate, at the age of seventy-three, to change the habits of a lifetime and, for the first time ever, "turn your private pen to composing a biting invective." Cicero's *De Senectute* (section 55) provides the script for Salutati's warning about age and experience favoring the elderly when it comes to rhetorical, rather than physical, competitions. Upon careful reading, Loschi's text lacks "order," "purpose," ability to persuade, and is replete with "commonplace clichés." Once again in a silent dialogue with himself that owes to Cicero as well as to Petrarch, Salutati writes: "I had to laugh to myself and think: 'The fellow who dictated this is immature either in age or in learning, motivated entirely by impulse and lacking any power of speech or reason [. . .].'" He also rephrases a passage in *Nicomachean Ethics* (I.4), where Aristotle had emphasized that young men lack experience as well as rational control and are thus unable of political participation; similarly, Salutati chastises the excessive self-confidence of his anonymous, unexperienced opponent: "when it comes to speech, it is harder than you may suppose for a young man to best an old one. Although age gives way to youth in all physical exercises, it usually surpasses it easily in speech, as old age is more loquacious."

[19] Salutati, *Political Writings*, 168–69.

Another text by Cicero that was widely employed in the intellectual circles of Florence was *De inventione*. Echoes of it loom large the way in which Salutati unmakes the arguments of Loschi about the primacy of either Milan or Florence, borrowing from the Roman oral in terms of both language and content. When criticizing the *Invectiva in Florentinos* for its ineffective opening, Salutati calls it a "vitiosum" and "commutabile exordium," following Cicero's *De inventione* and the spurious *Rhetorica ad Herennium*—that is, an "inept beginning" wherein identical slurs could easily apply to any contingent target. "Is there any lord, any prince or any community at all"—Salutati asks—"against which these accusations could not be hurled, if one wants to give way to uncontrollable rage?" Shifting from Loschi's mishandling of rhetorical technicalities to his rival ideological agenda, he caustically continues: "If the selfsame words were directed against your lord, who would make the case that they are wide of the mark? What else has to be changed but the word 'tyrant' in place of 'citizens' and the singular for the plural?"[20]

Salutati follows in the footsteps of Cicero—and his critique of Mark Antony in the second *Philippic*—also at the beginning of the third paragraph of *Contra maledicum*. Loschi (whose first name, Antonio, is reminiscent of Mark Antony) has overlooked, according to Salutati, that his whole argument rests on shaky premises ("by simply denying what is said, the entire case falls to pieces") and has thus made "a schoolboy error." These lines rephrase Cicero's statement that "to make an objection to an adversary that the latter can overturn with a word, halting the prosecution's efforts"[21] disqualifies someone both as an orator and as man. A few lines later, Salutati draws again on *De inventione* to reject Loschi's whole enterprise as a "turpis argumentatio": namely, a slanderous and deliberate attempt to undermine the solid reputation of someone. And with a brilliant, good-humored twist of words, he claims it is hard to believe that someone named Loschi calls the Florentines "blind": the Latin word "Luscus" means, in fact, both "sightless" and "doubtful."

Loschi's invective does not meet the basic standards of rhetoric also for its careless terminology, as Salutati contends appealing to Cicero as the supreme judge on rhetorical matters:

> Nothing is further from eloquence than to use words that are unclear or that have a sense different from your meaning. The sibyls and the oracles

---

[20] Quoted from Baldassarri, "Hard Times," 73–74.
[21] Quoted from ibid., 74.

may speak in this way, not orators, whose worst vice, as the greatest orator Cicero tells us, is to "distance oneself from daily speech and the customary practices of common sense.[22]

Unfolding at the very beginning of the fifteenth century, the Loschi-Salutati controversy set the stage for later and influential projects, bringing classical rhetoric to bear on contemporary and divisive political questions. Leonardo Bruni—the disciple as well as the successor of Salutati as the chancellor of the Florentine republic—authored what would become one of the most widely read and discussed rhetorical compositions of Italian Humanism.

Between Aristotle and Cicero: Bruni's Militant Painting of Florence

Notoriously celebrated as a vigorous expression of the political and philosophical ideals at the core of humanist political thought, as well as a vibrant manifesto of Quattrocento Florentine republicanism, Bruni's *Laudatio Florentinae Urbis* (Panegyric of the City of Florence) has recently found renewed prominence among historians and political theorists. As is well known, Bruni argues and seeks to demonstrate that the republic of Florence is the natural heir of ancient Rome, capable of pursuing freedom at home and expansionism abroad, and that the institutions and values of its popular government play a vital role to continuously promote virtue across the citizenry at large. By doing so, as someone aspiring to replace Coluccio Salutati as the chancellor of the Florentine Republic, Bruni interestingly gives an unprecedented democratic twist to the educational and moral vision championed by Petrarch. Italian humanists should not focus exclusively on the soulcraft of political elites; they should also encourage and actively sustain the development of citizens' intellectual potential, itself a fundamental precondition for a virtuous republic capable of merging freedom and glory. It is this "adaptive pressure"[23] that makes the *Laudatio* a source to mine for capturing the afterlives of Petrarch's reformist agenda at the crossroads of rhetoric and politics.

[22] Ibid.
[23] Hankins, *Virtue Politics*.

The cornerstone of Bruni's rhetorical masterpiece, one that owes significantly to the moral and political philosophy of Aristotle, is that Florentines' virtue is a matter both of distinguished ancestry and of habitual practice. Not only does Florence legitimately claim a place of prominence by hereditary right; it also deserves to shine most brightly on the chessboard of Italian and foreign affairs because it has developed and internalized the habit of sound behavior by means of practical reasoning. Accordingly, it paradigmatically exemplifies two beliefs at the core of humanist virtue politics: namely, that the legitimacy of political authority is, first and foremost, a moral one, grounded in excellence of character and intellect; and that membership in the ruling class is ultimately a question of merit more than birth, of proven virtue more than wealth and lineage.[24] Descending from the most magnificent founders of ancient times (the citizens of Rome), they are by default the noblest of all peoples, "for they are born from such parents who surpass by a long way all mortals in every sort of glory."[25] Even more importantly, as Bruni puts it, no war waged by Florence can be unjust, since the Florentines notoriously attack only for defensive reasons or to reappropriate territories after unlawful dispossessions.

This argument has important implications considering the historical and political context of the *Laudatio*. Writing soon after Florence's victorious self-defense against Gian Galeazzo Visconti and amidst Florence's ongoing attempts to conquer Pisa (which will eventually succeed in 1406), Bruni legitimizes *ex ante* any expansionistic project that, within the Mediterranean, the "daughter of Rome" might pursue. Again, the Florentine republic deserves to thrive beyond its borders not simply due to its glorious ancestry but, most importantly, because of its virtuous behavior, which shines through the widest number of its citizens. Bruni revisits and turns on its head Aristotle's famous dualism between the principle of quantity and that of quality: unlike other political communities, wherein educated and honorable individuals are just a fraction of the entire citizenry, Florentines stand out for the excellence of its majority. In Florence alone—Bruni writes, swimming against the tide of humanist republicanism—the greater part (*maior pars*) and the better part (*melior pars*) coincide. While Venetian humanist Lauro Quirini will continue to follow in the footsteps of Aristotle and contend, against the supporters of popular government, that "the greater part overcomes the

---

[24] See ibid., 39.
[25] Quoted from ibid., 220.

better one in a regime ruled by many" (*In multitudine praeterea maior pars meliorem vincit, De republica* (1449-1450), Bruni celebrates Florence for the quality of its quantity. By doing so, as Hankins has recently emphasized,[26] he expands the scale of virtue—no longer a quality of individuals or the few— and ascribes a moral personality to political regimes—a conglomeration of parts wherein the dominant one gives traction to the whole and determines its behavior.

The history of Florence—Bruni further claims—is filled with examples of its integrity, humbleness, and liberality, in times of war and peace alike, to the point that the Florentine republic has acquired the status of the common homeland of citizens and exiles across Italy. The rhetorical trope of dual citizenship owes significantly to Cicero's *De legibus*, wherein loyalty to Rome—the *communis patria* of all—demanded a higher allegiance than to the membership in the original political community. Petrarch himself, in a letter to Stefano Colonna, had described Rome as "communem patriam" and "matrem nostram" and, in another passage of *Fam*, as "the common country of everyone, head of public affairs, queen of the world and of cities."[27] However, already in the oration that Bruni took as the primary model for his *Laudatio* (i.e., Aelius Aristides's *Panathenaicus* in praise of Athens), the rhetoric of the *duplex patria* was functional to the ideological project of the author (though, in other compositions, the orator had celebrated Rome and rejected Greek nativism). "All of the Greeks," Aristides had written, "each privately called his original land his country, but all named Athens their common home"; a few paragraphs later, he referred to the object of his apology as "the country and common hearth of the race by its admission of those from everywhere."[28] While Baron called Bruni's enumeration of the virtues of Florence "long and tedious,"[29] as if they were but an almost literal borrowing from Aristides's eulogy of Athens, Hankins has emphasized the innovations of the *Laudatio* when detailing the credentials of Florentine virtue.[30] Florence's status as *princeps populus*—a phrase that Bruni had

---

[26] Cf. ibid., 222.
[27] Quoted from ibid., 583, n.22.
[28] Quoted from ibid., 584, n.26.
[29] Hans Baron, *The Crisis of the Early Italian Renaissance: Civic Humanism and Republican Liberty in an Age of Classicism and Tyranny* (Princeton, NJ: Princeton University Press, 1966), 193.
[30] For a more detailed analysis, see Antonio Santosuosso, "Leonardo Bruni Revisited: A Reassessment of Hans Baron's Thesis on the Influence of the Classics in the *Laudatio Florentinae Urbis*," in *Aspects of Late Medieval Government and Society: Essays Presented to J. R. Lander*, ed. J. G. Rowe (Toronto: University of Toronto Press, 1986), 25-51.

already employed in his *De Tyranno* and that he took from Livy's description of Rome—is demonstrated by its being not simply a safe place for those who are unfairly exiled, but also a bulwark against actual and potential tyrants. At the same time, it is at the level of conceptual analysis and historical context, more than in the list of human virtues, that Aristides's oration provided the ideal template for Bruni.[31] Despite its limits vis-à-vis prior and more influential sources (from the funeral speech of Pericles in the version of Thucydides to the *Panegyricus* of Isocrates), the *Panathenaicus* allowed for striking and more fitting analogies between the two cities.

Aristides's praise of the geographical position of Athens, felicitously combining the advantages of plains and mountains, inspires Bruni's remarks on how Florence epitomizes the golden mean between the steep Apennines and the luxuriant hills of Tuscany. Aristides's eulogy of the constitutional virtue of Athens, perfectly blending rule by one, few, and many, resonates in Bruni's celebration of the mixed government of Florence and its harmoniously organic interplay of institutions and offices. And the passages of the *Laudatio* emphasizing the intellectual leadership of Florence echo those in the *Panathenaicus* acclaiming Athens for its unrivaled cultural traction. However, the most important similarity lies in the geopolitical role of Athens and Florence in facing oppressive and counter-hegemonic projects in their respective areas. Just like the former had been, according to Aristides, the savior of Greece during the Persian wars, the latter becomes, in the portrait that Bruni paints, the champion of republican freedom in the wars against Gian Galeazzo Visconti.

As Hankins has pointed out, Bruni distinguishes neatly between the lawful expansion (*amplitudo*) of the Florentine Republic, pursued with integrity and the ability to offer protection (*patrocinium*) to weaker populations, and the oppressive lordship embodied by Visconti and his imperialism. Once again, the influence of Cicero's *De officiis*—a text that was highly influential among Italian humanists—is palpable in the deliberate use of the term "patrocinium" to qualify Florence's role as the "protectress" (*antistes*) of Italy. The word and the concept were, in fact, rooted in the intellectual repertoire of the *ius gentium* and described a form of subjection without servitude[32]—a voluntary support, or protectorate, granted by a superior state to its provinces within a legitimately hierarchical order. Cicero, in a passage quoted

---

[31] See Baron, *The Crisis of the Early Italian Renaissance*, 193–96.
[32] See Adam Woodhouse, "Subjection without Servitude: The Imperial Protectorate in Renaissance Political Thought," *Journal of the History of Ideas* 79, no. 4 (2018): 547–69.

also by Petrarch in his *De vita solitaria*, made a subtle yet important distinction between a protectorate (*patrocinium*) and an empire (*imperium*): while the former relies on "acts of kind service," such as "the fair and faithful defense" of allies,[33] the latter is all about greed, corruption, and injustice. In some of his later writings—specifically, Book I of *History of the Florentine People* (1415–1416), *On the Origins of Mantua* (1418), and, to a lesser extent, *The Constitution of the Florentines* (1439)—Bruni developed Cicero's insight even further. He presented Florence as a first among equals (*primus inter pares*) within a federation of free cities, united by a shared heritage, that would resemble the pre-Roman Etruscan League and offer a more egalitarian and effective paradigm of interstate governance. Lasting more than a thousand years, the federal model crafted by the Etruscans became an ideal reference for Bruni also in the realm of political practice, when he was a chancellor of Florence and, just like his mentor and predecessor Salutati, he routinely advocated for the federal leadership of Florence against, and as an alternative to, the centralized, exploitative domination by Milan under Gian Galeazzo and Filippo Maria Visconti.

Whether Bruni's account of Florence—its history, institutions, and public virtues—should be read as a shameless piece of propaganda or as a skillfully crafted and deliberately exaggerated representation according to the requirements of epideictic rhetoric, is a question worth considering. As Hankins noted, partly in reaction to Baron,[34] Bruni himself felt the need to respond to the earliest critics of his *Panegyric of Florence* who had dismissed it as a venomous distortion of reality. In a letter of 1440 to his long-term acquaintance Francesco Pizolpasso, archbishop of Milan, he calls it a "rhetorical exercise," a "boyish trifle" written when he was "fresh out of Greek class"; to support his self-defense, he recalls the nature and goals of this specific genre ("for a critic should consider this, too," as he reminds his detractors). "In civic panegyrics," in fact, "the speech is directed to those whom you wish to praise"; it "demands an audience" and, unlike judicial oratory and historical narrative, it is not supposed to respect the truth. Adorned with ekphrastic descriptions, panegyrics can extol past and present events "above the truth" (*supra veritatem*), "for the sake of rhetorical embellishment" (*ornandi causa*).[35] Yet, as Italian "civic humanists" knew too well, Cicero

---

[33] Quoted from Hankins, *Virtue Politics*, 584 n.31.
[34] Hankins, "Rhetoric, History, and Ideology," 160.
[35] Quoted from ibid., 161.

had urged orators and historians alike to master the art of *ornatio*, as to inspire their readers more cogently, "let some truths stand out more clearly"[36] (*Brutus*), and paint human vices and virtues as vividly as possible (*Epistulae familiares*). The likeliness of truth by means of plausible *exempla*, in fact, poignantly ties the audience to the orator and allows the historian to teach and inspire his public more effectively than by just presenting unadorned facts. Having forged his style through the reading of Cicero and closely following in the footsteps of the classical rhetorical tradition, Bruni simply does not see rhetoric and history as mutually exclusive. This intellectual and methodological axiom reflects extensively on his writings, allowing him to nuance the line between fact and fiction, sincerity and honesty, in the interest of edification and reform.

At the same time, modern readers must not neglect the specific political and moral philosophy that underpins the *Laudatio*, with its emphasis on virtuous behavior as the ground for political legitimacy and the connection it makes between virtue (individual, collective, and across generations), political equality, and political liberty. Aristotle's *Rhetoric* was a key text for the Italian humanists who wrote on nobility of character and its public implications, as it linked the praise of noble qualities to the scope and purpose of a panegyric and equated the extolment of a man's virtue with the call for a generalized behavior in line with it. Yet, Bruni pushes such time-honored tropes in new directions. He calls for "an enlivening competition in the virtues to be poured in the spirits of citizens" as the foundation of healthy republics. He also emphasizes the intergenerational dimension of this fervor for probity, so that each new progeny can actualize its inherited virtue and enliven, "as though in a mirror," the connection between past, present, and future (as he argues a few years after the *Panegyric* in the preface to his translation of Plutarch's *Life of Aemilius Paulus*, written in 1407–1409). Finally, free institutions and the equality typical of popular government are crucial for encouraging and safeguarding virtuous behavior among citizens, turning its zealous pursuit by those in office into a public school of virtue (as Bruni will repeat in 1427 in the *Oration for Nanni Strozzi*, a text that—just like the *Laudatio*—significantly bends historical facts to ideological purposes). In a passage of this second civic panegyric, Bruni eulogizes Florentine's institutional life according to the foundational principles of humanist "virtue politics":

---

[36] Quoted from ibid., 167.

We do not tremble beneath the rule of one man who would lord it over us, nor are we slaves to the rule of a few. Our liberty is equal for all, obeying only to the laws, and is free from the fear of men. The hope of attaining distinction [or office] and of raising oneself up is the same for all, provided one applies industry, has talent, and follows a sound and serious way of life. Our city looks for virtue and probity in its citizens. Anyone who has these qualities is thought to be sufficiently well born to govern the republic.[37]

Conclusion

The writings of Bruni—and his civic panegyrics specifically—encapsulate the intellectual creed of Italian humanism. They compellingly and consistently emphasize the foundational role of *studia humanitatis* (including the study of rhetoric) in the zealous pursuit of virtue, the importance of integrity and nobility of character in the construction of political legitimacy, and the relevance of all of the above for the preservation of political freedom and equality. They also remind us of the breadth and depth of fifteenth-century civic humanists' mastery of the rules and sources of classical rhetoric, dexterously employed on the battlefield of eloquence and bended to serve rival political agendas (as in the Loschi-Salutat controversy). At the same time, Bruni's work provides a striking term of comparison to capture the fault lines separating the champions of humanist "virtue politics," such as Petrarch and Bruni, and the Columbus of a new political world in the early sixteenth century—Machiavelli. The two Florentines authored two majestic histories of their common city—Bruni's *History of the Florentine People* (1415/1416–1442) and Machiavelli's *Florentine Histories* (1520–1525)—that differed profoundly in terms of purposes, audiences, and lessons drawn, thus amplifying the "great gulf" between their moral and political philosophies.[38] Though mining the political history of Florence through the same sources, their respective analyses and prescriptions reveal significant divergences in terms of their account of the shortcomings of the republic and the most effective solutions. Once again, Bruni makes a case for a virtue-centered approach to the pathologies of Florentine politics: following diligently in the footsteps of Aristotle, he identifies the "popolo"—a term broadly encompassing the

---

[37] Quoted from Hankins, *Virtue Politics*, 227.
[38] Ibid., 476.

middle classes of Florentine society—with the living repository of moderation and civic virtue, capable of taming the equally disruptive extremes of arrogance (in the case of the magnate families) and incivility (in the case of the lowest strata). On his account, the predominance of vice over virtue is what made Florence endlessly plagued by internal divisions, and government based on meritocratic inclusivity and civic friendship is the only way out of the quicksand of factionalism. Francesco Patrizi of Siena—one of the leading intellectuals right before the generation of Machiavelli and Guicciardini—will encapsulate the core idea of Italian humanism when, in his *How to Found a Republic* (1461/1471), he will present the empowerment of virtue-driven individuals as the foremost condition for any republican government to last. Machiavelli, on the contrary, does not share in this axiomatic belief: virtue, traditionally understood, has no preservative power in the realm of public affairs. He firmly rejects the humanist conceptualization of good government as the natural byproduct of rational self-control by properly trained statesmen. Consistent with his realism and his signature emphasis on the "effectual truth" of things, the secretary of the Second Chancery of the Republic of Florence is primarily concerned with what human beings do, not with what they should do. According to him, a reform of public affairs, especially in Florence, is possible only by rethinking the way in which the various parts of society interact, without excluding any of them; by embracing and channeling conflict as a healthy venue to vent competing interests; by resisting the naïve expectation that a public competition of virtue will enliven the citizenry at large. It demands, as Hankins poignantly put it, "a wise legislator to improve its institutions, not a humanist educator to teach virtue to its elites."[39] The difference between these two accounts of political leadership and, more generally, of politics—the humanists' in the early Renaissance and Machiavelli's at the dawn of a new century—could not be more vivid.

---

[39] Ibid., 481.

PART II
MODERN AND CONTEMPORARY THEMES

7

Demagoguery, Populism, and Political Culture in Cooper's *The American Democrat*

Daniel Kapust

Introduction

Demagoguery has, in spite of America's recent experience with the phenomenon, seen less interest than populism among political theorists.[1] If we take demagoguery to be, as Knott describes it in a recent monograph, a form of politics "appealing to public prejudices" with the result that demagogues "lead the people to betray their true interests," and populism to be an anti-elitist and anti-pluralist form of politics, this is not all that surprising.[2] After all, we are living in something of a populist moment, and while populists will often be labeled demagogues, the latter term has gone out of fashion in scholarly discourse, Knott's fine book notwithstanding. As Roberts-Miller, an important rhetoric scholar working on demagoguery, described it in 2005, "rhetoricians have moved away from the topic of demagoguery."[3]

Contemporary interest in populism and the relative neglect of demagoguery are not entirely surprising, then, and yet such a turn is striking in the American context given that, as Tulis has remarked, one of the most canonical

---

[1] There are exceptions, notably Knott's *The Lost Soul of the American Presidency: The Decline into Demagoguery and the Prospects for Renewal*. Roberts-Miller remarks, "It's a commonplace that we live in an era of demagogues." Patricia Roberts-Miller, *Demagoguery and Democracy* (New York: The Experiment, 2017), 1.

[2] Stephen F. Knott, *The Lost Soul of the American Presidency: The Decline into Demagoguery and the Prospects for Renewal* (Lawrence: University Press of Kansas, 2019), 5. On populism, anti-elitism, and anti-pluralism, see both Jan-Werner Müller, *What Is Populism?* (Philadelphia: University of Pennsylvania Press, 2016) and Cas Mudde and Cristobal Rovira Kaltwasser, *Populism: A Very Short Introduction* (Oxford: Oxford University Press, 2017).

[3] Patricia Roberts-Miller, "Democracy, Demagoguery, and Critical Rhetoric," *Rhetoric & Public Affairs* 8, no. 3 (2005): 461.

texts in American political thought—the *Federalist*—"literally begins and ends with" demagogues, with both Ceasar and Tulis suggesting that the federal system was designed, at least in part, to check demagoguery.[4] But it is also surprising for a less obvious reason: America produced a writer who, in the midst of its nineteenth-century period of democratization, identified demagoguery as one of the chief problems of American political life while seeking to educate his readers about its dangers and its signs. That writer is James Fenimore Cooper, and the text is his 1838 *The American Democrat*.[5]

Cooper has seen better days in terms of critical interest, at least if we take to heart Person's claim that Cooper's "reputation and the presence of his novels even on college reading lists have waned in recent years."[6] His place in English literature departments aside, to say that *The American Democrat* has gotten little attention from *political theorists* is uncontroversial; a search of *JSTOR* within political science journals for the terms "the American democrat" and "Cooper" yields only fifteen hits, of which only four appeared after 1990, and only one of which is centrally concerned with Cooper himself.[7] This paucity is in spite of the fact that Cooper was one of America's first great novelists, and that *The American Democrat* features a variety of arguments akin to what we can find in his contemporaries Tocqueville and Mill— arguments about the tyranny of the majority, or the threat that democracy poses to individualism.[8] To be sure, this neglect may reflect, at least in part, both the history of the book's production and the reaction with which the book was met. John Orville Taylor had invited Cooper to write the book "for a series he had recently launched"; Cooper completed the book's manuscript in September 1837, but the series never came to be, and Cooper wound up publishing it on his own.[9]

---

[4] Jeffrey K. Tulis, "The Rhetorical Presidency," in *The Rhetorical Presidency* (Princeton, NJ: Princeton University Press, 2017), 27.; James Ceasar, *Presidential Selection* (Princeton, NJ: Princeton University Press, 1979), 318–27.

[5] On this point, see Caroline Winterer, "Classical Oratory and Fears of Demagoguery in the Antebellum Era," in *Classical Antiquity and the Politics of America: From George Washington to George W. Bush*, ed. Michael Meckler (Waco, TX: Baylor University Press, 2006).

[6] Leland Person, "Introduction," in *A Historical Guide to James Fenimore Cooper*, ed. Leland S. Person (Oxford: Oxford University Press, 2007), 4.

[7] The piece I have in mind, and with which I generally agree, is Chris Barker, "Demagoguery and Mental Independence in James Fenimore Cooper's Political Writings," *American Political Thought* 4, no. 4 (2015): 588–611.

[8] Railton notes, "Though it appears doubtful, it is possible that Cooper had read at least part of the Frenchman's study." Stephen Railton, *Fenimore Cooper: A Study of His Life and Imagination* (Princeton, NJ: Princeton University Press, 1978), 165.

[9] This choice was just as well for, as Franklin puts it, "Cooper's self-publication . . . no doubt protected him from the negative effects that wider circulation and notice would have caused." As

The book itself also seems to have been controversial in substance: Mencken, who penned an introduction to the 1931 edition, called it "the shrewdest and the most offensive" of Cooper's writings about America after his return from an extended stay in Europe.[10] Because the work was the product of "the first American to write about Americans in a really frank spirit"[11] and because it was so critical of American democracy, "poor Cooper got the name of a sniffish and unpatriotic fellow, and was accused of all sorts of aristocratic pretension, immensely obnoxious to the free citizens of a free and glorious state."[12]

Yet Cooper's book is of interest precisely because of its pedagogical aims, given both the moment in which it was written and Cooper's focus on demagoguery.[13] It is also of interest from the perspective of the history of political thought because it takes part in a long tradition of anti-demagogic texts, ultimately traceable to Plutarch. Unlike Plutarch, however, Cooper's account straddles two different ways of approaching the problem of demagoguery, the first of which is consonant with the decidedly pejorative account common in late-eighteenth- and early-nineteenth-century America (with its origins in Plutarch), and the second of which focuses less on the character of the demagogue and more on what demagogic speakers do. The first account, I'll suggest, is moralistic (or Plutarchean), while the other is discourse-centered, a point I'll make through a turn to the work of Patricia Roberts-Miller. I'll also suggest that Cooper's account of demagoguery is illuminating in light of contemporary concerns with populism. To put things schematically, Cooper's flattering demagogue is—despite his not using the term "populist" or "populism"—recognizably populist, whether we look to the account of Mudde or Müller: his demagogue is anti-elitist and, at times, anti-pluralist. I will argue that Cooper's moralistic account suffers from structural defects common

---

Cooper himself wrote of the work in July 1838, "Democrat sells slowly." Wayne Franklin, *James Fenimore Cooper: The Later Years* (New Haven, CT: Yale University Press, 2017), 185–87. Or, as Railton remarks, "*The American Democrat* was neither published in Europe nor purchased in America." Railton, *Fenimore Cooper: A Study of His Life and Imagination*, 169.

[10] H. L. Mencken, "Introduction," in *The American Democrat*, by James Fenimore Cooper (Indianapolis, IN: Liberty Fund, 1959), xi.

[11] Cooper remarked that the book could also have had the name "something like 'Anti-Cant.'" Quoted in Franklin, *James Fenimore Cooper: The Later Years*, 188.

[12] Mencken, "Introduction," x–xi.

[13] As Watts put it, "As historians of post-revolutionary America have demonstrated ... by the 1820s the roots of a growing market society had begun to undermine the foundations of a traditional, hierarchical republic." Steven Watts, "Through a Glass Eye, Darkly," *Journal of the Early Republic* 13, no. 1 (1993): 60.

to *all* moralistic accounts of demagoguery, while his discourse-centered account points toward ways in which demagogic—and populist—appeals would find less purchase in political discourse through a process of mass education and the elite practice of rhetoric.

I'll make this argument in three phases. In the following section, I'll briefly describe the accounts of demagoguery and populism—from the work of Roberts-Miller and Müller, respectively—that I'll be relying on in this chapter, and explain how the two accounts relate to each other. To put things schematically, I'll suggest that while all populist political actors are demagogues, not all demagogues are populists. Then, I'll make the case for reading Cooper's *The American Democrat* in light of an anti-demagogic tradition inaugurated by Plutarch. I do so by discussing Cooper's potential knowledge of Plutarch, the ways in which Plutarch shaped pejorative accounts of demagoguery in late-eighteenth-century America, and Plutarch's account of demagoguery in *How to Tell a Flatterer from a Friend* and the *Life of Alcibiades*. *The American Democrat* is the focus of the subsequent section, in which I enumerate just why Cooper was so worried about demagoguery given the centrality of public opinion to American political life, before turning from Cooper's diagnosis to his treatment of the problem. I conclude by exploring the weakness of some of Cooper's moralistic solutions, while suggesting that other themes in his book—especially those involving mass education and elite discourse, and his diagnosis of the relationship between demagoguery and what we might term populism—are interesting potential remedies to demagogic rhetoric *and* populist politics.

Demagogues and Populists

Prior to turning to my analysis, though, I want briefly to introduce Roberts-Miller's account of demagoguery, an account that I find quite fruitful, and put it into conversation with two prominent accounts of populism.[14] Roberts-Miller delineates two ways of thinking about demagoguery, tracing one to Plutarch, for whom "demagogues are rhetors just looking out for themselves who pretend to be populists and who rouse the ignorant masses through

---

[14] While I focus on her more recent *Demagoguery and Democracy* and *Rhetoric and Demagoguery*, Roberts-Miller's 2005 article, "Democracy Demagoguery, and Critical Rhetoric," is also quite helpful. Patricia Roberts-Miller, "Democracy, Demagoguery, and Critical Rhetoric," *Rhetoric & Public Affairs* 8, no. 3 (2005): 459–76.

appeal to emotion."[15] A demagogue on the traditional account, then, speaks falsely, is vicious, feigns populism, and is strategic. The problem with such an account—which Roberts-Miller rejects—is that we rarely know if a speaker is lying or the reality of a person's character, not all appeals to populism are demagogic (and vice versa), and the demagogue may in fact be "sincere and honest," rather than strategic.[16] For Roberts-Miller, such an account of demagoguery replicates arguments from identity that are in fact the stuff of demagoguery: "Demagoguery is about identity. It says that complicated policy issues can be reduced to a binary of us (good) versus them (bad)."[17] In other words, such an account recreates the very in-group/out-group dynamics that create the space for demagoguery in the first place (the demagogue is not like us or our leaders). Instead, Roberts-Miller offers the following definition:

> Demagoguery is *discourse* [emphasis added] that promises stability, certainty, escape from the responsibilities of rhetoric by framing public policy in terms of the degree to which and the means by which (not whether) the outgroup should be scapegoated for the current problems of the in-group.[18]

This way of thinking about demagoguery focuses on rhetoric (as she puts it elsewhere, demagoguery is "a damaging way to argue when the stakes are high") and what it does, rather than the speaker's character or the truth value of statements embedded in rhetoric.[19] With respect to solutions, most important for Roberts-Miller is that we cultivate practices that lend themselves to public deliberation, rather than try to figure out if a rhetor is a good or bad person and describe them as such.

Now a few words about populism, for which I am indebted to the analysis of Jan-Werner Müller. For Müller, populism is "a particular *moralistic imagination of politics*," an imagination that has two key features. First, populist politics is anti-elite, pitting the "people against elites who are deemed corrupt or in some other way morally inferior."[20] Second, populist politics is

---

[15] Roberts-Miller, *Demagoguery and Democracy*, 21.
[16] Roberts-Miller, *Demagoguery and Democracy*, 31.
[17] Roberts-Miller, *Demagoguery and Democracy*, 8.
[18] Roberts-Miller, *Demagoguery and Democracy*, 33. Compare the definition in Patricia Roberts-Miller, *Rhetoric and Demagoguery* (Carbondale: Southern Illinois University Press, 2019), 173: "Demagoguery is a polarizing discourse that promises stability, certainty, and escape from the responsibilities of rhetoric through framing public policy in terms of the degree to which and means by which (not whether) the out-group should be punished/scapegoated for the current problems of the in-group."
[19] Roberts-Miller, *Rhetoric and Demagoguery*, 172.
[20] Müller, *What Is Populism?*, 19–20.

anti-pluralist, in that "populists claim that they, *and only they*, represent the people." As such, populism involves "a *pars pro toto* argument and a claim to exclusive representation."[21] It is thus "an exclusionary form of identity politics," pitting the people against both corrupt elites and, in certain forms of right populism, non-elite out-groups.[22]

Suffice to say, Roberts-Miller's account of demagoguery shares key features with Müller's account of populism. Both rely on claims about identity and are, in fact, forms of identity politics; both rely on the construction of in- and out-groups; and both tend to equate a *part* of the people with the *whole* of the people. What differentiates Roberts-Miller's demagogue from Müller's populist, it seems to me, is that the populist is necessarily anti-elite, while the demagogue need not be—any out-group will do (though of course plenty of demagogues are anti-intellectual, or deploy the trope of what Roberts-Miller terms, following Saurette, "epistemological populism").[23] And while the right populist may well focus their energy on stigmatizing lower-status out-groups, not all populists do so; the demagogue will, however, likely (though not always) scapegoat not simply out-groups but marginalized out-groups—racial, religious, or other minorities.

Cooper and the Anti-Demagogic Tradition

I'll turn now to the case for locating Cooper in a moralistic anti-demagogic tradition with origins in Plutarch. This case is twofold, centering, first, on the likelihood that Cooper would have known Plutarch's works, at least in English, and, second, on the way in which Plutarch's account of demagoguery shaped how writers understood the phenomenon in late-eighteenth- and

---

[21] Ibid., 20.

[22] Ibid., 3, 23. Mudde and Kaltwasser's account shares much with Müller. The definition of populism is "a thin-centered ideology that considers society to be ultimately separated into two homogeneous and antagonistic camps, 'the pure' people and the corrupt elite,' and which argues that politics should be an express of the volonte generale (general will) of the people." Mudde and Kaltwasser, *Populism: A Very Short Introduction*. Like Müller, they distinguish between pluralism and populism (7), but unlike Müller, they also draw a sharp distinction between populism and what they term elitism, which holds "that 'the people' are dangerous, dishonest, and vulgar, and that 'the elite' are superior ... in moral, but also ... cultural and intellectual terms" (7). Also unlike Müller, their account relies on the Rousseauean concept of the general will, and thus puts populism in opposition to representative democracies. As a result, populism would seem to go hand in hand with both representation and modern democratic theory and practice, a point suggested in, e.g., their claim that "[s]cholars of populism share the idea that it is a modern phenomenon" (21).

[23] Roberts-Miller, *Rhetoric and Democracy*, 133.

early-nineteenth-century American intellectual life. Not only, then, do I think it is reasonable that Cooper would have known Plutarch and that Plutarch's account of demagoguery illuminates Cooper's; I also think that given the educational project of *The American Democrat* it is fruitful to read the text in the anti-demagogic tradition.

Let's start by turning to Cooper's likely knowledge of Plutarch. Cooper grew up on the frontier, spending a good deal of his earliest years in Otsego, New York. Nonetheless, he "was provided amply with the physical comforts and luxuries which could be transported into [New York's] interior."[24] Cooper's father was very successful—judge, member of Congress, large landowner—and we know from Cooper himself that when his father had a large home constructed for the family, it featured a library: "This room had two windows; one on the east, and one on the south, and the book cases stood in a recess, between the end of the pantry and the partition beyond."[25] Cooper does not describe the contents of the library, though his daughter, Susan Fenimore Cooper, later related that her father "always read a great deal, in a desultory way. Military works, travels, Biographies, History—and novels!"[26]

Cooper's father sent him to study in Albany with Reverend Thomas Ellison in 1801, study that included a good deal of Latin, especially Cicero and Virgil. There, Franklin writes, Cooper improved on a "basic facility with Latin" that he had first studied in Burlington, New Jersey, with the result that, as Cooper later wrote to William Jay, his fellow student with Ellison and son of John Jay, in a "fictitious letter," that Ellison "compelled you and me to begin Virgil with the Eclogues, and Cicero with the knotty phrase that opens the oration in favour of the poet Archias."[27] Indeed, suggests Franklin, Ellison would have had Cooper learning "to scan Latin as well as to pronounce and translate it correctly," study that "went far beyond what Cooper and Jay were to encounter even in their classes at Yale College."[28] While Cooper's Latin was thus quite good, and would have met the prerequisites for matriculating at

---

[24] His sister, Hannah, wrote of James and their brothers that they "show plainly they have been bred in the Woods," and are thus "very wild." Quoted by James Franklin Beard, *The Letters and Journals of James Fenimore Cooper*, Vol. I (Cambridge, MA: Harvard University Press, 1960), 4.

[25] James Fenimore Cooper, *The Legends and Traditions of a Northern County* (Cooperstown, NY: The Freeman's Journal Co., 1936), 202.

[26] Ibid., 183.

[27] Wayne Franklin, *James Fenimore Cooper: The Early Years* (New Haven, CT: Yale University Press, 2007), 46.

[28] Ibid., 46.

Yale[29] (he did not graduate, having been expelled for disciplinary reasons), he fell short of one of the entry requirements for Yale: the ability to read Greek. His father arranged for him to be tutored in Greek, with the result that he began his formal studies at Yale in February 1803. From the sound of it, he never mastered Greek.[30]

Cooper would likely not have read Plutarch in Greek. But even if he didn't, there is good circumstantial reason to think that he would have known Plutarch given how widely circulating Plutarch was in late-eighteenth- and early-nineteenth-century America—Richard writes that "Translations of Plutarch's *Lives* flooded the early American republic," and Reinhold describes eighteenth-century America as "a veritable *aetas Plutarchana*."[31] As Wright argued, evidence regarding the offerings of "general stores" and advertisements in newspapers illustrate that "standard translations of the Greek and Roman classics, particularly Plutarch's *Lives*, were exceedingly popular" on the frontier.[32] Richard thoroughly documents the wide variety of late-eighteenth- and early-nineteenth-century American figures who knew Plutarch well, including both John and John Quincy Adams, Alexander Hamilton, and Benjamin Franklin. Franklin, intriguingly, invoked demagogues from Athenian history (presumably including Alcibiades) to criticize those in Britain advocating war against the colonies.[33] Richard also shows Plutarch's popularity in the following century, including, among nineteenth-century literary figures, Hawthorne, Emerson, and Thoreau. If, then, Cooper was anything like late-eighteenth-century American writers or his nineteenth-century peers, he would have known Plutarch. And while I have not found any direct mentions of Plutarch by name in Cooper's writings, there is a likely reference to Plutarch in his 1823 novel, *The Pilot*, in which the character Edward Griffith quotes the Latin phrase "*vox et preterea nihil*," a phrase that echoes "a Spartan's description of a nightingale plucked of its feathers, according to Plutarch."[34]

---

[29] As recorded in *The Laws of Yale-College*, "no one shall be admitted, unless he shall be found able to read, translate, and parse Tully, Virgil, and the Greek Testament, and to write true Latin in prose." Yale College, *The Laws of Yale-College* (New Haven, CT: Thomas Green and Son, 1800), 9.

[30] Franklin cites Cooper's "half-boast" in a letter about his study of Greek at Yale: "he had 'never studied but *one* regular lesson in Homer'" (Vol. I, 47).

[31] Carl J. Richard, "Plutarch and the Early American Republic," in *A Companion to Plutarch*, ed. Mark Beck (Oxford: Blackwell, 2013), 598; Meyer Reinhold, *Classica Americana: The Greek and Roman Heritage in the United States* (Detroit: Wayne State University Press, 1984), 252.

[32] Louis B. Wright, *Culture on the Moving Frontier* (Bloomington: Indiana University Press, 1955), 116.

[33] Carl J. Richard, *The Founders and the Classics: Greece, Rome, and the American Enlightenment* (Cambridge, MA: Harvard University Press, 1994), 210

[34] James Fenimore Cooper, *Sea Tales: The Pilot and Red Rover*, edited by Kay Seymour House and Thomas L. Philbrick (New York: Library of America, 1991), 88, 888.

That much on the case, albeit largely circumstantial, I want to make for Cooper's likely knowledge of Plutarch given his background and context. The other case I want to make for reading Cooper with Plutarch and the anti-demagogic tradition has to do with how he, and many other Americans, understood demagoguery, an understanding that was decidedly negative and emphasized the dishonest, irrational, and self-interested nature of demagogues. Cooper's use of the term "demagogue" ("a leader of the rabble," 120), to which I return below, echoes what we find in Webster's 1806 *Compendious Dictionary*: "a ringleader of a rabble or a faction."[35] This is a usage that we find in a range of late-eighteenth-century sources. Take, for instance, the *Federalist*: the first and last *Federalist Papers* treat the threat of demagogues, as noted above with Tulis. In *Federalist* 1, Hamilton puts the problem—and danger—succinctly:

> a dangerous ambition more often lurks behind the specious mask of zeal for the rights of the people, than under the forbidding appearances of zeal for the firmness and efficiency of government. History will teach us, that the former has been found a much more certain road to the introduction of despotism, than the latter, and that of those men who have overturned the liberties of republics, the greatest number have begun their career, by paying an obsequious court to the people . . . commencing demagogues, and ending tyrants.[36]

Hamilton's demagogues are obsequious courtiers: ambitious and deceptive, feigning zeal for the people.

In addressing the problem of the demagogue, Hamilton echoes concerns voiced at the Constitutional Convention. In Madison's notes on the convention,[37] the term "demagogue" (or "demagogues") appears eleven times. George Mason has the most theoretically sophisticated account of demagoguery and its dangers to republican government. Mason argues that, while demagoguery is an intrinsic danger in republican governments,

---

[35] James Fenimore Cooper, *The American Democrat* (Indianapolis: Liberty Fund, 1959), 120. Noah Webster, *A Compendious Dictionary of the English Language* (New Haven, CT: Hudson & Goodwin, 1806), 80.

[36] Alexander Hamilton, John Jay, and James Madison, *The Federalist*, edited by George W. Carey and James McClellan (Indianapolis: Liberty Fund, 2001), 3.

[37] The version consulted is James Madison, *The Debates on the Adoption of the Federal Constitution*, Vol. 5, edited by Jonathan Elliot (Washington, DC: LENOX HILL Pub. & Dist. Co. (Burt Franklin), 1827). I consulted an electronic version available via: https://oll.libertyfund.org/title/elliot-the-debates-on-the-adoption-of-the-federal-constitution-vol-5.

the design of the federal system will help to eliminate the threat of demagoguery:

> He admitted that notwithstanding the superiority of the Republican form over every other, it had its evils. The chief ones, were the danger of the majority oppressing the minority, and the mischievous influence of demagogues. The Genl. Government of itself will cure them. As the States will not concur at the same time in their unjust & oppressive plans, the General Govt will be able to check & defeat them, whether they result from the wickedness of the majority, or from the misguidance of demagogues.[38]

Mason's demagogues engage in injustice and oppression and, through their pernicious influence, can mislead the people of the states.

This brief survey of late-eighteenth-century figures suggests that common usage treated demagogues and demagoguery in a fashion that is decidedly pejorative, emphasizing the negative moral qualities of the demagogue (ambition, dishonesty, pandering), or the negative qualities of the people (the rabble) the demagogue seeks to mobilize. What we see in Webster, Hamilton, and Mason reflects one of the classic definitions of demagoguery in twentieth-century scholarship, advanced by Charles W. Lomas: "Demagoguery may be described as the process whereby skillful speakers and writers seek to influence public opinion by employing the traditional tools of rhetoric with complete indifference to truth. In addition, although demagoguery does not necessarily seek ends contrary to public interest, its primary motivation is personal gain."[39] Such an account centers on the fact that demagoguery involves "irrationality, populism, and emotionalism."[40]

In this regard, they are all reminiscent of Plutarch, a writer with whom eighteenth-century American intellectual culture was deeply familiar. I'm following, in making this claim about Plutarch's moralized account of demagoguery, Melissa Lane, who argues that Plutarch played a key role in the history of the term. With Plato, demagogue and related terms can be neutral or pejorative. When neutral, it can be made pejorative by the addition of an adjective (e.g., *aischra demegoria* at *Gorgias* 503a). Or, by contrast, it can be pejorative on its own, as in *Statesman*, where the term is put in opposition to the term "statesman," and demagogue (or rather *demalogikon*) has

---

[38] Madison, *The Debates on the Adoption of the Federal Constitution*, 415.
[39] Quoted in Roberts-Miller, "Democracy, Demagoguery, and Critical Rhetoric," 460.
[40] Ibid., 461.

a decidedly negative connotation. Aristotle, in turn, takes the term and gives "it a mainly, though not exclusively, pejorative sense"; this is especially the case at *Politics* 4.4.[41]

With Plutarch the term takes a form that is recognizable in the decidedly negative connotation of late-eighteenth-century American English that we've just surveyed. Plutarch, as Lane shows, distinguishes between the statesman and the demagogue, but unlike Plato, the distinction was not grounded "in an epistemological analysis." Those who studied philosophy, for Plutarch, might be statesmen rather than demagogues, but this was a function of philosophy helping to develop moral virtue rather than imparting particular knowledge. As a result, in Plutarch's writings, "the statesman-demagogue distinction became even more ardently moralistic while ever less clearly informative," and the term "demagogue" stands in need of no adjective to be made pejorative.[42]

Plutarch makes claims about or uses the term "demagogue(s)" across his writings,[43] but I want to focus on two texts in particular: his essay *How to Tell a Flatterer from a Friend* and the *Life of Alcibiades*. I've written elsewhere about Plutarch's essay *How to Tell a Flatterer from a Friend*, and given that the text isn't the focus of this chapter, and that Cooper may not have known it, in any case,[44] I won't say too much about it here. I do, though, want to make several points about the text given the relationship I'll try to describe between Plutarch and Cooper. First, and foremost, the essay is a sort of pedagogical text, seeking to provide Plutarch's immediate audience—C. Julius Antiochus Philopappus—and those like him with advice to combat flatterers. Philopappus, descended from the royal family of Commagene and, presumably, those like him are in special need of such advice given what Plutarch says of flatterers: "where renown and power attend, there do they throng and thrive."[45] Second, the essay provides its readers with a series of tests by which they can examine (*elengchetai* at 52.a) those they suspect of flattery and

---

[41] Melissa Lane, "The Origins of the Statesman–Demagogue Distinction in and after Ancient Athens," *Journal of the History of Ideas* 73, no. 2 (2012): 190.

[42] Ibid. 194.

[43] Plutarch uses three terms related to demagoguery: *demagogeo*, *demagogia*, and *demagogos*. As far I can tell, he uses these three words roughly seventy times across his corpus. For the details of their locations, see Daniel Wyttenbach, *Lexicon Plutarcheum*, Vol. I (Hildesheim, Georg Olms Verlagsbuchhandlung, 1962), 390–91.

[44] Reinhold, *Classica Americana*, 259, suggests that, prior to Emerson in particular, the *Moralia* was "little appreciated."

[45] Plutarch, *How to Tell a Flatterer from a Friend*, in *Moralia*, Vol. I, trans. Frank Cole Babbitt (Cambridge, MA: Harvard University Press, 2005), 49d.

figure out if they are "really like-minded," or rather "merely imitating" those they are pursuing. Third, the essay juxtaposes flattery with frank speech (*parrhesias* at 59a), positing that the friend speaking frankly deploys frank speech against "errors that are being committed; the pain which it causes is salutary and benignant."[46] Fourth, and finally, Alcibiades serves as the key example of a person who is both a flatterer *and* a demagogue.

Indeed, Plutarch refers to Alcibiades as "the greatest" of all flatterers and demagogues (*ton megalon... kolakon kai ta ton demagogon hon ho megistos Alkibiades*).[47] Alcibiades is marked less by ignorance than vice and, especially, the fact that he was adept at conforming his behavior to that of the audience with which he sought to ingratiate himself: "by making himself like to all these people and confirming his way to theirs he tried to conciliate them and win their favor [*edemagogei*]."[48] Alcibiades is thus something of an archetypical flatterer [*kolax*], in that "he has no abiding-place of character to dwell in, and... leads a life not of his own choosing but another's... he is constantly on the move from place to place, and changes his shape to fit his receiver."[49] Plutarch's flatterer-cum-demagogue and, by extension, Alcibiades, is like the chameleon (*chamaileontos*): "the chameleon can make himself like to every colour except white, and the flatterer, being utterly incapable of making himself to another in any quality that is really worthwhile, leaves no shameful thing unimitated."[50]

Arch-flatterer and demagogue: such themes are on full display in Plutarch's *Life of Alcibiades*, a text that, unlike the *Moralia*, would have been in wide circulation in late-eighteenth- and early-nineteenth-century America given the circulation of the *Lives* as a whole.[51] There, Plutarch likens Alcibiades to a chameleon, using just the same metaphor as in *How to Tell a Flatterer from a Friend*: "He had, as they say, one power which transcended all others, and proved an implement of his chase for men: that of assimilating and adapting himself to the pursuits and lives of others, thereby assuming more violent changes than the chameleon."[52] Alcibiades, that is, is even more flexible

---

[46] Ibid., 59d.
[47] Ibid., 52e.
[48] Ibid., 52e–f.
[49] Ibid., 52b.
[50] Ibid., 53d.
[51] While I've focused on the *Life of Alcibiades*, Plutarch uses the term "demagogue" or related terminology roughly seventy times, and Dryden's popular translation of the *Lives* features at least eighteen instances of the term.
[52] Plutarch, *Life of Alcibiades*, in *Plutarch's Lives*, Vol. 4, trans. Bernadotte Perrin (Cambridge, MA: Harvard University Press, 1959), 23.4.

than the chameleon; whereas the chameleon cannot make itself "white," Alcibiades, by contrast, "could associate with good and bad alike, and found naught that he could not imitate and practice."[53] Alcibiades had been driven to enter the public eye due largely to "his love of distinction and love of fame [*tes philotimias . . . kai tes philodoxias*]," each of which was the target of "his corrupters."[54] Ambitious and able to change his character, in effect, to suit his audience, no less than Demosthenes described Alcibiades as "a most able speaker in addition to his other gifts," and Plutarch reports that Alcibiades himself "thought that nothing should give him more influence with the people than the charm of his discourse [*tes tou logou charitos*]."[55] Once he entered political life, "he immediately humbled all the other popular leaders [*tous allous demagogous*]," a usage suggesting that Alcibiades, too, was a demagogue, for Plutarch.

What set him upon the path of eloquence? Plutarch reports that Alcibiades first happened to go to the Assembly when money was being disbursed to the people; hearing "a shout," he too offered the people funds. After he had done so, "The crowd clapped their hands and shouted for joy—so much so that Alcibiades forgot all about the quail which he was carrying in his cloak, and the bird flew away in a fright."[56] Plutarch's judgment of Alcibiades is as harsh as it is instructive for later accounts of demagoguery, with Plutarch describing the "exceeding wantonness of Alcibiades, and the stain of dissoluteness and vulgarity upon all his efforts to win the favour [*charin*] of the multitude [*tois pollois*]."[57] Though, to be fair to Alcibiades, while Plutarch describes it as "a disgrace to flatter the people for the sake of power [*to kolakeuein demon epi toi dunasthai*]," it is preferable to the "injustice" of Coriolanus, to whom Alcibiades is compared. In any case, Alcibiades is a case study in Plutarch's account of demagoguery: ambitious, adaptable, manipulative, and vicious.

Demagogic Threats to Democracy

Thus far, I've made the case for reading Cooper with Plutarch and the antidemagogic tradition he inaugurated. With this in mind, I want now to turn to

---

[53] Ibid., 23.4.
[54] Ibid., 6.2.
[55] Ibid., 10.2.
[56] Ibid., 10.1.
[57] Plutarch, *Comparison of Alcibiades and Coriolanus*, in *Plutarch's Lives*, Vol. 4, 1.3.

Cooper's *The American Democrat* to explore both his understanding of the problem of demagoguery and his broader pedagogical project. With respect to the latter, I refer to it as pedagogical because the work was, in Cooper's own words, aimed at "a commencement towards a more just discrimination between truth and prejudice."[58] The book is also a friendly critique of American democracy written by, as Cooper puts it of himself, "as good a democrat as there is in America."[59] The need for such good information is due in no small part to the fact that "in a democracy, the delusion that would elsewhere be poured into the ears of the prince, is poured into those of the people."[60] Structurally, then, the American people stand in a relationship to their deluders analogous to that of a prince and his courtiers, or Plutarch's addressee and his flatterers. And Cooper himself states, in his Preface, that the book "is written more in the spirit of censure than of praise, for its aim is correction," and what he intends to correct in particular are "popular errors" whose effects can be magnified by the sheer power of misled or erroneous "popular opinion."[61]

Why does America need such an education, for Cooper? America is a republic, "a government in which the pervading acknowledged principle is the right of the community," and thus "the sovereignty of the people."[62] Given the nature of the American republic, we can better understand why Cooper seeks to correct what he calls "popular errors"; as he remarks, "in a nation so much controlled by popular opinion, [errors] not only lead to injustice, but may lead to dissension. It is the duty of every citizen to acquire just notions of the terms of the bargain before he pretends to a right to enforce them."[63] And if it is their duty to acquire these notions, he views it as his duty to help impart them through the medium of print.[64]

Among the notions he wants to impart is the positive value of individualism. Cooper gives such high value to individualism that he states,

---

[58] Cooper, *The American Democrat*, xxiii.
[59] Ibid., xxiv.
[60] Ibid., xxiv.
[61] Ibid., xxvi, 19, 25.
[62] Ibid., 2.
[63] Ibid., 19, 25.
[64] In fact, Cooper had hoped, according to Beard, for *The American Democrat* to be a text used in schools, and Cooper also suggests, in a passage to which we return below, that both "the art of printing" and "cheap publications" have the effect of making the public as a whole less of "a rabble." In the end, as Beard (*The Letters and Journals*, Vol. 1, xxvii) points out, the book "was conceived for use as an elementary-school text." (Cooper's discussion of printing and publication is on page 120 of the text.)

"Individuality is the aim of political liberty," adding that "freedom of action and of being" are key ingredients in making someone "a freeman."[65] American democracy endangers individuality: "Numbers . . . may oppress as well as one or a few, and when such oppression occurs, it is usually of the worst character."[66] America's foundation in "publick rule" is at odds with individualism, and hence liberty. At the same time, "All greatness of character is dependant on individuality."[67] So, too, is happiness. Cooper's worry is that as the power of public opinion and the depth of public rule increase, so, too, will threats to individuality in America.

Public opinion, then, reigns in America and, because of its power, "the fraudulent and ambitious find a motive to mislead, and even to corrupt the common sentiment, to attain their ends."[68] Public opinion's power can bring about "private hypocrisy, causing men to conceal their own convictions when opposed to those of the mass."[69] "Mediocrity" is the endpoint of this elevation of public opinion, and the result is that America lacks the elevated cultural standards of other countries. But public opinion does not simply impede artistic and intellectual endeavor; it also tends to supplant the law and, in doing so, we see "the precise form in which tyranny is the most apt to be displayed in a democracy."[70]

In democracies, "men defer to publick opinion, right or wrong, quite as submissively as they defer to princes."[71] Cooper later urges the following as a set of principles "to be impressed on every man's mind, in letters of brass":

> That, in a democracy, the publick has no power that is not expressly conceded by the institutions, and that this power, moreover, is only to be used under the forms prescribed by the constitution. All beyond this, is oppression, when it takes the character of acts, and not unfrequently when it is confined to opinion.[72]

Readers of his account of public opinion and its dangers ought, then, to keep its danger in mind and, as would be the case with any power-holder, "The

---

[65] Ibid., 231.
[66] Ibid., 231.
[67] Ibid., 232.
[68] Ibid., 82.
[69] Ibid., 82–83.
[70] Ibid., 84.
[71] Ibid., 86.
[72] Ibid., 185.

publick ... is to be watched, in this country, as in other countries kings and aristocrats are to be watched."[73]

But the greatest threat to American democracy, given the power of public opinion, is demagoguery and, when we think back on what Cooper says about the dangers of public opinion—his use of the terms "misleading," "ambition," "fraud," and the like—we can see that demagogues and would-be demagogues are often on his mind, even if unmentioned. As he puts it in a chapter titled, aptly enough, "Of the Disadvantages of Democracy," "the people are peculiarly exposed to become the dupes of demagogues and political schemers, most of the crimes of democracies arising from the faults and designs of men of this character." In this first discussion of demagogues, then, demagogic qualities are familiar from Plutarch and the writers surveyed above. The people, in democracies, may act wrongly through "ignorance," but this ignorance—especially given the difficulty citizens in mass democracies have in seeking "to scrutinize and understand character"—is compounded by the activities of demagogues.[74] Thus, for Cooper, "The misleading of publick opinion in one way or another, is the parent of the principal disadvantages of a democracy, for in most instances it is first corrupting a community in order that it may be otherwise injured."[75] That the people are the objects of such characters' manipulations and deceits is unsurprising: as we saw above, "in a democracy, the delusion that would elsewhere be poured into the ears of the prince, is poured into those of the people."[76] Like Plutarch's powerful as they face flatterers, the American people are too easy a mark for demagogues.

We first encounter at length the nature and danger of demagogues, however, in the context of Cooper's discussion of "the duties of publick station," where he remarks, "The peculiar danger of a democracy, arises from the arts of demagogues."[77] In this discussion, he criticizes the would-be voter "who gives his vote, on any grounds, party or personal, to an unworthy candidate," as such a voter "violates a sacred publick duty, and is unfit to be a freeman."[78] Cooper emphasizes the duties of the individual citizen—duties which, when carried out, check "the peculiar sins of a democracy," all of which are rooted "in the democratical character of the institutions."[79] The particular concern

[73] Ibid., 187.
[74] Ibid., 81.
[75] Ibid., 85.
[76] Ibid., xxiv.
[77] Ibid., 100, 101.
[78] Ibid., 102.
[79] Ibid., 104.

in this chapter is public opinion, from which emerges "the particular form in which tyranny exhibits itself in a popular government." What he has in mind is, in essence, what we might elsewhere see termed tyranny of the majority: "in a democracy, resisting the wishes of the many, is resisting the sovereign, in his caprices."[80]

Cooper turns his full attention to demagogues, however, in the chapter titled "On Demagogues," beginning with a definition of the term ("a leader of the rabble"). For Cooper, the term's significance has shifted with the advent of printed literature, the result of which is that "cheap publications were placed within the reach of the majority," such that not *all* individuals can be said to be part of the rabble any longer.[81] What makes a group a rabble is that it loses "sight of that reason and respect for their own deliberately framed ordinances."[82] The demagogue can be understood by reference to their "peculiar office... to advance his own interests, by *affecting* [my emphasis] a deep devotion to the interests of the people." The term "demagogue," then, is pejorative in just the way it was for Plutarch, and Cooper's use relies upon the duplicity, ambition, and selfishness of the rhetor. Demagoguery is thus a function of intention—pursuing one's own interests—and deception (affectation). And it is in democracies, above all regimes, that demagogues are to be found, for there, "the body of the community possessing the power, the master he pretends to serve is best able to reward his efforts."[83] Given this dynamic, "[h]e who would be a courtier under a king, is almost certain to be a demagogue in a democracy."[84]

Cooper's Proposed Treatment for Demagoguery

How, then, does Cooper seek to educate his readers against the danger of demagogues, danger magnified by the sheer power of public opinion in America? Partly, he provides his reader with "some of the rules" that allow us to distinguish between true and false friends of the people, or what he terms "those who labor in behalf of the people on the general account, and those who labor in behalf of the people on their own account."[85] First, he

---

[80] Ibid., 103. On this point, and "despotic public opinion," see Barker, "Demagoguery and Mental Independence," 594.
[81] Ibid., 120.
[82] Ibid., 120–21.
[83] Ibid., 121.
[84] Ibid., 123.
[85] Ibid., 121.

points to the demagogue's "motive," which he thinks we can observe in the demagogue's actions. If we observe someone "constantly telling the people that they are unerring in judgment, and that they have all power," then we can be confident that we are dealing with a demagogue.[86] The people are plainly not unerring in their judgment, and they do not have all the power in a system of constitutional government. The demagogue is, as with Plutarch, a kind of flatterer, and the demagogue engages in flattery to manipulate the people ("the people are flattered, in order to be led").[87] But demagogues don't just flatter the people; they *elevate* the people, putting "the people before the constitution and the laws." That is, demagogues subvert the normal order of things, in which the law and the constitution are of fundamental importance and take precedent over the immediate will of the people.

Moreover, demagogues engage in divisiveness; thus what Cooper terms the "local demagogue" blurs the distinction between part and whole when it comes to the people. Indeed, this is one of the local demagogue's tells—"while loudest in proclaiming his devotion to the majority, he is, in truth, opposing the will of the entire people, in order to effect his purposes with a part." The most reliable "test" of the demagogue is to see whether the demagogue "does not distinguish between the whole people and a part of the people," identifying a subpopulation with the people as a whole. Demagogues will pretend to defend or advocate for the rights of a subset of the nation writ large and, in doing so, will go against "the will of the nation."[88] That is, the demagogue speaks as if supporting the desires or rights of the people as a whole, when the demagogue is in fact engaging in a dishonest form of synecdoche.

Having explained the "local demagogue," Cooper provides a character sketch of the demagogue:

> Usually sly, a detractor of others, a professor of humility and disinterestedness, a great stickler for equality as respects all above him, a man who acts in corners, and avoids open and manly expositions of his course, calls blackguards gentlemen, and gentlemen folks, appeals to passions and prejudices rather than to reason, and is in all respects, a man of intrigue and deception, of sly cunning and management, instead of manifesting the frank, fearless qualities of the democracy he so prodigally professes.[89]

---

[86] Ibid., 121.
[87] Ibid., 122.
[88] Ibid., 122.
[89] Ibid., 123.

It would be hard to put together a more moralistic portrait of the demagogue—this demagogue is dishonest, vicious, and manipulative.

Armed with a character sketch and some rules for picking up on demagogic appeals, Cooper's reader is, in a sense, equipped to sniff out the demagogue. But Cooper doesn't just try to provide his readers with a set of tools that will allow them to spot a demagogue. He also provides them with the sort of information about government, writ large, and American government, in particular, that he thinks they require in order to avoid being duped by demagogue's fallacious arguments. Thus Cooper moves, concept by concept, through his discussion—equality writ large, and American equality; liberty; the advantages of democratic regimes compared to non-democracies, along with the disadvantages of democracy, and a variety of other topics. Take equality, for example: Cooper distinguishes between what he calls equality of condition and equality of rights. The prior "is incompatible with civilization, and is found only to exist in those communities that are but slightly removed from the savage state."[90] By contrast, the latter characterizes democracies and includes "civil and political" rights, and thus "all men are equal before the law."[91] If citizens have equal rights, there is "an absence of privileges"; what equal rights do not mean, though, is that there will be no "artificial inequalities," which themselves derive from "the inevitable consequences of artificial ordinances."[92] The upshot of his account of equality is that it both equips his readers with sharper understandings of the concept, and makes clear that the role of government is "to abstain from fortifying and accumulating social inequality as a means of increasing political inequalities."[93] A reader armed with such notions about concepts fundamental to the American regime would, presumably, be less susceptible to manipulation regarding these principles.[94]

It isn't simply a matter of trying to enlighten public opinion on the limits to which it ought to adhere, or on the fundamental character of the American republic, though; Cooper wants, too, to provide a model for his readers to emulate, or perhaps to recognize, in political life. To make this point, it's worth noting another danger found in the chapter on demagogues: those who "in their desire to be moderate, lend themselves to the side of error."[95] They do

---

[90] Ibid., 45.
[91] Ibid., 46, 47.
[92] Ibid., 47, 52.
[93] Ibid., 54–55.
[94] On this point, see Barker, "Demagoguery and Mental Independence," 601.
[95] Ibid., 125.

this out of a desire to prevent harm, thinking that the only way to provide "safe direction ... to the publick mind" is by paying respect "to prejudices, and ignorance, and even to popular jealousies."[96] Such individuals, though not demagogues, "deceive themselves" in their rhetorical strategy, for while they do not flatter the people, they indulge them, and they do not pursue the common good, just as they misunderstand how to deal with the errors of the public. Rather than kowtow to the whims of the masses in a misguided effort to steer them toward justice, Cooper holds that "on all publick occasions on which it is necessary to act at all, the truth would be the most certain, efficient, and durable agency in defeating falsehoods, whether of prejudices, reports, or principles."[97]

If the doubtful moralists are little better than demagogues, what sort of character *does* Cooper commend? He seeks to impress upon his readers the importance of a certain sort of character—the character and the duties of the republican citizen, mass or elite. Many of these duties are oriented toward the prevention of demagoguery, or at least having demagogues in political office. Take, for instance, what he has to say in the chapter "On the Duties of Publick or Political Station." There, he emphasizes that what he terms "the publick duties of the private citizen" are of fundamental importance to political life, for should the citizen be "careless of his duties," the result will be "the triumph of abuses, peculation and frauds."[98] These duties entail, in part, sheer vigilance with regard to officeholders (he doubts "that the publick servant who is not watched, will be true to his trust"). This is especially the case in America, which is characterized by "self-government," a form of rule that entails the "imperious duty of every elector to take care and employ none but the honest and intelligent, in situations of high trust."[99] Cooper is thus attuned to the duties of both political elites (witness his disdain for the doubtful moralists) *and* non-elite citizens who, in their exercise of the civic virtue of vigilance, can prevent demagogues from taking power.[100]

And it is here that Cooper raises, in a passage encountered above, the "peculiar danger of a democracy"—namely, "the arts of demagogues"—and suggests a way of ameliorating their sway: "It is a safe rule, the safest of all,

---

[96] Ibid., 124.
[97] Ibid., 125.
[98] Ibid., 100–1.
[99] Ibid., 101.
[100] In this regard, I differ somewhat from the argument of Barker which, while I find it generally persuasive, seems to me to overemphasize Cooper's elitism. See Barker, "Demagoguery and Mental Independence," 591.

to confide only in those men for publick trusts, in whom the citizen can best confide in private life."[101] Cooper holds that the virtuous private individual—"honest, frank, above hypocrisy and double-dealing"—is the individual who ought to be entrusted with political power, while the opposite individual is simply a "knave." As a result, Cooper drives home that any citizen "who gives his vote, on any grounds, party or personal, to an unworthy candidate, violates a sacred publick duty, and is unfit to be a freeman."[102] Similarly, the virtuous democratic citizen ought to "watch himself, as under a government of another sort he would watch his rulers."[103]

But the duties that I find most interesting, from the perspective of political rhetoric (and demagoguery *qua* rhetoric), are those involving how one ought to go about speaking to one's fellow citizens. Behind these duties is a challenge: how to convince the public to watch, and limit, itself in its exercise of power, formal and informal. These duties center around the quality of candor, "a proof of both a just frame of mind, and of a good tone of breeding." It is "a sentiment that proves a conviction of the necessity of speaking truth, when speaking at all; a contempt for all designing evasions of our real opinions; and a deep conviction that he who deceives by necessary implication, deceives willfully."[104] The individual possessing candor would not, then, be a demagogue or one of Cooper's "doubtful moralists"; such an individual would speak in a fashion that accords with the public's "right to be treated with candor." It is a "manly and truly republican quality" and, if absent, "the institutions are converted into a stupendous fraud."[105] The weight of candor and the standing of frank-speaking individuals are thus elevated. That they need such elevation reflects the fact that, for Cooper, "a tyranny of opinion" might prevent individuals from engaging in frank speech, and he suggests that a variety of circumstances characterizing America, ranging from social equality to the legacy of those "religionists who first settled the country," combine to impede the sort of candor he views as central to democratic vitality. "There is," he writes, "no doubt that these combined causes have had the effect to make a large portion of the population less direct, frank, candid and simple in the expression of their honest sentiments, and even in the relation of facts, than the laws of God, and the social duties

[101] Ibid., 101–2.
[102] Ibid., 102.
[103] Ibid., 104.
[104] Ibid., 143.
[105] Ibid., 144.

require."[106] As evidence of these effects, Cooper provides a list of expressions that, in his mind, indicate the pressure not to engage in frankness: "I guess," "I conclude," "I some think," "I shouldn't wonder, if such a man had said so and so," expressions that he thinks are deployed even when speakers are perfectly certain that they are correct. Such mundane expressions are "beneath the frankness of freemen."[107] In what sense, though, is candor connected to liberty? "Candor has the high merit of preventing misconceptions, simplifies intercourse, prevents more misunderstandings than equivocation, elevates character, inculcates the habit of sincerity, and has a general tendency to the manly and virtuous qualities."[108] Candor, in short, aids those who seek to check the demagogue through public speech. And the sort of character that he has in mind, I think, when talking about candor is what he terms a gentleman, or rather an "American gentleman."[109] Such a character is noble and ennobling, and Cooper works hard to persuade his readers to value such an individual more than the cloying demagogue.

This individual—the gentleman—plays a vital role in American political life, foremost "to be a guardian of the liberties of his fellow citizens."[110] This individual will always pronounce "the true principles of government, avoiding, equally, the cant of demagogueism [sic] with the impracticable theories of visionaries."[111] Part of his defense of gentlemen having a prominent place in America is, to be sure, a bit off-putting—"The danger to the institutions of denying to men of education their proper place in society, is derived from the certainty that no political system can long continue in which this violence is done to the natural rights of a class so powerful."[112] Or, in other words, social and intellectual elites are dangerous—working together, "they will be found too powerful for the ill-directed and conflicting efforts of the mass."[113] This rather dire warning aside, Cooper also makes clear that the gentleman and the aristocrat are not identical, just as he thinks it erroneous to hold "that a democrat can only be one who seeks the level, social, mental and moral, of the majority."[114] Inculcating a willingness to allow "every one to be the undisturbed judge of his own habits and associations,

[106] Ibid., 145.
[107] Ibid., 145.
[108] Ibid., 146.
[109] Ibid. 112.
[110] Ibid., 112.
[111] Ibid., 112–13.
[112] Ibid., 113.
[113] Ibid., 114.
[114] Ibid., 116.

so long as they are innocent," means that democracy can be made compatible with social inequality—inequality that is necessary since "the alternative would be to reduce the entire community to the lowest."[115]

Demagoguery and Rhetorical Culture

At this point in my analysis, one thing is clear: Cooper's demagogue is more than reminiscent of Plutarch's flatterer-cum-demagogue. We may recall, for instance, that Plutarch tells us that the flatterer will affect to speak frankly; so, too, Cooper's demagogue affects honesty and intimacy with the public as well, pretending to side with the people; we may note here the scorn Cooper pours on those who use the expression "they say": "Designing men [who] endeavor to persuade the publick, that already 'they say,' what these designing men wish to be said."[116] Just as the frankness of Plutarch's flatterer "is not genuine or beneficial," the frankness of the demagogue is false.[117] Similarly, Plutarch's flatterer does not seek to engage with or strengthen reason, as would a true friend; rather, "the flatterer's talk adds nothing to the thinking and reasoning powers, but only promotes familiarity with some amorous pleasure, intensifies a foolish fit of temper, provokes envy, engenders an offensive and inane bulk of conceit."[118] Cooper's demagogue, too, addresses the passions rather than reason.

Just as we can hear echoes of Plutarch's anti-demagoguery in Cooper's account of the demagogue and some of his solutions, we see a similar difficulty in his prescriptions insofar as they involve claims about the rhetor's character. On the one hand, if we take demagoguery to be "*obviously* [emphasis added] false rhetoric on the part of corrupt and self-serving political elites who are manipulating their followers," then figuring out who is and isn't a demagogue shouldn't be all that hard.[119] Cooper's character portrait of the demagogue emphasizes that the demagogue is a "man of intrigue and deception, of sly cunning and management."[120] Yet, on the other hand, we very rarely know the depths of any public figure's character and our perceptions

---

[115] Ibid., 118.
[116] Ibid., 233.
[117] Plutarch, *How to Tell a Flatterer from a Friend*, 51d.
[118] Ibid., 61d–e.
[119] Roberts-Miller, *Demagoguery and Democracy*, 23.
[120] Cooper, *The American Democrat*, 123.

of their character are strongly conditioned by our sense of personal identity and group membership. Indeed, such an account of demagoguery—centering on character—is, itself, rooted in just the sort of identity claims that demagogues generally exploit: "it says that the world is very simple, and made up of good people (us) and bad people (them)."[121]

Not only does such a moralizing account of demagoguery run into real conceptual difficulties; while Cooper is clear that he prefers representative to direct democracies—small, direct democracies "are liable to popular impulses, which, necessarily arising from imperfect information, often work injustice from good motives"—he is also quite clear that larger democracies suffer their own problems.[122] In larger democracies, the people "are unable to scrutinize and understand character with the severity and intelligence that are of so much importance in all representative governments, and consequently the people are peculiarly exposed to become the dupes of demagogues and political schemers."[123] This dilemma undercuts some of Cooper's own advice about how to protect ourselves against demagogues. As we saw him argue above, "It is a safe rule, the safest of all, to confide only in those men for publick trusts, in whom the citizen can best confide in private life." If an individual is, in fact, honest, it will be evident—"honesty colors a whole character."[124] But knowing if someone is honest or dishonest has to do with their comportment in private life ("He who in private is honest, frank, above hypocrisy and double-dealing, will carry those qualities with him into publick, and may be confided in"), and there is little reason to think that citizens in large democracies will have much insight into their peers' private qualities. This, then, is not the best argument Cooper makes about demagogues, and it's not one that I think will pay much in the way of dividends as we try to face up to the threat—and presence—of demagogues in our own political culture. We simply do not have access all that often to the sorts of evidence that will let us know if someone is trustworthy in the private sphere (while we might imagine that there is a heuristic that allows us to circumvent this problem, heuristics are not foolproof).[125] Nor do we have the sort of information that allows us to determine whether what someone

---

[121] Roberts-Miller, *Demagoguery and Democracy*, 24.
[122] Cooper, *The American Democrat*, 180.
[123] Ibid., 81.
[124] Ibid., 102.
[125] On this point, see Christopher Achen and Larry Bartels, *Democracy for Realists: Why Elections Do Not Produce Responsive Governments* (Princeton, NJ: Princeton University Press, 2017), 36–41.

is saying is manipulative or not. This way of seeking to meet the dangers of the demagogue is subject, then, to the same sorts of difficulties that Plutarch's advice was subject to.

But these are not the only arguments that he makes about them, either, and what I want to do now is turn to his emphasis on individualism and social inequality, for it is here that we can see just how similar Cooper's demagogue is to a latter-day populist. A good entry point is the role the gentleman plays in American democracy. Cooper's American gentlemen are *not* aristocrats, even if it is the case that "in their ordinary habits and tastes they are virtually identical."[126] Where they differ, for Cooper, is in "principles" and "deportment." Most importantly, the democratic gentleman, "recognizing the right of all to participate in power, will be more liberal in his general sentiments." What he will not do, however, is give up "his own independence of vulgar domination, as indispensable to his personal habits." Here, Cooper emphasizes the political role of the gentleman: "The same principles and manliness that would induce him to depose a royal despot, would induce him to resist a vulgar tyrant."[127] Cooper also envisions such an individual playing a key role in the intellectual and cultural life of the American people, a role extending beyond ensuring the cultural trappings of "civilization," and entailing that he "be a guardian of the liberties of his fellow citizens."[128] Such an individual avows "at all times the true principles of government, avoiding equally, the cant of demagogueism [sic] with the impracticable theories of visionaries, and the narrow and selfish dogmas of those who would limit power by castes."[129] And such an individual will play a key role in fostering a viable democratic political culture. Thus Cooper hopes that "a firm union of all the intelligent of a country, in the cause of plain and obvious truths, would exterminate their correlative errors," and rectify public opinion.[130] Truth can and does defeat falsehood, but it can only do so by avoiding what he terms a "mistaken forebearance."[131]

How would such an individual speak? As it turns out, Cooper tells us a few things in this regard. In the chapter "On Language," where Cooper engages in an unfortunate amount of pedantry ("'Creek,' a word that signifies an *inlet*

---

[126] Cooper, *The American Democrat*, 119.
[127] Ibid., 119.
[128] Ibid., 111, 112.
[129] Ibid., 113.
[130] Ibid., 125.
[131] Ibid., 126.

of the sea, or of a lake, is misapplied to running streams, and frequently to the *outlets* of lakes"), he also has some interesting things to say about style. He says these in the context of describing "the most certain evidences of a man of high breeding" as "simplicity of speech; a simplicity that is equally removed from vulgarity and exaggeration."[132] This individual—"a gentleman"—speaks in a fashion that is "deliberate and clear, without being measured."[133] The gentleman, "cannot but know that the highest quality of eloquence, and all sublimity, is in the thought,rather than in the words, though there must be an adaptation of the one to the other."[134] Plain speaking, equipped with knowledge, deliberate, clear, avoiding affectation—this is the style, and the rhetoric, of the gentleman who is, like Cooper himself, "as good a democrat as there is in America."[135]

Cooper remarked that he might have titled *The American Democrat* "Anti-Cant," and such a term is instructive, highlighting the role he hoped the book would play in fostering an elite culture characterized by candor and persuading his readers that democratic elites—that is, elites who agree that social inequality should not translate into political inequality and that all citizens should, even if unequal in many respects, stand before the law as equals—have a vital role to play in public life. To revisit Roberts-Miller in light of the theme of cant, a culture that supports deliberation and that would be less amenable to demagoguery would be characterized by four principles in its deliberations. The first, part of what she terms "rhetorical fairness," is a principle holding that "whatever the argument rules are, they apply equally to everyone in the argument."[136] Just as rules ought to apply equally to all, so, too, do participants in argument have the responsibility of "representing one another's arguments fairly, and striving to provide internally consistent evidence to support their claims," and participants should also (the third principle) "strive to be internally consistent in terms of appeals to premises, definitions, and standards."[137] Last, and not least, participants in a debate must act in good faith—they must accept that they "can be proven wrong, and that they can imagine abandoning, modifying, and reconsidering" their claims as they argue.[138] These attributes of a deliberative rhetorical culture

---

[132] Ibid., 147, 153.
[133] Ibid., 153.
[134] Ibid., 154.
[135] Ibid., xxiv.
[136] Roberts-Miller, *Democracy and Demagoguery*, 125.
[137] Ibid., 125.
[138] Ibid., 126.

are, I suggest, precisely the attributes of the speech deployed by Cooper's gentleman, whether in spoken or written language.

Now, that much on demagoguery. What are we to make of Cooper as having something to say about populism, a point with which I began this chapter? The term does not feature in his book, and we should not expect it to, given that the term does not enter usage in American English until the late nineteenth century. Yet if we follow both Müller and Mudde and Kaltwasser, and take populism to rest upon both anti-elitism and anti-pluralism, I would suggest that when Cooper is talking about demagoguery, he is talking about something that is recognizably populist. Take, for example, the harms that Cooper associates with the "tyranny of opinion" and demagoguery more broadly: we see that "a large portion of the population [becomes] less direct, frank, candid and simple in the expression of their honest sentiments, and even in the relation of facts."[139] Candor—as opposed to demagogic flattery— "has the high merit of preventing misconceptions."[140] And candor would, while difficult to cultivate, lead to a different sort of political-communicative style—we may recall how attuned Cooper is, in this regard, to the deference paid to common opinion in the hedging that characterizes the speech of so many: "I guess," "I conclude," "I some think," "I shouldn't wonder, if such a man had said so and so." Though mundane, Cooper thinks such hedging is "beneath the frankness of freemen."[141] Cooper's democratic gentlemen counter the demagogue, to be sure, but his democratic gentlemen are also "men of education" who espouse "the true principles of government."[142] His democratic gentlemen counter the majority, and are by all appearances social and intellectual elites.

As to his demagogue and, in particular, what he terms the "local demagogue," we should remind ourselves of Müller's keen observation that populism involves "a *pars pro toto* argument and a claim to exclusive representation."[143] This mode of argument is part of the reason why Müller sees populism as incompatible with pluralism, producing "an exclusionary form of identity politics," with an undifferentiated people beset by elites. Let us revisit what Cooper says about the local demagogue: this demagogue engages in a sort of *pars pro toto* argument, or a synecdoche, to use the classical

---

[139] Cooper, *The American Democrat*, 145, 25.
[140] Ibid., 146.
[141] Ibid., 145.
[142] Ibid., 112–113.
[143] Müller, *What Is Populism?*, 20.

rhetorical term. What such a demagogue does is identify the whole with what is at best a part, and "while loudest in proclaiming his devotion to the majority, he is, in truth, opposing the will of the entire people, in order to effect his purposes with a part."[144] Such a demagogue, who, in Roberts-Miller's terms, speaks with the aim of "the reduction of political questions to us versus them," is recognizably a populist as well.[145]

[144] Cooper, *The American Democrat*, 122.
[145] Roberts-Miller, *Demagoguery and Democracy*, 36.

8
Anti-Parliamentary Politics
Populist Momentum in Historical Perspective

Kari Palonen

Introduction

Populism illustrates how the two major concepts of European politics from the mid-nineteenth century onward, namely democracy and parliamentarism, have not only different histories but also different reputations in contemporary debates. The core rhetorical *topos* of populism is that of "the people," and therefore populists as a rule claim to support democracy, even more than others do. This identification is, of course, both conceptually and historically a *non sequitur*, when it fails to ask who "the people" are, and how this kind of unit could "rule."

During the twentieth century, democracy has become a widely accepted "descriptive-normative concept."[1] Already Robert Michels, in the second edition of *Die Soziologie der Parteiwesens in der modernen Demokratie*, in 1925, claimed that even the enemies of democracy admitted that it could be overthrown only in a democratic way, that is, by relying on popular will (*Volkswillen*).[2] Parliamentarism never gained such support and has, on the contrary, remained controversial among many adherents of democracy, notably among the populists.

The parliamentary form of democracy, based on representation, has long been understood as the second-best choice in both popular and academic language. Parliamentarism is seldom defended on its own merits, and both activists and theorists are still searching for ways to complement or

---

[1] Quentin Skinner, "Empirical Theorists of Democracy and Their Critics," *Political Theory* 1, no. 3 (1973): 281–304; John Dunn, *Setting the People Free: The Story of Democracy* (New York: Atlantic books, 2005).

[2] Robert Michels, *Zur Soziologie des Parteiwesens in der modernen Demokratie* (Stuttgart: Kröner, 1925, [1970]), 6.

replace it with more "direct" or "participatory" forms of democracy. It is my point in this chapter that anti-parliamentarism, whether populist or not, is characterized by a longing to overcome politics. Similarly to older currents of anti-parliamentarism, populism is both unable and unwilling to recognize the contingent and controversial quality of all politics.

By the parliamentary style of politics, I don't mean merely parliamentary government or the system of government's political responsibility to parliament, the origins of which lie in Sandys's Motion in 1741.[3] On the contrary, I emphasize the parliamentary *way* of doing politics, which contains a wider spectrum of topics, including the freedom of members, the rhetoric of debate, and the procedural style of doing politics, as well as an intense playing with political time.[4]

During the postwar decades, parliaments were frequently regarded, both among scholars and political actors, as having lost powers, to the advantage of governments and bureaucracies. The replacement of the parliamentary French Fourth Republic with the semi-presidential Fifth Republic, as well as new longings for "participatory democracy" since the 1960s are quite obvious signs of such decline. Nonetheless, the renaissance of parliaments in the post–World War II period could also be worth closer attention, due to the lack of a theorizing of this revival.[5]

Since the 1990s, there have been strong signs of growing academic interest in political representation[6] and in the parliamentary style of politics. Parliaments have also been understood in a wider sense than that of a system of government; this has included rising interest in the rhetoric, culture, time, and procedure of parliaments.[7] At least in countries such as Britain[8] or

---

[3] Tapani Turkka, *The Origins of Parliamentarism: A study of Sandys' Motion* (Baden-Baden: Nomos, 2007); William Selinger *Parliamentarism from Burke to Weber* (Cambridge, UK: Cambridge University Press, 2019).

[4] Kari Palonen, *Parliamentary Thinking: Procedure, Rhetoric and Time* (London: Palgrave Macmillan, 2018).

[5] See the introductory chapter of Pasi Ihalainen, Cornelia Ilie, and Kari Palonen, *Parliament and Parliamentarism* (Oxford: Berghahn, 2016).

[6] Frank Ankersmit, *Aesthetic Politics* (Stanford, CA: Stanford University Press, 1996); Ankersmit, *Historical Representation* (Stanford, CA: Stanford University Press, 2001); Ankersmit, *Political Representation* (Stanford, CA: Stanford University Press, 2002); Nadia Urbinati, *Representative Democracy: Concept and Geneaology* (Chicago: University of Chicago Press, 2006).

[7] Ihalainen et al., *Parliament and Parliamentarism*; Cornelia Ilie, *European Parliaments under Scrutiny* (Amsterdam: Benjamins, 2010); Selinger, *Parliamentarism from Burke to Weber*; Cyril Benôit and Olivier Rozenberg, *Handbook of Parliamentary Studies* (Cheltenham, UK: Edward Elgar, 2020).

[8] Paul Evans, *Essays on the History of Parliamentary Procedure* (London: Bloomsbury, 2017).

within the European Union,[9] parliaments have strengthened their position in various ways.

A frequently neglected aspect of parliamentary politics concerns the status of parliamentarians, which conceptually speaking cannot be dealt with exclusively in terms of the struggle between parties inside and outside parliament. The old tradition of free speech and the free mandate of members, and more generally the freedom from dependence of parliamentarians,[10] has today enabled what could be called the *rule of professional politicians*, as opposed to officials, experts, courts of law, and so on.[11] As such, it has become one of the most vocal points in the militant critiques of parliamentarism.

Historically speaking, parliamentarism is linked to *parler* or *parlare*, and thus refers to a *rhetorical style* of politics. Walter Bagehot spoke in this sense of "a government by discussion," which "at once breaks down the yoke of fixed customs."[12] The parliamentary culture of politics operates through the medium of a rhetoric of debating *pro et contra*. In rhetorical terms, the parliamentary style relies on the deliberative genre, dealing with the strengths and weaknesses of every issue on the agenda. As such, it operates in contrast to the forensic genre of the courts and to the epideictic rhetoric of acclamation in referenda and presidential elections, as well as to the diplomatic rhetoric of negotiation, which includes the relationships between multi-cameral assemblies. The necessity of reaching decisions prevents inaction, but at the same time marks a final step in the debate that can be taken only after weighing opposite alternatives.[13]

The deliberative genre of rhetoric is even more explicit in the *procedural style of* parliamentary politics. Debates *pro et contra* are conducted in different stages of plenary and committee sessions in a "parliamentary" manner. The fair play principle, the free and equal chances of the parliamentarians to act politically, provides a regulative idea of the procedural politics. An item can be properly understood only if it is debated from opposite perspectives and confronted with alternative proposals. A nineteenth-century rhetoric

---

[9] See, e.g., Claudia Wiesner, *Inventing the EU as a Democratic Polity: Concepts, Actors and Controversies* (London: Palgrave Macmillan, 2018).
[10] In the sense of Skinner, "Empirical Theorists of Democracy and Their Critics."
[11] Walter Bagehot, *The English Constitution*, ed. Paul Smith (Cambridge, UK: Cambridge University Press, 1867); Max Weber, *Parlament und Regierung im neugeordneten Deutschland* (Berlin: Dunker & Humblot, 1918).
[12] Walter Bagehot, *Physics and Politics* (Boston: Beacon Press, 1872), 117, 135.
[13] Kari Palonen, "Parliamentary and Electoral Decisions as Political Acts," in *The Decisionist Imagination*, ed. Daniel Bessner and Nicolas Guilhot (Oxford; New York: Berghahn, 2019), 85–108.

professor, James De Mille, put the point of the parliamentary debate as follows: "[t]he aim of parliamentary debate is to investigate the subject from many points of view which are presented from two contrary sides. In no other way can a subject be so exhaustively considered."[14] It is in this sense that procedure enjoys in the parliamentary style of politics both a conceptual and a practical priority over all results achieved by parliamentary decisions.[15]

A final aspect of parliamentary politics lies in *playing with time*, that is, in spending enough time for parliamentary deliberations, but also in saving time when necessary. The procedural character of the politics of parliamentary debate consists of a series of successive debates in plenum (e.g., three readings, report stage) and in committees, with each stage dealing with the item on the agenda from a different angle. Procedural tools, such as amendment or adjournment motions, as well as the question of order, allow parliamentarians to interrupt the debate, to reset the agenda, or to delay the debate. From early on, parliaments have known rules to limit the time of deliberations. In nineteenth-century Westminster, the extended agenda and a growing willingness of members to speak at the plenum necessitated reforms concerned with managing the scarcity of time, with such instruments as the *cloture* (motion to end the debate) and the *guillotine* (determining the end of debate in advance) problematizing the distribution of time between both members and the items on the agenda as fairly as possible.[16] Governments have tried to turn these instruments into means of weakening parliamentary control, but parliaments have invented countermeasures.[17]

In this chapter, I shall first present some historically relevant forms of anti-parliamentary politics, emphasizing the differences between them and the *topoi* of the parliamentary style of politics. At the end of each section, I shall provide some commentaries and examples of how the populist language of politics relates to these versions of anti-parliamentarism. My point is to show that all of these aspects of anti-parliamentarism are on the populist agenda, and that at the same time there are considerable differences between them.

---

[14] James De Mille, *Elements of Rhetoric* (New York: Harper, 1882), 473.
[15] Kari Palonen, *From Oratory to Debate: Parliamentarisation of Deliberative Rhetoric in Westminster* (Baden-Baden: Nomos, 2016).
[16] Josef Redlich, *Recht und Technik des Englischen Parlamentarismus* (Leipzig: Duncker & Humblot, 1905); Kari Palonen, *The Politics of Parliamentary Procedure: The Formation of the Westminster Procedure as a Parliamentary Ideal Type* (Leverkusen: Budrich, 2014).
[17] Gilbert Campion, *An Introduction to the Procedure of the House of Commons* (London: Macmillan, 1958); Evans, *Essays on the History of Parliamentary Procedure*.

Against Parliamentary Government: Old and New Ideas

The classical form of anti-parliamentarism defends the monarchist reaction to the fall of the *ancien régime*. The parliamentarization of government received its first impetus in Britain in the parliamentary polemic against the Walpole government, the first vote of no confidence for Walpole, and his final resignation.[18] The first anti-parliamentary reaction was that of King George II from 1760s, who wanted to retain his intervention in the formation of government and to take back from parliament the decisive role in bringing a government to fall. This monarchist, later also presidentialist, reaction against the parliamentary government has remained the classical form of opposition to parliamentarism.

In Germany, the monarchist defenders of the old order were after 1848 ready to accept a kind of "constitutional" government as a moderate alternative to the parliamentary regime. Such a regime could not dispense with a parliament with independent powers, above all regarding the annual budget, but it never allowed the parliament to overthrow the government save to elect a new one. The real political leader was the *Reichskanzler*, and the chancellor Otto von Bismarck was the most famous anti-parliamentary leader in the nineteenth century.[19]

This "reactionary" form of anti-parliamentarism, however, differs from the "counter-revolutionary" opposition to the parliamentary regime. A nationalistic "new right" arose in France and Germany in the 1880s and 1890s.[20] Its aim was getting rid of the parliamentary control of government and administration, not in order to return to a pre-constitutional monarchy but to end parliamentary disorder, which it considered a betrayal of the unity of the nation or the state. For this purpose, what was said to be needed was a regime that either claimed to dissolve the parliament forever or retained solely a facade of it, a decorative assembly that kept the executive beyond the reach of parliamentary control.

The "*gouvernement direct*" of Moritz Rittinghausen became a popular slogan of left-wing anti-parliamentarism in the aftermath of the failure of the 1848 revolution.[21] Anarchists and Marxists rejected the separation between

---

[18] See, for example, Turkka, *The Origins of Parliamentarism*.
[19] For Bismarck's anti-rhetorical rhetoric, see Hans-Peter Goldberg, *Bismarck und seine Gegner. Die politische Rhetorik im kaiserlichen Reichstag* (Düsseldorf: Droste, 1998).
[20] See the discussion in Tuula Vaarakallio, "'Rotten to the Core': Variations of French Nationalist Anti-System Rhetoric," PhD Dissertation in Political Science, *University of Jyväskylä*, (2004).
[21] Pierre Rosanvallon, *La démocracie inachevée* (Paris: Gallimard, 2000), 159–162.

the legislative and executive powers, as Marx put it in his essay on the Paris Commune of 1871: "The Commune was to be a working, not a parliamentary body, executive and legislative at the same time."[22] August Bebel, the historical founder of the German Social Democrats, presented in his *Die Frau und der Sozialismus* one of the few descriptions of a communist utopia. Although Bebel sat for decades in the *Reichstag*, in his utopia not only the state but also parliaments have disappeared in favor of a Saint-Simonian vision of replacing politics with administration: "The great and yet so petty parliamentary struggles, in which the men of the tongue imagine that they rule and direct the world through their speeches, have disappeared; they have given way to administrative bodies and delegations."[23]

Although populists of today might still long to get rid of parliaments and politicians, they would hardly be ready to accept an omnipotent bureaucracy. Present-day populists do not straightforwardly reject the parliamentary form of government, but try to instrumentalize it to their own purposes. Once they reach a parliamentary majority, they tend to change the electoral rules and parliamentary procedures in a way that renders the removal of the populist government very difficult. The present-day government in Hungary, for instance, uses a number of legal and administrative measures to render its majority permanent, as if only the ruling party expresses the true will of the people. In this view, an opposition victory would falsify this will, and therefore no "fair chance" should be given to the opposition, as we also clearly see in Donald Trump's conduct after losing the 2020 presidential election.

In France, Boulanger and others supported the old Bonapartist device of plebiscites as an example of direct rule of the people,[24] a tool that is still on the agenda of populist parties. The Five Star Movement in Italy originated in an extreme belief in referenda, including inside the party itself, and the True Finns recently proposed a referendum in Finland on the European Union's crisis package. Another major anti-parliamentary device for the populists

---

[22] "[d]ie Kommune sollte nicht eine parlamentarische, sondern eine arbeitende Körperschaft sein, vollziehend und gesetzgebend zu gleicher Zeit." Karl Marx, Der Bürgerkrieg im Frankreich, [1871], in *Marx-Engels Studienausgabe IV* (Frankfurt am Main: Fischer 1966), 213.

[23] "Die großen und doch so kleinlichen parlamentarischen Kämpfe, bei denen die Männer der Zunge sich einbilden, durch ihre Reden die Welt zu beherrschen und zu lenken, sind verschwunden, sie haben Verwaltungskollegien und Verwaltungsdelegationen Platz gemacht." August Bebel, "Die Frau und der Sozialismus," last modified January 31, 1999, http://www.mlwerke.de/beb/beaa/beaa_481.htm.

[24] Vaarakallio, "'Rotten to the Core': Variations of French Nationalist Anti-System Rhetoric."

has been the strengthening of powers of presidents as incarnations of the unity of the people.[25]

However, retaining the parliament as an expression of the unity of the people was supported by Hermann Göring as the president of the *Reichstag* in December 1932: "Parliament is currently the only place where the will of the German people can be made known (hear! listen, Left!), and at this point the will of the German people must be heard."[26] A façade Reichstag, seldom convened, persisted in the National Socialist regime until 1942.[27]

Anti-Parliamentary Sermons against Professional Politicians

The parliamentarization of government and the democratization of the electorate brought neither all power to the people, nor the rule of ungovernable masses or "the mob." The nineteenth-century reforms of parliament, representation, and government were brought about as a byproduct of professional politicians, who soon obtained the decisive positions both in government and parliament.[28] A common trait of the different anti-parliamentary currents consists in their permanent polemics against professional politicians.

In this critique there are multiple strains, which are not always compatible with each other. The core idea is the unity of the people in the sense of an identity between the rulers and the ruled. This can be realized in a Hobbesian manner, as an incarnation of the people in the leader, or in the (vulgar-) Rousseauean vein as the rejection of political representation as an usurpation of popular sovereignty by representatives. Carl Schmitt has managed a strange synthesis of Hobbes and Rousseau with a thesis that "the people" (*das Volk*) can only act by acclamation, as opposed to the election and the parliamentary-style deliberation:

> Only the truly gathered people is a people, and only the truly gathered people can do what specifically belongs to the activity of this people: they

---

[25] Carl Schmitt, *Verfassungslehre* (Berlin: Duncker & Humblot, 1928).
[26] "Daß das Parlament zurzeit die einzige Stelle ist, an der der Wille des deutschen Volkes kundgetan werden kann, (hört! Hört! links) und an dieser Stelle muß der Wille des deutschen Volkes gehört werde" (December 6, 1932).
[27] "Negotiations of the German Reichstag and Its Predecessors Structure of the Offer," Verhandlungen des Deutschen Reichstags, https://www.reichstagsprotokolle.de/index.html.
[28] See Weber, *Parlament und Regierung im neugeordneten Deutschland*.

can acclaim, that is, express their approval or rejection by simple shouting, shouting high or low, cheering a leader, or a proposal, the king, or anyone else, or refuse acclamation by silence or murmuring.[29]

Schmitt understands that in a referendum, the direct "participation" of the electorate does not mean having a real choice between alternatives, but serves for identification with the system. In a referendum campaign, there is nothing left to deliberate, only to acclaim or refuse to do so. Due to the pre-given questions and the yes-or-no vote itself, the no-alternative does not make much difference for the regime. The no-vote is a powerless expression of a protest without an alternative, although it may sometimes be effective, if the political leader commits to linking his or her fate with that of the referendum, as de Gaulle did in 1969.

Another device also supported by Schmitt in *Verfassungslehre* is the presidential system that follows the Hobbesian model of the incarnation of the people in the president. Complementary measures could be those weakening the parliamentary powers, such as a radical reduction of the number of parliamentarians, as well as of parliamentary sitting days, or the non-payment of salaries and compensations. All of these are today commonplaces in the populist repertoire. In short, every parliamentary representative remains suspicious of populist parties. That some of these parties' adherents also tend to dispute the legitimacy of the populists' own representatives might be a major reason why the parliamentary groups of populist parties so frequently split.

As an example of a "populist epistemology" suspicious of representatives, we can quote the slogan of the legendary Finnish populist leader Veikko Vennamo, "kyllä kansa tietää."[30] To get the rhetorical point, I would translate it as "the people do know better (than politicians)," or "you (the politicians) cannot deceive the people." This view assumes that, first, in line with the Rousseauean rejection of the legitimacy of representation, the knowledge of "the people" is held to be authoritative, and, conversely, politicians are liable to errors, especially those who have "never done ordinary work" but rise

---

[29] "Erst das wirklich gesammelte Volk ist Volk und nur das wirklich gesammelte Volk kann das tun, was spezifisch zur Tätigkeit dieses Volkes gehört: es kann *akklamieren*, d.h. durch einfachen Zuruf seine Zustimmung oder Ablehnung ausdrücken, Hoch oder Nieder rufen, einem Führer oder einem Vorschlag zujubeln, den König oder irgendeinen anderen hochleben lassen, oder durch Schweigen oder Murren die Akklamation verweigern." Schmitt, *Verfassungslehre*, 243–244.

[30] "Veikko Vennamo," Wikipedia, last modified September 9, 2022, https://en.wikipedia.org/wiki/Veikko_Vennamo.

directly—as the typical caricature puts it—from student unions or the party youth apparatus to parliament. The political skills of such parliamentarians remain suspicious because they have lost all contact with the moods of "the people," an unerring source of knowledge in the populists' rhetoric.

Populist politicians have extended the knowledge claim to a sanctification of the people's political judgments, too. This has led to a celebration of popular opinions and prejudices and to a condemnation of all attempts to change them. Timo Soini, the political heir of Vennamo and leader of the True Finns until 2017,[31] expressed the point in his identification with the "meat-eating hetero-men." This is a metonymy in praise of "ordinariness" and an attempt to delegitimate alternative ways of living as topics on the political agenda, with an additional, implicit edge against the rise of women to political leadership.

Parliamentarians are suspicious because they must confront thorough debates on specific items on the parliamentary agenda, especially in committees. Such encounters with unknown topics and opposite standpoints might lead them to revise their judgments. Against the independent judgment of parliamentarians, another slogan of Vennamo can be quoted, namely his denunciation of *pelin politiikka*, the politics of gaming or gambling, directed against the tactics of politicking at the cost of "the people." In this suspicion toward parliamentarians, we could also see a historical similarity between the populists and the traditional left in justifying a quasi-imperative mandate.

Anti-Rhetorical Rhetoric

Older forms of anti-parliamentarism needed the parliament in order to have a target for their militant attacks. The British writer Thomas Carlyle already collected many of the later anti-parliamentary *topoi* in his *Latter-Day Pamphlets*.[32] Carlyle's critique is directed above all against the rhetorical character of parliamentary regime, "the National Palaver," doomed to remain powerless: "Your National Parliament, in so far as it has only that question to decide, may be considered as an enormous National Palaver existing mainly

---

[31] "Timo Soini," Wikipedia, last modified October 27, 2022, https://en.wikipedia.org/wiki/Timo_Soini.

[32] Thomas Carlyle, *Latter-Day Pamphlets*, 1850, http://www.gutenberg.org/files/1140/1140-h/1140-h.htm.

for imaginary purposes." Carlyle advocates, in line with the monarchist reaction, a return to merely advisory parliaments, without an emphasis on the rhetorical powers of its members.[33]

A historical example of separating debating and voting between different assemblies is the Napoleonic regime of the Consulate and Empire. The Senate elected both the Tribunat, as the debating assembly, and the Corps législatif, in which no debate was possible.[34] Even later, the French parliamentary tradition, focusing on the legislation as the main task of the parliament, gave the decisive role to the vote, understanding debate merely as a preparation to enable voting.[35]

In Britain, tendencies to strengthen the government's position in parliament have persisted, partly in order to prevent parliament from exhaustion, due to its own success, including the extended agenda and the growing willingness of members to speak at the plenum. Behind the obstruction campaign of Irish members around Charles Parnell in the 1870s and early 1880s was also an anti-parliamentary Irish nationalism, which sought to paralyze the entire British parliamentary government.[36] Elsewhere, in particular in the Habsburg Empire, the Czech and other nationalists took obstruction tactics to their extreme and partly managed to destroy the parliament's reputation. An obstructive speech was no longer a *voice* in the Hirschman[37] sense, an intervention in debate, nor merely a way to spoil the precious time of the parliament, but was instead an attempt to destroy the very parliamentary idea of "politics by discussion."

Similar critiques of *bavardage*[38] could also be heard among left-wing anti-parliamentarians. The poet Georg Herwegh parodied the *Paulskirche* Parliament of 1848 with a poem called *Zu Frankfurt an dem Main*, every strophe repeating: "In Parla-parla-parliament, the talking never ends!"[39] To the Carlylean lamentation of the parliament as a talk-shop corresponded

---

[33] Ibid.

[34] Jean Garrigues, *Histoire du Parlement de 1789 à nos jours* (Paris: Colin, 2007), 102–30.

[35] Philipp Valette and Benôit Saint-Marsy, *Traité de la confection des lois, ou examen raisonnée des règlements suivis par les assemblées legislatives françaises, compare aux forms parlementaires de l'Angleterre, des États-Unis, de la Belgique, de l'Espagne, de la Suisse etc.* (Paris: Joubert, 1839).

[36] Redlich, *Recht und Technik des Englischen Parlamentarismus*; Palonen, *The Politics of Parliamentary Procedure.*

[37] Albert O. Hirschman, *Exit, Voice and Loyalty* (Cambridge, MA: Harvard University Press, 1970).

[38] As Mill summarizes this critique in John Stuart Mill, *Considerations on Representative Government* (Buffalo, NY: Prometheus Books, 1861).

[39] "Im Parla-Parla-Parlament. Das Reden nimmt kein End!", *Zu Frankfurt an dem Main*, quoted from *Volksliedsarchiv*, created 1848, http://www.volksliederarchiv.de/text1533.html.

the German expression *Schwatzbude* (or "Chatterbox"), which has been attributed to the leading Social Democrat, Wilhelm Liebknecht.[40]

Behind such views, across the spectrum, lies the old idea that rhetoric per se is suspicious, if not entirely condemnable. Strikingly anti-rhetorical are the scientistic and technocratic claims, which in their radical version look to dispense with parliaments, or in more moderate versions to subordinate them to the knowledge claims of officials, experts, and specialists. An older version was the German *Beamtenstaat*, in which even ministers were selected among officials who claimed to rule over parliamentarians due to their superior knowledge. Max Weber, in his pamphlet *Parlament*, submitted such claims to a thorough critique, not only illustrating rhetorical devices by which parliamentary committees and their members could hold such a rule of officialdom in check, but also disputing the very concept of knowledge as possession in favor of a procedural and rhetorical view of knowledge as debate, accentuating Westminster parliamentary practices as its historical model.[41]

Ignoring or discarding the Weberian view, the idea that parliamentary decisions should be based on "scientific knowledge" is surprisingly widespread today. Its practical instruments seem, however, not to go beyond calls for replacing parliamentary committees by commissions of outside experts. How and why parliaments should follow their advice—frequently controversial within the commissions—without debating it in an ordinary parliamentary manner remains unanswered. On occasion, technocratic governments of experts have been formed to respond to various crises, but they have hardly been a political success.

Despite being programmatically anti-rhetoricians, modern populists, such as Vennamo and Soini in Finland, exercise in their own sense a highly rhetorical form of politics, frequently with success. Their rhetoric is, of course, not that of the deliberative genre of parliamentary debate, judging the strengths and weaknesses of motions on the agenda or arguments presented in the debate. Like the older labor movement, populists instead use the parliament as a platform for speaking publicly to "the people," without any intention of converting the parliamentary majority toward their own views; instead, their parliamentary speeches are instrumentalized for use in electoral campaigns.

---

[40] Elfi Pracht, *Parlamentarismus und die deutsche Sozialdemokratie 1867–1914* (Pfaffenweiler: Centaurus, 1990).
[41] Weber, *Parlament und Regierung im neugeordneten Deutschland*, 235–48; Kari Palonen, *"Objektivität" als faires Spiel. Wissenschaft als Politik bei Max Weber* (Baden-Baden: Nomos, 2010).

Their rhetoric is that of the epideictic genre, of praise and blame, in which an un-nuanced, black-and-white dualism between praise and blame is maintained, and no questions about the criteria of praise and blame are asked. In classical terms, the rhetorical genre is *acclamatio*, the rhetoric of applauding or denunciating. Compared with old nationalist or totalitarian movements, we could perhaps claim that what today's populists acclaim are mainly abstractions such as "the people," whereas certain reservations are shown even toward populist leaders themselves. The contrast to the acclamation is militant denunciation of the adversaries of "the people," among which all other parties and politicians, without distinction, tend to be counted. Again, this tendency is shared by both right- and left-wing populists, with slight differences in the identification of who and what are denounced.

The populists and nationalists interpret the "sovereignty of the people" not an as extension of, but as a counter-concept to, parliamentary sovereignty à la Westminster. Whereas for Walter Bagehot, parliamentary debate forms the model for debates outside parliament and has been replicated in associations, meetings, newspapers, and so on, populist rhetoric treats parliamentary speeches as extensions of a permanent electoral campaign.[42] For populists, parliament is a kind of mandate of the majority to realize their electoral program. Thus, the "debate" between the governmental majority and oppositional minority would be limited into a contest between acclamation and counter-acclamation for the ratification of government motions.

Although such a tendency can also be observed in governments led by non-populist parties, in no cases has it reached such an extent as in populist governments, with Victor Orbán's government in Hungary as the extreme case. The parliamentary debate on the strengths and weaknesses of motions on the agenda has been replaced by rhetoric on the legitimacy not only of the government, but also of the opposition as such, preventing the opposition from gaining any fair chances to win the next elections.

The relationship between populists and technocrats is an intriguing one. In the polemic against rhetoric and professional politicians, they are on the same side. Some studies indicate that support for populist parties—such as the True Finns—is strongest among specialist professions based on narrow, unilinear training, such as engineers. However, for the populists, science and expertise appear as alienated from the experiences, opinions, and judgments

---

[42] Bagehot, *The English Constitution*.

of "the people" as the world of politicians. The Trump administration was a striking expression of this contrast. The populist demand that the parliamentarians should be "ordinary people"—or even "ordinary men"—instead of professional politicians, leads to dilettantish politicians, unable to criticize and control officials, experts, and specialists. The appeal to the unerring knowledge of the "ordinary people" is another myth, strategically cultivated by populists, but also one that contributes to their internal splits.

Against Formal Procedures

If the anti-rhetorical effect lies in playing things against words, reality against mere rhetoric, the anti-procedural effect consists in playing substance against form, the results against the modus of proceeding. Businessmen-politicians, such as the former Finnish prime minister Juha Sipilä, cultivated their anti-politician image by extending the "results or out" criterion from business to governments, changing politics, to use Hannah Arendt's terminology, from action to fabrication. In addition, parliamentary proceduralism has been criticized as a waste of time when action is urgent, as a delay that in practice equals inaction.

The simplest form of procedural anti-parliamentarism turns against parliamentary "method" as a complex set of moves, in the name of direct action. This may assume different forms across the political spectrum, such as revolutionary or lynching masses, an avant-garde claiming to do better than the elected representatives, or a popular reaction claiming immediate action against parliamentary formalities demanding thorough treatment of an issue. The Sartrean figure of *groupe-en-fusion* in *Critique de la raison dialectique* is a formal ideal type that contains equally well the unorganized egalitarian activism that Sartre illustrates with the capture of the Bastille on July 14, 1789,[43] and the anti-Semitic lynching mob, a parallel figure already briefly sketched by Sartre in his *Réflexions sur le question juive*.[44]

The revolutionary *république une et indivisible* is the historical paradigm of a "parliamentary Rousseaueanism." In this view, parliaments are in principle dubious because of their tendency to split participants into proponents and opponents of a cause on the basis of the separate items on the agenda. This

---

[43] Jean-Paul Sartre, *Critique de la raison dialectique* (Paris: Gallimard, 1960), 453–68.
[44] Jean-Paul Sartre, *Réflexions sur la question juive* (Paris: Gallimard, 1946), 34–38.

anti-deliberative view is close to the Hobbesian[45] or Napoleonic ideal: the members of an assembly vote but do not deliberate. For many critics, the parliamentary government only appears acceptable when it embodies the general will represented by its majority as expressed in the elections.

This form of anti-parliamentarism does not dispense with parliaments as such, but merely with their procedural style of politics, which it regards as an obstacle to reaching the majority's programmatic aims. The parliament is then reduced to being solely an assembly that represents the unity of the nation without deliberating between political alternatives. The parliament appears as a *pars pro toto*, an assembly representing the entire people, instead of an assembly deliberating *pro et contra* the single items on the agenda, which would dissolve the unity as an illusion. The quoted references to Göring and Orbán allude to such a pseudo-parliament.

An anti-procedural majoritarianism is strong among parties based on a definite interest, task, or mission, such as nationalists, socialists, populists, agrarians, and economic liberals. For example, the early socialists defended an electoral version of parliamentary government with the assumption that under universal suffrage (women not always included), the working class would regularly comprise the immense majority of the voters. They saw the working class vote as a mere registration of "objective interests," and, hence, a failure to win a socialist majority would be the result of sinister machinations. If parliamentary elections did not result in a majority for the "party of the working class," accusations that the elections had been manipulated were repeatedly presented, and parliamentarism was renounced as a "bourgeois" regime. This was further strengthened by a belief in a "scientific" worldview.[46]

The minimalist parliamentarism that appeals to the authority of the majority shares much of anti-parliamentarism's anti-rhetorical and anti-procedural pathos in reducing the role of the deliberative process in parliamentary politics. For anti-parliamentarians, a thorough and fair debate according to parliamentary procedure almost equals an obstruction of the "will of the people" (*vox populi, vox Dei*).

This anti-proceduralism equally manifests itself in presidentialism, which turns the president into supreme arbiterm and plebiscitarianism,

---

[45] Richard Tuck and Holly Hamilton-Bleakley, "Hobbes and Democracy," in *Rethinking The Foundations of Modern Political Thought*, ed. Annabel Brett and James Tully (Cambridge, UK: Cambridge University Press, 2006), 171–90.

[46] For France, see Marc Angenot, *La démocratie, c'est le mal* (Laval: Les Presses de l'Université de Laval, 2003); for August Bebel's scientistic rhetoric, see Goldberg, *Bismarck und seine Gegner. Die politische Rhetorik im kaiserlichen Reichstag*.

in which—unlike in the strict majoritarian interpretations of parliamentary government—the parliament even tends to lose the epideictic role of ratification to "the people." Anti-proceduralism unites presidential plebiscitarianism, from Louis Bonaparte to Charles de Gaulle, with the role of referenda in the Swiss type of a semi-plebiscitary regime appealing to "the people" as a veto against parliament's decision. As observed above, the point of a referendum is that a question is set for the voters in advance and from above; they can only answer yes or no, without any possibility to discuss the fairness of the formulation of the question or the conditions of the referendum. Indeed, we can ask whether a fair referendum, at least beyond purely local issues, is possible at all.[47]

All of these classical anti-formalistic and anti-procedural aspects are included in the rhetorical repertoire of present-day populists. The new feature, in their case, lies in the extensive—and in a formal sense also innovative (yet thoroughly partisan)—use of the new communication and information technologies of the so-called social media. These media have so far escaped a great deal of procedural, parliamentary-style regulation, which leaves them open to arbitrary declarations. The rhetoric of the social media "like" is simply a version of the epideictic genre of acclamation.

The procedural and rhetorical idea of parliamentary, debate-centered politics holds that that in politics, no single "right" decision exists; decisions should be left open and achieved only by means of the confrontation of possible (procedural) and actual (rhetorical) alternatives in the preceding debate. Such proceduralism would endanger the persistence of the conventional opinions and prejudices at the core of the populist style of (anti-) politics.

Anti-Parliamentary Politics against Time

The rhythm of contemporary politics is frequently experienced as a hectic one, and the questions under debate seem to require urgent decisions to be resolved. In a diametrically opposite sense, parliamentary politics operates with thorough debates that both "demand time" in the quantitative sense and use time as a major medium of doing politics as such. Time is not only a medium that allows reflection and "second thoughts" on issues, but has been

---

[47] Ankersmit, *Historical Representation*.

built into the procedures, institutions, and practices of parliamentary politics: patience is a major parliamentary virtue. This holds in particular for the regular items on the parliamentary agenda, namely for budgets, legislation, and international treaties in particular, whereas a vote of confidence or parliamentarians' questions to the government can be dealt with in a single event.

The close link between time and procedure appears, for instance, in adjournment motions, which may serve as interruptions to the current debate, delaying the moment requiring a stand or a silent rejection (*adjournement sine die*), for which no member is held easily responsible among outsiders. Amendment motions resetting the agenda of alternatives, raising procedural questions of parliamentary "order," demands for cloture, and replies and explanations of votes are in Westminster legitimate interruptions of a debate, which might provoke a reconsideration of stands on the motion on the agenda. The different stages of parliamentary debate also contain occasions for the parliamentarians to reconsider the item each time from a new perspective, each of which contains a chance to alter their stands or their justification. These are examples of how dealing with time is an inherent part of dealing with the items on the agenda in parliamentary-style politics.[48]

This highly time-sensitive quality of parliamentary politics, carefully formed in Westminster and other parliaments over centuries, is a major target of criticism on the agenda of anti-parliamentarians of all colors. Accelerating the stream by which motions pass parliament has been a frequent demand of governments in order to counter the scarcity of time. The demand for urgent decisions is no longer reserved for extraordinary situations, but is a corollary of the claims that the entire pace of history has been accelerating.[49] Such claims are frequently presented in the name of "progress," regarding which government and administration have been seen as more reliable agents of change than parliaments.

Equally important are, however, parliament's interventions against vested interests and rooted practices, which current members in their thorough but slow deliberations have come to consider as no longer acceptable or legitimate. An example that is militantly debated today is the traditional, quasi-natural division of humanity into the dyad of men and women. In matters

---

[48] See Palonen, *The Politics of Parliamentary Procedure: The Formation of the Westminster Procedure as a Parliamentary Ideal Type*.
[49] Hartmut Rosa, *Beschleunigung. Die Veränderung der Zeitstrukturen in der Moderne* (Frankfurt am Main: Suhrkamp, 2005).

disputing the legitimacy of this divide, already taking a parliamentary initiative is the provocative point. The anti-parliamentary rhetoric of reaction is here clearly directed against the politicization of the issue, which for an order's defenders endangers the "nature of things," or at least a tradition worth maintaining.

Considering the populist variants of anti-parliamentarism, it is not uncommon to see them joining the forces of "progress" in demanding rapid changes to realize some "reform," although, for example, the German AfD is highly divided between market absolutists and nationally restricted social reformers. The reform demands are presented as if the issue would be a simple matter of will, realizable at one stroke, without the complicated parliamentary deliberations. Or an immediate stop to something, immigration above all, is demanded, without worrying about the conditions and realizability of the demand. In these demands, populist politics appears to consist of instantaneous moves, opposed by sinister forces.

More politics aiming at terminating all subsequent politics is included in present-day populists' vocal demands to move backward; in this sense, their anti-parliamentarism is analogous to the Marxist view of the "last battle." The ultra-nationalist True Finns demanded in the 2019 parliamentary and European elections *Suomi takaisin!* ("Give us Finland back!" or "Return to Finland!"), and I saw an analogous poster for the Austrian FPÖ in the EU elections. Of course, the obvious point was to call for leaving the European Union, or at least ignoring its demands at home. Behind this surface level there lies, however, a myth of a past golden age, to which a time machine would bring us back, if the populists could gain power. Within the party, it is easy to identify factions of businessmen who wanted back the unfettered capitalism within national borders of the 1980s, of health specialists and social workers who wanted to restore the reformist 1960s and 1970s without foreigners, or of traditionalists who longed for a return to the simple rural and Christian moral order assumed to have remained prevalent into the 1950s. Again, political acts are seen as instantaneous acts of willing, without considering the changed conditions and the grounds of opposing such a rhetoric of reaction in a literal sense.

Its sensitiveness to playing with time as inherent in the very activity of politics is one of the main strengths of parliamentarism. Such a complicated and even delicate politics requires learning that is hardly possible elsewhere than in parliamentary practice. The populists' and other anti-parliamentarians are unable and unwilling to regard time other than as an adverse force in politics. From the parliamentary perspective, all this shows a lack of elementary political literacy, because time cannot be separated from the content of the issues.

Conclusion

In an important triad of books, Frank Ankersmit[50] has defended representation as a constitutive political act. The core formula is: *representation creates both the represented and the representatives.*[51] This view provides a major justification for parliamentary politics. The founding act of both parliament and elections is itself already a political move. The representatives, members of parliament, do not act on their own behalf, but are legitimized by the act of representation as the basis of their free mandate and free speech. Even more important is that the represented, the citizens or "the people," are equally politically created and do not possess any natural right to power. They are invited to do politics in elections and in taking stands on the issues on the parliament's agenda.

Some conservative, technocratic, or meritocratic versions of political assemblies, estate diets, or meetings of corporations do, on the contrary, assume a kind of natural right for their favorite types of the represented, differing in each version. Some of such versions of anti-parliamentarism, at least so-called epistocracy, still play a role in contemporary anti-parliamentarism.

The situation is different with the conceptions that have to do with the naturalization of the people. Even though the justification for a direct democracy of the soviets, or citizens' councils, still plays some role, much more important are the plebiscitarian and presidentialist ideas of representing "the people" by acclamation. A naturalistic view of popular sovereignty is also assumed in the extreme versions of the renaissance of the lottery principle, although most of these versions instead regard lotteries as complements to elected parliaments.[52] Their dispute is with the procedure of electing members, rather than with the parliamentary mode of debating *pro et contra*.

Oddly enough, contemporary populists seem not to be found among those who support the lottery method, which is surely the most complete

---

[50] Ankersmit, *Aesthetic Politics*; *Historical Representation*; *Political Representation*.
[51] See Ankersmit, *Political Representation*, 115.
[52] Hubertus Buchstein, *Demokratie und Lotterie* (Frankfurt am Main: Campus, 2009).

method of producing an assembly as a miniature of the electorate. It is obvious that if the people are understood as a unity, a random selection out of it already contains too much contingency in order to retain "the people" as the sovereign. Populist parties and candidates have, in contrast, succeeded in elections during the past decade, but the question arises: Would elected representatives be less alienated from the people than randomly selected ones? The history of the populist parties, on the contrary, tends to hint that not a few of their parliamentarians have begun to consider themselves as "elected" in the religious sense, which already creates a distance from "the people."

The converse side of the populist focus on electoral victories lies in an underestimation of both the requirements and possibilities of parliaments as media of political agency, especially in the Western European parliamentary regimes. Their defense of "nameless" rank-and-file members of parliament resembles Lenin's famous example of simplification of politics in the soviets so that any cook would be able to handle them. For other parliamentarians, the populists appear as hopeless political dilettantes who are not interested in learning the requirements of the parliamentarian's "craft," or even in attending committee meetings, as was the tendency with French Front National members. I am convinced that if populist groupings ever reached a majority in a Western European parliament, the parliamentarians would be able to use their different parliamentary resources as power shares against populist majorities and governments.

The populist parties have been quite spectacular, and academic interest in them has been massive. Chantal Mouffe, the main contemporary political theorist of left-wing populism, claims: "[i]n recreating political frontiers, the 'populist moment' points to a 'return of the political' after the years of post-politics."[53] Her target is the "consensus of the centre" consisting of a "bipartisan alternation of power between centre-right and centre-left parties,"[54] drawing the consequence: "[p]olitics has therefore become a mere issue of managing the established order, a domain reserved for experts."[55] Mouffe attributes the shaking of this constellation to both left- and right-wing populist parties, but sees also a major difference "in the composition of the 'we' and in how the adversary, the 'they,' is defined."[56]

---

[53] Chantal Mouffe, *For a Left Populisms* (London: Verso, 2018), 6.
[54] Ibid., 17.
[55] Ibid., 17.
[56] Ibid., 23.

Mouffe's argumentation relies on certain assumptions which I regard as questionable. One of them is the Schmittian[57] or structuralist assumption of the "ontological" priority of "the political" over "mere politics."[58] Although she has replaced Schmitt's concept of the enemy (*Feind*) with that of the adversary and thus has taken a step toward the parliamentary direction, her point is that in the consensus between established parties, no adversaries are left either, and politics has become reduced to mere management by experts. She sees the point of the populist moment as a return to a clear Schmittian-type either-or dualism between "us" and "them."

Judged from a parliamentary perspective, Mouffe, in a very conventional manner, appears to reduce politics to the level of majorities in elections and parliament and to the corresponding view of the government versus opposition divide. In rhetorical language, the priority of the political, the reading of current political disputes, as well as the longing for a clear unidimensional political divide, presented in a partisan manner as one between "us" and "them," can all be regarded as an affirmation of the epideictic genre, that is, of the politics of applauding or not applauding—with the left- and right-wing populists offering competing views of the nature of "us" and "them." Without denying the tendency toward marginal political differences between the "mainstream" parties in Europe, this concerns above all the electoral-cum-governmental dimension of parliamentary politics. When the rhetorical, procedural, and temporal dimensions are considered, the situation appears much more nuanced, though the competing types of professional politicians cannot be compared with experts.

Read in view of the history of parliamentary politics, the populists—and their academic defenders such as Mouffe—appear much less original than they are considered today. They have reworked old anti-parliamentary *topoi*, rather than inventing something new; or perhaps their novelty consists in a further simplification of these *topoi*, for example in terms of the "us" versus "them" divide. Such a view of politics can be understood as a very narrow one, if judged in terms of political literacy, for which the parliamentary style of politics offers much more complex and nuanced resources.

In parliamentary terms, the talk of consensus appears instead as an optical illusion that disappears with a more nuanced, multilevel political reading of parliamentary debates. The relative weaknesses of contemporary politics

---

[57] Carl Schmitt, *Der Begriff des Politischen* (Berlin: Duncker & Humblot, 1932).
[58] Chantal Mouffe, *On the Political* (London: Verso, 2005).

refer, rather, to the dominance of the government-versus-opposition divide in parliament, as well as to the overestimation of the electoral dependence of parliamentarians on their own parties. Instead of the focus on government, parties, and elections, a more parliamentary type of professional politician could be needed.[59] Such parliamentarians could apply their political imagination in employing their procedural competences, their sense for nuances in the parliamentary type of deliberative rhetoric, and their ability to cleverly use complex chances in playing with parliamentary time.

---

[59] On the ideal of a back-bencher, see Paul Flynn, *How to Be an MP?* (London: Biteback, 2013).

9
Vilfredo Pareto on Rhetoric and Populism

Giovanni Damele

Introduction

Together with Gaetano Mosca and Robert Michels, Vilfredo Pareto is considered one of the "founding fathers" of classical elitism.[1] After spending most of his life working as an engineer and industrial manager and, later, as the successor of Léon Walras in the chair of political economy at the University of Lausanne, in the latter part of his life Pareto devoted himself mainly to the study of sociology. This study, as is well known, was condensed into the monumental (and often cumbersome) *Trattato di Sociologia Generale*, published in 1916 and translated into English by Arthur Livingston in 1935 with the title *The Mind and Society*.

---

[1] The paternity of the theory gave origin to the (not so) "small controversy" between Mosca and Pareto: Mosca claimed the paternity with a short article published in 1907 on "La Riforma Sociale," under the title *Piccola polemica* ("small controversy"), which Pareto never directly answered (even though he partially edited a note of the *Manuel d'économie politique*, in which he quoted the French politicians Paul Deschanel and Gustave de Lamarzelle and the British jurist and historian Henry J. Sumner Maine, but not Mosca). The controversy continued as late as the 1930s, opposing Mosca (who died in 1941) to scholars and students of Pareto (who died in 1923). As a matter of fact, Mosca published his *Teorica dei governi e governo parlamentare* in 1884 and further developed his theory in the first edition of the *Elementi di scienza politica* (1896), while Pareto began to develop its sociological theory with an article entitled "Una applicazione di teorie sociologiche," published in August 1900 in the *Rivista italiana di sociologia* (Vol. 4, 401–456, July–August 1900), and developed a definitive version of his "elite theory" only in the first edition of his *Trattato di sociologia generale*, published in Italian in 1916 (Firenze: Barbera) and in French in 1917 and 1919 (Paris: Payot et Cie). It seems fair, today, to recognize that Mosca developed the idea (which, in itself, is neither new nor original) into a coherent theory before Pareto and that the latter was probably in some respects influenced by the former. However, while Mosca's theory is mainly confined to the field of political theory, Pareto's approach has a broader range, analyzing the relationship between (ruling) minorities and (ruled) majorities in different fields of social life, and was developed from the field of political economy, while recognizing the limitations of the model of the so-called *homo oeconomicus*. In addition, Mosca always criticized the choice of the term "elite"—which, according to him, implies a (positive) value judgment—always preferring to it expressions such as "political class" or "ruling class." However, it seems fair to assume that Pareto's terminological choice has been mainly due to linguistic reasons: we should not forget that Pareto's first language was not Italian, but French.

Giovanni Damele, *Vilfredo Pareto on Rhetoric and Populism* In: *Populism, Demagoguery, and Rhetoric in Historical Perspective*. Edited by: Giuseppe Ballacci and Rob Goodman, Oxford University Press. © Oxford University Press 2024.
DOI: 10.1093/oso/9780197650974.003.0010

The conventional account of the political sociology of Vilfredo Pareto highlights its antiparliamentary, antidemocratic dimension.[2] Various authors suggested a direct link between Pareto's elitism and the fascist view on the relationship between the crowds and their leader.[3] More generally, Pareto, together with other elitists (such as Michels, Mosca, and Moises Ostrogorski), has been described as one of the interpreters of a "disenchantment of democracy," having "exposed democracy's fundamental elitism" by "stressing that the people's contribution to democracy is little more than the participation in the selection of their rulers." From this premise, they draw the conclusion that "any additional involvement of the people can [...] be seen as disturbing, pathological and overloading the system."[4] According to this viewpoint, their work should be read together with the contemporary literature on crowd psychology. With their work, Mosca, Pareto, and Michels further developed the argument of authors such as Gustave Le Bon, Gabriel Tarde, and Scipio Sighele, according to which "crowds subordinate reason to the irrational influence of the leader and the group," stressing "the weakness of rationality in politics" and "arguing that subconscious suggestion dominates politics in mass society."[5] Their "realist" or "Machiavellian" distrust of parliamentarism[6] and their elitism have been said to be based on a "conventional antidemocratic critique of the masses," which "identified mass society with the rule of irrational emotions, uncontrollable impulses, and dangerous passions."[7]

---

[2] Zeev Sternhell, Mario Sznajder, Ashéri Maia, and David Maisel, *The Birth of Fascist Ideology: From Cultural Rebellion to Political Revolution* (Princeton, NJ: Princeton University Press, 1996), 31–32, 252. See also Andreas Kalyvas, *Democracy and the Politics of the Extraordinary: Max Weber, Carl Schmitt, and Hannah Arendt* (Cambridge, UK: Cambridge University Press, 2009), 70.

[3] See, e.g., James W. Vander Zanden, "Pareto and Fascism Reconsidered," *The American Journal of Economics and Sociology* 19, no. 4 (1960), 399–411. According to him, "Pareto can best be understood as a precursor of fascism. In particular, four main aspects of his work stand out conspicuously in this regard: first, his intense anti-intellectualism and anti-rationalism; second, his quasi-biological theory of the elite; third, his militant vilification and hatred of democracy; and fourth, his glorification of force as an instrument of acquiring and maintaining power" (411). In an early review of the translation in English of the *Trattato*, Ellsworth Faris said that "a reading of the fourth volume reveals an extraordinary correspondence" between Pareto's view and Italian fascism. Faris, "An Estimate of Pareto," *American Journal of Sociology* 41, no. 5 (1936): 667.

[4] Yves Mény and Yves Surel, "The Constitutive Ambiguity of Populism," in *Democracies and the Populist Challenge*, ed. Yves Mény and Yves Surel (New York: Palgrave, 2002), 5.

[5] Ellen Kennedy, "Hostis Not Inimicus: Toward a Theory of the Public in the Work of Carl Schmitt," in *Law as Politics: Carl Schmitt's Critique of Liberalism*, ed. David Dyzenhaus (Durham, NC: Duke University Press, 1998), 102–3. See also Giovanni Damele, "Crowds, Leaders, and Epidemic Psychosis: The Relationship between Crowd Psychology and Elite Theory and Its Contemporary Relevance," *Frontiers in Political Science* 4 (October 2022), 1–10.

[6] Jan-Werner Müller, *A Dangerous Mind: Carl Schmitt in Post-War European Thought* (New Haven, CT: Yale University Press, 2003), 215.

[7] Andreas Kalyvas, *Democracy and the Politics of the Extraordinary: Max Weber, Carl Schmitt, and Hannah Arendt* (Cambridge, UK: Cambridge University Press, 2009), 70.

An alternative, although not less conventional, interpretation sees Pareto as an author who (together with his elitist fellows) realistically recognized that a liberal oligarchy can be considered a "lesser evil," given the premise of the ineluctability of an oligarchic form of government.[8] Or, less indulgently albeit more convincingly, this interpretation considers Pareto as an author who, despite his deep and polemical pessimism (disguised as "pure science") sowed the seeds for a realistic approach to the study of contemporary democracy: a (liberal) democratic elitism.[9]

More recently, both of these interpretations have been contested by challenging the dominant interpretation of "liberal elitism" without, in doing so, accusing the classical elitists in general, and Pareto in particular, of proto-fascist attitudes. Natasha Piano recently highlighted how the conventional account minimized the role of what she considers one of Pareto's and Mosca's main concerns: "containing plutocracy in the age of mass politics." According to Piano, far from being "celebrations of an elite-enabling and mass-constraining model," their criticisms of "plutocracy advancing under a democratic guise," open "possibilities for democracy" through a "self-conscious confrontation with fundamental obstacles to human flourishing."[10] More concretely, their work on "political transparency" and plutocratic domination may even serve "as a subversive tool in disrupting the domination of a particular ruling class."[11] As for Pareto, Piano notes that "his analysis does not impute to the masses an inherent cognitive incapacity for participating in politics" and that "the dominant class-based binary that animates his political writings is not one of elites versus masses but rather the distinction between speculators and rentiers."[12] Consistently interested "in economic inequality," Pareto, according to Piano, "sought to combat the plutocratic tendencies of liberal capitalism" and denounced modern parliamentary systems as "plutocracy's handmaiden," an "inherently deficient system."[13]

Frequently seen as an antidemocratic proto-fascist, Pareto, who admired the Swiss (direct) democracy,[14] can be reinterpreted, according to this view,

---

[8] Raymond Aron, *Main Currents in Sociological Thought*, Vol. 2 (Harmondsworth, UK: Penguin Books, 1977), 174.
[9] Giovanni Sartori, *The Theory of Democracy Revisited*, Vol. 1 (Chatham, NJ: Chatham House, 1987), 48.
[10] Natasha Piano, "Revisiting Democratic Elitism: The Italian School of Elitism, American Political Science, and the Problem of Plutocracy," *The Journal of Politics* 81, no. 2 (2019): 525
[11] Ibid., 527.
[12] Ibid., 528.
[13] Ibid., 527–28.
[14] Sartori, *The Theory of Democracy*, 47.

as an opponent of liberal parliamentarism based on an oligarchic representative system. Reframing the tradition of these Italian theorists, Piano reveals that the later reception of Pareto and Mosca was flawed by an elitist bias, just as the traditional interpretation of Machiavelli—one of Pareto's main sources—obscured his anti-elitist critique.[15] The result is an intriguing reversal of the meaning of the title of James Burnham's classical book of 1943— *The Machiavellians: Defenders of Freedom*—which reunited under the same label both Machiavelli and the classical elitists. Now the members of the Italian school can be considered as "Machiavellians" not because of their elitism, but because of their "anti-elitist pessimism."[16]

Interestingly enough, one of the consequences of this interpretation is a reconfiguration of Pareto, a classical elitist thinker, which focuses on his criticisms of the plutocratic oligarchy, with the result of giving to his arguments an almost populistic nuance. This is particularly true when we consider the well-known argument of Ernesto Laclau, according to which "populism is not an ideology but a mode of construction of the political, based on splitting society in two and calling for the mobilization of 'those at the bottom' against the existing authorities."[17] Certainly, as I noted above, Piano insists that Pareto does not emphasize the populist opposition of "elites" and "masses." However, also making reference to Pareto's late work *The Transformation of Democracy*, Piano argues that the Italian sociologist preeminently demonized plutocracy as "the greatest nemesis of political life per se" or "the most insidious problem," because "it creates room for the 'devious' measures that speculators use to dupe the masses." For him, "the speculators that reign through modern representative governments are the perpetrators of injustice."[18]

This interpretation, however, raises a further question. Can Pareto's "pessimistic, vigilant outlooks" really help us develop, as Piano claims, "our own dispositional strategy that emboldens future democratic containment

---

[15] See John P. McCormick, "Machiavelli against Republicanism: On the Cambridge School's 'Guicciardinian Moments.'" *Political Theory* 31, no. 5 (2003): 615–43.

[16] See, e.g., Piano, "Revisiting Democratic Elitism," 532: "The Italians worried that leaders perverted the democratic process; Schumpeter expressed suspicious views of the elite leadership's competence in organizing politics for the future." The "anti-elitist pessimism remained consistent among them," even if "the tone of their respective pessimisms resulted in different conclusions that should not be divorced from their expressed political prescriptions."

[17] Ernesto Laclau, "Logiques de la construction politique et identités populaires," in *Les gauches du XXIe siècle: Un dialogue Nord–Sud*, ed. Jean-Louis Laville and José Luis Coraggio (Lormont: Le bord de l'eau, 2016), 151. Quoted in Pierre Rosanvallon, *The Populist Century: History, Theory, Critique* (Medford: Polity, 2021), 17.

[18] Piano, "Revisiting Democratic Elitism," 528.

or reversal of plutocratic domination"?[19] And, if yes, in what sense? Without a doubt, Pareto was a staunch critic of plutocracy, which he basically interpreted as a sign of degeneration of the political system. However, in order to answer those questions, I think that we need to come back to two interpretive issues. First, far from occupying a "substantially secondary place,"[20] the theory of elite circulation plays a crucial role in Pareto's sociopolitical theory. When we pay attention to it, we can see that the "dominant class-based binary" relation of "elites versus masses" is at least as important as "the distinction between speculators and rentiers." Second, if it is (at least partially) true that Pareto's analysis "does not impute to the masses an inherent cognitive incapacity for participating in politics," it is also important to understand the pivotal function attributed by Pareto to emotions and "sentiments" in the field of politics. It is precisely by acting on this dimension that "speculators" can succeed in their "protracted, deliberate efforts ... to 'gull' the lower classes ... into supporting their own self-interested ends."[21] Thus, the combination of "sentiments" (in Pareto's terms) and "cognitive capacity" (in Piano's words) actually frames the political relationship between rulers and ruled, dominators and dominated. Finally, once we understand these two aspects of Pareto's thought (the centrality of elite-circulation and that of sentiments), his relevance to the analysis of contemporary political phenomena—and of populism, in particular—becomes even clearer.

The Force of the Sentiments and the Sentiment of Force: Elites and Their Circulation

Pareto famously distinguishes between logical, non-logical, and illogical actions. In a frequently quoted paragraph of his *Trattato*, he affirms:

> we apply the term logical actions to actions that logically conjoin means to ends not only from the standpoint of the subject performing them, but from the standpoint of other persons who have a more extensive knowledge—in other words, to actions that are logical both subjectively and objectively

---

[19] Ibid., 537.
[20] Michelangelo Bovero, *La Teoria dell'elite* (Torino: Loescher, 1975), 47.
[21] Piano, "Revisiting Democratic Elitism," 528.

in the sense just explained. Other actions we shall call non-logical (by no means the same as "illogical").[22]

Thus, non-logical actions are subjectively, but not objectively, logical. They are, in a sense, the result of an *ex post* pseudo-rationalization: a kind of facade legitimation of irrational behaviors. "People," Pareto notes in another frequently quoted paragraph of the *Trattato*, "feel a need for covering their non-logical conduct with a varnish of logic."[23] This observation leads to the fundamental psycho-sociological distinction between "residues" and "derivations." While the former are "more stable" and "substantial," the latter are "fairly variable" and "contingent." "Residues" correspond *directly* to non-logical conduct, while "derivations" correspond to it *indirectly*. Being "the manifestation of the need of logic that the human being feels," derivations clothe the residues "with logical or pseudo-logical reasonings."[24] Thus, derivations are basically theories, or also, in political context, "ideological systems," while residues represent the emotional and irrational ground of our discourses and our conduct.

Initially, Pareto gives a preliminary, broader definition of "derivations." They comprise, he affirms, "logical reasonings, unsound reasonings, and manifestations of sentiments used for purposes of derivation: they are manifestations of the human being's hunger for thinking."[25] However, this definition is immediately narrowed in the same paragraph: "If that hunger were satisfied by logico-experimental reasonings only, there would be no derivations," Pareto recognizes. This "human hunger for thinking is satisfied in any number of ways; by pseudo-experimental reasonings, by words that stir the sentiments, by fatuous, inconclusive 'talk.'" At this point, Pareto concludes, "derivations come into being." They are somewhere in between logico-experimental theories and purely instinctive behaviors: "they do not figure at the two extreme ends of the line," but "in the intermediate cases."[26]

From this psychological premise, Pareto comes to a sociological conclusion. The various distributions of residues—and of their correspondent derivations—give rise to the phenomenon of social heterogeneity. According to Aron, Pareto makes the movement of society depend on four variables,

---

[22] Vilfredo Pareto, *The Mind and Society* (New York: Harcourt, Brace, 1935), § 150.
[23] Ibid., § 975.
[24] Ibid., § 798.
[25] Ibid., § 1401.
[26] Ibid., § 1401.

which are "in a state of mutual dependence," namely "interests, residues, derivations, social heterogeneity." Thus, the "general mechanism of society"[27] may be understood considering the "psychic make-up" by virtue of which "human beings are heterogeneous and unequal, and fall into different social strata."[28]

Indeed, starting from the observation of the pure fact of social heterogeneity, it is then possible to distinguish "a class of the people who have the highest indices in their branch of activity" and to give to that class "the name of elite."[29] The "elite" can be further divided into two strata: "a governing elite, comprising individuals who directly or indirectly play some considerable part in government, and a non-governing elite, comprising the rest."[30] Pareto's theory of the elite can, thus, be analyzed into "static" and "dynamic" forms. While the static form identifies the heterogeneous distribution of "inclinations, sentiments, attitudes,"[31] the dynamic form analyzes the circulation of "classes" with different "psychic make-up." In political terms, this means that, according to Pareto, an ideally constant circulation between governing and non-governing elites, a moderate "openness" (through co-optation, election, or other forms of selection) of the governing elites toward those "who have the highest indices in their branch of activity," leads to a healthy equilibrium between conservative and innovative forces and allows the substitution of "decadent elements no longer possessing the residues suitable for keeping them in power."[32] This equilibrium, however, can only be "ideal." In reality, inertia and the inevitable tendency of the governing elite to defend its power and the privileges associated with it "slows down" class-circulation, leading to the accumulation of "decadent elements" among the members of the governing elites and preventing the entry of "suitable" new elements. The lack of circulation increases the pressure in the social body and the probability of "explosions" of revolutionary outcomes, whose result is the violent substitution of the old with a new elite.[33]

Pareto defines the circulations of elites as the manner in which the individuals of a given population, and their attitudes, "intermix" between the

---

[27] Aron, *Main Currents*, 160.
[28] Samuel E. Finer, "Introduction," *Vilfredo Pareto: Sociological Writings*, ed. Samuel E. Finer (London, Pall Mall Press, 1966), 14.
[29] Pareto, *The Mind and Society*, § 2031.
[30] Ibid., § 2032.
[31] Ibid., § 2041.
[32] Ibid., § 2057.
[33] Ibid., §§ 2057–58.

two strata of the "elite" and the "non-elite." In order to understand this mix, he catalogues all the main residues into different classes, the first two by far being the most relevant in the political field. With his characteristically idiosyncratic vocabulary, he names these two classes "instinct of combinations" (Class I) and "persistence of aggregates" (Class II). As a matter of fact, these two "classes" correspond to the "foxy" and the "leonine" attitudes to which Machiavelli famously refers in the eighteenth chapter of *The Prince*. While the former includes the characteristics of the dynamic and astute individuals, the latter represents, in the "psychological mix-up," the conservative part and the proclivity to use force whenever necessary for the defense of a certain position.

Furthermore, Pareto associates with the prevalence of one class or the other two anthropological ideal types: the "speculators" and the "rentiers." We should not be deceived by the economical origins of these two labels, which come from Pareto's background: they apply to every field of human actions and, above all, to the political one. While the rentiers are willing to defend their position—or to conquer new positions—with force, the speculators follow "lines of least resistance": they maximize their utility, minimizing the resistance of others, essentially in an opportunistic way. Incidentally, here we can meet a common point between Pareto's sociological analysis and his liberal political ideas about the risks of the exponential growth of the state in all its manifestations (bureaucracy, militarism, protectionism, etc.). The larger the state, Pareto insists, the greater are the opportunities for enrichment for the speculators, which results in an inevitable disequilibrium in the higher stratum of the society and, in particular, in the governing elite. More generally, and, Pareto seems to suggest, independently from other circumstances, in the higher stratum of the society, "Class II residues [persistence of the aggregates] gradually lose in strength," to the point of not being "reinforced by tides upwelling from the lower stratum."[34] Residues of the kind of the "instinct of the combinations" gradually prevail, precisely because through them, people follow "lines of least resistance." Thus, we can integrate what was said above: the ideal equilibrium among residues, in the governing elite, can be unbalanced not only by a prevalence of "conservative" attitudes—which ultimately leads to a sclerosis—but also by the opposing prevalence of "speculators," which increases the velocity of class circulation, to the point of destabilizing the persistence of the elite.

[34] Ibid., §2048.

As a matter of fact—as Natasha Piano acutely understood—Pareto seems far more concerned by the destabilization created by the prevalence of Class I residues, than by the sclerosis created by the prevalence of Class II residues. In order to understand this point, we should come back to the problem of the "decay" of the "upper stratum" of society, which Pareto also calls "aristocracy." In some cases, or "in the beginning," Pareto notes, "the majority of individuals belonging to such aristocracies actually possess the qualities requisite for remaining there."[35] When this occurs, "military, religious, and commercial aristocracies and plutocracies" are "parts of the governing elite" or even "the whole of it." In other words, "military, religious, and commercial aristocracies and plutocracies" are made by victorious warriors, prosperous merchants, and opulent plutocrats that are "each in his own field . . . superior to the average individual." "Under those circumstances," Pareto concludes, "the label correspond[s] to an actual capacity." However, "as time goes by, considerable, sometimes very considerable, differences arise between the capacity and the label." Thus, aristocracies "decay not in numbers only," but also "in quality."[36] Interestingly enough, with the aim of explaining the meaning of this "quality," Pareto adds that "they lose their vigour" and "that there is a decline in the proportions of the residues which enabled them to win their power and hold it."[37] It is fair to conclude that this "decline" is directly related to the resistance to using force whenever necessary.

This relationship not only is explicitly articulated by Pareto himself, but also is revealed by quotations that we may find in various parts of his work, and particularly by quotations taken from the third volume of Hippolyte Taine's *magnum opus*, *Les origins de la France contemporaine*, dedicated to the "Jacobin conquest." Taine's role as a major source of inspiration for the literature of the so-called psychology of the crowds has been widely recognized, most recently by Laclau. According to him, Taine "formulated in the crudest and most uncompromising way" two "crucial assumptions which

---

[35] Ibid., §§ 2051–52.
[36] Hence, his famous claim that "history is a graveyard of aristocracies" (§ 2053). Pareto seems to consider this process as ineluctable and not as a pathological state that can be avoided. See, e.g., § 2260: "Such phenomena, long the subject of remark, are usually described as aberrations, or 'degenerations,' of 'democracy'; but when and where one may be introduced to the perfect, or even the merely decent, state from which said aberration or 'degeneration' has occurred, no one ever manages to tell. The best that can be said is that when democracy was an opposition party it did not show as many blemishes as it does at present; but that is a trait common to almost all opposition parties, which lack not so much the will as the chance to go wrong."
[37] Pareto, *The Mind and Society*, § 2054.

have dominated much of the early stages of mass psychology": the first, "that the dividing line between rational forms of social organization and mass phenomena coincides, to a large extent, with the frontier separating the normal from the pathological"; the second, "that the distinction between rationality and irrationality would largely overlap with the distinction between the individual and the group."[38]

Pareto's reading of Taine is critical (as always): sometimes he shares his main assumptions, but in other cases he criticizes his interpretation of the causes and reasons of the French revolution. Even more than the image of the "irrational" crowd, what Pareto mainly finds in Taine's historiographical accounts is the representation of an elite in decadence, the aristocracy, whose fate parallels, from his viewpoint, the decadence of the late-nineteenth-century bourgeoisie.[39] In both cases, the source of the decline is identified by Pareto in the inability of the elite—and in particular the ruling elite—to resort to the use of force when necessary. According to Taine, quoted by Pareto, "at the end of the 18th century, a horror of blood prevailed in the upper, and even in the middle class; refinement of manners and idyllic dreams had weakened the militant will power." At this point, Pareto adds a comment: "And today again the French bourgeoisie indulges in sweet dreams." Then, the quotation continues: "Everywhere the magistrates were forgetting that the maintenance of society and civilization is infinitely more valuable than the lives of a handful of offenders and fools. They forgot that the primary objective of government, as it is of the police force, is the preservation of order through force."[40] Basically, Pareto accepts this reconstruction, but rectifies the interpretation. According to him, "it was not only education which deprived them of active courage, it was a combination of circumstances, including, among others, their sentimental follies." Following the same path, "the bourgeois of today who, in their speeches and their writings, flatter the enemy and lick the boots 'of the poor and humble,' are ripe for the rope, and they will let themselves be despoiled and killed without offering resistance."[41]

Thus, more than an imbalance of "cunning," decadence seems to be typically caused by an excess of it, and a reluctance to use force. From this viewpoint, Pareto seems to distance himself from Machiavelli, who ultimately

---

[38] Ernesto Laclau, *On Populist Reason* (London: Verso, 2005), 29.
[39] See Vifredo Pareto, *The Rise and Fall of the Elites: An Application of Theoretical Sociology* (Totowa, NJ: Bedminster Press, 1968), 61: "the elite of that time resembled the bourgeoisie of today."
[40] Hippolyte Taine, *La conquête Jacobine*, quoted in Pareto, *The Rise and Fall*, 61.
[41] Pareto, *The Rise and Fall*, 60, n.29.

thought that vulpine astuteness was more important than leonine force. However, the other side of the scale is not less important. As Pareto noticed in his *Les systèmes socialistes*, the liberal elites had also lost the power of influence because they thought they could "direct the masses through reason alone," whereas people can be spurred to action only "by engaging with their feelings and with their interests."[42] Emotions are particularly relevant in the political field, and interests and their relevance define a particular type of political regime. Let us begin with the relevance of *persuasion* through *emotion* in Pareto's sociopolitical theory.

Emotions and Persuasion

Human beings, Pareto affirms, "feel a certain need for logic, but readily satisfy it with pseudo-logical propositions."[43] Derivation seems to respond to this "need," thus satisfying a "psychic" necessity. In part, we verbalize our irrational motivations with pseudo-rational justifications because we need to feel that our actions are not founded on irrational or, say, "pre-rational" grounds. Even when we fail to obtain a logical-rational justification in the proper sense, the pseudo-rationalization still satisfies us. It is important to remember, at this point, that the distinction between logical and non-logical actions implies, from Pareto's viewpoint, the distinction between subjective and objective judgment about them.

However, there is a second—not less relevant—function performed by the derivations. In paragraph 168 of the first volume, Pareto affirms that "theoretical discussions [...] are not [...] very serviceable" for directly modifying human conduct. They may be indirectly effective for modifying a psychic state. However, "to attain that objective, appeal must be made to sentiments rather than to logic and the results of experience." Thus, he concludes, "in order to influence people thought has to be transformed into sentiment." If we consider that, according to Pareto, "derivations are manifestations of sentiments,"[44] than we can understand the centrality of the "derivations" in what we may call a theory of persuasion included in the *Trattato*.[45]

---

[42] Vilfredo Pareto, *Les systèmes socialistes. Cours professé à l'Université de Lausanne*, Tome Premier (Paris, V. Giard & E. Birère, 1902), 66–67.
[43] Pareto, *The Mind and Society*, § 2086.
[44] Ibid., § 1746.
[45] Pareto's general theory of sociology is relevant for argumentation theory in general and for rhetoric in particular. This specific topic was approached by Norberto Bobbio in a paper published

Persuasion, in a political context, is mainly obtained through derivations, which are, in turn, based on emotions. Thus, ultimately, the residues and their verbalizations play a crucial role in the sociopolitical context. Indeed, according to Pareto, "a derivation which merely satisfies that hankering for logic which the human being feels, and which neither is transmuted into sentiments nor re-enforces sentiments, has slight if any effect on the social equilibrium." "In order to influence society," Pareto concludes, "theories have to be transmuted into sentiments, derivations into residues."[46] This persuasive force is particularly relevant in a social context. With a characteristically realistic approach, Pareto insists that "we shall [. . .] not stop with the reflection that a certain argument is inconclusive, idiotic, absurd, but ask ourselves whether it may not be expressing sentiments beneficial to society, and expressing them in a manner calculated to persuade many people who would not be at all influenced by the soundest logico-experimental argument."[47] According to Pareto, the analysis of this persuasive force is not limited to the demagoguery of the political speculators. Political communication in general is largely a matter of emotive persuasion. In some paragraphs, Pareto actually makes reference to people who "would not be influenced by logico-experimental discourses," in others, to "human beings" in general. For instance, in paragraph 1397 we may read that "human beings are persuaded in the main by sentiments," that is, residues, and that "we may [. . .] foresee, as for that matter experience shows, that derivations derive the force they have, not, or at least not exclusively, from logico-experimental considerations, but from sentiments." We may conclude that derivations, with their process of verbalization and pseudo-rationalization, strengthen or intensify already existing sentiments: "Once the derivation is accepted it lends strength and aggressiveness to the corresponding sentiments, which now have found a way to express themselves."[48] The "effects of derivations," we are told by Pareto, serve "primarily to give greater strength and effectiveness to the residues that they express."[49]

---

in 1961 on "Pareto and Argumentation Theory": "Pareto e la teoria dell'argomentazione," *Revue Internationale de Philosophie* 15, no. 58 (1961): 376–99). The topic has been also approached by Francesco Aqueci, *Le funzioni del linguaggio secondo Pareto* (Berne: Peter Lang, 1991); and Pier Paolo Portinaro, "Sofismi e derivazioni. Bentham e Pareto," in *Vilfredo Pareto: a 100 anni dal Trattato di sociologia generale*, ed. Pier Paolo Portinaro (Torino: Accademia delle Scienze), 31–55. This section of the article is largely indebted to these three texts.

[46] Pareto, *The Mind and Society*, § 1746.
[47] Ibid., § 445.
[48] Ibid., § 1747.
[49] Ibid., § 2201.

Moving from these premises, Pareto outlines—in the third book of *The Mind and Society*—what we may call a theory of argumentation. From paragraph 1543 to 1686 we find, indeed, what we may consider a treaty of rhetoric and a book of fallacies. These paragraphs correspond to the chapter devoted to the analysis of the fourth class of derivations, called, in Pareto's terminology, "verbal proofs." These are, in a sense, derivations par excellence,[50] since the whole activity of "derivation" is developed, according to Pareto, through language. These "verbal derivations" are "obtained through the use of terms of indefinite, doubtful, equivocal meaning and which do not correspond to any reality."[51] Pareto, as in other cases, further divides the class into subcategories, marked with Greek letters. The first, IV-α, includes "indefinite terms," that is, "terms that do indeed arouse indefinite sentiments but otherwise correspond to nothing real." IV-β includes "terms designating things and arousing incidental sentiments, or incidental sentiments determining choice of terms."[52] "Derivations of this type," Pareto says, "play an important role in judiciary eloquence and in politics," being "very effective in persuasion" because "the sentiments that are set in motion by the language used work upon the auditor unawares." For example: "In the Italo-Turkish war of 1912, Arabs who brought information from the Turco-Arab camp to the Italians were called 'informers'; those who carried information from the Italian camp to the Turks and Arabs, 'spies.'" The force of an argument such as the latter depends on the "sentiments" associated with certain words. The fact that these "sophistries [...] continue to be so lavishly used" despite the fact that "so many writers all the way from Aristotle to Bentham have been sign-boarding" their fallacious nature, clearly shows that "their force lies not in the argument, which, to tell the truth, is childish, but in the sentiments that they stir."[53] Thus, a term like "freedom" can mean "nowadays [...] the exact opposite of what it meant fifty years ago." However, "the sentiments that it stirs are the same—in other words, it designates a state of things of which the average auditor approves."

The next category, IV-γ, consists of "terms with numbers of meanings, and different things designated by single terms," which, in turn, designate a certain "accord with certain sentiments," carrying with it "the assent of

---

[50] Bobbio, "Pareto e la teoria dell'argomentazione," 387.
[51] Pareto, *The Mind and Society*, § 1543.
[52] Ibid., § 1552.
[53] Ibid., § 1552 n.

the believer." It is the case of terms or expressions such as "highest good" or "state of nature."[54] A word like "truth," Pareto notices, on the one hand, "signifies accord with the facts—what is sometimes called 'experimental' and 'historical' truth." On the other hand, "it designates mere accord with certain sentiments, which carries with it the assent of the believer." Between these two extremes "there are any number of intermediate significations."[55] Sub-class IV-δ consists of metaphors, allegories, and analogies, "much used by metaphysicists and theologians."[56] Finally, sub-class IV-ε represents "the extreme limit in verbal derivation": "vague, indefinite terms" which correspond "to nothing concrete" and end "as a mere jingle of words." Few of them "are for the consumption of the ignorant, who halt in stupefaction before the strangeness of the terms, and imagine that they must conceal some profound mystery." Most "are for the use of metaphysicists, who feed on them day in and day out and end by imagining that they stand for real things."[57]

Another interesting aspect, from a rhetorical point of view, is the centrality attributed by Pareto to enthymemes. According to him, derivations are frequently constructed through enthymemes, intended as strategic devices, not as means for economizing the cognitive resources of the audience.[58] The "enthymematic" dimension is, thus, relevant in order to understand the difference between persuasive and logico-experimental discourse. Pareto stresses that "the qualities that make a good derivation out of a reasoning are oftentimes the opposite [...] of the qualities which would make it a sound logico-experimental reasoning."[59] The enthymematic structure of an argument, for instance, conceals its erratic path. The "derivation

---

[54] Ibid., §§ 1556–67.
[55] Ibid., § 1567.
[56] Ibid., §§ 1614, 1616.
[57] Ibid., § 1686.
[58] Pareto gives an example, making reference to the Kaiser Wilhelm's claim that he ruled by divine right, a claim that was considered by the German opposition as an "flat contradiction with the 'modern conception of the state.'" The "modern conception of the state," Pareto says, "is another abstraction." "The conception voiced by the German Kaiser is held by many people living today. Why then is it not entitled to be called a 'modern conception'? An enthymeme is involved. Suppose we state it: 'The Kaiser's conception is contrary to the modern conception of the state; therefore it is bad.' [The major premise has been suppressed.] The completed syllogism would be: [Major premise:] 'Everything that is contrary to the modern conception of the state is bad.' [Minor premise:] 'The Kaiser's conception is contrary to the modern conception of the state.' [Conclusion:] 'Therefore the Kaiser's conception is bad.' The major premise was suppressed as calling attention to the weak point in the argument." Pareto, *The Mind and Society*, §§ 1522, 1525.
[59] Ibid., § 1772.

follows some path, any path, that will bring the two points together," since "ordinarily the point of departure and the point of arrival are known in advance."[60] In spite of these characteristics, human beings usually do not have any difficulty "in devising and accepting sophistical derivations of that type," precisely because, as we already know, at the same time "they feel a certain need for logic" and they are ready to satisfy it "with pseudo-logical propositions."[61]

Demagoguery and Government by Speculators

The Machiavellian dyad of fox and lion, reflected in the Paretian distinction between "Class I" and "Class II" residues, becomes a main criterion, in the *Trattato*, for a taxonomy of governments. It is easy to understand that the prevalence of the "vulpine" dimension is to be found in what Pareto calls the "government by 'speculators.'"[62] Starting from the premise of the "scientific" objectivity, Pareto does not associate an ethical value judgment to the speculators, "as with other elements in the social order." It is important to note that, according to Pareto, "the speculators are not to be condemned from the standpoint of social utility because they do things that are censured by one or another of the current ethical systems; nor are they to be absolved from any given ethical standpoint because they have proved socially beneficial." The utility depends upon, again, "the relative proportions of speculators to persons strong in Class II residues, either in the population at large or in the governing classes." And the problem, according to Pareto, is always the possibility of a "great decline in the Class II residues in our masses at large or even merely in our governing classes."[63] More generally, in modern democratic governments, given the need to obtain widespread consensus, the extent of clientelism and other abuses related to elections and parliaments increases, while the benefits initially generated by the combinatory and innovative skills of the hegemonic class of speculators decrease rapidly.[64] Thus, Pareto recognizes that the hegemony of the speculators can have a beneficial

---

[60] Ibid., §1590.
[61] Ibid., §2086.
[62] Ibid., § 2275.
[63] Ibid., § 2254.
[64] Silvano Belligni, "Arte dei governi, spoliazione e democrazia. La teorica della corruzione in Vilfredo Pareto," in *Economia, Sociologia e Politica Nell'opera Di Vilfredo Pareto*, ed. Corrado Malandrino and Roberto Marchionatti (Firenze: Leo S. Olschki, 2000), 360.

impact in terms of social development. However, in the long run, the imbalance in the distribution of the residues among the governing class will necessarily lead to negative consequences.

The prevalence of the vulpine characteristics underlies two distinct subtypes of government, depending on whether "intelligence and cunning" are "used chiefly to play upon" sentiments or interests.[65] The first case (II-a) corresponds to religious or hierocratic governments.[66] The second case, "which," Pareto carefully notes, "does not necessarily imply disregard of sentiments," results in "governments like the demagogic regimes in Athens" or "the very important type of government flourishing in our day," that is, government "by speculators." While "class-circulation is generally slow in the subtype II-a," it is "rapid, sometimes very rapid, in subtype II-b," attaining "its maximum velocity under the system of our contemporary speculators." In both cases, "Class I residues predominate as compared with Class II residues." Indeed, "to play artfully, shrewdly, and with success upon both interests and sentiments requires a governing class possessing combination instincts in high degree and unencumbered with too many scruples."[67]

According to Pareto, speculators therefore govern both by means of demagoguery (acting on feelings, through persuasive discourses) and by means of clientelist practices, acting on interests. The fact that this second aspect characterizes the "plutocratic" government of speculators does not mean that the first is less important. Speculators have, thus, a competitive advantage, represented by their ability to replace force with cunning. While the use of force always implies a "cost"—not in economic terms, but in physical and emotional terms—the use of cunning and demagoguery makes it possible to govern without brutality, while the economic costs of clientelism can be passed on to the community as a whole (public debt).

The evolution from governments in which Class II residues predominate toward governments in which Class I residues are prevalent is seen by Pareto as a triumph of demagogic over military elites. This "circulation," in turn, further accelerates as the "plutocratic" elites of contemporary political speculators impose themselves. The final result, as we already now, is an alteration, or, better, an unbalancing among the ruling classes and the power elites themselves. At the end, Pareto concludes, "such regimes may degenerate into

---

[65] Pareto, *The Mind and Society*, § 2275.
[66] Ibid., § 2274.
[67] Ibid., § 2276.

government by shrewd but cowardly individuals who are easily overthrown by violence, whether from abroad or from within."[68] Again, the degeneration of the elite is clearly, from Pareto's viewpoint, mainly a decline in terms of capacity for self-defense, which leaves the pluto-democratic elite of speculators exposed to the risk of being replaced by more determined and aggressive counter-elites.

Conclusion

We can return to Taine and to how his historiographical account of the French revolution was interpreted by Pareto in analogy with the situation of the liberal European bourgeoisie between the nineteenth and early twentieth centuries. The crucial point is that, both for Taine and for Pareto, the absence of leaders is tantamount to the absence of organization: "a multitude being simply a herd." In 1789, the mistrust of the Parisian multitude "of its natural leaders, of the great, of the wealthy, of persons in office and clothed with authority" was, according to Taine, "inveterate and incurable."[69] So was, Pareto noticed, the mistrust of the industrial proletariat toward the bourgeoisie. Certainly, the liberal, plutocratic elites were able to deceive the masses. And it was also possible to find common interests between the bourgeoisie and the proletariat. As Pareto acutely underlines, "[e]ven though the interests of speculators and workers do not correspond completely, it happens that certain members of both classes find it profitable to operate in the same way—to impose themselves upon the state and use it to exploit the remaining social classes."[70] From the viewpoint of the bourgeoisie, however, this strategy represents a double-edged sword. Indeed, Pareto notices, faced with the challenge arising from the mobilization of the subordinate classes, led by the socialists and trade unions, the bourgeois ruling classes, rather than adopting with determination the repressive methods and the intransigence that the situation requires, entered instead into compromises and parliamentary alliances with their enemies, with the aim of depriving

---

[68] Ibid., § 2276.
[69] Hippolyte A. Taine, *The Ancient Régime* (New York: Henry Holt & Co., 1876), 379. Pareto made a direct reference to this page in an article (*Cronaca*) published in the "Giornale degli Economisti" in January 1894. Now in Vilfredo Pareto, *Oeuvres Complètes*, Vol. 22, *Écrit sociologiques mineurs*, ed. Giovanni Busino (Genève: Droz, 1964), 721–23.
[70] V. Paretos, *The Transformation of Democracy* (New Brunswick (NJ), Transaction Books, 1984). 55.

them of their natural political leaders. In the long run, this strategy, Pareto argues, cannot succeed. Faced with the evident irreconcilability between the interests of the two classes, the greater determination and aggressiveness of the subordinate class (where, unlike the bourgeois elites, the residues of Class II predominate) will prevail over the cunning of the ruling class. In the latter, moreover, the scarce propensity to force favors the spread of "humanitarian sentiments," which thus leaves it even more defenseless in the face of the probable revolutionary outcome.

Once again, Pareto's debt to the famous eighteenth chapter of Machiavelli's *Prince* is evident. There, the Florentine Secretary introduces the political qualities of the lion and the fox: force and astuteness. But just as important to Pareto's analysis is Machiavelli's sixth chapter, where he explains why "all armed prophets succeed, whereas unarmed ones fail": because "the people are fickle" and "it is easy to persuade them about something, but difficult to keep them persuaded." Hence, "when they no longer believe in you and your schemes, you must be able to force them to believe."[71] In the end, Class I residues are not self-sufficient. When the subordinate classes no longer trust the elites, they must be able to resort to force whenever necessary to defend their position.

As Femia argues, resonating with Aron's interpretation of Pareto's elitism, the "critique of demagogic plutocracy" which we find in his writings may be interpreted as "a desire to safeguard liberal individualism against the encroachments of the leviathan state."[72] There is, indeed, a strong link between this critique and that of the gigantism of the state caused by the demagogic and clientelist government of the "speculators." But there is also something more, which can help us to illuminate other contemporary phenomena, related to the crisis of liberal democracies. If we consider Pareto's analysis of the degeneration of the liberal elites into demagogic plutocracies within the broader picture of the "circulation" of power elites, populism clearly appears just like any other political strategy of substitution of an old elite with a new one.

---

[71] Niccolò Machiavelli, *The Prince* (Cambridge, UK: Cambridge University Press, 2019), 21. The same point is repeated by Machiavelli in the *Discourses*, applied not to individuals but to states, resorting to the example of Venice: "having seized a great part of Italy—and the greater part not with war but with money and astuteness—when it had to put its forces to the proof, Venice lost everything in one day." Niccolò Machiavelli, *Discourses on Livy* (Chicago: University of Chicago Press, 1998), 22.

[72] Joseph V. Femia, *The Machiavellian Legacy: Essays in Italian Political Thought* (New York: St. Martin's Press, 1998), 159.

Here, Pareto's approach based on the demystification of political "derivations" helps us to illuminate the phenomenon. As Nadia Urbinati acutely—and famously—noted, "despite its grassroots discourse, populism boils down to the manipulation of the masses by the elites."[73] It may start "as a phenomenon of mass discontent and participation," but ultimately populism represents "a strategic politics of elite transformation and authority creation."[74] Pareto's analysis, as presented above, can only be understood—in my opinion—in the context of the general process of elite circulation. The recourse to demagoguery, as well as patronage tactics, motivated by political action conducted along lines of least resistance, must be understood against the background of a fundamental imbalance that characterizes plutocratic regimes. It is important to note that, according to Pareto, states of disequilibrium can assume a pathological connotation not only due to an excess of rigidity (sclerosis), but also due to an excess of openness, which impedes the stabilization of the governing elites. The same recourse to demagogic techniques of persuasion does not differ from "ordinary" persuasive strategies in terms of quality. Ultimately, as I have tried to show, Pareto claimed that persuasive strategies, in the political arena as well as others, always rely on feelings, on the irrational side of the human soul. The point, therefore, is not so much whether or not Pareto assumes the incapacity of crowds to elevate their reasoning, but a general characteristic of the human psyche that appears even more evident in the political arena. It is the circumstances of the rule of "speculators"—understood as a stage in the wider process of circulation of the elites—which further accelerate these dynamics. Finally, the elites of the "speculators" gradually lose the ability to defend their position, the inclination to use force, and appear destined to succumb.

Pareto's analysis not only warns us against the risks inherent in the "demagogic" phases of politics, and about the "discursive" characteristics of these phases. It also draws our attention to the role of force, whether it is used to protect a political position or to conquer it. The alternative to its use—as liberal democratic elitism will better understand—is precisely the institutionalization of the conflict, not only as a neutralization of violence, but also as a possible stabilization of the precarious balance in the process of elite circulation.

---

[73] Nadia Urbinati, "Political Theory of Populism," *Annual Review of Political Science* 22, no. 1 (2018): 111–27.

[74] Nadia Urbinati, *Democracy Disfigured: Opinion, Truth, and the People* (Cambridge, MA: Harvard University Press, 2014), 157.

10
Palaces for the People
How and of What Should Public Buildings Persuade Citizens in a Democracy?

Jan-Werner Müller

Im Bauwerk soll sich der Stolz, der Sieg über die Schwere, der Wille zur Macht versichtbaren; Architektur ist eine Art Macht-Beredsamkeit in Formen, bald überredend, selbst schmeichelnd, bald bloss befehlend.

[In a building, pride, victory over gravity, the will to power should become visible; architecture is a kind of eloquence in matters of power through forms, sometimes persuading, sometimes flattering, sometimes simply commanding.]

—Nietzsche[1]

Introduction

Just before Christmas 2020, in the dying days of his administration, Donald Trump took time off from his busy schedule promoting the Big Lie about having won the presidential election and preparing fraudulent slates of electors to help him hold on to power: he found occasion to issue an executive order entitled "Promoting Beautiful Federal Civic Architecture."[2] The order made "classicism" the preferred style for new federal buildings, stopping just short of banning modernism from government construction

---

[1] Friedrich Nietzsche, *Götzen-Dämmerung* (Leipzig: Naumann, 1889), 64–5.
[2] This chapter draws on my "January 6 and the Possessive White Male," *Project Syndicate*, January 2022, https://www.project-syndicate.org/commentary/january-6-white-male-resentment-by-jan-werner-mueller-2022-01, and my "Seats of Power," *Project Syndicate*, June 2023, https://www.project-syndicate.org/commentary/design-of-legislative-chambers-facilitates-democratic-politics-by-jan-werner-mueller-2023-06.

entirely.[3] This aesthetic intervention—justified in the name of "beauty," like many other things Trump said and did (or at least pretended to do)—came with a larger set of prescriptions as to how U.S. history was to be properly understood: the President's "1776 Commission" mandated a specific understanding of the American past, to be fed directly into patriotic education across the whole country.[4] Had Trump been re-elected, or gotten away with stealing the election, new visual strategies for federal buildings would have been combined with a larger pedagogy aimed at making the country feel good about itself again—and beautiful.

The man who built plenty of other "palaces" around the world and in the United States—including "Trump Palace" on the Upper East Side of New York City and plenty of other edifices which are actually quite modernist on the outside—did not get to realize his vision of new "beautiful" federal buildings; in fact, his supporters ended up significantly damaging an existing one on January 6, 2021.[5] As so often in Trump's presidency, it felt more like a prop was being presented to the public, as opposed to any kind of long-term plan: a cartoonish image—made for TV audiences—was supposed to persuade citizens that something important had happened: in January 2017, an enormous pile of papers had "proved" that the real estate developer had properly divested from his business; in 2020, another large stack of papers was expected to demonstrate conclusively that there really existed a "beautiful" healthcare plan. Now, the slapdash Commission report—and vague visions of Greek- and Roman-looking buildings—was meant to prove that the United States was a proper and proud democracy (and not, perhaps, a polity inextricably linked to legacies of slavery).

This curious episode still leaves one with difficult questions about how "palaces," or other building types, for that matter, might plausibly communicate something about commitments to democracy. Historically, plenty of democratic, or at least proto-democratic, legislatures that claimed to be based on the people's will have simply occupied existing edifices designed for very different purposes: Westminster is a former church; the French

---

[3] "Promoting Beautiful Federal Civic Architecture," Executive Office of the President, Federal Register, published December 23, 2020, https://www.federalregister.gov/documents/2020/12/23/2020-28605/promoting-beautiful-federal-civic-architecture. The order's title proposed initially had been "Make Federal Buildings Beautiful Again."

[4] "The 1776 Report," The President's Advisory 1776 Commission, published January 2021, https://trumpwhitehouse.archives.gov/wp-content/uploads/2021/01/The-Presidents-Advisory-1776-Commission-Final-Report.pdf.

[5] "Trump Palace," The Trump Organization, https://www.trump.com/residential-real-estate-portfolio/trump-palace-new-york.

National Assembly sits in what had been an aristocratic palace, as does the French Senate; the first postwar West German parliament met in a former pedagogical academy; until 2023, India's Lokh Sabha sat in an edifice created by and for the Raj. From time to time, a choice is posed whether to stick with makeshift solutions or to build anew: Westminster burned down in the nineteenth century, but it was decided to rebuild in Gothic style; the French state, unlike during the French Revolution, at one point would have had enough funds to build a new house for the National Assembly, but it never did; German members of parliament kept complaining that their chamber actually felt like a university where they were being lectured at from on high,[6] while one of the parliament's presidents, Christian Democrat Richard Stücklen, also missed "splendor"; the spaces for the Indian parliament were considered far too small (that concern, among others, justified the enormous building project in Central Vista undertaken under Narendra Modi). In such debates, the question becomes central: What should a democratic "palace"—a term regularly used in the relevant discussion—look like? Is it supposed to persuade the people that it is really theirs? Or is that very suggestion perhaps opening a path to the "stormings" of parliaments, with "mobs" incited by populist leaders determined to remove supposedly illegitimate elite usurpers of the people's space? After all, violent attempts to enter what some citizens referred to as "our house" were undertaken in Berlin in August 2020, in Washington, D.C., in January 2021, and in Brasília in January 2023.

The word "palace" goes back to a specific place: the Palatine hill in Rome. There, emperors were competing to erect magnificent private residences, while continuing the tradition of creating or at least embellishing forums to commemorate military triumphs. "The Caesar must build," Pliny wrote;[7] that imperative referred not just to self-glorification and projecting power across society, but also to the need to gain subjects' support through eminently useful projects: for instance, Caesars, from Julius Caesar to Napoleon, a self-declared successor to the Roman emperors, also brought water to cities (or at least proper sewage systems).

There is, of course, every reason democracies should also improve the built environment for all. But do they also have to build a type of *palatium*, edifices that, historically, were manifestations of social hierarchy and, at

---

[6] Heinrich Wefing, *Parlamentsarchitektur* (Berlin: Duncker & Humblot, 1995).
[7] Heinrich Wefing, *Kulisse der Macht* (Berlin: Deutsche Verlags-Anstalt, 2001).

least to some degree, keeping the people at a distance?[8] If there are palaces at all, what should they signal? A glorification of the citizenry as a collective actor? That might conjure up the problematic image of a single, homogeneous people, when the people are never one, but can only ever appear in the plural, as Jürgen Habermas once put it.[9] While "the people" are not a single actor, there is always the possibility that someone claiming to incarnate the people will try to occupy the place—and the palace—once reserved for a single actor claiming a unique kind of legitimacy: namely, the king.[10]

To deny that possibility of usurping place and palace of the people (and to make sure all kings' heads have been cut off properly in modern political theory), should one perhaps switch then to a glorification of democracy as a set of political ideals—or a set of procedures?[11] Contrary to what is sometimes asserted, democratic procedures are *not* invisible: they are codified somewhere; and citizens, and especially professional politicians, can be observed following them. The fact that they are often ritualized also makes them easier to follow. But can such observations somehow be translated into spatial configurations, or, for that matter, an iconographic program which might then be attached to buildings serving democratic purposes?

In 1831, John Quincy Adams wrote:

> Democracy has no forefathers, it looks to no posterity; it is swallowed up in the present, and thinks of nothing but itself. This is the vice of Democracy, and it is incurable. Democracy has no monuments. It strikes no medals. It bears the head of no man on a coin; its very essence is iconoclastic.[12]

---

[8] Historically, palaces, as opposed to the homes of tyrants, were meant to be relatively accessible. Alberti wrote: "But this is how they differ: A royal palace should be sited in the city centre, should be of easy access, and should be gracefully decorated, elegant and refined, rather than a house. But that of a tyrant, being a fortress rather than a house, should be positioned where it is neither inside nor outside the city. Further, whereas a royal dwelling might be sited next to a showground, a temple, or the houses of noblemen, that of a tyrant should be set well back on all sides from any buildings." Quoted in Eamonn Canniffe, *The Politics of the Piazza: The History and Meaning of the Italian Square* (Farnham, UK: Ashgate, 2008), 102.

[9] Jürgen Habermas, *Faktizität und Geltung: Beiträge zur Diskustheorie des Rechts und des demokratischen Rechtsstaats* (Frankfurt am Main: Suhrkamp, 1994), 607.

[10] Of course, for the king, private residence and public function could not really be separated. Kings were dressed by aristocrats in the morning, and they were watched by aristocrats as they consumed their dinners at night.

[11] The diagnosis that social and political thought has still not cut off the king's head—that we operate within a downright medieval imaginary, in fact—goes back to Foucault, of course.

[12] John Quincy Adams, *Memoirs of John Quincy Adams, Comprising Portions of His Diary from 1795 to 1848*, ed. Charles Francis Adams (Philadelphia: J. B. Lippincott & Co., 1876), 433. There are, it turns out, no Adams monuments. But he was the first president to be honored with a library and had numerous places named after him—indeed, more abstract, though hardly iconoclastic, forms of veneration.

The argument was put forward by a deeply embittered politician, someone disenchanted by democracy and therefore perhaps prone to claim that democracy could never be enchanted. But the thought has proven influential and is regularly invoked to support the point that democracy resists all concrete incarnation. What's more, according to Adams, democracy is not just self-obsessed, and an impotent symbol-maker, but also incapable of giving an account of its past and its future.

The United States has evidently not followed Adams's line of reasoning: it has plenty of heads of men (and now even women) on coins and dollar notes; and it keeps creating monuments to particular individuals, even when other democracies have long opted for a more abstract form of self-representation (or even a general wariness to any self-representation). But these are just facts; they hardly answer the question about democracy's proper self-representation and what might be suspected is a fundamental iconographic deficit. Monuments, the glorification of statesmen (or even rebels) on coins, and so on—maybe these are in fact leftovers from a pre-democratic political imagination; maybe, without realizing it, we are operating in the king's shadow, after all.[13]

Or are such concerns ultimately animated by an unfounded fear of the concrete and a deeply problematic anxiety of embodiment that could even lead to a weakening of democracies, as democrats are speechless—and imageless—in the face of Trumpian (or smarter authoritarians') visions of "beauty"?

In this chapter, I shall break the question of possible "democratic palaces" down into four elements: first, the relationship of democracy to monumentality, which, on the most basic level, is a means to draw attention and signal where a polity seeks to invest its resources: Jefferson, for instance, desired the Capitol to be "a durable and honorable monument to our infant republic." But should democratic authority really seek to impress? Attention, especially political attention, is always in short supply, and one may wonder whether, as Olúfẹ́mi O. Táíwò puts it, we should direct "what little attentional power we can control at symbolic sites of power rather than at the root political issues that explain why everything is so fucked up."[14]

---

[13] Philip Manow, *Im Schatten des Königs: Die politische Anatomie demokratischer Repräsentation* (Frankfurt: Suhrkamp, 2008).
[14] This observation is based on a larger account of "attentional injustice" in Olúfẹ́mi O. Táíwò, *Elite Capture: How the Powerful Took over Identity Politics* (London: Pluto Press, 2022), 72.

Second, there is the long-standing discussion whether democracy might be associated with particular styles and also particular materials. Think of the view that classicism is indissolubly associated with Rome and Athens, as they are said to be the paradigm cases for republicanism and democracy, respectively; or consider the conventional thought that glass means transparency and that transparency in turn is a core feature of democracy. Here the issue is the "clothing" of buildings, so to speak, not size.[15]

Third, and on a related note: Ought democracy to come with a particular iconographic program? Should contemporary democracies venerate individuals in order to persuade citizens of political values? And, if not, should they display only allegorical representations? Or is even that inappropriate, in line with Adams's claims?

Finally, and, as I will suggest, most important: What spaces should buildings devoted to democracy provide, and what political dramaturgies ought they to produce, or at least suggest? To be sure, spaces do not determine human conduct (even if behavior can re-codify the meaning of spaces); but how spaces enable, and disable, movement, and how they create particular flows, is usually intentional and carries political meaning. Steen Eiler Rasmussen, in his classic *Experiencing Architecture*, analyzed the dramaturgy of absolutist palaces; in particular, he noted the "dynamic spatial planning with rhythmical series of rooms in which none is treated as an independent unit." These, he argued, were "entirely in keeping with the whole system of Absolutism," for the royal residence

> was formed like an eel trap, that is to say, all movement went in one direction only, each room opening on to another and all leading to a symbol of the regime: a royal statue, a throne room, or an audience chamber presided over by the all-powerful king himself. Though Baroque layouts were not—like Peking—used for processions, they were designed as though they were.[16]

The dramaturgy of absolutism was inevitable movement to the king, the center of everything. But what, if anything, might constitute a democratic dramaturgy?

---

[15] The notion of a clothing—*Bekleidung*—of buildings goes back to Gottfried Semper. See Gottfried Semper, *Der Stil in den technischen und tektonischen Künsten oder Praktische Ästhetik* (Frankfurt am Main: Verlag für Kunst und Wissenschaft, 1860).
[16] Steen Eiler Rasmussen, *Experiencing Architecture* (Cambridge, MA: MIT Press, 1964), 142.

The chapter will suggest that there is neither a uniquely democratic style nor a uniquely democratic building material. There is also no self-evident democratic iconography. But it does not follow that democracy is somehow beyond all representation and embodiment, let alone that every embodiment is populist in a pernicious, authoritarian sense. It is true that democracy does pose special problems for processes of symbolic condensation partly because of its internally plural character—it's not just the people who can ever appear in the plural—but, again, this does not imply that democracy is therefore necessarily bereft of visual strategies to persuade citizens of its merits and inspire them to engage in ongoing democratic practices.

More important than representations are spaces that can facilitate such practices. However, just as there isn't a single people, there is also not just one democratic practice (and hence not a single dramaturgy). One must do many different things, according to different rhythms, in a well-functioning democracy; even a very basic desideratum of democracy like accountability requires different spaces: the dramatic back-and-forth in something like Prime Minister's Question Time, when partisans are meant to highlight that there are alternatives in politics, is not the same as patient questioning of bureaucrats in a committee hearing. Also, debating is not the same as negotiating, which in turn is not the same as building capacities for collective action among citizens who might be meeting for the first time—something that, as I shall argue toward the very end of the chapter, is particularly important outside of parliamentary assembles.

How Size Matters

On a basic level, the investment in conspicuous public buildings can serve to signal the importance that a collective assigns to particular functions—size, one might say, follows function. Whether a conscious choice along such lines is made is a question that needs to be answered with historical evidence.[17] Wilhelm II really did not want the cupola of the Reichstag—the parliament building he had grudgingly conceded to his subjects at the

---

[17] Harold Laswell, the highly influential American political scientist, built a whole theory on this notion in his very last book: Harold Laswell, with Merritt B. Fox, *The Signature of Power: Buildings, Communication, and Policy* (New Brunswick, NJ: Transaction Books, 1979).

end of the nineteenth century—to be higher than that of his palace, Unter den Linden; plenty of surviving documents from the German Empire make that clear.

What complicates matters is the fact that, since the totalitarian regimes of the twentieth century, there is the pervasive thought that monumentality is in and of itself somehow undemocratic; it constitutes what the Germans call an *Überwältigungsarchitektur*—an architecture meant to overwhelm individuals. Less obviously, if the most monumental buildings serve a regime's self-representation, this would appear to signal a primacy of politics (and, according to one line of reasoning about totalitarianism, a subjugation of society).

Lewis Mumford, in an influential article, highlighted the difficult relationship of democracy to monumentality, what he called democracy's "grudging attitude" toward monuments. Yet his core argument had nothing to do with fears of totalitarianism; rather, he claimed that a democracy would shy away from monumentality primarily because governments would be loath to spending vast resources on monuments, as opposed to schemes that improved the day-to-day lives of citizens.[18] As Mumford put it, "to raise all living standards to a decent level, at least to the 'minimum of existence,' is the aim of modern man: not to elevate and sanctify one side of life at the expense of every other aspect."[19]

Countries eager to signal distance to a totalitarian past consciously built in a modest way, to the point of self-effacement.[20] Historically, such efforts coincided with the early Cold War period when the International Style was promoted as inherently "free" and "democratic," contrasting with a Stalinist approach that was monumental, nationalist, and baroque all at the same time. Bonn and Karlsruhe—seats of the West German government and of the country's constitutional court, respectively—turned out to be prime examples of an architecture seeking to avoid even a hint of a primacy of the political: when a new Chancellery was built in the 1970s, Helmut Schmidt likened it to the office of a local savings bank (plenty of others probably thought an anti-monumental gesture was a good thing for a post-totalitarian, and self-consciously anti-totalitarian, society).

---

[18] Lewis Mumford, "Monumentalism, Symbolism and Style," *Architectural Review* 105 (1949): 173–80.
[19] Ibid., 179.
[20] Michael Z. Wise, *Capital Dilemma: Germany's Search for a New Architecture of Democracy* (Princeton, NJ: Princeton Architectural Press, 1998).

By contrast, during the 1970s, the East German government erected a monumental *Palast der Republik* in the middle of Berlin, on the very site where the Prussian royals' palace had once stood (in 1950, GDR leader Walter Ulbricht had ordered what remained of the palace after World War II to be blown to bits); Ceaușescu destroyed large swaths of central Bucharest to clear space for his sprawling *Palatul Parlamentului* (also known as *Casa Republicii* and *Casa Poporului*). These were icons of a supposed devotion to the people; they also often combined multiple functions—entertainment such as cinemas and dance halls, bars and restaurants, and fun sports like bowling—all in the name of facilitating a classless, fraternal socialist way of life: they were versions of the building as a "social condenser."[21] But, unlike the king's palace, the people themselves could not really reside in the edifices meant to glorify them; often enough, they were relegated to cheap prefab housing far away from the palaces at the heart of capital cities, a reality that might have made observers all the more skeptical of palatial self-representations of political systems.

Yet, as Herfried Münkler has pointed out, there is nothing necessarily progressive or, for that matter, democratic about *minimizing* the visibility of political authority.[22] Violence is easily visible; authority is not. Showing where political authority resides is *prima facie* preferable to effacing it; at the very least, it becomes a target for public attention and possibly protest. Yet making authority visible will not make authority automatically accountable: visibility is not the same as "assessability," and that in turn is not the same as accountability.[23] In other words, what is successfully hidden can hardly become subject to political judgment, but visibility does not guarantee that one can truly assess matters of collective concern; even if one can assess them, still further institutional mechanisms and practices are required to make those exercising authority accountable. None of this means that buildings in the service of democracy—such as, most obviously, parliaments—must overshadow everything else. But an authority that has no location, and does not identify itself to the public, is as such incompatible with basic intuitions

---

[21] Michał Murawski, *The Palace Complex: A Stalinist Skyscraper, Capitalist Warsaw, and a City Transfixed* (Bloomington: Indiana University Press, 2019).
[22] Herfried Münkler, "Sichtbare Macht: Das Reichstagsgebäude als politisches Symbol," in *Kunst, Symbolik und Politik: Die Reichstagsverhüllung als Denkanstoß*, ed. Ansgar Klein, Ingo Braun, Christiane Schroeder, and Kai-Uwe Hellmann (Wiesbaden: VS, 1995), 249–58.
[23] I adopt the important distinction between accessing and assessing from Onora O'Neill, "Media Freedoms and Media Standards," in *Ethics of Media*, ed. Nick Couldry, Mirca Madianou, and Amit Pinchevski (New York: Palgrave, 2013), 21.

about democracy. As we will see in a moment, this argument in favor of visibility is not the same as the conventional valorization of "transparency" as particularly democratic, nor does it point to a singularly correct way to configure spaces in the service of facilitating democracy.

Democratic Styles, Material for Democracy?

Plenty of political leaders have insisted that public buildings must exhibit a particular style and rhetoric, appealing to specifically political, as opposed to broadly aesthetic, considerations in the process. What they have often really meant, though, is *national* styles: legislatures, but also edifices housing the executive, are meant to be expressions of *national* cultural traditions. British politicians associated themselves with the Gothic, for instance, when they discussed whether Westminster ought to be rebuilt in classical style after the great fire in 1834 (to be sure, they were also worried that classicism, much discussed as an alternative at the time, was not only the style of supposed "republican temples," but also most clearly associated with revolutions).

Yet again, we are operating in the shadow of totalitarianism here. For that association of the classical with attractive egalitarian political values was put into question in the twentieth century, as "stripped classicism" became widely perceived as the signature style of Nazism. Cartoonish images of megalomaniacal projects—most prominently Albert Speer's gigantic hall and *via triumphalis* in Berlin—have entered the collective consciousness and can easily be conjured up in both popular culture and professional art criticism.

Yet that is a false collective memory, so to speak. Fascism adopted many architectural theories and styles—especially, but not only, in Italy, where strands of modernism were promoted long after they had become officially condemned in Nazi Germany, alongside much more traditional approaches. Even in the Third Reich, what actually prevailed—and what was actually built, as opposed to Speer's monstrous plans for Berlin—was a mixture of monumentality, "the classical" (as Speer himself liked to put it) and a variety of the modern—a "monumentalized modernity."[24] A similar style and, for that matter, similar spaces were created in democracies in the course of the 1930s, sometimes also invoking ideals of collective mastery over

---

[24] Christian Welzbacher, *Monumente der Macht: Eine politische Architekturgeschichte Deutschlands 1920–1960* (Berlin: Parthas, 2016).

history: looked at from a bit of distance, the Federal Reserve building can easily be imagined as the office building dealing with monetary policy in a thousand-year *Reich.*

Nazi architecture certainly sought to overwhelm; it also, less obviously, promoted a kind of uniformity through over-long rows of windows and arcades that appears to leave the viewer with no possibility to find an individual hold in the edifice—unlike Gothic cathedrals, which might also overwhelm, but which, through their individual masonry and ornaments, allow the single believer to find their own approach, when it comes to connecting the building to worship and faith.[25] Nazi architecture sought to coerce viewers into adopting a particular perspective, focusing on the leader holding forth from a balcony; the sheer mass of edifices and "people material" were meant to reinforce the imaginary of a homogeneous *Volksgemeinschaft.* What ultimately makes the most obvious difference with buildings like Senate House in London or some enormous "republican temples" built in Washington, D.C., in the interwar period, though, were the iconographic program, most notably a cult of future sacrifice and even death that had no equivalent in the democracies at the time (or since, for that matter): the Nazis, uniquely, sought to build memorials for war dead *in advance.*[26]

If fascist architecture foreshadowed war, military logics and war materials, one would think, must have been central to fascism's approach to building. That partly explains the intuition behind fashioning supposedly democratic architecture out of glass, for no fortress can be made of such fragile material; and no warriors will want to be on full display. Glass has also been said to persuade citizens about a commitment to "transparency" as a core democratic feature, a tendency particularly strong in West Germany in the postwar period: politicians connected the notion of democracy to the public, the notion of the public to the idea of porousness, and porousness to transparency though glass.

Yet lack of transparency is hardly the most striking characteristic of totalitarianism. What's more, totalitarianism sought to create spectacles in which totalitarian subjects were all supposed to be both fully united and visible

---

[25] I am grateful to Erika A. Kiss for this point.
[26] Dietmar Schirmer, "State, Volk, and Monumental Architecture," in *Berlin—Washington 1800–2000*, ed. Andreas Daum and Christof Mauch (Cambridge, UK: Cambridge University Press, 2013); Winfried Nerdinger, "A Hierarchy of Styles: Architecture between Neoclassicism and Regionalism," in *Art and Power: Europe under the Dictators 1930–45* (London: Thames and Hudson in association with Hayward Gallery, 1995).

to each other, albeit not in their individual differences, of course; only as forming a homogeneous collective actor.[27] Nazi architects emphasized the importance of *Schaubarkeit*; Mussolini even declared: "*il fascismo è una casa di vetro in cui tutti possono guardare*."

This statement found expression in one of the most remarkable buildings constructed during the "twenty black years" in Italy: Giuseppe Terragni's Casa del Fascio in Como. Terragni's cube featured large glass windows and doors, suggesting a seamless connection between the fascist people and their representatives on the inside. Terragni himself promoted this notion; he published montages of his building and large fascist rallies. While by all accounts modernist in style and a prime example of Italian *razionalismo* (a Nazi *Rationalismus* would have been unthinkable), the building was also cleverly inserted into the city landscape to suggest a continuity with the Roman Empire: Terragni effectively created a vertical version of the Roman *castrum*, while also alluding to a combination of later elements of Italian architecture, such as the *torre del comune* and the Renaissance assembly hall.[28] As Terragni's own montages with the masses suggested, Mussolini's imperative to create a glass house for fascism meant that the people would relate to fascism as a spectacle of power: the building was as much a temple and a monument as it was an office building ostensibly open to the people.

The impression of the Casa as really temple-cum-monument was strengthened by the edifice's iconographic program: an unplastered, visibly damaged concrete column (behind glass!) in the middle of the office of the *segretario generale* was supposed to invoke the heroic street fighting of the *squadristi*.[29]

Of course, one building does not prove that the intuitions behind West Germany's postwar "transparent state" were mistaken.[30] More important is the argument—alluded to above—that visibility might not ensure actual comprehension; and comprehension is likely to remain powerless without means of political participation. It's a long way from "seeing" to political accountability, with many complicated steps in between.

---

[27] See Miguel Abensour's interpretation of Nazi architecture as aiming at "compactness" in his *De la Compacité: Architectures et Régimes Totalitaires* (Paris: Sens & Tonka, 1997).

[28] Kurt W. Forster, "BAU gedanken und GEDANKEN gebäude: Terragnis Case del Fascio in Como," in *Architektur als politische Kultur*, ed. Hermann Hipp and Ernst Seidl (Stuttgart: Reimer, 1996), 253–71.

[29] Ibid.

[30] Deborah Ascher Barnstone, *The Transparent State: Architecture and Politics in Postwar Germany* (New York: Routledge, 2005)

The step from seeing to understanding poses the least obvious difficulty: total transparency can in fact be a tool to obscure things. Overwhelming audiences with information allows one to claim that everyone can "see" everything; but it might take a long time to comprehend what information means. What is behind glass might be fully visible, but the objects themselves can remain opaque; what's more, the glass also separates us from them; the separation becomes visible only in the moment when glass is shattered (which also puts into doubt the notion that the Casa del Fascio signified the "immediate" relationship between the leader and the masses).[31]

How politics really functions can never directly be read off visual orders, stylistic choices, or, for that matter, the deployment of particular materials. German politics did not become more transparent because of large windows; nor is Norman Foster's famed "transparent" dome atop the Reichstag in Berlin proof that German politics is more accessible to its citizens (the supposed placing of the sovereign, the people, on top of the parliament is also ironic in light of the fact that Germany usually keeps the sovereign as a collective actor safely at a distance; referendums at the federal level are prohibited, for instance). If anything, citizens, and tourists, become a spectacle for each other, with little connection to the inaudible, and for the most part actually invisible, political goings-on far below.

In any case, the underlying assumption that parliamentary politics should be as transparent as possible is problematic. A fully transparent parliament is probably a largely powerless one; there is no need for difficult committee negotiations and the hard work of compromises behind closed doors, because what deputies individually think and want is irrelevant in the first place.

Having said that, we should remember that "seeing through" as a political demand and glass as material are not the only possible understandings of transparency. According to György Kepes, a theorist associated with the New Bauhaus who taught at the Massachusetts Institute of Technology for many years, we might think of transparency very differently: an overlapping without obscuring, or, put differently, "interpenetration without optical destruction." This is a question of organization and spatial relations, as opposed to the qualities of one material. The literal kind of transparency is relatively easy to achieve in architecture; the organizational kind requires careful design of different spatial relations.[32]

---

[31] Jeffrey T. Schnapp, "The People's Glass House," *South Central Review* 25 (2008): 45–56.
[32] Colin Rowe and Robert Slutzky, "Transparency: Literal and Phenomenal," *Perspecta* 8 (1963): 45–54. Rowe and Slutzky contrast Bauhaus and Garches to underline the difference between

This conception might still invite the objections just leveled against "transparency kitsch": after all, seeing all the relevant parts and, translated into politics, recognizing how the different parts hang together, is also compatible with being condemned to political passivity. A system of divided powers, or checks and balances, can aim at "interpenetration without destruction," but the spatial relations among different buildings devoted to different powers—think of the Praça dos Três Poderes in Brasília—do not explain how the powers actually interact. That leaves transparency as creating variable spaces for politics, with different sequences and sizes of spaces—a less literal understanding of Kepes's theory, one focused on dramaturgies appropriate for democracy to which I'll turn toward the end of this chapter.

Icons of Democracy?

If an iconographic program can at least sometimes make the difference between fascist and democratic buildings, it is imperative to determine if there is a clear and distinct iconography of democracy. As we saw, Adams denied that there could be such a thing. Democracy is about the people as a collective actor, but differences, even conflicts, within the collective are—on all plausible understandings of democracy —legitimate. The king is one, and his two bodies—the physical and the body politic he represents—can be represented as unitary;[33] democracy might need embodiments, but certainly no single body can ever represent a democratic body politic.

Those instituting democracy in the modern world—most obviously the French Revolution's chief culture warriors—suffered intense anxieties about the polity's lack of unity. One solution they thought of in response was to ensure unity through rituals demonstrating unanimity. After a majority vote in the National Assembly, ballots were burned and a unanimous decision was staged as the final, official one.[34] Various attempts to render

---

the literal and phenomenal notions of transparency; and they enthuse about Le Corbusier's transparency as organization of space in particular: "Le Corbu's planes are like knives for the apportionate slicing of space. If we could attribute to space the qualities of water, then his building is like a dam by means of which space is contained, embanked, tunneled, sluiced, and finally spilled into the informal gardens alongside the lake" (54). I am grateful to Erika A. Kiss for drawing my attention to the importance of Kepes's theories and helping make sense of them.

[33] Ernst Kantorowicz, *The King's Two Bodies: A Study in Medieval Political Theology* (Princeton, NJ: Princeton University Press, 2016).
[34] Manow, *Im Schatten*.

the republic, and the people, for that matter, legible in the form of a single symbol proved unsuccessful: Hercules statues were created to remind citizens of their strength as a united collective actor; when that proved too abstract, Voltaire himself was presented as Hercules.[35] In 1848, a grand competition was held to find the Republic's definitive figuration—and promptly abandoned.[36]

There are, in the end, two reasons to remain at least somewhat skeptical about iconographies of democracy. One is that democracy's complex set of ideals is difficult to render in any single symbolic condensation. That is not to say that monarchy (or contemporary dictatorship) is necessarily simple, let alone simplistic in its self-representation. But they have evidently a person available in the way democracy does not; they also have adjacent images of glorification which can easily stand in for the leader: just think of Erdoğan's palace in Ankara, reflecting the Ottoman-Seljuk style which he has relentlessly promoted as an anti-republican Turkish cultural (and religious) identity.[37] Democracy cannot so easily find an expression for its core dynamics of unity-in-difference and cohesion-through-conflict (though the less well-known conception of transparency discussed above might be a candidate).

Then there's a less theoretical, on one level rather banal, problem: the vast majority of traditional allegories, from Cesare Ripa's late-sixteenth-century emblem book *Iconologia* onward, are probably incomprehensible to citizens today. Just what do snakes have to do with democracy? Why are figures of the republic flanked by bare-breasted women with a mirror? Most people could not tell. Many might recognize statues of particular statesmen, but what is the meaning of such statues, beyond vaguely pointing at exemplars of political virtue? One needs to have read the history to be literate about the icon; all too often, iconographic programs presume an understanding which they are supposed to create in the first place.

Not that everyone in the past would have been familiar with relevant texts. But precisely because it is easier to access texts today—which is not to say that everyone is necessarily paying more attention to texts—it also appears

---

[35] Rolf Reichardt, *Das Blut der Freiheit. Französische Revolution und demokratische Kultur* (Frankfurt am Main: Fischer, 2002)

[36] Albert Boime, "The Second Republic's Contest for the Figure of the Republic," *Art Bulletin* 53 (1971): 68–83; Marie-Claude Chaudonneret, *La Figure de la Republique: Le Concours de 1848* (Paris: Éd. de la Réunion des musées nationaux, 1987).

[37] Bülent Batuman, *New Islamist Architecture and Urbanism: Negotiating Nation and Islam through Built Environment in Turkey* (London: Routledge, 2018).

more feasible to contextualize an iconographic program. And that matters because any simple glorification is today *prima facie* under suspicion: *pace* Adams, democracy will not bring down all statues, but in recent years plenty of statues *have* been brought down because who and, especially, what was represented could no longer possibly give the impression of being a proper subject of veneration: colonialism and more or less subtle endorsements of the old South, to name only the most obvious.

Removal is not the only possibility. There are ways to contextualize, and, in particular, create transparency in Kepes's sense of keeping different elements in view, establishing relations without any "optical destruction." Rather than just removing a street name, it can be left in place, disowned by a polity, and complemented with a new sign, with a new name, and an explanation of the change. Such strategies of raising awareness of the past beyond the simplistic choice of glorification or destruction can be complemented online, allowing citizens to move between physical and virtual spaces.

An iconography communicating ambivalence, or even absences, is one thing; another is one drawing on substitutions that undermine any unreflective veneration of the original. A statute like Kehinde Wiley's "Rumors of War" was, according to Wiley, meant to "use the language of equestrian portraiture to both embrace and subsume the fetishization of state violence"; it was put up in Times Square for two months and eventually moved to a permanent home at the end of Monument Avenue in Richmond, Virginia (among plenty of Confederate statues). The same strategy of subversion is exemplified by Hans Haake's installation in the Reichstag, reading, "To the Population," an ironic variation of the official inscription "To the German People" on the front of the building: the latter, designed by Peter Behrens, cast from cannons surrendered in the Franco-Prussian War and mounted in 1916, was both a (characteristically awkward) attempt by Wilhelm II to gain popular legitimacy during the war, and a quite accurate expression of how the Kaiser viewed the political system: it was his choice to hand his Volk a parliament, *von Kaisers Gnaden*. Haake not only reminds the people that the word *Volk* can no longer be used innocently; he also, in an ironic mode meant to spur reflection, repeats the gesture, using Behrens's very design. Deputies have been invited to bring soil from their constituencies to fill the space around the neon "Der Bevölkerung" sign; there is now a wild garden (which anyone can "access" through a webcam documenting the uncontrolled growth of greenery from across the country).

The Dramaturgies of Democratic Spaces

I want to argue that what really matters is having spaces that enable different democratic practices. Such spaces can suggest different dramaturgies through different layouts and sequencing of spaces; they can also have important variations in intensity and atmosphere.[38]

"Debating chambers" is often used as shorthand for parliaments. But that is a misunderstanding, often consciously encouraged by critics of parliamentarism: Carl Schmitt held that the original ideal of parliament—with the word derived from *parlare*—relied on the notion that "truth," or at least rational policies, would emerge from free and open discussion. There are indeed moments when speakers confront each other with arguments in front of packed parliaments, the UK's Prime Minister's Question Time being an obvious example. But these are exceptional moments; and only in authoritarian states are assemblies always filled with attentively listening (and compliant) deputies.[39] The notion of legislatures as providing a stage for what Schmitt also derided as a *clasa discutidora* misses an important element of actual, working parliaments:[40] parliamentary procedures are not primarily designed to enable a freewheeling exchange of views; rather, they aim at reaching collectively binding decisions: even the longest filibuster can eventually be brought to an end. Second, what is staged as a debate seldomly holds any surprises: the very fact that an issue comes to the floor means that it has already been decided.

There is little evidence that even memorable debates in which parties leave their members free to vote their conscience (or, rather, their political judgement) were decided by the force-less force of the better argument (the 1991 debate as to whether to move the capital to Berlin is often mentioned as a glorious hour of parliamentarism; in fact, the best predictor of an individual's vote was how close their home was to Bonn). But none of this is to suggest that debates are dispensable, or even worse, that we should dismiss them as ideological facades in the way Schmitt did. It is crucial to dramatize conflicts in front of the citizenry; the drama of an intense parliamentary debate is much more likely to make people understand what's at stake than

---

[38] Holger Kleine, *Raumdramaturgie: Inszenierung und Typologie von Innenräumen* (Basel: Birkhäuser, 2017).

[39] Florian Meinel, *Die Vertrauensfrage* (Munich: C. H. Beck, 2019).

[40] Schmitt adopted the term—shorthand for the liberal bourgeoisie that made its home in an assembly of notables in the nineteenth century—from Spanish arch-reactionary Donoso Cortés.

deliberations in which fundamental political differences might not be articulated clearly; it is also crucial that government representatives and an opposition confront each other in a legible way: it should become clear which side stands for what (obviously, this is less true for presidential systems; neither the president nor the cabinet has an assigned place—forming part of a comprehensible dramaturgy centered on accountability—as is the case in parliamentary systems).[41]

For the most part, the real work of parliaments happens in committees, sometimes visible, sometimes not so visible (German deputies are fond of describing the Löbe Haus, with its large cylinder-like elements as "the engine room of democracy," as most committees meet there). Here the naïve normative endorsement of total transparency is particularly unhelpful. Whereas debates can serve to dramatize differences to the public—an eminently important function—committees tend to do the slow, hard work of accountability (which hardly ever takes the form of a "gotcha"-question in front of rolling cameras; in Germany most inquiries, often de facto criticisms, by the opposition are answered in writing).[42] Not least, committees are the site where an opposition can have most of an influence; and for that, the dramatization of conflict is sometimes precisely to be avoided.

Different legislatures work in very different ways, of course. Any suggestion that there could be an "ideal form"—be it oblong benches à la Westminster or the circle, sometimes said to facilitate consensus—is naïve. Still, the choice is not arbitrary, and different considerations can help in making it: government and opposition confronting each other is a straightforward way of dramatizing conflict; it also underlines the notion—far from obvious to anyone until the middle of the nineteenth century—that the opposition is legitimate and functions as a "government-in-waiting." The House of Commons—far too small to accommodate all members on its benches simultaneously—created the sense of crowds and urgency which Churchill deemed essential for the highly adversarial understanding of democracy practiced in the United Kingdom. As he put it, "a small chamber and a sense of intimacy are indispensable."[43] The fact that British parliamentarians have no fixed place—and no desks at all—also strengthens the sense that parties

---

[41] See also Stefan Rummens, "Staging Deliberation: The Role of Representative Institutions in the Deliberative Democratic Process," *Journal of Political Philosophy* 20 (2012): 23–44.

[42] Meinel, *Vertrauensfrage*, 48; Christoph Schönberger, *Auf der Bank: Die Inszenierung der Regierung im Staatstheater des Parlaments* (Munich: C. H. Beck, 2022).

[43] Winston Churchill, "A Sense of Crowd and Urgency," *Australasian Parliamentary Review* 16 (2001): 12–15; here 13.

are there to oppose each other in words, not to work, individually and collectively, on policy detail; the fact that members address the Speaker, and cannot see colleagues on the same side, might suggest that one's own side needs no persuading (it could also be seen as evidence for the ghost of the king in parliament: as they address the Speaker—as they are supposed to, officially—members are really addressing the Crown in Parliament).[44]

The American Senate has long ceased to be the world's "greatest deliberative body" (a view usually attributed to President James Buchanan, one of the most spectacular failures in office); in fact, it is doubtful that this description ever applied outside a few decades in the twentieth century (in the nineteenth, senators physically attacked each other on the floor). But the configuration and equipment of the chamber make it clear why, in principle, it is not an absurd notion. What Thomas Jefferson imagined as a "natural aristocracy" was to convene in a calm atmosphere, with each senator working studiously at their desk, not immediately subject to partisan "crowd" behavior, and ideally free from Churchill-style "urgency" (leading to rash decisions). Half-circles make for inter-visibility, as on the Athenian Pnyx and subsequently in the city's Theater of Dionysus. If partisan lines are not already clear, and if outcomes are not already decided before being debated on the floor, it might really matter that one can catch cues about the reactions of allies, potential allies, and, sometimes, outright political adversaries.

The one form that finds the least support in any plausible theory of democracy is the "classroom model": teachers have elevated seats at the front, everyone else sits in rows facing them. The Duma looks like this. Konrad Adenauer would have preferred this configuration, with the executive visibly elevated above deputies. It is easy to read it as vaguely authoritarian, but one might also understand this kind of direct confrontation, in systems where government and parliament are entirely separated, as an awkward attempt to suggest accountability—except that the image of all rows filled with deputies has precisely become an emblem of authoritarianism, not of anything like a particularly strong check on executives.[45]

Different spaces suggest different dramaturgies. They can force encounters or make it easy to avoid them. One of the vexing—though not entirely new—political challenges of the past few years is which stance politicians should adopt vis-à-vis what, for shorthand, one can call authoritarian populists

---

[44] Manow, *Im Schatten*.
[45] Hans Maier, "Parlamentsreform—aber wie?," *Merkur* 23 (1969): 515–26.

(some of whom have appeared in parliaments in Sweden and Spain for the first time). Should they be excluded entirely, from coalitions for sure, but perhaps also from any cooperation in committee work? Or ought one to have some hope for strategies of "moderation through inclusion"? According to such strategies, once they are actually made responsible for addressing real problems, extremists will have to stop spending all their time on grandstanding (and hate-mongering), and start to deal with politics in a pragmatic fashion.

These dilemmas will not be solved by architects. But it is not an entirely trivial footnote to the debates about the far right that different spaces might facilitate different strategies of relating to what are sometimes euphemistically called "parliamentary newcomers." Some spaces are so small and create such intimacy (just as Churchill wished) that one might be forced to engage one another; others are so large that the far right itself can stick with tactics of shunning (as in: "we shun 'the mainstream' before 'the mainstream' can shun us"), of self-isolation, and, not least, of self-radicalization.

Self-radicalization, social scientists tell us with an unusual degree of confidence, is more likely to happen in homogeneous groups. It is not true—contrary to what was presented as an instant diagnosis of contemporary political ills in 2016 or so—that something known as "the internet" necessarily creates "filter bubbles" and "echo chambers." This facile, though at the time also oddly comforting, technological determinism repeated a long-established pattern—radio gave us Hitler, TV made McCarthy inevitable. But the diagnosis failed to distinguish between "the internet" and the business model of particular platforms, some of which can indeed be described as "incitement capitalism," based on the monetization of anger (including anger sparked by demonstrable falsehoods).[46]

While we need to resist entering an echo chamber about echo chambers—faithfully confirming to each other that filter bubbles are the cause of all political problems—we also do need to understand how parliaments today function differently on the basis of new technological affordances: in some cases, deputies do spend more time curating their image online than engaging colleagues in the supposed "halls of power"; they will also communicate incessantly with other party members through short messages in "chat

---

[46] Andrew Guess, Benjamin Lyons, Brendan Nyhan, and Jason Reifler, "Avoiding the Echo Chamber about Echo Chambers: Why Selective Exposure to Political News Is Less Prevalent than You Think," *Knight Foundation White Paper*, accessed June 1, 2020, Topos_KF_White-Paper_Nyhan_V1.pdf (kf-site-production.s3.amazonaws.com).

groups" more than with speeches, or, more important still, the hard work of negotiating.[47]

Too often, what happens in the plenary is no longer aimed at persuading either anyone physically present or what might be presumed as a general public; rather, it is designed to produce instant material for tweets—which in turn are only designed for fundraising. In one of his most celebrated observations on how changing media were transforming society (and politics) in the 1930s, Walter Benjamin claimed that the then crisis of democracy should be understood as a crisis of the exhibition—*Ausstellbarkeit*—of political human beings; film in particular, he ventured, led to theaters and parliaments being deserted, as the stage actor was being replaced with the movie star, and the great debater with the dictator.

It's today simple to represent, and even more so, to mis-represent dramaturgies unfolding in legislatures instantly (think of Senator Ted Cruz being observed during an important committee hearing as he searched for himself on Twitter, after a particularly outrageous set of statements). Unlike Trump's props—which followed the logic of TV shows—online snippets can pass for conclusive proof, if edited cleverly: they really show the relevant details, unlike Trump's cartoonish piles of paper, even if the details are framed in a profoundly misleading way.

"Whose House? Our House!"

Having moved into debating chambers and committee rooms to examine the dramaturgy suggested by them, it is time to turn toward the exterior again, or, rather, to consider transitions between inside and outside. Getting close to legislatures retains major practical and symbolic significance: ideally, people—not *the* people—should have spaces outside legislatures to protest and contest the collective decisions of representatives (but without denying the legitimacy of representatives, in the way the January 6th insurrectionists did).

Some gestures toward access and inclusion of the people are symbolically more plausible than others; some might even succeed in actually making a

---

[47] Justus Bender, "Karl Lauterbach ist bei Signal!," *Frankfurter Allgemeine Zeitung*, published July 31, 2022, https://www.faz.net/aktuell/politik/inland/karl-lauterbach-ist-bei-signal-was-politiker-in-chatgruppen-treiben-18208445.html.

popular presence felt. Robespierre famously wanted 12,000 citizens on the galleries of a National Assembly which was never built. Inside the Reichstag plenary, the galleries are large (larger than in the House of Commons, for instance) and intrude into the circular space. Here, again, the citizens watching are elevated above their representatives, but in way that makes them a presence hard to ignore—one that might even, to a degree, be uncomfortable for professional politicians. Of course, citizens still have to behave themselves—but the dynamics of the space inside the parliament is clearly different from a traditional theater setting, where citizens might simply get the message that they are the spectators of the great game of politics.

Across from the Reichstag, the Löbe building features a ground floor that resembles a street (and that continues what should have been the civic forum on the outside). The street as a site of democratic contestation and citizens acting in concert is symbolically brought into the official house of the government; it is evidently meant as a reminder that there is more to democratic politics than formal procedures.

Of course, with ever tighter security it can seem that the internal street only adds insult to civic injury. What still merits consideration, though—quite apart from the bureaucratic obstacles to overcome before entering galleries or meeting one's deputy in their office—is how individuals might experience a way in, comparable perhaps to the manner in which the Gothic cathedral, unlike Speer's architecture, was meant to be accessible. Especially in large, diverse, and especially in federal, states, one way is to enable citizens to connect what might *prima facie* be an intimidating structure with the local worlds they know. The representation of the individual states in the Congress building's Hall of the People is an attempt to provide such connections; Lutyens's allusions to India's diversity in his government architecture another (an aspect that largely disappears with the new parliament constructed under Modi).[48]

Liminal spaces are particularly promising for "bringing the people in," but large open spaces just outside assembly buildings also matter. Once again, the anxieties about unity by the French revolutionaries, and the answers they attempted, are particularly instructive: they sought to hold festivals where citizens watched *each other* as much as any official performances, which held out the promise of deepening fraternal feelings. After all, Rousseau had

---

[48] John Parkinson, "How Legislatures Work—and Should Work—as Public Space," *Democratization* 20, no. 3 (2013): 438–55. I am grateful for Pratap Mehta for the point about Delhi's new parliament.

already recommended festivities in which the people, not a king or nobles, are the main actors.[49] In his advice to the Poles, he argued that they should institute festivities and "many public games where the good mother country delights in seeing her children at play" (in contrast with "shut-in halls" and "dissolute effeminate theaters" in which people would just passively consume and be isolated from each other).[50] The Swiss philosopher-cum-political consultant advocated making "these games attractive to the public by organizing them with some pomp ... so that they become a spectacle." He continued that it was then "a fair assumption that all honest folk and good patriots will regard it a duty and a pleasure to attend them."[51]

After the French Revolution, crowds were indeed drafted to partake in large marches and festivals—sometimes holding up placards with sentences from Rousseau's books. These elaborate fêtes revisited the central locations of the Revolution, like a Catholic procession marking the ascension to freedom. They concluded on open fields where the people, or so it was hoped, could experience themselves as a collective actor.[52] Festivals were not just to focus the mind of a usually distracted citizenry, but to activate it politically.

In the 1790s, the republican festival became increasingly dominated by military parades; mutual, and often unchoreographed, interaction among citizens was de-emphasized in favor of spectacles that stressed the republic's strength, especially vis-à-vis outside powers that posed a permanent threat to the democratic experiment unfolding in the hexagon. Instead of the processions, Louis-Marie La Revelliere-Lepeaux, deputy of the National Assembly and later a member of the Directory, proposed a giant amphitheater around an altar of the fatherland (which, to be sure, remained faithful to the notion that the people also ought to observe each other—and adore their own adulation of the fatherland).

Of course, all such talk of giving citizens a sense of the legislature as a "palace of the people" and "allowing them a way in" and "making them adore each other" sounds different after 2021. "This is our house!" the January 6th insurrectionists kept yelling (similar rhetoric had been heard among those

---

[49] Jean-Jacques Rousseau, "Considerations on the Government of Poland," in *The Social Contract and Other Later Political Writings*, ed. Victor Gourevitch (Cambridge, UK: Cambridge University Press, 1997), 177–260. See also Mona Ozouf, *La fête revolutionnaire 1789–1799* (Paris: Gallimard, 1976), who writes of the basic idea that the legislator makes laws for the people, but festivities make the people for the laws—something that explains the Revolution's *"festomanie"* (p. 20). See also Reichardt, *Das Blut der Freiheit*.
[50] Rousseau, "Considerations," 182.
[51] Ibid., 191.
[52] Ozouf, *La fête*; and Reichardt, *Das Blut der Freiheit*.

trying to "take" the Reichstag in August 2020); rather than seeing Congress's Hall of the People as a representation of their particular federal identities, the Trump storm troops literally shit in (and possibly on) it.

The issue is not the desirability, let alone the permissibility, of large demonstrations in front of legislatures; it also not whether citizens should not try to get under the skin of professional politicians—all of that is fine, one would think. What was particular—and in need of explanation—about January 6th was that those who declared themselves "the real people" did not just occupy their house, but also vandalized it. One key is to be found in a phenomenon that characterizes far-right parties and movements in otherwise very different countries: the promise to restore entitlements to white men who think that women, nature, and even the machinery of democracy, including the buildings which house that machinery, are ultimately something like their personal property.

Not enough thought has been given to the basic fact that the Capitol was "taken," and that those who entered it displayed an astonishing sense of entitlement, with "This is our House" as its most obvious expression. Observers at the time noted that some of the insurrectionists behaved almost like tourists, but tourists generally—and God-fearing conservative ones in particular—know that they are not supposed to just grab, deface, or outright destroy what they see.

To get at the deeper meaning of the events, a concept recently coined by the German philosopher Eva von Redecker is helpful: "phantom possession," a term inspired by well-known phenomena such as phantom pain and phantom limbs.[53] White men used to be entitled to certain things, and even human beings, as their de facto property: the natural environment was just there for the taking; women were simply expected to provide sex, care, and all kinds of other services (and, not least: to let their reproductive capacities be subject to men's control).

True, territory conquered by colonialists was first declared *terra nullius* (even if there had been someone there before), and it could then be bought and sold; by contrast, it was not true that women could be sold like property (whereas men could indeed always buy sexual services).

But coverture still meant that women were effectively under the control of men (and it is easy to forget that in some Western democracies wives could

---

[53] Eva von Redecker, "Ownership's Shadow: Neoauthoritarianism as Defense of Phantom Possession," *Critical Times* 3 (2020): 33–67.

not accept employment without their husband's consent until the 1970s, while marital rape was not outlawed until the 1990s). As W. E. B. Du Bois famously pointed out, the right to feel superior to, and outright oppress, certain groups compensated poorer whites for some of the domination they suffered themselves; it generated a "psychological wage" in addition to the monetary one.[54]

One of the hallmarks of modern property is that you can do with it more or less what you want. At the limit, that includes the right to destroy it. The British jurist William Blackstone famously described property as "that sole and despotic dominion which one man claims and exercises over the external things of the world"; the Code Napoleon included a right to abuse and even destroy property. The legal dimension is one thing; the psychological one another: it can seem that destruction proves that something is really mine; after all, I can do with it whatever I want, no matter how abusive. That disastrous dynamic becomes visible when men try to kill a woman they claim to love, rather than put up with her emancipation (literally, the exit from property, or *mancipium*).

It might not come as a surprise, then, that the vast number of the insurrectionists were men, with many displaying military gear and pretending to engage in combat against the very group—enemies of the U.S. constitution—they themselves constituted. The man who put up his feet on a desk in Nancy Pelosi's office, from which he also stole mail, no doubt tried to assert "despotic dominion." Destruction might seem to make the phantom real—and the pain go away.

Explaining to committed far-right people what democracy is really about, or that they are in fact destroying the thing they claim to value, can be beside the point, if their underlying assumption remains: if it's not exactly as I want it, I'd rather destroy it, including what is supposed to be "my House"; and for sure, no one else (and especially not majorities consisting of Black and Brown people) can have it.

The Other Palaces of the People

The "stormings" of 2020, 2021, and 2023 in Berlin, Washington, D.C., and Brasília, respectively, do not invalidate the arguments for having the

---

[54] W. E. B. Du Bois, *Black Reconstruction in America* (New York: Simon and Schuster, 1997).

people get close to the politicians. But they do force us anew to consider whether—beyond large demonstrations, delegations visiting deputies, or school classes being dutifully shepherded through parliaments on an annual civic excursion—there are ways of "bringing the people" close or even in.

One possible answer is offered by edifices mentioned earlier: the multi-use "culture palaces" in state socialist countries. Of course, one can object that the fact that bowling happened next to the *Volkskammer* in the Palace of the Republic precisely demonstrated that the latter was in the end as inconsequential as the former. There is an argument to be made for clearly communicating the "dignity of legislation" to citizens; putting parliamentary work-spaces next to entertainment venues constitutes a failure to do so.[55] One of the (many) problems with Trump's privatization of government work at Mar-a-Lago was that it turned politics into a spectacle; another was that the rules of access could no longer be traced back to a process of democratic decision-making, to put it mildly; instead, they conformed to the logic of a private club driven by the profit motive.

There is a strong argument for separation, then. But it has to go together with one in favor of properly financing the kinds of spaces which state socialists rightly lauded as "social condensers" and as expressions of civic pride. Not just state socialists, though: in the nineteenth century, the United States put a lot of money, and artistic effort, into buildings for the post office (the remarkable palace on Pennsylvania Avenue in D.C. was of course privatized and eventually became the Trump International Hotel); Andrew Carnegie demanded "palaces for the people"; and sociologists have rightly emphasized the importance of "third spaces"—not private homes, not workplaces, and also not directly political ones—for people to meet and engage in practices of cooperation—which create stronger bonds and possible bridges to groups one does not regularly encounter.[56] The public library—ideally complemented by a truly public square—remains the prime example of such a space, but others are easily imaginable: think of public swimming pools or community youth centers.[57]

---

[55] Jeremy Waldron, *The Dignity of Legislation* (New York: Cambridge University Press, 1999)
[56] Eric Klinenberg, *Palaces for the People: How Social Infrastructure Can Help Fight Inequality, Polarization, and the Decline of Civic Life* (New York: Crown Publishing Group, 2018)
[57] Till van Rahden, *Demokratie: Eine gefährdete Lebensform* (Frankfurt am Main: Campus, 2019).

Conclusion

So, what might one say, in the end, about the design of palaces of the people and the possibilities for them to persuade the people that legislatures are really theirs? These edifices should certainly signal that something important happens in them—collectively binding decisions are made here, decisions that will eventually authorize the state's coercion of those who resist them. Such buildings should dignify, but not glorify; they should be serious, but not severe ("severity" is one truly common denominator of fascist architecture—no such thing as irony or playfulness in fascism). Arguments for visibility and dignity do not translate into a demand for gestures in the form of instantly comprehensible icons; for one thing, few such icons exist, and, second, a concentration on one icon—always a temptation—is likely to do injustice to democracy's pluralistic character.

There are neither uniquely democratic styles nor singularly democratic materials, contrary to what received wisdom—be it about the classical or the Gothic or the supposedly self-evident connection between democracy and transparency—might suggest. What matters much more are the spaces inside and just outside designated democratic buildings, spaces for assembly in particular: legislatures' inside spaces ought to be appropriate for the different dramaturgies of democracy; in particular, they must allow for the dramatization of conflict, but also for the much less dramatic practices of accountability and policymaking.

True, this risks democracy itself becoming a spectacle, yet another thing to be consumed more or less passively. In that sense, all arguments for how to stage debates, deliberations, and negotiations rely on the assumption that it will still be possible to find a proper public for them—a public which does not have to be "open-minded," but which grasps the seriousness and is prepared to view the goings-on from multiple perspectives (including a consideration of how others might view—intervisibility, again). Architecture can help in sustaining such a public; but, we must remind ourselves, it cannot create it.

11
Reconstructing Pluralism and Populism
Not "Opposites" but a More Complex Configuration

Mark Wenman

Introduction

The widespread emergence of populist movements in many parts of the world has been a defining feature of democratic politics, especially following the global financial crisis of 2008. As advocates of a left-wing populism like Chantal Mouffe and Nancy Fraser have said, this reflects the declining hegemony of neoliberalism;[1] as inequalities rise, wage growth stagnates, opportunities decline, and mainstream parties offer no solutions, populism is likely to persist. A very substantial literature has emerged seeking to comprehend this most significant political development of our times. Despite important distinctions between left- and right-wing varieties, as well as specificities of national context, political scientists and political theorists have sought to delineate the core characteristics of populism. These efforts have reanimated these disciplines and have opened significant questions about the relationship between populism and other key terms in political discourse, most notably democracy, liberalism, and pluralism. This chapter engages these discussions, and I aim to bring greater focus to the important question of the relationship between populism and pluralism. I present a conceptual and historical reconstruction of "pluralism," outlining how pluralism can help address the challenges presented by populism, while also countering the misleading claim that populism is the "opposite" of pluralism. In addition, I touch on the rhetorical style characteristic of populism and pluralism to further illustrate this conceptual and historical reconstruction.

---

[1] Chantal Mouffe, *For a Left Populism* (London; New York: Verso, 2018); Nancy Fraser, *The Old Is Dying and the New Cannot Be Born* (London and New York: Verso, 2019).

The predominant view is that populists are "anti-pluralist" (Jan-Werner Müller), or that populism is the "opposite" of pluralism (Cas Mudde and Cristóbal Rovira Kaltwasser).[2] However, the counter-view has also been articulated: that certain forms of left-wing populism can, and do, accommodate pluralism (Benjamin Moffitt).[3] The advocates of these respective viewpoints outline what they mean by "pluralism," but only briefly; and to a considerable extent, the key characteristics of pluralism are underdetermined in these discussions. On closer examination, I show that these authors refer to different ideas when they invoke this key term. These differences partly reflect alternative meanings of pluralism in political theory and political science, but this indistinctness also mirrors the more general fate of this term, where there has been a wide proliferation of "pluralism," and associated notions such as "difference" and "diversity," over several decades in the context of postmodernism, multiculturalism, and identity politics. As Anne Philips said in 1993, "contemporary work in political philosophy positively groans under the weight of diversity, plurality, and difference."[4] Since then, the weight of this polysemy has only become more intense. It is therefore important to disaggregate the various meanings associated with pluralism, and my objective is primarily to differentiate the tradition of American political pluralism from other iterations. The presentation of pluralism as the "opposite" of populism reflects widely felt concerns about the authoritarian tendencies within populism. I share those concerns, and I agree that pluralism can help mitigate against these tendencies. However, when we reconstruct the American tradition of pluralism and separate this from alternative meanings, we see that it is nonetheless misleading to describe pluralism as the opposite of populism, because, from the American pluralist perspective, pluralism and populism are very different phenomena and so can't simply be compared as opposites.

For Müller, populists are "anti-pluralist" because they threaten individual rights and civil liberties and delegitimize the opposition.[5] Moffitt thinks this is not always the case and cites various left-wing examples, including Podemos, Syriza, and La France Insoumise, who, on his account, "extend

---

[2] Jan-Werner Müller, *What Is Populism?* (London: Penguin Books, 2017); Cas Mudde and Cristóbal Rovira Rovira Kaltwasser, *Populism: A Very Short Introduction* (Oxford: Oxford University Press, 2017); see also William Galston, *Anti-Pluralism: The Populist Threat to Liberal Democracy* (New Haven, CT; London: Yale University Press, 2018).
[3] Benjamin Moffitt, *Populism* (Cambridge, UK: Polity, 2020).
[4] Anne Phillips, *Democracy and Difference* (Cambridge, UK: Polity, 1993), 139.
[5] Müller, *What Is Populism?*, 3–4.

their conception of the people to include minority groups."[6] He is more circumspect about the main Latin American examples—Hugo Chávez, Evo Morales, and Rafael Correa—and their record with respect to pluralism.[7] While not unimportant, the issue of whether we can, or cannot, identify some instances of populism that accommodate social diversity and/or respect individual rights is not the most significant question for understanding the relationship between populism and pluralism. Later in the chapter, I demarcate three different strands of pluralism in late-twentieth- and early-twenty-first-century social and political theory, which I refer to respectively as modes of *ethical*, *metaphysical*, and *political* pluralism. This helps to differentiate the uses of this term in current debates. For example, Müller and Moffitt are ultimately referring here to ethical pluralism, which they also associate with liberalism. However, one thing that emerges from the appraisal later in this chapter is that there is no intrinsic relationship between ethical pluralism and liberalism. Indeed, I argue that we need to dissociate pluralism from liberalism if we are to find an adequate response to the authoritarian tendencies within populism.

We need to do so because liberalism is, at its core, an anti-political doctrine concerned with demarcating a private space of freedom from politics. Isaiah Berlin gets to the heart of the matter, when he says liberalism is strictly indifferent to the political question of "who governs me?," focusing instead on the entirely different problem of "how far does government interfere with me?"[8] The key objective in liberalism is therefore to demarcate constitutional limits or firm boundaries to the legitimate scope of governmental power, to ensure a negative space of "non-interference" where the individual is free "to do or be what he is able to be," essentially "unobstructed by others."[9] As waves of communitarian and republican critics have said, this has had a corrosive impact on the quality of public life and public debate,[10] and Mouffe was correct when she perceived, back in the 1990s and the following decade, that the predominance of liberalism in the academy, and of liberal individualism more generally throughout society, would likely lead to a resurgence of right-wing

---

[6] Moffitt, *Populism*, 27, 72, 83–88.
[7] Ibid.
[8] Isaiah Berlin, "Two Concepts of Liberty," in *Political Philosophy*, ed. Anthony Quinton (Oxford: Oxford University Press, 1982), 148.
[9] Ibid., 141, 143.
[10] E.g., Benjamin Barber, *Strong Democracy* (Los Angeles; London: University of California Press, 1984); Michael Sandel, "The Procedural Republic and the Unencumbered Self," in *The Self and the Political Order*, ed. Tracy Strong (Oxford: Blackwell, 1992); Quentin Skinner, *Liberty before Liberalism* (Cambridge: Cambridge University Press, 1998).

extremism, understood as an effort to re-politicize issues that have increasingly been treated as private or simply administrative concerns.[11] So, while populism, and especially its right-wing versions, present a danger to individual liberty and the rule of law, we misstep if we place too much emphasis on upholding liberal values in response to this predicament. While civil liberties and the principles of constitutionalism are important, we should look elsewhere for a more *political* response to the authoritarian tendency within populism. Thankfully, we find alternative resources in a rather different account of pluralism.

Müller is right to stress the importance of political checks and balances, but this idea has only ever had, at best, a muted and peripheral status within the traditions of liberalism. This idea is central, however, for the mid-twentieth-century tradition of political pluralism, developed by a series of prominent American political scientists, including David Truman, Earl Latham, Charles Lindblom, Nelson Polsby, and most notably Robert Dahl. This tradition of pluralism was developed amidst the famous community power debates of the 1950s, and, not unlike contemporary discussions, this was also a highly productive moment in political science; the pluralists focused primarily on empirical questions about the distribution of power in society, but this generated a rich series of theoretical debates about the nature of power and about the status of different political regimes that ran into the 1960s and beyond. This was also a context where the question of the relationship between authoritarianism and democracy was a pressing issue, given the recent collapse of nascent democracies in central and southern Europe before the war, as well as the rise of McCarthyism in the United States. Mudde and Rovira Kaltwasser are therefore right to cite specifically this tradition of pluralism as offering important insights into contemporary populism.[12]

There is, however, a certain irony in this tradition receiving a generally positive reception in contemporary debates, because this "pluralism" has also come under repeated criticism over the past half century and was for a long time dismissed as nothing more than an ideological defense of the American system in the context of the Cold War. I revisit and push back on several criticisms, because this conception of political pluralism offers crucial

---

[11] E.g., Chantal Mouffe, *On the Political* (London; New York: Routledge. 2005).
[12] Mudde and Rovira Kaltwasser, *Populism*, 7–8, 81; Cristóbal Rovira Kaltwasser, "The Ambivalence of Populism: Threat and Corrective for Democracy," *Democratisation* 19, no. 2 (2012): 184–208; "The Responses of Populism to Dahl's Democratic Dilemmas," *Political Studies* 62, no. 3 (2014): 470–87.

insights, not just for understanding the current emergence of populism, but also for how we should respond to the authoritarian tendencies within populism. The section "Populism and American Political Pluralism" later in this chapter presents a conceptual and historical reconstruction of American pluralism outlining the explanatory tools we can recover from this approach. Here, I challenge Mudde and Rovira Kaltwasser's misleading claim that populism represents the "opposite" of pluralism—because pluralism in this tradition designates the key qualities of a particular kind of democratic system, whereas populism is best understood as a distinct manifestation of the popular will, and one that emerges from within a pluralist system. The challenge then is—in the subsequent section—to examine the causes and consequences of the emergence of populism from within pluralism, and this also clears the way for an account of the normative principles that we can extract from this tradition, that is, to bring to bear on the threats posed by populism, which I explore in the final section of the chapter. However, each of these discussions first requires a more detailed understanding of the authoritarian tendency within populism, and more generally the relationship between populism and democracy, so it is to these much-discussed issues that first I turn in the next two sections.

The Authoritarian Tendency in Populism

Notwithstanding discussions about what kind of thing populism is—an ideology, discourse, a political strategy, or style[13]—there is a predominant view in the literature about how populism manifests itself. Despite differences in content and their policy agenda, left- and right-wing populisms, in northern and southern Europe, North and South America, and elsewhere, invoke a binary division of the political space by pitting the "authentic" will of the people against conventional leaders (e.g., in political parties, business, and media organizations) who are depicted as representatives of a "corrupt elite."[14] Populist rhetoric is therefore deeply polarizing; political opponents are portrayed as "enemies of the people," and there is no room for legitimate

---

[13] For a helpful overview of these alternatives, see Moffitt, *Populism*, ch. 2, and Paulina Ochoa Espejo, "Populism and the Idea of a People," in *The Oxford Handbook of Populism*, ed. Cristóbal Rovira Kaltwasser, Paul Taggart, Paulina Ochoa Espejo, and Pierre Ostiguy (Oxford: Oxford University Press, 2017), 618–22.
[14] Müller, *What Is Populism?*, 19–20; Mudde and Rovira Kaltwasser, *Populism*, 5.

dissent from the aims of the populist movement, or the populist leadership, with their unique claim to embody the popular will.[15] Mudde and Rovira Kaltwasser invoke the idea of the "general will" to elucidate these characteristics of populism.[16] Indeed, the Rousseauean ideal has made a powerful impression on numerous stands of modern democratic theory, and this helps to explain populism, as well as the tensions between populism and pluralism. In short, Rousseau inaugurated a very high standard for modern democratic theory and practice, with his key distinction between the "general will," which carries strong normative connotations, and a mere "will of all."[17] The former is associated with legitimate and authentic decision-making, where citizens reason together in a disinterested fashion to generate a public will that represents something like the common good, whereas the latter is depicted instead as merely an aggregation of particular interests and so does not carry these same connotations.[18] For Rousseau, it is a key characteristic of the "general will" that it cannot be represented, hence his stress on direct intercourse between citizens as they work collaboratively toward agreement in small face-to-face communities, with the ideal outcome being one of unanimous agreement around a common enlightened viewpoint. By way of contrast, in populism the emphasis is instead on the role of charismatic leaders who supposedly embody the popular will on account of their personal qualities, often over and above existing party organizations.[19] So the details of how the popular will is mobilized are very different, but populism nonetheless leverages the strong normative connotations of unity and authenticity associated with the "general will." For Müller, it is this depiction of the unity of the popular will that is at the root of populism's "anti-pluralism." As he puts it, there "can be no populism ... without someone speaking in the name of the people as a whole."[20]

This account helpfully identifies key characteristics of populism, evident in right- and left-wing versions, from Donald Trump and Jair Bolsonaro to Chávez and Morales, and it is this characteristic binary division of the political space, combined with rhetoric of the "authentic" people versus the "corrupt" elite, and the claim to represent the unity and authenticity

---

[15] Müller, *What Is Populism?*, 4.
[16] Mudde and Rovira Kaltwasser, *Populism*, 16.
[17] Jean-Jacques Rousseau, "On the Social Contract," in *Jean-Jacques Rousseau: The Basic Political Writings* (Indianapolis, IN; Cambridge, UK: Hackett, 1987), 155.
[18] Ibid.
[19] Mudde and Rovira Kaltwasser, *Populism*, 4, 43, 63; Müller, *What Is Populism?*, 33, 35, 40.
[20] Müller, *What Is Populism?*, 20.

of the people-as-a-whole, which is key to understanding the authoritarian tendency within populism. The exemplary theoretical account of populism in these terms has been formulated by Ernesto Laclau. In the current literature, Laclau's "radical democratic" approach is denounced for his outright endorsement of populism, and as too abstract to account for empirical cases.[21] Despite these criticisms, Laclau's account of how populism is manifested has nonetheless influenced the generally accepted description of populism outlined above.[22] I briefly touch on his approach here because it further illustrates the authoritarian tendency within populism. In Laclau's account, the binary division of the social space is a necessary condition for the articulation of a popular will, because as he sees it, this is the only way a series of disparate political demands can begin to see themselves as equivalent, that is, in their common opposition to the prevailing authorities, who are seen as unable or unwilling to satisfy their various demands.[23] This is how the established authorities come to be seen as the "corrupt elite," blocking what is still at this point a disparate set of demands, until one of those demands begins to function as representative of them all, simultaneously mobilizing and embodying something like the "general will."[24] Moreover, Laclau explained this articulation of "the people" with reference to the figures of speech, and he stressed the pivotal moment of synecdoche, whereby a part embodies the whole of "the people." Admittedly, Laclau also stressed how this moment of fullness is inherently precarious and unstable; but nonetheless, in his theory, democratic politics is staged around a struggle by various actors to stand in for or represent the people-as-a-whole. Müller objects that the "idea of the single, homogenous, authentic people is a fantasy."[25] To which Laclau would reply, "yes," but it is because the "general will" is a fantasy that it is such a powerful mobilizing trope in democratic politics.

Commentators have for a long time pointed out the authoritarian tendency in Laclau's rendering of democratic politics, because the part representing

---

[21] See, e.g., Moffitt, *Populism*, 25; Rovira Kaltwasser, "The Ambivalence," 192; Nadia Urbinati, *Me The People: How Populism Transforms Democracy* (Cambridge, MA: Harvard University Press, 2019), 52.

[22] I am grateful to Gulshan Ara Khan for this observation, as well as for many other helpful discussions on the relationship between populism, democracy, and pluralism.

[23] Ernesto Laclau, *On Populist Reason* (London; New York: Verso, 2005); "Populism: What's in a Name?," in *Populism and the Mirror of Democracy* ed. Francisco Panizza (London and New York: Verso, 2005), 148–9.

[24] Ibid.

[25] Müller, *What Is Populism?*, 3.

the whole can lead to a dangerous concentration of power.[26] He tended to brush off these concerns, but anxieties around the authoritarian tendency manifested in real-world examples of populism have become a major theme in contemporary debates. The concern is that, despite appeals to an authentic popular mandate, populism threatens a perilous concentration of power, and that populists are contemptuous of institutional constraints on the popular will, such as a free press and the integrity of free and fair elections, as well as individual liberties and the rights of minorities. I refer to these propensities respectively as the oligarchic and despotic tendencies in contemporary populism. In particular, right-wing populist leaders use social media to denigrate migrants and other minorities, and so right-wing populism is understood as a clear and present danger to basic rights and civil liberties. But these tendencies are also evident in left-wing populism, for instance in the prominent Latin American examples, where press freedoms have been curtailed and the judiciary crammed with loyalists to the regime. So, we should pause before supporting Mouffe and Fraser in their recent endorsement of left populism, and Laclau's approach is invoked here precisely because it neatly illuminates the authoritarian tendency associated with the current phenomenon of populism.

Populism and Democracy

It is also evident from what's been said that populism emerges from within democracy, and so we need to examine further the relationship between populism and democracy, as a prelude to an analysis of the relationship between populism and pluralism. Here again, Müller and Mudde and Rovira Kaltwasser's respective contributions are instructive. For Müller, populism is a "degraded form of democracy that promises to make good on democracy's highest ideals," but is, in fact, anti-democratic, because "democracy requires pluralism and the recognition that we need to find fair terms of living together as free, equal, but also irreducibly diverse citizens." Democracy therefore "necessarily involve[es] checks and balances (and, in general, constraints on the popular will)."[27] By way of contrast, for Mudde and Rovira Kaltwasser

---

[26] See, e.g., Mark Wenman, "Laclau or Mouffe? Splitting the Difference," *Philosophy and Social Criticism* 29, no. 5 (2003): 581–606; Gulshan Ara Khan, "Pluralisation: An Alternative to Hegemony," *The British Journal of Politics and International Relations* 10, no. 2 (2008): 194–209.

[27] Müller, *What Is Populism?*, 3, 6, 9.

the relationship is more ambiguous, and "populism can work as either a threat to or corrective for democracy."[28] On their account, populism aims to empower "groups that do not feel represented by the political establishment," enables the participation of ordinary people, and can be commended for "politicising issues that are not discussed by the elites but are considered relevant by the silent majority," such as "immigration in western Europe or the policies of the so-called Washington Consensus in Latin America."[29] Indeed, left-wing populists such as Chávez and Morales illustrate the progressive side of populism, because they have "successfully politicised the dramatic levels of inequality in their countries."[30] For Mudde and Rovira Kaltwasser, populism is therefore better understood as a form of "democratic extremism" and hence a threat to liberal democracy, or, more precisely, to the liberal element in "liberal democracy,"[31] in the sense that "by claiming that no institution has the right to constrain majority rule, populist forces can end up attacking minorities and eroding those institutions that specialise in the protection of fundamental rights."[32] Noting how the idea of "illiberal democracy" has been adopted as a badge of honor by Hungary's Viktor Orbán, Müller thinks this is a dangerous conclusion that plays into the hand of the populists: "This supposed criticism confirms the Hungarian prime minister as exactly what he wants to be: an opponent of liberalism. At the same time, he ... and all other populist leaders get to keep 'democracy,' which, for all the disappointments over the last quarter century, remains the most important ticket to recognition on the global stage."[33] We should therefore "stop the thoughtless invocation of 'illiberal democracy.' Populists damage democracy as such, and the fact that they have won elections does not give their projects automatic democratic legitimacy."[34]

There is a lot packed into these brief exchanges, and the central point is Müller's claim that pluralism, understood as checks and balances and constraints on the popular will, is inherent to democracy. If this is correct,

---

[28] Mudde and Rovira Kaltwasser, *Populism*, 79.
[29] Ibid., 18, 19, 82, 84; see also Rovira Kaltwasser, "The Ambivalence," 198.
[30] Mudde and Rovira Kaltwasser, *Populism*, 84. See also Mudde and Rovira Kaltwasser "Exclusionary vs. Inclusionary Populism: Comparing Contemporary Europe and Latin America," *Government and Opposition* 48, no. 2 (2012): 47–174.
[31] Mudde and Rovira Kaltwasser, *Populism*, 84.
[32] Ibid., 84.
[33] Müller, *What Is Populism?*, 56.
[34] Ibid. This view is shared by, among others: Stefan Rummens, "Populism as a Threat to Liberal Democracy," in *The Oxford Handbook of Populism*, ed. Cristóbal Rovira Kaltwasser, Paul Taggart, Paulina Ochoa Espejo, and Pierre Ostiguy (Oxford: Oxford University Press, 2017); Urbinati, *Me The People*, 10.

then we see how populism is a threat to democracy "as such," both in the real world and in Laclau's theory, because in neither case is there any emphasis on the importance of political checks and balances. However, if checks and balances are not inherent to democracy, then we see instead the viability of Mudde and Rovira Kaltwasser's counterclaim that populism can be a legitimate expression of democracy, mobilizing a popular will around issues that have been kept off the political agenda by mainstream parties and elites, while nonetheless representing a threat to individual liberties. Curiously, both these accounts are right, and wrong, about the relationship between populism and democracy, and this can be illustrated through the introduction of a conceptual distinction between democracy as "moment" (of popular will formation) and as a "form" (or system of government). The predominant understanding of democracy in political science, most political theory, and more generally throughout society, is that "democracy" equates with the political institutions that have been consolidated in Western societies since the eighteenth century and subsequently also in many other parts of the globe, characterized by popular sovereignty through free and fair elections, competitive party politics, constitutional protections of civil liberties, and so on. This common-sense understanding reflects a deeper assumption, which runs through the entire Western tradition from antiquity, that sees democracy as principally a system of government. As authors such as Sheldon Wolin and Jacques Rancière have illustrated, this tendency, which was inaugurated by ancient critics of democracy, notably Plato and Aristotle, "ascribes to democracy a proper or settled form."[35] Yet it is also possible to think of democracy instead as something like an indeterminant, and therefore unruly, capacity for popular self-determination—that is, as an authorizing "moment," rather than a "form" or system of government.[36]

This distinction throws helpful light on the question of the relationship between populism and democracy, because if we conceive of democracy, in the first instance, as a temporary mobilization of the popular will, bracketing for a moment any perceived consequences for democracy as a system of government, then it seems evident that populism is a genuine expression of democracy. In other words, for good or ill, the populist binary division of

[35] Sheldon Wolin, *Politics and Vision: Continuity and Innovation in Western Political Thought* (Princeton, NJ; Oxford: Princeton University Press, 2004), 601, 603; Jacques Rancière, *Disagreement: Politics and Philosophy* (Minneapolis; London: University of Minnesota Press, 1999), ch. 4.
[36] Rancière, *Disagreement*, ch. 4.

the social space, the rhetoric of the "authentic" people versus the "corrupt" elite, and the claim to personify the people-as-a-whole do represent a genuine democratic "moment," and it is foolhardy to dismiss populism as merely an anti-democratic menace to democracy "as such." The idea of democracy as an instituting "moment" is primarily associated with extra-constitutional modes of politics such as widespread civil disobedience and moments of revolution. Wolin describes how in these circumstances, the popular will, mobilized en masse in the public square, makes itself felt by "protesting actualities and revealing [new] possibilities."[37] These have been a recurrent feature of modern politics and are generally seen as empowering citizens, evident, for example, in the 1963 March on Washington, in the fall of the Berlin Wall and subsequent collapse of the Soviet Union, and in the Arab Spring. Populist leaders try to tap into this extra-institutional source of democratic power by using referenda and other mechanisms to mobilize a popular will outside the main channels of representation. However, democracy as an instituting moment was also a decisive force in Berlin in January 1933, and the collapse of the Weimar Republic is the exemplary case of the more widely evident phenomena of an inherent authoritarian *possibility*, when democracy manifests as an unruly moment. This was most clearly expressed by Carl Schmitt, who observed—with the clarity of proximity—that, if the essence of democracy is "an identity between law and the people's will," then "in an emergency, no other constitutional institution can withstand the sole criterion of the people's will, however it is expressed."[38]

Müller objects that on Schmitt's view, "Caesaristic methods not only can produce the acclamation of the people but can be a direct expression of democratic substance and power."[39] In other words, Schmitt stresses a correlation between democracy and an inherent possibility for the emergence of authoritarian and dictatorial forms of power. For Müller, such a view only makes sense if we disregard democracy as a system of government composed of institutions of checks and balances. However, we need to concede the validity of Schmitt's insight when we see democracy as, first and foremost, a pre- or extra-institutional indeterminant power of ordinary citizens to join together and manifest a democratic "moment." Often this will be for the good, but such a fortuitous outcome can't be predetermined,

---

[37] Wolin, *Politics*, 603.
[38] Carl Schmitt, *The Crisis of Parliamentary Democracy* (Cambridge, MA: MIT Press, 1988), 15, 26.
[39] Müller, *What Is Populism?*, 52.

and democratic will formation always runs the risk of degenerating into more concentrated (oligarchic) and arbitrary (despotic) forms of power. So it appears to follow that we should not only see populism as a genuine expression of democracy, but that the authoritarian tendency within populism is also a genuine expression of potentialities inherent within democracy. In other words, rather than populism being anti-democratic, it is better understood as a contemporary reminder of democracy's much-evidenced capacity for self-harm, which has, of course, been noted across the centuries, from nineteenth-century concerns about the tyranny of the majority (variously in Alexis de Tocqueville and John Stuart Mill), back to Aristotle's astute insights into the power of the demagogues. Or, at least, these seem to be the inferences when we conceive of democracy as an instituting moment. However, while we need to understand and value democracy in these terms because this is repeatedly how ordinary citizens challenge the status quo and bring new possibilities into being, this is not the whole story. This conception of democracy needs to be joined with an equivalent appreciation of democracy as it is more commonly understood (i.e., as a system of government). Here, "radical" right- and left-wing critics—from Schmitt to Laclau and Rancière—coalesce on an outright rejection of "mainstream" democratic institutions, presented as mere contrivances to "police" otherwise authentic expressions of the popular will.[40] Laclau's claim that the articulation of a populist moment is synonymous with politics exemplifies this disregard for democracy as a set of institutional constraints.[41] Against this view, I think one of the most profound achievements of modern societies, in contrast to the instability of ancient Greek democracy, has been to craft institutions that have facilitated something like popular self-determination that is *relatively durable* or able to *persist over time*. Claude Lefort captures something of the profundity of this achievement when he describes modern democracy as a fundamental "mutation in the symbolic order," where social and political conflict comes to be recognized and valued as "constitutive of the very unity of society."[42] In contrast to early modern European sovereignty "embodied in the person

---

[40] Rancière, *Disagreement*. For a recent illustration of this outlook, see Alain Badiou, Pierre Bourdieu, Judith Butler, George Didi-Huberman, Sadri Khiari, and Jacques Rancière, *What Is a People?* (New York: Columbia University Press, 2016). This collection includes many important insights into the discursive construction of "the people," but nothing on the positive role that institutions can play in sustaining self-government over time.
[41] Laclau, "Populism," 47.
[42] Claude Lefort, *Democracy and Political Theory* (Cambridge, UK: Polity Press, 1988), 16–18.

of the prince," through the consolidation of institutions such as periodic elections for legislative and executive office, sovereignty in modern democratic systems remains inherently divided. As Lefort puts it, the "locus of power becomes an empty space."[43]

There are many different accounts of what is most ingenious in this development. One prominent view is the idea that, in modernity, democracy comes to be increasingly articulated with liberalism, and that liberalism—manifest above all in constitutional protections of individual rights—places necessary limits on democracy's capacity for self-harm. This is exemplified in Jürgen Habermas's famous description of democracy and liberalism as "co-original" for modern politics.[44] This view has recently been reiterated by Stefan Rummens, to dismiss populism as entirely illegitimate (i.e., as all "threat" and no "corrective") and therefore to be tolerated, at best, on the margins of public opinion, but to be excluded from participating in government at all costs.[45] While these sentiments are understandable, especially given the challenges posed by right-wing populism, this view reiterates post-political liberalism as a theory of absolute constraints on political power, rather than a theory of checks and balances. However, as we have said, liberalism is blind to its complicity in the reasons for the emergence of populism in the first place; so rather than simply dismissing populism as anti-democratic, we need a more political response to the authoritarian tendency within populism. We turn instead, then, to the tradition of American pluralism, which represents an exemplary account of modern democracy as a system of government, and to Dahl's work on "polyarchy," which has played a significant role in shaping the now common-sense understanding of democracy in these terms. In this approach, there is room to acknowledge populism as a genuinely democratic "moment," one that presents both a corrective and a threat to democracy as a "system" of government; the focus is precisely on the importance of political checks and balances, designed to counter such threats; and, in this account, liberalism plays, at best, only a limited and qualified role. However, before we turn to this discussion, we first need to briefly disaggregate several other meanings of "pluralism."

---

[43] Ibid.
[44] Jürgen Habermas, "Constitutional Democracy: A Paradoxical Union of Contradictory Principles?," *Political Theory* 29, no. 6 (2001): 766–81.
[45] Rummens "Populism."

Alternative Modes of Pluralism

Müller and Mudde and Rovira Kaltwasser disagree on the relationship between populism and democracy, but broadly agree that populism is "antipluralist" or the "direct opposite" of pluralism.[46] However, what exactly does it mean to invoke "pluralism" in these discussions? Müller emphasizes checks and balances; he also cites Habermas's argument that "the people can only appear in the plural."[47] Mudde and Rovira Kaltwasser cite the tradition of American pluralism, which they contrast with the binary division characteristic of populism, stressing how the pluralists understood society instead as "divided into a broad variety of partly overlapping social groups with different ideas and interests."[48] However, in each of these discussions the meaning of pluralism is somewhat underdeveloped, and this underdetermined quality is set against a broader context where, as I have said, there has been a wide dissemination of this term throughout social and political theory over the last forty years. As Steven K. White said in 2002, one of the key challenges of contemporary political theory is to "not let pluralism become a platitude."[49] But it has become a platitude, and so in this section I disaggregate several different meanings of "pluralism," before outlining the American tradition in more detail in the following section.

Amidst the different usages, it is possible to identify three different meanings of "pluralism," that each circulate in contemporary social and political theory, and I distinguish these here respectively as *ethical, metaphysical,* and *political* pluralism. The idea of ethical pluralism has been very influential, for example in anglophone moral philosophy, to the point where this is broadly taken for granted as the starting point for most of the major strands of moral and political theory over the past half century. This idea is clearly articulated in the work of Berlin, who stressed how a diversity of incompatible, and often incommensurate, values form the bedrock of ethical life, and so this value of "pluralism" is understood as a necessary condition of any ethical or moral decision-making.[50] This underlying ethical condition is subsequently reflected in the multiplicity of lifestyle choices which

---

[46] Müller, *What Is Populism?*, 3, 9; Mudde and Rovira Kaltwasser, *Populism*, 7, 81, 95.
[47] Müller, *What Is Populism?*, 4.
[48] Mudde and Rovira Kaltwasser, *Populism*, 7.
[49] Stephen K. White, "Pluralism, Platitudes, and Paradoxes: Fifty Years of Western Political Thought," *Political Theory* 30, no. 4 (2002): 472–81.
[50] Isaiah Berlin, *The Crooked Timber of Humanity: Chapters in the History of Ideas* (London: John Murray, 1990), 79–80.

have become an obvious feature of contemporary societies. This is what John Rawls called the "fact of pluralism," that is, of a society comprising multiple different conceptions of the good life.[51] In part, it is this understanding that Müller has in mind when he says that populists are anti-pluralist, and it is, more explicitly, this pluralism that Moffit references when he says that some forms of left-wing populism articulate a conception of the people that is receptive to a plurality of different values and lifestyles.

This conception of pluralism is instructive, and the populist emphasis on the unity and authenticity of the popular will presents a challenge to this understanding of pluralism; right-wing populism, especially, represents a danger to ethical and lifestyle pluralism. The problem, however, is that nothing incontestable about political institutions, practices, or principles follows from the "fact" of ethical pluralism. Berlin sought to defend liberalism as the normative principle to emerge from an acknowledgment of the foundational status of ethical pluralism, and, despite their differences, Berlin and Rawls represent an exemplary account of liberalism as the appropriate response to this acknowledgment. However, as commentators have shown, it is not self-evident that the liberal priority of protecting a space for individual moral choice follows necessarily from ethical pluralism.[52]

What if, for example, we take the group, rather than the individual, as the proper locus of ethical life? Then ethical pluralism might give rise instead to multiculturalism, and a defense of group rather than individual rights as the appropriate normative political principle.[53] Without wishing to defend multiculturalism, I cite these claims here to illustrate that a vindication of liberalism does not follow necessarily from a recognition of ethical pluralism. In fact, a wide divergence of positions in political theory over the past several decades—liberalism and multiculturalism, deliberative and agonistic democracy—all start from an acknowledgment of ethical pluralism but proceed to elaborate a range of divergent views about how we should respond. The more important question is what political principles and institutions follow from an acknowledgment of ethical pluralism, and what these tell us about how to respond to populism.

Müller is right to stress the importance of checks and balances and constraints on popular power, but Habermas responds to the underlying

---

[51] John Rawls, *Political Liberalism* (New York: Columbia University Press, 1996).
[52] John Gray, *Enlightenment's Wake* (Abingdon, UK: Routledge, 2007), 199.
[53] E.g., Bhikhu Parekh, *Rethinking Multiculturalism: Cultural Diversity and Political Theory* (London: Red Globe Press, 2006).

condition of ethical pluralism with an emphasis on the need for reasoned agreement and consensus, rather than checks and balances and mutual constraints. His approach absorbs much of the high moral criteria of Rousseau, and places considerable burden on citizens to leave their particular interests behind as they reason together toward common ends.[54] And while the "coming of age" of deliberative democracy might involve a belated acknowledgment of the need to make room for compromises and bargaining, these are still secondary and derivative principles in an approach to democratic will-formation that remains predicated on the normative standard of disinterested and enlightened agreement, ultimately derived from Rousseau.[55] In other words, if it is a theory of checks and balances that we want in response to populism, Habermas and the traditions of deliberative democracy are not the obvious source, and so we need to look elsewhere for a vindication of these principles.

Another source of "pluralism" in contemporary social and political theory stems from what we might term "metaphysical pluralism." I use this term provokingly because this idea is most evident in a range of theories influenced by postmodernism, and postmodernism is supposed to be committed to a critique of philosophy and a rejection of metaphysics. Remarkably, however, in these theories, pluralism—or an entire set of substitute terms, such as difference, diversity, multiplicity, heterogeneity, the multitude—is presented as something like an irreducible quality of all relationships. These claims are usually derived from one of two sources, either observations about the wonderous diversity observed in nature or manifest in the incessant play and polysemy of language.[56] However, whichever of these sources is appealed to, they broadly coalesce around an emphasis on "difference" and "diversity" as an irreducible quality of the lived experience; so that, in the words of William James, an important forerunner of this approach, from every claim to identity "something like a pluralism breaks out."[57]

---

[54] E.g., Habermas, "Three Normative Models of Democracy," in *Democracy and Difference: Contesting the Boundaries of the Political*, ed. Seyla Benhabib (Princeton, NJ: Princeton University Press, 1996); "Reconciliation through the Public Use of Reason," in Habermas, *The Inclusion of the Other* (Cambridge, MA: MIT Press, 1988).

[55] James Bohman, "The Coming of Age of Deliberative Democracy," *Journal of Political Philosophy*, 6, no. 4 (1998): 399–425.

[56] Exemplified respectively in Gilles Deleuze, *Pure Immanence: Essays on Life* (New York: Zone Books, 2001), and Jacques Derrida, *Of Grammatology* (Baltimore, MD; London: John Hopkins University Press, 1976).

[57] William James, *A Pluralistic Universe* (London: Longmans, Green and Co., 1909), 37.

These insights capture important aspects of our lived experience. However, as with the discussion of ethical pluralism above, nothing obvious about political institutions or principles follows from this acknowledgment of pluralism as an irreducible feature of life and language. What's more, there is a tendency among these broadly postmodern approaches to read optimistic political consequences directly into this (post) metaphysical assumption. So, for example, those who defend Laclau's approach will say that there is no need to be unduly concerned about his stress on a concentration of power, with the part standing in for the whole, because "society is never fully sutured," or the "nodal points" or "empty signifiers" are "never entirely fixed," and this is because the popular will is always articulated within a discursive terrain that is itself constitutively unstable, because of the irreducible play of language. The problem with these sorts of claims is that a (post) metaphysical assumption about the inherent plurality in language has assumed the role we would otherwise look for in institutions of political checks and balances. There is nothing in Laclau's theory about the prescriptive role of political institutions in constraining popular power, but we do find exactly these claims in one of the two distinct accounts of "political" pluralism in twentieth-century democratic theory.

These two traditions of "political pluralism" are the English and American versions, articulated respectively in the aftermath of the First and Second World Wars. These approaches share a mistrust of centralized forms of power and place considerable emphasis on the role of groups, or secondary associations, in the political process. English pluralism was more explicitly normative and manifested above all in the claim that authority (not power as influence, but recognized legal authority) ought to be wrestled away from the state and dispersed throughout the various groups in society. Based on this principle, prominent pluralists like G. D. H. Cole and Harold Laski advocated for quasi-corporatist institutions and complex systems of functional representation.[58] Although versions of this theory have been resurrected in more recent democratic theory,[59] these approaches do not offer a credible response to the rise of populism. Indeed, the institutional proposals advocated by the English pluralists were predicated on an assumption of an underlying unity of social purpose that now looks antiquated and naïve.

---

[58] E.g., G. D. H. Cole, *Self-Government in Industry* (London: Bell and Sons, 1922); Harold J. Laski, *Authority in the Modern State* (New Haven, CT: Yale University Press, 1919).

[59] Paul Q. Hirst, *Associative Democracy: New Forms of Economic and Social Governance* (Cambridge, UK: Polity Press, 1996).

By way of contrast, in the tradition of postwar American political science, "pluralism," which for Dahl is mostly used interchangeably with "polyarchy," refers to a particular kind of political regime, where power (as influence, rather than a designated legal authority) is unequally distributed, but nonetheless still sufficiently dispersed for the system to approximate the principle of democratic self-rule. Here, in other words, pluralism doesn't signify a property of ethics, lifestyles, life, or language, but rather denotes the key attribute of a political system: one where, crucially, political checks and balances play a central role in preserving a capacity for self-government over time. I agree with Mudde and Rovira Kaltwasser that this tradition of pluralism offers important insights for understanding contemporary populism, as well as providing resources for how to tackle the authoritarian tendency within populism, and it is to these points that I turn in the rest of this chapter.

Populism and American Political Pluralism

Joseph Schumpeter's *Capitalism, Socialism, and Democracy* (1942) is a good starting point for understanding mid-century American pluralism. This text also exemplifies a pivotal moment in twentieth-century democratic theory, with Schumpeter rejecting the idealism of what he called the "classical theory" and seeking to redefine democracy as a system of government appropriate to modern complex societies.[60] Rather than a participatory arrangement for realizing the "general will," the democratic system is a procedural mechanism for free competition for political leadership, characterized above all by periodic elections for positions of legislative and executive office.[61] From the early 1950s, Dahl and Lindblom acknowledged Schumpeter's contribution, and they were equally dismissive of the Rousseauean ideal, "as it never was, and probably never can be."[62] The pluralists agreed with Schumpeter on the importance of developing a theory of the democratic system that accounts for modern conditions "characterised by enormous scale and considerable social pluralism."[63] However, whereas Schumpeter emphasized competition

---

[60] Joseph Schumpeter, *Capitalism, Socialism and Democracy* (London: Allen and Unwin, 1970), 252.
[61] Ibid., 270, 271.
[62] Robert A. Dahl and Charles E. Lindblom, *Politics, Economics and Welfare*, 2nd ed. (Chicago; London: University of Chicago Press, 1976), 283; Dahl, *Dilemmas of Pluralist Democracy* (New Haven, CT; London: Yale University Press, 1982), 140, 204.
[63] Robert A. Dahl, *Democracy and Its Critics* (New Haven, CT; London: Yale University Press, 1989), 291.

for political leadership, the pluralists also perceived a considerable role for societal interest groups, during and between elections, and highlighted their influence over policy formation and outcomes.[64] This is the leitmotif of American pluralism, their stress on the so-called group basis of politics. The pluralists understood society as "fractured into ... hundreds of small special interest groups,"[65] and they depicted government decision-making as, to a large extent, a manifestation of the balancing and negotiation between groups.[66] Indeed, one of the central features of American pluralism—and one at the root of American pluralists' emphasis on the importance of political checks and balances—was an uncompromising rejection of the idea that democracy can deliver an "attainable harmony of interests."[67] Against Marxist, Rousseauean, participatory, and deliberative versions of this idea, the pluralists insisted that interests are perpetually formed, and reformed, around prevailing policy areas, and that they are also cross-cutting and inherently competitive, so the most we can expect from the democratic system is a balancing and adjustment between groups.[68]

The question of the degree of equality between these competing interests (i.e., whether political power is concentrated or more widely dispersed) is, for the pluralists, an empirical question.[69] This is a second theme for which the pluralists are well known: their intervention in the so-called community-power debates that took place in the 1950s. Against those who argued that the system of power was so concentrated in America (either at the state[70] or the federal level[71]) that, in reality, "democracy" was just a shallow veneer for a de facto "power elite" operating behind the scenes, Dahl's influential *Who Governs?* concluded instead that power was more widely dispersed. The local politics of New Haven, Connecticut, the subject of Dahl's study, was a

---

[64] Dahl and Lindblom, *Politics*, 283.

[65] Nelson Polsby, *Community Power and Political Theory* (New Haven, CT: Yale University Press, 1963), 118.

[66] The pioneer of this view is of Arthur Bentley, and this position is widely shared in the tradition of postwar pluralism. See Arthur F. Bentley, *The Process of Government: A Study of Social Pressures* (New Brunswick, NJ: Transaction, 1995), 222; David Truman, *The Governmental Process* (New York: Alfred A. Knopf, 1962), vii, 33; Earl Latham, "The Group Basis of Politics: Notes for a Theory," *The American Political Science Review* 46, no. 2 (1952): 376–97, 383; Polsby, *Community*, 120.

[67] Dahl, *Dilemmas*, 186.

[68] Bentley, *The Process*, 202, 264–65; Latham, "The Group Basis," 390; Truman, *The Governmental Process*, 27, 516; Polsby, *Community*, 115; Dahl and Lindblom, *Politics*, xxii; Dahl, *Dilemmas*, 158.

[69] For a classic statement to this view, see Robert A. Dahl, "A Critique of the Ruling Elite Model," in *Readings in Modern Political Analysis*, ed. Dahl and Deane E. Neubauer (Englewood Cliffs, NJ: Pentice Hall, 1968); see also Polsby, *Community*, 113.

[70] See Floyd Hunter, *Community Power Structure* (Chapel Hill: University of North Carolina Press, 1953).

[71] See Charles W. Mills, *The Power Elite* (New York: Oxford University Press, 1956).

political system where "any active and legitimate group will make itself heard at some stage in the process of decision making."[72] The key reason for this relative dispersal of power, from the pluralist perspective, is what they called "non-cumulative inequalities" in "resources of political influence."[73] In other words, groups can call upon "different kinds of resources for influencing officials": for example, wealth, social status, knowledge, popularity, charisma, and the sheer weight of numbers. But these resourses are "unequally distributed," such that groups with "access to one kind of resource are often badly off with respect to many other resources."[74] This dispersal effect is further compounded by the fact that groups have "incompletely overlapping memberships," and that different groups have varying degrees of influence in distinct policy areas, so that a single pattern of concentrated power is "unlikely to reproduce itself in more than one issue area."[75]

However, these debates extended beyond an exchange of competing empirical observations and gave rise to a set of rival claims about how we define modern democratic systems. As Dahl pointed out, since antiquity, Western political thought has defined different political regimes in terms of *the relative degree of concertation of power within a political system*. Given the observed relative dispersal of political influence, Dahl reaches for a term to describe this kind of system and concluded that over the past two centuries New Haven had been transformed from "oligarchy" to "pluralism."[76] He also repeatedly used the term "polyarchy" to describe a political system defined by an unequal distribution of political power, but where that inequality did not reach a sufficient threshold to cross over into "oligarchy," defined by the presence of a single ruling elite.[77] Notwithstanding widespread misrepresentation, the pluralists did not emphasize an equal distribution of power or influence. To the contrary, they stressed instead "extensive inequalities in the resources different citizens can use to influence one another."[78] But crucially, in a pluralist system, these inequalities did not accumulate to the point of enabling the concentrated dominance of a single "elite."[79] In a pluralist system

---

[72] David Nicholls, *Three Varieties of Pluralism* (London: Macmillan. 1974), 25.
[73] Robert A. Dahl, *Who Governs?* (New Haven, CT: Yale University Press, 1961), 11, 70.
[74] Dahl, *Who Governs?*, 228; Polsby, *Community*, 118.
[75] Polsby, *Community*, 113, 118.
[76] Dahl, *Who Governs?* 11, 70.
[77] Robert A. Dahl, *Polyarchy: Participation and Opposition* (New Haven and London: Yale University Press, 1971).
[78] Dahl, *Who Governs?* 1; See also Dahl, *Dilemmas*, 40.
[79] Dahl, *Polyarchy*.

"the democratic goal is [therefore] still roughly and crudely approximated, in the sense that non leaders exercise a relatively high degree of control over leaders."[80]

Mudde and Rovira Kaltwasser are right to single out this tradition of pluralism as providing important insights into the contemporary emergence of populism. However, Dahl's efforts to define pluralism as a distinct kind of democratic regime are also crucially different from contemporary efforts to define populism. The various contemporary presentations of populism—as an ideology, discourse, a political strategy, or style—each reveal certain aspects of this phenomenon, but the generally received view is that populism is something that emerges *within* democratic systems, rather than being a new kind of regime. It is therefore misleading to define populism as the "opposite" of pluralism, as this term is understood in American political science. Mudde and Rovira Kaltwasser emphasize that populism is predicated on a binary division of the political space, and this contrasts with the pluralist emphasis on a dispersal of different groups throughout society.[81] But this emphasis on a diversity of competing interests is not the key criterion of pluralism. It is rather the implications of this diversity for the relative concentration of power within the system, and in turn what this implies for a proper definition of the democratic regime. Mudde and Rovira Kaltwasser also note this aspect of pluralism,[82] but they don't explore what it means for the relationship between populism and pluralism. If they had done so, they would need to acknowledge that we are talking about two different kinds of phenomena. One is a definition of a distinctive system of democratic government; the other is a particular manifestation of a democratic "moment," or a mode of popular-will formation, that emerges from within this system. In *Who Governs?* and other key pluralist texts, the opposite of pluralism is "oligarchy," and so the operative question about the relationship between populism and pluralism is: What are the implications of the emergence of populism—with its rhetoric of the "authenticity" and "purity" of the people versus the "corrupt" elite, and its emphasis on synecdoche, the part standing in for the whole—for the concentration of power within the system? The concern is that populism leads to a dangerous concentration of power, but this does not make populism the opposite of pluralism. Instead, it is better

---

[80] Dahl and Lindblom, *Politics*, 275.
[81] Mudde and Rovira Kaltwasser, *Populism*, 7–8.
[82] Ibid.

understood as a particular type of democratic moment, one which risks tipping the system over into oligarchy.[83]

In fact, it was precisely this kind of dynamic that Dahl and Lindblom understood as definitive of modern politics; remember that they were writing against the backdrop of McCarthyism. In contrast to the erroneous reading that the pluralists stressed an inbuilt tendency toward equilibrium,[84] they presented polyarchy instead as inherently precarious. As Dahl and Lindblom put it, the "struggle to maintain a polyarchal organisation is never won; it is always on the verge of being lost."[85] Here, we also need to consider Mudde and Rovira Kaltwasser's additional claim that populism is not only the oppositive of pluralism, but also the opposite of elite theory.[86] On their account, populism and elite theory share a binary division of the political space, but the positive and negative terms in these polarities are reversed, with a positive valuation of the people against the corrupt elite in populism, and the reversal of these estimations in elite theory. Again, however, this is to compare two different kinds of phenomena. Unlike populism, elite theory—whether in the critical American version of someone like C. Wright Mills or the earlier Italian iteration in the work of Vilfredo Pareto, Gaetano Mosca, and Robert Michels—was, like pluralism, characterized by an attempt to define the key characteristics of modern democratic regimes on the basis of the extent of the concertation of power within the system.[87] Unlike the pluralists, however, the elite theorists observed that the concentration of power was such that the system was best defined in terms of a hierarchical "power elite." We have seen that Dahl arrived at different conclusions, but, to further complicate matters, he also acknowledged a central premise of "elite theory," which is that there are inbuilt tendencies toward oligarchy in modern societies.

---

[83] Takis Pappas perceives the difficulty with describing populism as the opposite of pluralism, because populism emerges from within a pluralist system. However, he focuses on the "manyness" of ideas and parties characteristic of pluralism, and brushes over the key point about the distribution of power within the system. He therefore unhelpfully describes "monism" as the opposite of pluralism, whereas Dahl avoids such abstract metaphysical notions, focusing instead on oligarchy (an illicit concentration of power) as the opposite of pluralism. See Takis S. Pappas, *Populism and Liberal Democracy: A Comparative and Theoretical Analysis* (Oxford: Oxford University Press, 2019), 30.

[84] Myron Q. Hale, "The Cosmology of Arthur Bentley," in *The Bias of Pluralism*, ed. William Connolly (New York: Atherton, 1969); Stanislaw Ehrlich, *Pluralism On and Off Course* (Oxford: Pergamon. 1982); Avigail I. Eisenberg, *Reconstructing Political Pluralism* (Albany: State University of New York Press, 1995).

[85] Robert A. Dahl and Charles E. Lindblom, *Politics Economics and Welfare* (New York: Harper Torchbooks, 1963), 281–82.

[86] Mudde and Rovira Kaltwasser, *Populism*, 7, 11; See also Müller, *What Is Populism?*, 3.

[87] Mills, *The Power*, and, e.g., Robert Michels, *Political Parties* (New York: Free Press, 1962), 377–92.

He adds, however, that in a polyarchic system, the "iron law of oligarchy" is nonetheless tempered in some important respects by a "counteracting law of reciprocity."[88]

So a more complex picture emerges from this reconstruction of American pluralism. Rather than simply conceiving populism as the oppositive of pluralism, the American pluralists understood pluralism, or polyarchy, as a particular kind of democratic regime, one where power is unequally distributed but nonetheless sufficiently dispersed to facilitate meaningful democratic governance. This system is precarious and always under threat from inbuilt tendencies toward oligarchy, or an illicit concentration of power. And populism is a particular democratic moment of popular will-formation, one that emerges from within polyarchy, but nonetheless runs the risk of generating an illicit concentration of power and tipping the system into oligarchy, particularly as a result of the stress it places on the part standing in for the whole.

In other words, the pluralist view corresponds with Nadia Urbinati's suggestion that we understand populism as part of the broader phenomena of the formation of elites; while populism emerges from within democracy, it nonetheless threatens to push democratic (pluralist) institutions to their limits and could produce the emergence of a new regime "that might well be authoritarian, dictatorial, or fascist."[89] One key question, therefore, is whether polyarchy has sufficient resources to prevent a populist moment from tipping the system over into oligarchy. This question is explored in the final section of the chapter. However, we have not yet said anything about the reasons why populism has emerged from within the polyarchic system. This is also a question where we find helpful observations in the American tradition of pluralism. As well as outlining the precariousness of polyarchy vis-à-vis the inbuilt tendency toward oligarchy, Dahl and Lindblom also reflected at length on the underlying conditions of polyarchy, and their later work was characterized by an increasing acknowledgment of the erosion and breakdown of those conditions. So it is to these points that we turn in the next section: How and why have the conditions of polyarchy broken down? How does this help explain the contemporary emergence of populism?

---

[88] Dahl and Lindblom, *Politics*, 279.
[89] Urbinati, *Me The People*, 7, 14.

The Broken Conditions of Polyarchy

Two well-known criticisms of American pluralism are particularly significant for understanding the contemporary emergence of populism. These are the claims that, because the pluralists focused on observable decision-making, they ignored the unarticulated or poorly articulated interests of disadvantaged groups;[90] and, relatedly that the pluralists were blind to the so-called second face of power, that is, to the "mobilization of bias" in the community that prevents "potentially dangerous issues being raised" as part of the normal democratic process.[91] These discussions appear to be the progenitor for Mudde and Rovira Kaltwasser's helpful explanation for the current emergence of populism: in a context where "people feel that they are not being (well) represented by the elites in power," populism emerges as an effort to re-politicize issues excluded from the political agenda, and thereby "give government back to the people."[92] This underscores how populism arises, in part, because of inbuilt deficiencies within polyarchic institutions. However, it is important to add that Peter Bachrach's and Morton Baratz's famous critique of pluralist theory misses its mark, because the postwar pluralists did recognize the role of something like the second face of power.[93] Similarly, against those who claimed that pluralism was designed to prevent the possibility of change,[94] the pluralists emphasized instead the need for the system to be open to new kinds of demands, and they were mindful of the dangers of what they called "immobilism," or the inertia built into the regime.[95] In other words, Dahl and Lindblom would be receptive to Mudde and Rovira Kaltwasser's insightful account of the reasons for the contemporary emergence of populism, and they would also likely connect this to their own more general account of the steady breakdown of the conditions of polyarchy.

---

[90] Peter Bachrach and Morton S. Baratz, "Two Faces of Power," *American Political Science Review* 56 (1962): 947–52; Stephen Lukes, *Power: A Radical View* (London: Macmillan, 1974).

[91] Bachrach and Baratz, "Two Faces," 947, 950, 952.

[92] Mudde and Rovira Kaltwasser, *Populism*, 10. Note also the parallels with Mouffe's account of the reasons for the emergence of right-wing populism.

[93] Robert A. Dahl, *A Preface to Democratic Theory* (Chicago and London: University of Chicago Press, 1956); 138; Truman, *The Governmental Process*, 512, 523.

[94] Herbert Marcuse, *One Dimensional Man*, (London: Routledge, 1964); Jack T. Walker, "A Critique of the Elitist Theory of Democracy," *The American Political Science Review* 60, no. 2 (1966): 285–95, 289; William Connolly, ed., *The Bias of Pluralism* (New York: Atherton, 1969); *The Ethos of Pluralization* (Princeton, MN: University of Minnesota Press, 1995); Eisenberg, *Reconstructing*, 158, 165.

[95] Dahl, *Who Governs?*; Robert A. Dahl and Bruce Stinebrickner, *Modern Political Analysis*, 6th ed. (NJ: Prentice Hall, 2003), 64; Truman, *The Governmental Process*, xli, xxxix.

Dahl repeatedly raised the question of the conditions of polyarchy throughout his work. This included not only summarizing the formal conditions of the democratic system—an inclusive suffrage, frequent and fair elections, a system of competitive party politics, the right to run for office, freedom of expression and of association, free access to information, and so on[96]—but also a set of reflections on the wider societal conditions for these institutions to be sustained. These wider societal conditions included, most importantly, a fair degree of socioeconomic equality, a fair degree of cultural commonality, and a society-wide acknowledgment of the importance and value of the democratic "rules of the game."[97] In the absence of these conditions, polyarchy cannot be sustained, because a pluralistic system requires citizens to take it in turn at being winners and losers in the game of cyclical democratic will formation; and today's losers will no longer have confidence that they can be tomorrow's winners in the absence of these wider societal conditions. Sadly, this also reads like a roll call of the conditions that have broken down in Western societies over the past four or five decades: the rough equality of the postwar welfare state era has given way to rising levels of poverty and to the almost unimaginable inequalities today between ordinary citizens and the super-rich; cultural diversity has increasingly taken the form of intense conflict around non-negotiable values or between competing identities in relations of reciprocal contempt; and, not surprisingly, these developments have also precipitated a deep erosion of democratic norms and values, exemplified in Trump's election denial claims and the extraordinary events following the outcome of the 2020 U.S. presidential election.

Dahl and Lindblom's interventions in the late 1970s and 1980s traced the early stages of these developments. They identified what they saw as the corrosive impact of increasingly uncompromising forms of "sub-cultural pluralism," of rising socioeconomic inequalities, and, most significantly, of the disproportionate power of large corporate interests over executive decision-making and policy outcomes.[98] Throughout these later writings, the pluralists became increasingly pessimistic that the democratic goal was still roughly approximated in contemporary "democratic" systems. Given

---

[96] Dahl and Lindblom, *Politics*, 278; Dahl, *Dilemmas*, 10–11; *Democracy*, 233, 260.
[97] Dahl, *A Preface*, 132–133; *Polyarchy*, 106–8; *Dilemmas*, 27; *Democracy*, 235, 255; *Who Governs?*, 225–226.
[98] See Dahl and Lindblom, *Politics*, xxxvii; Lindblom, "The Market as Prison," *The Journal of Politics* 44 (1982): 324–36, 326, 335; Dahl, *Polyarchy*, 108; "Pluralism Revisited," in *Three Faces of Pluralism*, ed. Stanislaw Ehrlich and Graham Wootton (Westmead: Gower, 1980), 25; *Democracy*, 235.

the subsequent acceleration of these trends, polyarchy today is broken, or almost broken, and this context provides the broader explanation for the contemporary emergence of populism.

However, it does not follow that modern democracy is simply a "neoliberal fantasy,"[99] or that we should rush to join Mouffe and Frazer in an endorsement of left populism. Mudde and Rovira Kaltwasser correctly highlight how left-wing populisms have had some success in re-politicizing the issue of inequality, but they also point out how this comes at considerable costs to (liberal) democratic institutions. Populism does reactivate democracy through challenging the status quo and reshaping the political agenda, but this does not preclude the possible emergence of alternative modes of democratic will-formation: alternative democratic "moments," that might have the same impact, without the corresponding appeal to a binary division of the political space, to a rhetoric of a "pure people" versus the "corrupt elite," or to the part standing in for the "whole."[100] In other words, we might envisage the possible emergence of alternative democratic "correctives" without the corresponding "threat" of overly concentrated power. A fuller account of what these alternative democratic moments might look like is beyond the scope of this chapter. What I do offer by way of conclusion is a brief reflection on several normative insights that emerge from the tradition of American pluralism, which might help inform how we begin to think about these challenges.

A Pluralist Response to Populism

We have seen that American pluralism was primarily an explanatory doctrine, but it is also apparent that the pluralist explication of modern democracy was informed by a set of normative claims, at the heart of which is an emphasis on the value of political checks and balances. Indeed, Dahl described the normative goals of pluralism in the following terms: pluralism

---

[99] Jodi Dean, *Democracy and Other Neoliberal Fantasies: Communicative Capitalism and Left Politics* (Durham, NC; London: Duke University Press, 2009).

[100] The prospect of the emergence of alternative types of democratic "moment" should also caution against Benjamin Arditi's account of populism as the "spectre" that necessarily haunts the democratic system from within. See Benjamin Arditi, "Populism as a Spectre of Democracy: A Response to Canovan," *Political Studies* 52, no. 1 (2004): 135–43. Although Arditi gives populism its due (i.e., as an unruly element within democratic institutions), his account has the unwarranted effect of presenting populism as the only contender for this role (i.e., by treating populism as the "internal periphery" of democratic politics), that is, as a necessary rather than contingent phenomena.

has the potential to help "minimise government coercion" of social life, "curb hierarchy," "prevent domination," and facilitate "mutual control."[101] Moreover, these ideals are derived from different canonical sources than the tradition inaugurated by Rousseau. Pluralism as normative political theory reaches back through Tocqueville to James Madison's account of the benefits of the separation of powers in the *Federalist* 10.[102] Whereas Rousseau invoked an idealized image of the ancient republics to emphasize small-scale, face-to-face decision-making as means toward a harmonization of interests in the "general will," Madison underscored instead the highly discordant character of the ancient republics, took it that the "causes of faction" were ineradicable or "in the nature of man," and sought to devise institutions that would, at best, permanently frustrate the "gradual concentration" of power in the hands of "the superior force of an interested and overbearing majority."[103]

Dahl and Lindblom described the central goal of this alternative approach as the "antique and yet ever recurring problem of how citizens can keep their rulers from becoming tyrants."[104] This suggests a negative ideal at the heart of pluralism: as we have seen, the aim is to prevent or inhibit an unhealthy concertation of power. Some prominent theorists have provided "minimalist" accounts of this alterative tradition, arguing that we should not expect democratic systems to deliver on ideals like social justice, or even the goal of self-government, but rather that the institutions of modern democracy simply prove their worth if they repeatedly facilitate a peaceful transfer of power.[105] While this negative function is important to the pluralists, who sought to avert the system tipping over into oligarchy, pluralism as articulated by Dahl and Lindblom is not (only) a minimalist theory of democracy. Instead, the goal is more affirmative: to facilitate self-government, over time, in which ordinary citizens have meaningful control on a sustained basis over the policy agenda and the outcome of governmental decisions. Lindblom calls this democracy through "partisan mutual adjustment," which allows for continuous "large scale coordination ... through mutual adjustment of

---

[101] Dahl, *Dilemmas*, 1, 32.
[102] Alexander Hamilton, John Jay, and James Madison, *The Federalist Papers* (London: Penguin, 1987); Alexis de Tocqueville, *Democracy in America* (London: Oxford University Press, 1946).
[103] Hamilton, Jay, and Madison, *The Federalist Papers*, 120, 123–25, 319.
[104] Dahl and Lindblom, *Politics*, 273.
[105] Karl Popper, *The Open Society and Its Enemies* (London: Routledge and Kegan Paul, 1962); Adam Przeworski, "Minimalist Conception Democracy: A Defence," in *Democracy's Value*, ed. Ian Shapiro and Casiano Hacker-Cordon (Cambridge, UK: Cambridge University Press, 1999).

persons not ordered by rule, central management, or dominant common purpose."[106]

Dahl identified three potential sites for the system of mutual restraints needed to sustain such a system. These can summarized as follows: a formal constitutional separation of powers (the Madisonian solution), societal checks and balances (exemplified in Tocqueville,[107] and also the main focus of twentieth-century pluralism), and what we might call the realm of pluralistic civic virtues (e.g., a responsibility to endorse democratic norms, and to uphold institutions designed to facilitate legitimate adversarial politics, such as free and fair elections, competitive party politics, and so on).[108] I close with a brief sketch of where we are with each of these potential sources of political pluralism in the context of the emergence of populism.

In the context of the Trump presidency, commentators have highlighted the limits of the U.S. constitution as a potential safeguard against the despotic tendencies within populism.[109] This assessment resonates with the pluralist view. Although Madison leaves an important legacy, and his contribution is widely acknowledged by the mid-century pluralists,[110] Dahl nonetheless cautioned against a narrow focus on the role of the constitution or the formal separation of governmental powers. As he put it, "no constitutional arrangements can produce a non-tyrannical republic" in the absence of a set of social checks and balances.[111] Ultimately, this is because governmental institutions are nested within, and reflect, the wider balances of political forces within society.[112] As Arthur Bentley put it, from the pluralist perspective there is "not a law passed that is not [in the end] the expression of force and force in tension."[113] This extends to the judiciary and those institutions whose primary function is to uphold the constitution. So while Dahl recognized the importance of an independent judiciary, he also stressed how legal institutions and the custodians of the law are, in the end, part of the wider balance of forces, rather than standing above or outside of them.[114]

---

[106] Charles Lindblom, *The Intelligence of Democracy* (New York: The Free Press, 1965), 4, 9.
[107] Tocqueville, *Democracy*, 129.
[108] Dahl, *A Preface*, 36.
[109] Steven Levitsky and Daniel Ziblatt, *How Democracies Die: What History Reveals about Our Future* (London: Penguin Books, 2018), 99–100.
[110] Dahl, *A Preface*, 4; Latham, "The Group Basis," 381; Truman, *The Governmental Process*, 4, 5.
[111] Dahl, *A Preface*, 83.
[112] Dahl, *A Preface*, 22.
[113] Bentley, *The Process*, 202.
[114] Dahl, *Democracy and its critics*, 189–90; Rovira Kaltwasser has noted this aspect of Dahl's theory; see Rovira Kaltwasser, "The Responses," 475.

By way of contrast, liberal theorists see a privileged role for constitutional courts, understood as the ultimate custodians of civil liberties and as a bulwark against governmental overreach, and they envisage constitutional law and lawyers as operating from an elevated place above the ebb and flow of democratic decision-making. These contrasting images reiterate the difference between pluralism and liberalism, and the pluralist understanding of the ultimately political underpinnings of juridical decision-making has recently been epitomized with the overturning of *Roe v. Wade*. This landmark decision further iterates the limited role of constitutional constraints in protecting against the threats posed by populism.

Given this context, it is not surprising that several commentators have appealed instead to the realm of pluralistic civic virtutes. Indeed, a robust defense of democratic norms seems vitally important given the relentless attack on these norms by Trump and those who have sought his endorsement. So in contrast to the populist rhetoric of the fullness and "authenticity" of the "general will," Paulina Ochoa Espejo has claimed that, instead, genuine democrats invoke claims about the people that are "self-limited"; Müller encourages actors to abandon rhetorical claims that "we, and only we, are the people," and to adopt instead the more modest assertion that "we are also the people"; and Steven Levitsky and Daniel Ziblatt have advanced norms of mutual tolerance and "institutional forbearance."[115] These claims parallel points articulated for many years by theorists of agonistic democracy. Mouffe and William Connolly have stressed the importance of a "the spiritualisation of enmity" as key to the success of modern democratic politics. From this agonistic viewpoint, democracies thrive when democratic actors confidently assert their respective viewpoints, while simultaneously acknowledging the inherent contestability of their positions (Connolly)[116] or seeking to overcome enmity through acknowledging their opponents as legitimate adversaries (Mouffe).[117] These pluralistic civic virtues are needed now more than ever, and it is vitally important that democratic actors inscribe these values into their ethos, pathos, and logos, for example in response to the current full-frontal attack on the integrity of free and fair

---

[115] Espejo, "Populism," 622–624; Müller, *What Is Populism?*, 39, 98; Levitsky and Ziblatt, *How Democracies Die*, 102–17. For comparable claims, see also Yascha Mounk, *The People vs. Democracy: Why Our Freedom Is in Danger and How to Save It* (Cambridge, MA: Harvard University Press, 2018).

[116] E.g., William Connolly, *The Ethos*; *Pluralism* (Durham, NC; London: Duke University Press, 2005).

[117] E.g., Chantal Mouffe, *The Return of the Political* (London; New York: Verso, 1993).

elections. This is a vital source of pluralism today, with, however, one significant caveat: it is equally important that this emphasis on a responsibility to democratic values does not settle too easily into a thin defense of the importance of civility, without addressing the underlying societal causes of the current emergence of populism.

Indeed, as we have seen, from the pluralist perspective it is the crosscutting tensions between relatively equal groups within society that is—over the long run—both the surest safeguard against tyranny, and key to sustaining self-government. It is also this aspect of pluralism that is most broken, on account of magnified and systemic inequalities and the rise of intense forms of cultural conflict. It follows that without significant intervention to address these broken underlying conditions of polyarchy, neither formal constitution protections, nor a shift in rhetorical styles toward a positive affirmation of democratic norms, are likely to provide a lasting response to the challenges posed by populism. To Dahl and Lindblom's credit, they did not shy away from these consequences. In their later work, they put forward a robust set of proposals for institutional reforms designed to redistribute wealth and access to political power (i.e., to level out the playing field of the societal balance of forces).[118] Key to these reforms would be recognition of the public accountability of "giant corporations," because this would enable political checks and balances to be introduced into the control and governance of these organizations, through a system of workers' democracy.[119] Appealing as this image may be, it is also very far removed from the current political agenda and the current context, which has seen the largest corporations grow in scope, wealth, and power far beyond that of their forebears at the time that Dahl was advancing these proposals in the early 1980s.

So we seem to have reached an impasse: to ensure the recovery of polyarchy, we need interventions in society and economy to address the current inequalities of wealth and power, but to achieve this aim we first need a political movement to challenge the status quo and put these issues effectively on the political agenda. At this point, various "left populisms" present themselves as possible contenders, as they have sought to address exactly these issues of systemic inequality and the disproportionate power

---

[118] Dahl and Lindblom, *Politics*, xxix–xliv.
[119] Robert A. Dahl, *After the Revolution? Authority in a Good Society* (New Haven, CT; London: Yale University Press, 1970), 13, 116–17, 129; *Dilemmas*, 183–85; "Pluralism," 23–25; Dahl and Lindblom, *Politics*, xxix.

of corporate capitalism. As Moffitt has argued, some of these movements are also partially receptive to the ethical and lifestyle pluralism outlined previously in the chapter. We could further bolster the pluralistic credentials of these movements through encouraging an emphasis on the pluralistic civic virtues of upholding democratic norms and the value of political checks and balances. However, through adding these layers of normative qualification, we effectively strip these left populists of their populism. So, we return, in conclusion, to the thought that whatever democratic "moments" might emerge to address the underlying issues of inequality and increasingly non-negotiable forms of cultural conflict, they will need to take some other semblance than the populist emphasis on the binary division of the social space combined with the part standing in for the whole. Or, at least, an alternative manifestation of "the people" will be needed if these movements are also going to help restore an effective system of polyarchy, rather than further tipping the system toward oligarchy.

12
Democracy, Plutocracy, and the Populist Cry of Pain

John P. McCormick

Introduction

As contemporary democracies succumb to unremitting plutocratic usurpation, populism has reemerged as a powerful political force.[1] So far, populism in its right-wing, xenophobic form has done nothing to ameliorate the problem of intensifying economic and political inequality. It remains to be seen whether more inclusive, egalitarian populist movements will gain the momentum necessary to propel a reversal of plutocracy's assault on democracy. In this chapter, I elaborate the reasons why both plutocracy and populism are phenomena endemic to electoral democracy: they are not, I argue, in any way peculiar to our own particular era in the history of representative government. Furthermore, I specify criteria that might be used to distinguish right-wing from progressive forms of populism; and, finally, I sketch the kinds of institutional reforms that progressive populist movements should pursue in efforts to counteract rampant economic and political inequality today.

The Necessity and Dangers of Populism

To set the stage, I begin with some observations on the present situation. In the United States and Western Europe, the parties of the political center—right-center *and* left-center—have been entirely bought by corporate and

---

[1] Thomas Piketty, *Capital in the Twenty-First Century*, trans. Arthur Goldhammer (Cambridge, MA: Harvard University Press, 2014); Benjamin Moffitt, *The Global Rise of Populism: Performance, Political Style, and Representation* (Stanford, CA: Stanford University Press, 2017).

financial interests such that public policy entails moderate or radical upward redistribution.[2] Here we encounter a perverse dynamic through which neoliberal politicians and right-wing populist movements mutually reinforce each other's ascendance. Using the specter of far-right populist parties taking power, centrist politicians secure electoral victories, and then govern to enact "austerity" policies that intensify material conditions which only serve to expand the far-right's appeal.

After congratulating themselves for rescuing the Enlightenment, civilization, and human decency by electorally defeating the xenophobic right, centrist politicians usually pivot to satisfy the policy preferences of the financial interests who, directly or indirectly, back their campaigns. Pursuing broadly "neoliberal" agendas, they immiserate middle-class and working-class citizens in ways that are now quite familiar: emasculating labor unions; cutting pensions; relaxing financial regulations; eliminating environmental, workplace, and product safety protections.[3] It should come as no surprise that the electorates of these democracies, in not entirely irrational ways, find populist appeals increasingly enticing.[4]

In the not so distant past—before circumstances had become so dire—I'd advocated for radical institutional reforms within contemporary democracy to address this growing crisis of economic and political inequality. Inspired by the most astute analyst of popular governments from earlier ages, Niccolò Machiavelli, I identified the following components of a robust, post-electoral model of popular government, one that might halt or roll-back plutocratic encroachment upon liberty and equality.

---

[2] Larry M. Bartels, *Unequal Democracy: The Political Economy of the New Gilded Age* (Princeton, NJ: Princeton University Press, 2009); Martin Gilens, *Affluence and Influence: Economic Inequality and Political Power in America* (Princeton, NJ: Princeton University Press, 2012); Benjamin I. Page and Martin Gilens, *Democracy in America?: What Has Gone Wrong and What We Can Do about It* (Chicago: University of Chicago Press, 2017); Kay Lehman Schlozman, Henry E. Brady, and Sidney Verba, *Unequal and Unrepresented: Political Inequality and the People's Voice in the New Gilded Age* (Princeton, NJ: Princeton University Press, 2018); Robert Kuttner, *Can Democracy Survive Global Capitalism?* (New York: W. W. Norton, 2018); and Anthony B. Atkinson, *Inequality: What Can Be Done?* (Cambridge, MA: Harvard University Press, 2018).

[3] Jeffrey A. Winters, *Oligarchy* (Cambridge, UK: Cambridge University Press, 2011); Mark Blyth, *Austerity: The History of a Dangerous Idea* (Oxford: Oxford University Press, 2015); David M. Kotz, *The Rise and Fall of Neoliberal Capitalism* (Cambridge, MA: Harvard University Press, 2017); William Davies, *The Limits of Neoliberalism: Authority, Sovereignty and the Logic of Competition* (Los Angeles: SAGE Publications, 2017).

[4] Carlos de la Torre, ed., *The Promise and Perils of Populism: Global Perspectives* (Lexington: University Press of Kentucky, 2014); John B. Judis, *The Populist Explosion: How the Great Recession Transformed American and European Politics* (New York: Columbia Global Reports, 2016); and Cas Mudde and Cristobal Rovira Kaltwasser, *Populism: A Very Short Introduction* (Oxford: Oxford University Press, 2017).

The constitutional features of this "Machiavellian Democracy" include: (1) public offices or assemblies that exclude the wealthiest citizens from eligibility; (2) appointment procedures for high office that combine lottery and election; and (3) political trials in which the entire citizenry, or a large segment thereof, acts as ultimate judge over the prosecution of political crimes such as corruption.[5] I argued that popular government was untenable unless economic elites were at least partially excluded from ruling, and unless the people were directly empowered to make laws and to judge political trials. I also took to heart the following Machiavellian imperative: common citizens can never fully enjoy civic liberty unless elites were, to a certain extent, afraid for their lives.

However, even more so now than only a few years ago, calls for institutional change beg a difficult question: How do we get there from here? Effective constitutional transformation requires the mobilization of mass movements that compel governing elites to enact, and economic elites to accept, fundamental institutional change. To repeat, thus far progressive movements have proven much less effective in organizing themselves in pursuit of institutional and policy change than have right-wing ones.

And yet I do not wish to give up on populism as such. In order to determine the means by which progressive institutional change might be achieved as an end, we must address the pressing issue of the relationship between populism and democracy in a plutocratic age. Populism, I will argue, is the necessary vehicle for realizing the effective reform of contemporary democracy. Nevertheless, populism, I will caution, potentially endangers precisely the kind of robust democracy that can only be achieved through populist means of mass mobilization.

Representative Democracy's "Cry of Pain"

The great French sociologist Emile Durkheim once declared socialism to be modern society's "cry of pain."[6] Socialism, Durkheim observed, was the outcry of persons suffering the excruciating pain of alienation, exploitation, and disaffection under the duress of modern, secular, commercial

---

[5] John P. McCormick, *Machiavellian Democracy* (Cambridge, UK: Cambridge University Press, 2011).

[6] Emile Durkheim, *On Politics and the State*, ed. Anthony Giddens (Stanford, CA: Stanford University Press, 1986), 99.

society. Promised unprecedented freedom, security, and happiness, modern individuals instead experience the agony of emotional *anomie* and material deprivation to which, in important ways, socialism appeared to be the definitive remedy. Populism, I contend, is modern, representative democracy's "cry of pain."

Populism is an inevitable occurrence in regimes that adhere to democratic principles, but where, in fact, the people do not rule. Exponents of populism decry painful insults and injuries caused by supposedly representative political systems that explicitly promise majorities the authority to govern, but that, in reality, do not facilitate popular rule in any substantive sense. Citizens of such systems are told that they are sovereign, that they wield fundamental political power; and yet their common, often painful and humiliating experience tells them that they exercise nearly no power at all. In fact, these democratic majorities do not rule; they merely choose which elites rule over them for finite periods of time. More often than not, when these political elites take power, they do not yield to the requests of the majorities that elect them, but rather leap to pursue their own interests—either directly, or by delivering on underhanded promises made to powerful economic actors—when they rule, rather than those of the majorities that elect them.[7]

Put simply, capitalism combined with electoral politics inevitably results in the proliferation of economic and political inequality. It should come as no surprise that the electorates of "democracies" that facilitate inequality perpetually find populist appeals enticing. Therefore, I believe that there are valid reasons to resist the overly alarmist reactions to populist politics characteristic of many progressive scholars and pundits today.[8]

To be sure, populism is certainly not an unmitigated good. An especially unattractive feature of populism, I would argue, is that it tends to reproduce many of the very same deficiencies of representative or electoral democracy: that is, it empowers others besides the people (say, a charismatic leader

---

[7] As Natasha Piano demonstrates, the so-called Italian Elite theorists—Mosca, Pareto, Michels—were especially trenchant critics of the plutocratic corruption and cooptation endemic to parliamentary democracies—however mistakenly they were later understood to be cheerleaders for "the iron law of oligarchy." See Natasha Piano, "Revisiting Democratic Elitism: The Italian School, American Political Science and The Problem of Plutocracy," *Journal of Politics* 81, no. 2 (2019): 524–38; Natasha Piano, *Democratic Elitism: The Founding Myth of American Political Science* (Cambridge, MA: Harvard University Press, 2024).

[8] Nadia Urbinati, *Democracy Disfigured* (Cambridge, MA: Harvard University Press, 2014); Jan-Werner Müller, *What Is Populism?* (Philadelphia: University of Pennsylvania Press, 2016); William A. Galston, *Anti-Pluralism: The Populist Threat to Liberal Democracy* (New Haven, CT: Yale University Press, 2018).

or an outsider political party) to act on behalf of the people—a scenario that is always at odds with democracy in principle and practice.

Indeed, populist politics puts modern democratic citizens in a peculiar bind: citizens demand policies that better reflect, or more faithfully enact, their preferences and interests than do policies produced through conventional electoral institutions. Populism, however, entrusts such popular demands to the custodial care of individuals or parties who still merely "represent" the people, much as electoral institutions do. In fact, these populist leaders or parties likewise only represent the people in highly tenuous ways. Populist leaders or parties may or may not deliver policy outcomes that actually improve the lot of common citizens; whether or not they do is entirely dependent on the competence or good faith of such elites—elites who too often prove entirely incompetent or self-interested.

History shows that populism does not always generate policies or institutions through which the people are empowered to more substantively and directly rule themselves. Very often, a party or a leader merely takes the place of electoral institutions, which are denounced, dismantled, and sometimes abolished on the grounds that they fail to allow the people to rule themselves—and then these populist parties or leaders proceed to rule in even less accountable ways than did the traditional elites who governed through conventional electoral means.

In such cases, populism undermines the kind of vigorous democratic politics that may only be achieved through populist means of mass mobilization. Therefore, the appropriate question is *not* whether democrats ought to renounce populism; but rather what kind of populism democrats should embrace. One way to evaluate whether a populist movement is progressive or reactionary, I suggest, is to examine whether the movement sets as its explicit goals institutional reforms through which citizens should and can rule themselves. Thus, populism, from a democratic perspective, ought not to serve as an *end* in itself—especially if it merely substitutes charismatic or party rule for government by parliamentary elites.

Rather, populist movements serve democratic ends when they set as an eventual *goal* the establishment of procedures and practices through which the people better and more directly rule themselves. Whereas a democracy where the people actually rule themselves is far preferable on normative grounds than most forms of populism, some form of populism will still be absolutely necessary in order to make modern electoral democracies more genuinely democratic. Paradoxically, then, a political movement in which the people do *not* rule is indispensable to the reform or the creation of contemporary political regimes where they actually *do*. This is why, although I am deeply skeptical of populism in many forms, I caution against overstated criticisms of it.

Disentangling Democracy, Populism, and Demagoguery

Democracy, I am arguing, is fundamentally different than populism. In a democracy, the people rule. Who are "the people"? "The people" constitute a citizenry that extends widely enough throughout the populace to include large numbers of individuals, and segments of society, who may genuinely be defined as poor. (This is why ancient critics often derided democracy as the horrible, scandalous, undesirable "rule by the poor.") What is "rule"? In a genuine democracy, the people "rule" through the following institutions: (1) legislative assemblies open to all citizens, not by assemblies composed exclusively of elites; (2) public offices distributed by lottery, not by election—that is, magistracies that are randomly distributed throughout the citizenry; and (3) through political courts comprising large subsets of randomly selected citizens, not judicial bodies composed of professional jurists, in which the people themselves decide what political crimes are and what punishments for them should be.

In democratic assemblies, every citizen is entitled to initiate and discuss law, and ultimate decisions are determined by simple majority vote—not through bicameral arrangements or by super-majoritarian measures that are so common within modern constitutions. In a democracy, any citizen who is willing and able to stand for office may submit their name for inclusion in the political lotteries that appoint public officials. And finally, former officials and, in fact, any citizen whatsoever, may be indicted by any other citizen, and put on trial before large citizen juries for offenses that threaten or undermine the democracy.

Obviously, this stylized description of democracy derives from the constitutions of ancient Greek democracies, especially Athens.[9] In my estimation, the further a regime deviates from the Athenian model of direct popular lawmaking and randomly distributed executive and judicial authority

---

[9] Mogens Herman Hansen, *The Athenian Democracy in the Age of Demosthenes: Structure, Principles, and Ideology* (Norman: University of Oklahoma Press, 1991).

among citizens, the less democratic is such a regime.[10] Modern electoral or representative democracies may be more "democratic" than ancient democracies in an important way: they (admirably) extend citizenship to even greater numbers of the poor; they (belatedly) abolished slavery; and they (eventually) granted full citizen rights to women.[11]

But modern democracies are much less democratic because they substitute representation for direct rule, and election for lottery; moreover, they entrust to professional judges or other officeholders, rather than to political amateurs among the citizenry, the task of punishing officials for political offenses.[12] A modern democracy therefore has much more "demos," but much less "kratos" than its ancient counterpart; it includes, as citizens, a larger proportion of the populace, but it politically empowers citizens far less substantively than did, of course, democratic Athens.

Such is democracy, but what about populism? Again, the term "populist" designates a movement characterized by popular mobilization, but one not necessarily oriented toward popular rule. Populism tends to manifest itself outside the institutions of government, through the workings of civic associations, social organizations, and mass demonstrations. Populism is "popular" in its genesis and its intention: large numbers of individuals and segments of society (but not always the majority of the populace) coalesce around an issue or program which is always cast as beneficial to the majority of the citizenry (or, too often, to the majority of "real" or "true" citizens).[13] A crucial difference, then, between contemporary populism and traditional democracy is this: populism ultimately charges an individual leader or a political party with the actual realization or concrete enactment of the policy goals espoused or expressed by the movement. In a democracy, by contrast, the people always decide.

Thus, when critics often identify "demagoguery" as a danger endemic to both populism and democracy, they confuse two distinct states of affairs. The successful *populist* demagogue will either attain office him- or herself, and then personally put into effect the policy program supported by

---

[10] Moses I. Finley, *Democracy Ancient and Modern* (New Brunswick: Rutgers University Press, 1985).

[11] Robert Alan Dahl, *Democracy and Its Critics* (New Haven, CT: Yale University Press, 1989).

[12] Bernard Manin, *The Principles of Representative Government* (Cambridge, UK: Cambridge University Press, 1997).

[13] Yuna Blajer de la Garza, "A House Is Not a Home: Citizenship and Political Belonging in Modern Democracies: France, Mexico, and the United States" (PhD Dissertation, Political Science Department, University of Chicago, 2019).

members of their movement (for instance, a Mussolini or Lenin); or they will use their prestige and political capital to influence officeholders unaffiliated with the movement to do so on behalf of their movement (for instance, a Martin Luther King or Gandhi). The *democratic* demagogue, alternatively, will attempt to persuade the formally assembled people to decide for themselves policies that purportedly benefit them (as in the examples of Pericles, Alcibiades, and Cleon). In a democracy, therefore, ultimate responsibility for the resulting law or policy rests with decisions of the people rather than, as in populism, with decisions by elites who act (whether at first, second, or third hand) in the people's name and/or on their behalf.

In this sense, "populism" did not exist in ancient democracies and democratic republics. In ancient Rome, Tiberius Gracchus may have proposed massive reforms aimed at economic redistribution; but the *populus Romanus* itself was ultimately entrusted to pass such legislation. On the contrary, the "plebeians" or the "demos" of modern republics rely entirely on agents to negotiate policies that hopefully ensure greater equality (for instance, agents such as labor unions in Western democracies); or they depend on agents who destroy existing and create new institutional arrangements so as to achieve a newly born equality (for instance, the Communist parties of twentieth-century Russia and China). On this definition, notable examples of populist movements would include: Jacobinism in Revolutionary France; the Chartist Movement in nineteenth-century Britain; Bolshevism and fascism in twentieth-century Russia and Italy; and the People's Party in the 1890s United States.[14] Today, the term is generally applied to Chavismo in Venezuela, far-right parties in Europe, and, most recently, to Trumpism in the United States.

The Recurrence of Populism in Modern Democracy

As mentioned before, populism is the flip side of the coin of normal politics in electoral democracies. Modern democracies ensure the rise to office of individuals who allow or encourage socioeconomic inequality to undermine political equality. Because elections either elevate to public office exclusively individuals who are themselves wealthy, or because the massive funding

---

[14] J. S. Maloy, *Democratic Statecraft: Political Realism and Popular Power* (Cambridge, UK: Cambridge University Press, 2013), 145–87.

required to mount successful electoral campaigns ensures that individual public officials (whether especially rich or not) are beholden to moneyed interests, electoral democracies are correctly characterized as inherently oligarchic or plutocratic regimes.

This differs from traditional democratic practice. Ancient democracies relied on an informal truce between rich and poor citizens: a compromise—a culturally enforced *noblesse oblige*—through which the demos would not excessively "expropriate the rich" so long as the wealthy did not use their vast economic resources and public prominence to undermine political equality and to corrupt democratic institutions.[15] Electoral democracies, on the contrary, structurally enforce this truce in ways that wildly favor wealthy citizens and, consequently, in ways that inevitably exacerbate sociopolitical inequality and that corrupt democratic institutions.[16]

This goes a long way toward explaining the emergence of populism in virtually every era of modern democracy. When poorer citizens within modern electoral democracies feel threatened by the economic advantages of the wealthy, they engage in left-wing populism to influence the outcomes of political machinery that they are prevented from controlling directly. When populism has been successful in protecting or advancing relative socioeconomic equality (for instance in Western Europe after each of the two World Wars), socioeconomic elites often respond by sparking right-wing populist movements aimed at rolling back or eradicating those egalitarian gains. Such right-wing populist movements invoke religious, ethnic, and/or cultural aspects of national identity; these ascriptive qualities appeal to commitments among poorer citizens that are often at odds with the poor's desire for socioeconomic and political equality.

Often in such circumstances, the principles of "liberty" or "equality" are given cultural, rather than political or economic, inflections. Elites appeal to the citizenry's non-economic, affective, or emotional ties, or to their fear of "foreign threats" to reconstitute national solidarity on grounds other than socioeconomic or political equality. Hence, critics often charge that the

---

[15] Josiah Ober, *Mass and Elite in Democratic Athens: Rhetoric, Ideology, and the Power of the People* (Princeton, NJ: Princeton University Press, 1991); Gordon Arlen, "Aristotle and the Problem of Oligarchic Harm: Insights for Democracy," *European Journal of Political Theory* 18, no. 3 (2016): 393–414.

[16] For a bottom-up account of the origins of social democracy, see Steven Klein, *Democratic Politics and the Welfare State: the Political Economy of Collective World-Making* (Cambridge, UK: Cambridge University Press, 2019).

American Tea Party movement is not a genuine "grassroots" phenomenon,[17] and that fascism and more recent far-right movements in Europe were and are more elite-driven than was Western European social democracy or even communism (both of which still were, of course, to great extents elite-directed).[18]

The examples of right-wing populism suggest that political enmity is more intensely generated by populist movements than it is within genuinely democratic politics. The demos or the plebeians of ancient Athens or Rome viewed, respectively, the oligarchs or patricians among the citizenry with intense suspicion; they monitored the latter's behavior with the strictest scrutiny, and they punished their political transgressions with severe measures. However, perhaps precisely because ancient citizens had direct access to mechanisms of rule, they did not feel the need to make outright enemies of their adversaries, as members of populist movements so often do. For instance, think of the following oppositions: Jacobins versus "aristocrats" or "émigrés"; communists and fascists versus the "bourgeoisie"; National Socialists versus "the Jews" and "Bolsheviks." In the United States, Trumpists identify their enemies, on the one hand, as criminally inclined, sexually predatory immigrants originating from "shithole countries," or, on the other hand, as an amorphously defined "liberal" intellectual-media class, purported purveyors of "fake news."

This dubious intensity may be attributed to the natural frustration that citizens feel within mere electoral democracies—which, as James Madison proudly exclaimed, practice the "total exclusion of the people in their collective capacity from any share" in government.[19] But, even under conditions characterized by large territorial states, average citizens perhaps should not have been excluded so drastically from modern schemes of democratic rule. As Machiavelli noted, charges of extremism and inconstancy that aristocratic critics have forever hurled at the people are much less applicable, and much less egregious, when the people themselves concretely judge, where they actually decide political matters. The people may clamor for all kinds of outrageous things when they are excluded from governing (such as killing all members of the aristocracy or annihilating the cities of foreign enemies);

---

[17] Theda Skocpol and Vanessa Williamson, *The Tea Party and the Remaking of Republican Conservatism* (Oxford: Oxford University Press, 2012).

[18] *Nazism, Fascism and the Working Class*, ed. Timothy W. Mason and Jane Caplan (Cambridge, UK: Cambridge University Press, 1995).

[19] James Madison, Federalist No. 63, in Alexander Hamilton, James Madison, and John Jay, *The Federalist Papers, With Letters of Brutus*, ed. Terence Ball (Cambridge: Cambridge University Press, 2003).

but, Machiavelli insists, they judge responsibly and correctly, when they are empowered to decide—at least, he insists, they decide more responsibly and correctly than elites do when similarly empowered to decide.[20]

In the realm of high theory, Carl Schmitt and Vladimir Ilyich Lenin are probably the foremost intellectual advocates of what I am calling populism.[21] Schmitt insisted that the people's "Will" was best realized by a plebiscitarily elected chief executive (e.g., the *Reichspräsident* of the Weimar Republic) or by a popularly "acclaimed" party leader who had succeeded in imposing "homogeneity" on the entire German *Volk* (i.e., Adolf Hitler). Lenin's "Democratic Centralism" similarly legitimated the Communist Party's claim to rule on behalf of the Russian proletariat. It is worth noting that progressive forms of populism, such as the turn-of-the-century People's Party in the United States, or Western European Trade Unionism in the twentieth century, have no such "grand theorists."

Perhaps for similar reasons, ancient democracy enjoyed scant intellectual advocates among philosophers and historians. Aristotle stands as the greatest "objective" analyst of ancient democracy, and, as mentioned above, Machiavelli—not, I believe, Jean-Jacques Rousseau[22]—is the most full-throated modern champion of "republican" institutions and practices that approximate ancient democracy.[23] Machiavelli, again, endorsed large assemblies where all citizens, regardless of birth or wealth, could initiate, discuss, and decide on laws, as well as pass judgment on the fate of elite citizens charged with political crimes. Moreover, he recommended offices, like the Plebeian Tribunate, for which wealthy and prominent citizens were

---

[20] Niccolò Machiavelli, *Discorsi* [1513–19], C. Vivanti, ed. (Torino: Einaudi-Gallimard, 1997) I.7–8, I.47, I.58.

[21] Carl Schmitt, *Constitutional Theory*, trans. Jeffrey Seitzer (Durham, NC: Duke University Press, 2008); Carl Schmitt, *Legality and Legitimacy*, trans. Jeffrey Seitzer (Durham, NC: Duke University Press, 2004); Carl Schmitt, *Der Hüter der Verfassung* (Tübingen: J. C. B. Mohr [Paul Siebeck], 1931); Carl Schmitt, "Der Führer schützt das Recht," *Deutsche Juristen-Zeitung* 38 (1934); Vladimir I. Lenin, *Essential Works of Lenin: "What Is to Be Done?" and Other Writings*, ed. H. M. Christman (Mineola, NY: Dover Publications, 1987).

[22] There is no sharper critic of Athenian democracy than Rousseau, who also recommended voting weighted in favor of wealthy citizens in large republics. See Jean-Jacques Rousseau, "Of the Social Contract, or Principles of Political Right" [1762], in *Rousseau: The Social Contract and Other Later Political Writings*, ed. Victor Gourevitch (Cambridge, UK: Cambridge University Press, 1997), 39–152; here: book IV, section 4, p. 133. See also John P. McCormick, "Rousseau's Rome and the Repudiation of Populist Republicanism," *Critical Review of International Social and Political Philosophy* 10, no. 1 (2007): 3–27; and John P. McCormick, *Reading Machiavelli: Scandalous Books, Suspect Engagements, and the Virtue of Populist Politics* (Princeton, NJ: Princeton University Press, 1991), 109–43.

[23] John P. McCormick, *Machiavellian Democracy* (Chicago: Cambridge University Press, 2012); John P. McCormick, *Reading Machiavelli* (Princeton, NJ: Princeton University Press, 2018).

ineligible: officials who wielded significant veto, legislative, and judicial authority within the Roman Republic. If such class-specific magistracies did not distribute offices as widely among common citizens as did Athenian political lotteries, they certainly distributed them more widely than do general elections in modern representative democracies.

Obstacles to Popular Mobilization

Allow me here to indulge some rather dark speculations before entertaining more hopeful possibilities in my concluding remarks. The post–World War II interregnum in the plutocratic assault upon modern democracy, one in which North American and European societies enjoyed relative economic equality, was a moment unprecedented in history—and one that will never be repeated again. At least in this one sense: it was a moment forged by socioeconomic elites who were profoundly chastened by the global catastrophes that they themselves created, most prominently, the Great Depression and World War II.[24] So thoroughly chastened, in fact, were these elites that they were more willing to share economic wealth—for the sake of future stability and even for the sake of justice—with less affluent members of their societies than had been any previous set of elites. Of course, we should not underestimate the impact of the Cold War on such elites: that is, the pressure they felt in having to compete, ideologically and geopolitically, with more economically egalitarian, if more politically repressive, communist adversaries.

Be that as it may, one might argue that the postwar social democratic moment will never be repeated because, in a world of dubiously controlled nuclear weapons and rapidly accelerating environmental degradation, the only conditions sufficiently dire to once again chasten elites are those that would culminate in the total destruction of the planet. By the time the socioeconomic elites who presently dominate the domestic and global economic order grasp the idea that they need to re-establish economic and political equality in order to save civilization, there will be no civilization left to save.

Of course, the eternally wise and wily Machiavelli did not live to witness the post–World War II conciliation between socioeconomic elites and common citizens in European and North American democracies. As far as

---

[24] Karl Polanyi, *The Great Transformation: The Political and Economic Origins of Our Time* (Boston: Beacon Press, 2001); Steven Klein, "Fictitious Freedom: A Polanyian Critique of the Republican Revival," *American Journal of Political Science* 61, no. 4 (2017): 852–63.

he was concerned, wealthy citizens could never be persuaded by words or reason to freely acquiesce in the creation of the socioeconomic conditions that make civic liberty possible: conditions that, as he put it, "keep the public rich but the citizens poor."[25] For Machiavelli, most emblematic of the wealthy's attitude toward redistribution necessary for civic health was the instance when the Roman Senate murdered Tiberius Gracchus in the public space of the Republic for proposing land reform legislation. In the Florentine's estimation, socioeconomic elites must be *compelled* to accept institutional arrangements that secure economic equality or at least political equality; otherwise, they will scuttle them in the most violent of ways.

Thus we return to the urgent question with which I began: How do we, in the present moment, undertake such an effort in elite compulsion? What kind of popular mobilization is necessary to pursue institutional reforms aimed at re-establishing equality, at least political equality? What kind of populism can demand the class-specific, lottery-based, directly legislative, and elite-sanctioning institutions that I mentioned at the outset?

Two obstacles immediately confront us: class-consciousness on the part of non-wealthy citizens (which may be insufficiently intense today), and also the concrete leverage that common citizens enjoy vis-à-vis socioeconomic elites (which may prove unobtainable). Ancient *demoi* and plebeians collectively threatened to withhold their war-making capacities from the state—they refused to fight!—in order to gain pro-democratic concessions from the oligarchs of their regimes. Later, worker-citizens in nineteenth- and twentieth-century North America and Europe achieved comparable results by withholding their labor power from industrial economies, or by threatening to withhold it.[26] Unfortunately, there doesn't seem to be an asset shared by modern "plebeians" comparable to military or labor power, the wielding or withholding of which would successfully extort democratic reforms from contemporary political-economic elites. Even if citizens protest more widely, and with greater intensity, against the growing economic inequality that is radically exacerbating political inequality today, what will they use to extract democratic reforms from modern oligarchs and their political proxies?

Consumer power is a possible, but—for several reasons—deeply unsatisfying answer. Even if, for instance, the internet were to better enable mass

---

[25] Machiavelli, *Discorsi*, I.37; McCormick, *Reading Machiavelli*, 45–68.
[26] Alex Gourevitch, *From Slavery to the Cooperative Commonwealth: Labor and Republican Liberty in the Nineteenth Century* (Cambridge, UK: Cambridge University Press, 2015).

consumers to coordinate their purchasing leverage against corporate power, it remains to be seen whether it could reproduce the political benefits historically afforded to democracy by citizens organized as armed forces or in trade unions. The close physical proximity, shared sacrifice, and cooperative action fostered by such military and economic arrangements created uniquely tight solidarity among soldiers and workers, enabling them to exercise formidable collective power against political and socioeconomic elites. I can think of no functional equivalent today.

Conclusion

So, at the heart of the crisis of democracy and the rise of populism today is the question: What can we do to keep economic inequality from translating into political inequality? Without a populist movement mobilized behind the effort, no institutional reform of electoral democracy seems possible in our plutocratic age. Nevertheless, allow me to revisit some of the institutional features of "Machiavellian Democracy." Two especially controversial features of such a model, especially among liberal or progressive academics, are: (1) legislative referenda, and (2) popularly judged political trials.

The exclamation, "Brexit!," is the obvious retort of critics who oppose legislative referenda. Brexit has provided the opportunity for leftist professors and pundits to voice their long-held and deep-seated distrust of common people's judgment. We have all heard or perhaps stated something like the following: "Average citizens are simply too stupid or uninformed to make decisions that carry the force of law—this is precisely why modern democracies depart from the practice of ancient democracies by empowering expert representatives to make decisions *for* common citizens." If one is comfortable with that argument, then one has to accept the inherent threat that elite-prerogative and plutocratic influence pose to political equality—a threat that is inevitably realized in practice.

Moreover, as Machiavelli pointed out centuries ago, those who so vigorously question popular judgment ignore the fact that privileged elites—that is, aristocrats and autocrats—often make demonstrably far worse decisions than do free citizens.[27] As for citizen apathy or ignorance: We know it is fairly certain that had the Brexit vote been repeated the very next day, after the

[27] Machiavelli, *Discorsi*, I.58.

"Leave" vote was public, voter turnout in Britain would have been astronomically higher and the outcome diametrically opposite. Politics—especially democratic politics—offers painfully difficult, but ultimately edifying lessons.

Admittedly, as many political realists like to point out, *any and all* non-electoral or extra-electoral measures can be circumvented by the power of private wealth: wealthy actors can bribe common citizens who attain office even through lotteries or class-specific arrangements; and the wealthy can flood the public sphere with disinformation that distorts decisions rendered through public referenda. But what if elites could be effectively deterred from engaging in such acts of political corruption? This is where another institutional aspect of pre-representative democracies proves so intriguing: popularly judged political trials where public officials or private citizens, indicted for corruption or treason, face the penalty of death. I have in mind here capital trials by large citizen juries like those that convicted Socrates in Athens and Coriolanus in Rome.

During the 2016 democratic primaries, Team Clinton declared publicly that the logical outcome of Bernie Sanders's presidential campaign was "to shoot every third person on Wall Street." Executing bankers, the Clintons averred, would accomplish nothing in the service of progressive politics. I'm not so sure.

With the examples of ancient democracies and republics in mind, Machiavelli insisted that fear of capital prosecution was the only—let me emphasize, *only*—way of deterring socioeconomic and political elites from steering public policy toward their own private self-enrichment. Let me emphasize that he encouraged neither pogroms nor purges. Rather, Machiavelli recommended legal, orderly judicial procedures; institutional modes through which as large a number of citizens as possible decided over the lives of elites indicted for political crimes. Such crimes might include: lying to initiate pointless wars that expend massive amounts of citizens' blood and treasure; perpetrating financial improprieties that trigger full-scale economic crises, which cost countless people their jobs, homes, and savings; and we might add, hypothetically, consorting with foreign enemies to corrupt public institutions for the sake of personal monetary and political gain,[28] to name just a few examples.

---

[28] Machiavelli, *Discorsi*, I.58; Sallust, *The Jugurthine War/The Conspiracy of Catiline*, S. A. Handford trans. (London: Penguin, 1964), 27–34.

Ancient popular governments, Machiavelli demonstrates, initially experimented with imprisonment and banishment as appropriate forms of political punishment. However, wealthy citizens often use their considerable resources to gain unwarranted pardons, to bust out of jail, or to return prematurely from exile. Lamentably, Machiavelli instructs us, there is no functional approximation for death. Indeed, death's exquisite finality is the only factor that gives pause to those who would use their wealth, as the Florentine puts it, "incorrectly"; that is, in continuous efforts to corrupt a political process meant to serve the many and not the few.[29]

The good liberal will protest that the Enlightenment has greatly advanced human flourishing and civic dignity by encouraging bans on capital punishment in the vast majority of liberal democracies. And just look at how successfully those regimes have stemmed the rising levels of economic inequality, political corruption, and autocratic lurching!

There's already too much capital punishment, especially in America, the good liberal will protest. Who could disagree? No country in this hemisphere goes about executing as large a number of their poor citizens as does the United States. Patriotic democratic citizens might therefore consider compensating for this fact by exempting the poor from the threat of execution: capital punishment should be reserved exclusively for wealthy citizens or public officials found guilty of political or economic corruption. Patriotic democratic citizens must issue threats of capital punishment, perhaps exclusively, to wealthy citizens or public officials convicted of economic or political corruption. Such a risk ought to be considered "the cost of doing business" for those of elite status in a healthy democracy—much like jury duty or paying taxes is for everyone else.

The point is this: so staunch an advocate of popular government as Machiavelli thought that citizens sell cheaply, very cheaply indeed, their commitments to freedom and equality, when they fail to defend such principles with the greatest severity—that is, when they fail to take recourse in the ultimate punishment to defend them.

---

[29] Machiavelli, *Discorsi*, I.5, I.37.

13
Populism, Celebrity Politics, and Politainment

Paula Diehl

Introduction

In recent years, an apparently new phenomenon has challenged scholars working on populism: a mixture of populism, celebrity politics, and media entertainment. Right-wing populist leaders like Donald Trump, Matteo Salvini, and Jair Bolsonaro have become masters of media entertainment by adopting populism, performing like celebrities, and producing "politainment." In doing so, they generate a new hybrid political phenomenon but, paradoxically, do not invent anything new. On the contrary, all three elements mentioned above were already known in democratic politics. Their novelty can be attributed to two different processes: on the one hand, the radicalization of the elements mentioned above, and, on the other hand, the hybrid arrangement they form. This chapter aims to disentangle the populism, celebrity politics, and politainment present in the new millennium and to show the continuities and innovations accompanying these new arrangements of populism.

Historically, the mix of celebrity politics and populism can be found in Eva Perón in the 1940s. Evita was a radio star and celebrity with a strong presence in mass media entertainment when she started her political career at the side of Juan Domingo Perón. Eventually, she became an icon of the populist movement in Argentina. At that time, however, mass-mediated political communication was limited to radio, print media, and cinema, while politainment was still unknown. Only with TV did politainment become a major element of political communication, emerging especially at the end of the 1990s after the crucial transformations in the media system worldwide. Silvio Berlusconi is perhaps the most famous populist producing politainment, the mix of entertainment and politics. Berlusconi adopted a new attitude to politics, fundamentally changing political communication in Italy. The novelty in politainment is that political performance embraces mass media hyperreality.

With the digital era, new changes radicalized the hyperreal character of media production and the corresponding attitude of consumers. Internet and social media brought further innovations to political communication, including not only new technical tools like digital manipulation of content and network communication (many-to-many), but also new forms of communication that blur the distinction between producers and recipients of mass media content. This passage from one-to-many media to many-to-many media was accompanied by a professionalization of the performance of the self and the radicalization of hyperreality in communication in general and in political communication in particular. Today, politicians like Trump, Salvini, and Bolsonaro integrate populism, celebrity politics, and politainment in their social media communication. Although the digital transformation was significant, the roots of politainment were already present in electronic media of the 1990s, as an examination of the performances of former Brazilian president Fernando Collor de Mello, Silvio Berlusconi, German chancellor Gerhard Schröder, and the former president of the Swiss Confederation Micheline Calmy-Rey shows.[1] My argument here is that both transformations (in the 1990s and in the new millennium) reshape the relationship between media and populism, facilitating the radicalization of populism, celebrity politics, and politainment, and giving birth to new hybrid arrangements of populism.

For democracy, the implications of these new arrangements cannot be overestimated. I argue that radicalization of celebrity politics and politainment blurs the borders between politics and entertainment, private and public, and, even more importantly, between reality and fiction. Against this background, populist claims about fake news and alternative facts need to be examined in a new light. Yet, concerning the question of reality and truth, the traditional logic of populism and the logics of celebrity politics and politainment do not go in the same direction. Whereas populism is a political logic claiming to speak the truth and the common will, celebrity politics and politainment introduce entertainment and hyperreality that, when radicalized, destabilize the same notions of reality and truth that populism

---

[1] Paula Diehl, "Zwischen dem Privaten und dem Politischen—Die neue Körperinszenierung der Politiker," in *Die Grenzen des Privaten*, ed. Sandra Seubert and Peter Niesen (Baden-Baden: Nomos Verlag, 2010), 251–65.

claims to defend. As a consequence, as I will argue further, the new populist arrangement fundamentally alters citizens' and representatives' relationship to politics. In order to grasp the effects of this new phenomenon (Donald Trump being the best example), its differences from traditional populist rhetoric need to be considered.

This chapter offers a contribution to the three key questions of this volume: To what extent is contemporary populism a distinctively modern phenomenon? To what extent does it have roots and precedents in earlier periods of political history? And how can studying populism in the light of rhetoric and the history of political thought help us answer these questions? This chapter addresses these questions conceptually and illustrates the historical transformations of populism in light of its relationship to mass media, using empirical examples such as Eva Perón, Berlusconi, and Trump. It begins by offering a complex and multidimensional definition of populism better suited to grasping its hybrid combinations with celebrity politics and politainment. In a second step, I discuss the concepts of celebrity politics and politainment and introduce the notion of hyperreality. Two major questions guide the last section of this chapter and the evaluation of the phenomenon: What is changing in populism? And what are the implications for examining the effects of these changes on democracy in our time?

The Complex Approach to Populism

In recent decades, scholarship on populism has grown significantly, producing rich and diverse conceptual and methodological approaches.[2] However, the old appraisal of populism as a chameleon-like phenomenon

---

[2] Yves Mény and Yves Surel, *Par le peuple, pour le peuple. Le populisme et les démocraties* (Paris: Faryard, 2000); Margaret Canovan, *Taking Politics to the People: Populism as the Ideology of Democracy* (London: Palgrave Macmillan, 2002); Cas Mudde, "The Populist Zeitgeist," *Government and Opposition* 39, no. 4 (Autumn 2004): 541–63; Ernesto Laclau, *On Populist Reason* (New York: Verso, 2005); Jan-Werner Müller, *What Is Populism?* (Philadelphia: University of Pennsylvania Press, 2016); Benjamin Moffitt, *The Global Rise of Populism: Performance, Political Style and Representation* (Stanford, CA: Stanford University Press, 2016); Rogers Brubaker, "Why Populism?," *Theory and Society* 46, no. 5 (2017): 357–85; Cristóbal Rovira Kaltwasser, Paul Taggartet, Paulina Ochoa Espejo, and Pierre Ostiguy, *The Oxford Handbook of Populism* (Oxford: Oxford University Press, 2017); Yannis Stavrakakis, "Discourse Theory in Populism Research: Three Challenges and a Dilemma," *Journal of Language and Politics* 16, no. 4 (2017): 523–34; Chantal Mouffe, *For a Left Populism* (New York: Verso, 2018); Paula Diehl and Till Weber, "Populism: Complex Concepts and Innovative Methods," *Polity* 54, no. 3 (2022): 503–8; *The Complexity of Populism: New Approaches and Methods*, ed. Diehl and Brigitte Bargetz (New York: Routledge, 2024).

that changes its colors according to the environment is still applied.[3] The reason for this is that populism can build very different combinations with distinctive ideologies[4] and with other phenomena such as celebrity politics[5] and mass media entertainment.[6]

In order to depict these new combinations, I propose a complex and multidimensional concept that considers populism as a fluid phenomenon. Instead of addressing populism as a category of actors, I offer a constructivist approach in which populism is considered as a practice that affects the shape of the political.[7] Therefore, I shift my attention to populism's particular way of "doing politics."[8] However, if populism is a specific way of doing politics, it does not always permeate politics coherently. Unlike other constructivist approaches, the complex concept of populism makes its incoherences visible. Populism does not necessarily permeate the ideology, communication, and social organization of politics in the same manner. Sometimes it does, building "perfect cases," such as those of Juan Domingo Perón and Eva Perón; but sometimes it does not, as Silvio Berlusconi illustrates. Indeed, on the ideological level, Berlusconi's appeal to popular sovereignty varies in intensity across time, and anti-elitism is missing from his rhetoric. In that rhetoric, there is no resentment toward the economic elites. Instead, the foe is characterized as the left and intellectuals. In the organizational dimension, Berlusconi's party varied in populist intensity during its historical evolution.[9] Yet Berlusconi's communication can be described as prototypically populist.[10] In sum, Berlusconi's case shows how populism can permeate ideology, political communication, and organization in different manners and to different degrees.

---

[3] Pippa Norris and Ronald Inglehart, *Cultural Backlash: Trump, Brexit and Authoritarian Populism* (Cambridge, UK: Cambridge University Press, 2019), 4.

[4] Cas Mudde and Cristóbal Rovira Kaltwasser, "Exclusionary vs. Inclusionary Populism: Comparing Contemporary Europe and Latin America," *Government and Opposition* 48, no. 2 (2012): 147–74.

[5] Gianpietro Mazzoleni, "Populism and the Media," in *Twenty-First Century Populism: The Spectre of Western European Democracy*, ed. Daniele Albertazzi and Duncan McDonnell (Hampshire, UK; New York: Palgrave Macmillan, 2008), 57.

[6] Paula Diehl, "For a Complex Concept of Populism," *Polity* 54, no.3 (2022): 518.

[7] Ernesto Laclau, *On Populist Reason* (New York: Verso, 2005); Pierre Ostiguy, "Populism: A Socio-Cultural Approach," in *The Oxford Handbook of Populism*, ed. Rovira Kaltwasser et al. (Oxford: Oxford University Press, 2017), 73–99; Nadia Urbinati, *Me the People: How Populism Transforms Democracy* (Cambridge, MA: Harvard University Press, 2019).

[8] Ernesto Laclau, *On Populist Reason* (New York: Verso, 2005); Chantal Mouffe, *For a Left Populism* (New York: Verso, 2018).

[9] Diehl, "For a Complex Concept of Populism," 516–17.

[10] Mazzoleni, "Populism and the Media," 49–64.

This fluid nature and the effects of populism can be grasped by analytically distinguishing among three major dimensions of populism: ideological, communicative, and organizational.[11] Populism can permeate political life in different ways, including incoherent ones, and can generate a variety of shapes and hybrid combinations.[12] In addition, populism should be treated as a phenomenon on a continuum, rather than an either/or question.[13]

Celebrity politics and politainment mostly interfere in the ideological and communicative dimensions, building the new hybrid combinations addressed in this chapter. Starting with the *ideological dimension*, the works of Margaret Canovan[14] and Cas Mudde[15] are unavoidable. Both understand populism as a "thin-centered ideology" incapable of providing a full political orientation. Further development of this notion makes it possible to analytically separate populism from the second, more robust, ideology added to it.[16] The approach of Canovan and Mudde detects three major features of populist ideology: the belief that politics should be the expression of the popular will; structural opposition between the people and the elite; and anti-elite resentment. Scholarship on the topic enriches this list by adding anti-institutional attitude, the "narrative of the betrayed people,"[17] the equation of the general will to the will of the majority,[18] and the centrality of a charismatic leader who builds a direct and immediate relationship to her/his followers. A further component of populism crucial for the understanding of its changes is the assumption that the truth is with the people, and that the leader knows it better and can speak it out.[19] The latter is crucial for the reflection proposed in this chapter.

---

[11] These three dimensions do not claim to be exhaustive. Policy, for instance, is one important dimension to be more intensively conceptualized and addressed by future research.
[12] Diehl, "For a Complex Concept of Populism."
[13] Ben Stanley, "The Thin Ideology of Populism," *Journal of Political Ideologies* 13, no. 1 (2008): 108; Claes H. De Vreese, Frank Esser, and James Stanyer, "Populism as an Expression of Political Communication Content and Style: A New Perspective," *The International Journal of Press/Politics* 23, no. 4 (2018): 4.
[14] Margaret Canovan, *Taking Politics to the People: Populism as the Ideology of Democracy* (London: Palgrave Macmillan, 2002).
[15] Mudde, "The Populist Zeitgeist."
[16] Mudde, "The Populist Zeitgeist"; Mudde and Rovira Kaltwasser, "Exclusionary vs. Inclusionary Populism."
[17] Pierre-André Taguieff, *L'illusion populiste: Essai sur les démagogies de l'âge démocratique* (Paris: Flammarion, 2007), 28; Paula Diehl, "Populist Twist: The Relationship between the Leader and the People in Populism," in *Creating Political Presence: The New Politics of Democratic Representation*, ed. Dario Castiglione and Johannes Pollak (Chicago; London: University of Chicago Press, 2019), 126–72.
[18] Paul Blokker, "The Populist Assault on the Constitution," in *Multiple Populisms: Italy as Democracy's Mirror*, ed. Paul Blokker and Manuel Anselmi (New York: Routledge, 2020), 198.
[19] Mény and Surel, *Par le peuple, pour le peuple*, 104–81.

When it comes to the communicative dimension, features described as populist discourse, language, style, and performance need to be considered. As is to be expected, the invocation of the people is a core element of populist communication.[20] From the linguistic and rhetorical point of view, populist communication is envisioned as speech "from below," while the elite is supposed to be on the top and the people on the bottom.[21] Its rhetoric is conflictual and polarizing; it makes heavy use of invective and produces a highly emotional and dramatic appeal. Along with Manicheanism, simple language, directness, and oversimplification are key elements of populist communication.[22] Concerning style, "bad manners," ordinary vocabulary, and vulgar expressions are crucial.[23] Performatively speaking, populist communication relies on a strong personalization, references to disadvantaged social classes, and mimetic body performance of the leader, who imitates the imagined people. This is the case when politicians dress down, eat simple food in public, or merge into the crowd.[24] Taboo breaking is another central feature of populism. Performatively, it articulates the idea of the unmediated opinion of the people and the critique of the "rules of the elite"; Trump and Bolsonaro are both well-known for such performances.

Populism and Mass Media Transformations in Historical Perspective

Looking at populism in the ideological and communicative dimensions, it is easy to identify the components operating in accordance with the logic of mass media:[25] oversimplification, immediacy, Manichaeism and the friend-foe dichotomy, dramatization, and strong emotional appeal. Populism builds a strong narrative, capturing mass media attention. It is the story of the betrayed people fighting together with the leader against the elites

---

[20] Moffitt, *The Global Rise of Populism*, 43.
[21] Martin Reisigl, "The Dynamics of Right-Wing Populist Argumentation in Austria," in *Argumentation*, ed. Frans H. Van Eemeren (New York: Ablex, 2007), 1133.
[22] Roberta Bracciale and Antonio Martella, "Define the Populist Political Communication Style: The Case of Italian Political Leaders on Twitter," *Information, Communication & Society* 20, no. 9 (2017): 1314.
[23] Moffitt, *The Global Rise of Populism*, 55–63.
[24] Paula Diehl, "The Body in Populism," in *Political Populism: A Handbook*, ed. Reinhard Heinisch, Christine Holtz-Bacha, and Oscar Mazzoleni (Nomos/Bloomsbury, 2021), 515–26.
[25] See, among others, Mazzoleni, "Populism and the Media"; Moffitt, *The Global Rise of Populism*, 76.

and bringing sovereignty back to the people. Trump's inaugural speech in 2017 is paradigmatic of this: "Today we are not merely transferring power from one administration to another, or from one party to another, but we are transferring power from Washington D.C., and giving it back to you, the people." In addition, populist scandals, taboo breaking, and personalization overlap with media logic. There is a systemic affinity between populism and mass media, and this affinity becomes more important the more the medium is dependent on commercial success. This was made very clear by CBS director Leslie Moonves, when he commented on Trump's presidential campaign in 2016: "It may not be good for America, but it's damn good for CBS."[26] Populism sells. This can explain why political actors adopting populism tend to get more attention than others from mass media, even if they refuse interviews or avoid direct contact with traditional media, such as the leader of the Five Star Movement, Beppe Grillo. Yet the affinity between mass media logic and populism not only reinforces populism, but also influences journalistic practices and routines,[27] contributing to the transformation of the media environment and the expectations of the audience concerning politics. In addition, there is a risk of contamination of the entire spectrum of mass-mediated politics. In order to compete with populists, mainstream politicians can adopt populist communication, creating what Cas Mudde has called "the populist Zeitgeist."[28] The intensity of populist contamination depends on both mass media mechanisms of resistance and on the counter-strategies of political competitors.

Although the compatibility of populism and mass media is independent of the specific medium—as long as it is a mass medium and technically reproducible—transformations in media technology, law, and economic systems have been crucial to the growth of populism and its combination with celebrity politics and politainment. From the historical perspective, new dynamics affecting populism emerged in line with new types of media and systemic changes, especially in the third age (the 1990s) and the fourth age (the new millennium) of political communication. From newspapers, film,

---

[26] Liza Collins, "Les Moonves: Trump's Run Is 'Damn Good for CBS,'" *Politico*, February 29, 2016, www.politico.com/blogs/on-media/2016/02/les-moonves-trump-cbs-220001.

[27] Amber E. Boydstun and Regina G. Lawrence, "When Celebrity and Political Journalism Collide: Reporting Standards, Entertainment, and the Conundrum of Covering Donald Trump's 2016 Campaign," *Perspectives on Politics* 18, no. 1 (2020): 128–43; Mojca Pajnik, "Transformations of the Media Sphere and Journalism: Amplifying Opportunity Structures for Populism," in *The Complexity of Populism*, ed. Paula Diehl and Brigitte Bargetz, 161–77.

[28] Mudde, "The Populist Zeitgeist."

and radio to TV broadcast, and finally to internet communication and social media, these changes need to be considered in the study of populism.

In the twentieth century, media history considers the two decades after World War II as the first age of political communication.[29] Newspapers, radio, and cinema were the dominant media at that time. They were all one-to-many media, in which one sender sends a message to many recipients. At that time, "much political communication was subordinate to relatively strong and stable political institutions and beliefs."[30] This is the media environment in which Eva Perón emerged as a celebrity and later as a celebrity politician. She was able to adapt her radio style and vocabulary to politics[31] and to capitalize on the identification with her personal life performed as a celebrity, transferring this identification to the populist project of Juan Domingo Perón. By presenting herself as a prototype of the poor shirtless people, Evita articulated her biography from poor child to successful actress using the populist perspective from below. She constantly reminded her followers "that she was born poor, a *descamisada* too, and that she could therefore understand their problems and their concerns."[32] In so doing, she became the "utmost representation of this popular Argentina," embodying "justice and plebeization" in the defense of the *descamisados*.[33] Compared with Berlusconi or Trump, Evita's celebrity politics was naïve and operated without irony.

With the spread of television in the 1960s, political communication entered the second age. TV quickly became the dominant medium, enlarging the audience and creating new social situations where the borders between the private and the public were blurred. "Much more than print media, television thrusts the personal, private realm into the public arena."[34] Political communication became more emotional, more personalized, and more of a mixture between the private and the public. "The campaigns on television are rarely about issues; they are about personality and style."[35] This facilitates the conditions for celebrities like Ronald Reagan to become politicians, on

---

[29] Jay Blumer and Dennis Kavanagh, "The Third Age of Political Communication: Influences and Features," *Political Communication* 16, no. 3 (1999): 212.
[30] Ibid.
[31] Marysa Navarro, "The Case of Eva Perón," *Signs* 3, no. 1 (1977): 238.
[32] Ibid.
[33] José Maurício Domingues, "The Imaginary and Politics in Modernity: The Trajectory of Peronism," *Thesis Eleven* 133, no. 1 (2016): 24.
[34] Joshua Meyrowitz, *No Sense of Place: The Impact of Electronic Media on Social Behavior* (New York; Oxford: Oxford University Press, 1986), 99.
[35] Meyrowitz, *No Sense of Place*, 100.

the one hand, and for the personalization of and identification with populist leaders, on the other. In addition, media transformations in the 1960s made entertainment a key requirement of political communication. According to Neil Postman, entertainment is intrinsic to television and has become "the natural format for the representation of all experience." In television, "all subject matter is presented as entertaining."[36]

The third age of political communication in the 1990s added a new turn to populist performances. This age was marked by the professionalized marketing style of campaign communication.[37] There were several different factors behind this development: first, the deregulation of mass media, allowing increasing commercialization and cartelization of media networks and facilitating the emergence of media moguls like Rupert Murdoch and Silvio Berlusconi; second, new technologies that made media consumption available independently of live broadcast; third, fragmentation of the audience by media products targeting specific audiences; and fourth, circulation of the same products through different media, facilitating mass media self-referentiality of content.[38] Media networks started developing mixed genres like infotainment and reality shows, further blurring the borders between reality and fiction. Although television was still a one-to-many medium, this was nevertheless an age of considerable change. Although entertainment was already a core feature of political communication in the 1960s, by the 1990s this characteristic of electronic media had become exacerbated. It is not surprising that, with the radicalization of the commercial conditions and the mixed genres like infotainment and reality shows, politainment emerged as a new tool of political communication. Indeed, populist politicians such as Berlusconi and the former Brazilian president Fernando Collor de Mello were different from celebrities who had become politicians. The latter, like Evita and Reagan, performed according to the politician's role. In contrast, Berlusconi and Collor de Mello did not perform like politicians, but imported entertaining performances into their offices, or performed their institutional roles in fictional frames like soap operas or comedy shows, often using deconstruction, irony, and mass media self-referentiality.

---

[36] Neil Postman, *Amusing Ourselves to Death: Public Discourse in the Age of Show Business* (Methuen, UK: Viking Penguin, 2005 [1985]), 87.
[37] Blumer and Kavanagh, "The Third Age of Political Communication."
[38] W. Lance Bennett and Lawrence M. Entman, *Mediated Politics: Communication in the Future of Democracy* (Cambridge, UK: Cambridge University Press, 2001).

In the new millennium, the situation became more complex. Today, mass media have built a hybrid ecosystem encompassing traditional offline media (such as print and television), as well as online media. New media technologies do not make old ones disappear; rather, they integrate traditional media in their platforms and are also an object of reporting in traditional media. Content can migrate from social media to TV and newspapers, or from traditional media to internet blogs and social media, and from there find its way back to traditional media, generating mass media intra-circulation and increasing self-referentiality. In addition, the fourth age of communication "seems marked by the growing chaos of multiple public spheres in which the spin of conventional parties and politicians interacts often chaotically with new forms of organization enabled by technology platforms and socially mediated information production and distribution."[39]

An important novelty of this new ecosystem is the emergence of network communication, connecting many senders to many recipients (many-to-many) and increasing the diversification of content, voices, and audiences.[40] "Everyone, anyone who wants it, is invited onto the stage. Via the social media platform of our choice, each of us can play a role, however small, in the social dramas of our time."[41] Internet users are both producers and consumers of content, and journalistic intervention is not necessary anymore. Trump's tweets, Salvini's Instagram posts, and Bolsonaro's WhatsApp and Facebook messages escape the control of journalistic gatekeepers. This institutional, unchanneled, and personalized communication often targets specific audiences and is better adapted to the increasingly individualized political orientation. There is a considerable change in the relationship of communication to political institutions and practices[42] affecting how individuals perceive and relate to politics, and making engagement with politics "an expression of personal hopes, lifestyles, and grievances."[43] In online media, personalization of content and its distribution are crucial elements of "the logic of connective attention," by which "taking public action or

---

[39] W. Lance Bennett, Alexandra Segerberg, and Curd Knüpfer "The Democratic Interface: Technology, Political Organization, and Diverging Patterns of Electoral Representation," *Information, Communication & Society* 21, no. 11 (2017): 18.

[40] W. Lance Bennett and Barbara Pfetsch, "Rethinking Political Communication in a Time of Disrupted Public Spheres," *Journal of Communication* 68, no. 2 (2018): 244.

[41] Alan Finlayson, "Rethinking Political Communication," in *Rethinking Democracy*, ed. Andrew Gamble and Tony Wright (Oxford: Wiley, 2019), 83.

[42] Ibid., 81.

[43] W. Lance Bennett and Alexandra Segerberg, "The Logic of Connective Action," *Information, Communication & Society* 15, no. 5 (2012): 743.

contributing to a common good becomes an act of personal expression and recognition or self-validation."[44] Although this practice need not necessarily be self-centered, it facilitates communication about personal life and "self-branding,"[45] which are crucial for celebrity politics. In addition, since users can manipulate and distribute content, they acquire knowledge about the production of media content, making a naïve attitude toward media content more difficult to sustain.

Social media interaction is self-referential, personalized, and fictionalized. It makes the borders between private and public, between reality and fiction, and between politics and entertainment almost undetectable. Trump's tweets, for instance, make it almost impossible to know to what extent they are fictional entertainment or political messages. The famous video posted by a user on Reddit in the last week of June 2017 and shared by Trump from his private Twitter account (@realDonaldTrump) and later from the POTUS account is a good example of the mechanisms involved in the fourth age of political communication. The video shows a man in a dark suit next to a wrestling ring where a wrestler is lying on the floor. His face is covered by the CNN logo—a digital manipulation carried out by the Reddit user. In this short video, another man in a suit runs over to the CNN man, wrestles him to the floor, and punches him three times. When the aggressor is finished, he stands up and walks away in a victorious, masculinist manner. The audience can then see his face: It is the president of the United States of America, Donald Trump.[46] The video quickly spread through social media, generating memes, and becoming the subject of news broadcasts and newspaper commentaries. It was a personalized manipulation of an older TV clip available in the internet, shared by an internet user, and adopted by the U.S. president as his own message, and reframed with hashtags such as #FraudNewsCNN or #FNN.[47] The video went into intra-media circulation in traditional and social media. In terms of content, this example shows how the populist logic delegitimizes intermediation as performed by the media and journalism, oversimplifies content, uses "bad manners," and provokes scandals. It was perfectly compatible with mass media logic and integrated

---

[44] Ibid., 753.
[45] Susie Khamis, Lawrence Ang, and Raymond Welling, "Self-Branding, 'Micro-Celebrity' and the Rise of Social Media Influencers," *Celebrity Studies* 8, no. 2 (2017): 191–208.
[46] The original video dates back to 2007 and came from a wrestling show, where Trump acted as a celebrity. There is no doubt that in 2017 it became a source of entertainment consumed and shared by different users.
[47] Both tweets (from @Potus and @RealDonaldTrump) were quickly deleted.

celebrity politics and politainment, making the borders between entertainment and politics, between reality and fiction, and between private life and public appearance fluid.

Celebrity Politics

How does celebrity politics work, and how does it affect populism? The core feature of celebrities is their ability to capture attention.[48] They enjoy a greater presence in mass media, having a "wider scope of activity and agency."[49] Celebrity news and performances are sources of pleasure for the audience. They are based on a special mix: Celebrities are perceived as authentic and situated in the private realm but, at the same time, they are public figures based on fiction. Celebrities present a "dramatic reality" to their audiences, "somewhere between fact and fiction."[50] Celebrities are heavily dependent on performances. "It is the symbolic power of the celebrity advertisement that matters, not its factual accuracy. Its authority is performative, its cultural power immediately felt."[51] To become a celebrity is not only to gain the attention of the mass media, but to perform accordingly. Through such performances, they are able to generate audience identification. At the same time,

> celebrities are treated, if not as a traditional power elite, as an elite with the power to anoint, however briefly. In a formal democracy, personal distinction, self-importance, glory, and honor are ideologically problematic and hard to achieve. Celebrities as an elite mediate this problem: they have been legitimated by popularity, distinguished by the fact that millions of eyes have dwelled on them, by the glamour of envy. To be acknowledged by them—to meet their eyes—is to briefly feel their power.[52]

This specific power can be used in politics and is compatible with populism.

---

[48] Alfred Archer, Amanda Cawston, Benjamin Matheson, and Machteld Geuskens, "Celebrity, Democracy, and Epistemic Power," *Perspectives on Politics* 18, no. 1 (2020): 27–42.
[49] John Street, "Celebrity Politicians: Popular Culture and Political Representation," *The British Journal of Politics and International Relations* 6 (2004): 436.
[50] Joshua Gamson, *Claims to Fame. Celebrity in Contemporary America* (Berkeley: University of California Press, 1994), 68.
[51] Jeffrey C. Alexander, "Barack Obama Meets Celebrity Metaphor," *Society* 47 (2010): 414.
[52] Gamson, *Claims to Fame*, 132.

John Street identifies two types of celebrity politics: politicians who act as celebrities, and celebrities who act as politicians, embracing political causes or advocating for specific political measures. For the purpose of this chapter, only the first case will be examined. It occurs when politicians adopt "the guise of celebrity politics."[53] Eva Perón, Berlusconi, Trump, Chávez, Bolsonaro, and Salvini share information about their lives with their audiences, perform in the manner of advertisements to present themselves as "super stars,"[54] and at the same time generate the illusion of intimacy described by Gamson. Lega leader Matteo Salvini, for instance, is very active on Instagram, posting photos and information about his love life and food preferences. The politicians mentioned above adopt populism in their communication and include populist ideology in their messages, even if the content of populist ideology can vary in degrees: Perón directly translated her biography into a populist narrative, while Trump adopted populist ideology in his speeches, but Berlusconi's populist ideology is more indeterminate.

In his approach to celebrity politics, Street includes celebrities who become politicians in the category of celebrity politicians. However, I think it is important to draw a distinction between a political actor who already enjoyed attention because of her or his celebrity status before becoming a politician, such as Eva Perón, Reagan, or Trump, and a politician adopting celebrity performances in order to gain more mass media attention, such as Hugo Chávez, Hans-Christian Strache, or Matteo Salvini. In the case of celebrities becoming politicians, a previous image shapes audience expectations toward playful consumption of their performances, even when these politicians occupy an office or official position. In the case of a politician adopting celebrity performances without having been a celebrity before, the expectations of the audience are connected to the official role, and a celebrity performance can run counter to these expectations; the resulting surprise can affect the audience positively or negatively, depending on the situation.

Perón illustrates the combination of populism and celebrity politics in the first age of political communication. Before she came to politics, she was already a famous radio star. Her life and her image were and still are a source of

---

[53] Street, "Celebrity Politicians," 437.
[54] Mark Wheeler, "Celebrity Politics and Cultural Studies within the United States and United Kingdom," in *Oxford Research Encyclopedia of Communication* (Oxford: Oxford University Press, 2016) https://repository.londonmet.ac.uk/3448/.

inspiration for the entertainment industry. Like all celebrities in show business, Evita generated the "illusion of intimacy."[55] Information about her private life, whether true or not, was shared with the audience and later with the followers of the Peronist movement. As a political actor, she was able to mobilize the illusion of intimacy to confer legitimacy on political messages and goals and to facilitate nearness to the people, reinforcing the populist immediacy of her connection with the public and stressing her outsider role as a politician.

After the third age of political communication, celebrity performances have become a common feature of politics in general,[56] not only of populism. Barack Obama, for example, capitalizes on both celebrity politics and politainment. His appearances on *The Ellen DeGeneres Show* illustrate this. In March 2014, Obama was introduced by the moderator as "my friend's [Michelle's] husband." In the show, he answered questions about his behavior during Michelle's absence, the food he was eating, and his sports routines, never without irony, but mixing performances of the private with his role as president.[57] A similar mix of performing the private in the public, political role and entertainment can be detected in Berlusconi's and Trump's appearances on talk shows, but in their cases, celebrity politics is based on egocentric comments about their own money, popularity, or supposed attractiveness.[58]

When adopted by politicians, celebrity performances blur the lines between information about private life and political speech; they make it unclear which frame is being applied in the situation, increasing the fluidity "between private emotion and public communication" already detected in television.[59] With internet and social media, however, the combination of populism and celebrity politics has become much more exacerbated, but also modified. Again Trump illustrates this phenomenon. He was already a celebrity, emerging in the age of reality shows, and managed to make the transition from TV celebrity to online celebrity. He participated in several talk shows,

---

[55] Gamson, *Claims to Fame*, 172.

[56] Boydstun and Lawrence, "When Celebrity and Political Journalism Collide," 129.

[57] "President Obama Appears on 'Ellen DeGeneres Show,'" YouTube, March 21, 2014, www.youtube.com/watch?v=2RN1A9rpArs.

[58] On July 18, 2015, the *New York Times* online published a quiz called "Name That Narcissist" about the authorship of such statements. Readers had the choice between Trump and Berlusconi, but in many cases, it was very difficult to pick the right answer: www.nytimes.com/interactive/2015/07/19/opinion/sunday/Frank-Bruni-Quiz-Trump-Berlusconi.html.

[59] Meyrowitz, *No Sense of Place*, 100.

promoted himself as a celebrity in interviews, and was a protagonist of reality shows like *The Apprentice* and of wrestling shows. Yet social media offer a specific infrastructure for communication, increasing personalization and emotional appeal, and facilitating its political exploitation. The "personality and celebrity element of social media hereby provides a sort of focal point around which the crowd can gather and millions of disaffected individuals, otherwise deprived of common organisational affiliation, can come together as an online crowd multiplying the power of each of its members."[60] This capacity is closely linked to celebrities' ability to provoke audience members' identification. Trump was able to transfer his image to the internet and social media and to perfectly adapt his performances to the new online media.

These identification dynamics help celebrities to gain power and to become a sort of elite. Celebrities' "epistemic power" is grounded on two related abilities: "the ability to influence what others believe, think, or know" and "the ability to enable and disable others from exerting epistemic influence."[61] Celebrities are invested with "credibility excesses" and therefore are perceived to be more credible than they really are.[62] Politically relevant is the fact that celebrities cannot be rendered accountable by institutional means. In addition, their credibility is not an outcome of a particular expertise, competence, or talent, and they do not need any expertise in or knowledge of public policies.[63] Moreover, celebrity's credibility is a product of identification and projection by the audience. Followers identify with the celebrity on a personal level and project their wishes, desires, fantasies, and anxiety onto the celebrity. In Freudian terms, identifying with someone means desiring to become like the object of identification. It "enriches" the ego "with the properties of the object,"[64] but it can turn into what Freud described as "being in love." Being in love is different from simple identification and describes a situation in which the object of love substitutes for the ego ideal: "The ego becomes more and more unassuming and modest, and the object more and more sublime and precious, until at last it gets possession of the entire self-love of the ego.... The object, has, so to speak, consumed the ego."[65] When

---

[60] Paolo Gerbaudo, "Social Media and Populism: An Elective Affinity?" *Media, Culture & Society* 40, no. 5 (2018): 751.
[61] Archer et al., "Celebrity, Democracy, and Epistemic Power," 28.
[62] Archer et al., "Celebrity, Democracy, and Epistemic Power," 29.
[63] Street, "Celebrity Politicians," 440.
[64] Sigmund Freud, *Group Psychology and the Analysis of the Ego* (Vienna: International Psycho-Analytical Press, 1922), 76.
[65] Ibid., 74–75.

celebrity consumers become fans, the risk of "being in love" increases. For "fans" of a given celebrity, that celebrity's credibility will be high and has a good chance of impacting fans' political preferences, since their relationship to the celebrity is based on admiration and "intimacy at a distance."[66] Admiration and identification, paired with intimacy at a distance, are crucial for celebrities and are typical tools of attracting mass media attention, but they also have a strong affinity with populist leadership and populist disintermediation of political representation. As I show elsewhere, identification with the populist leader can also turn into "being in love" and make it possible for the leader to replace the will of the followers with his or her own will, producing unlimited trust. The problem here is that this decreases and can even destroy accountability.[67] When combined with celebrity politics, the populist threat of obfuscating democratic accountability increases.

Further, in celebrity politics, identification can take two different shapes of performance: "'superstar' celebrity politicians" and "'everyday' celebrity politicians."[68] While "superstar celebrities" stress their difference from "normal people" and present themselves as glamorous, "everyday celebrities" do the contrary, showing their similarities to the audience. What gives power to the "superstar celebrity" is exactly her/his capacity to be extraordinary. In his interviews with celebrity watchers in the 1990s, Gamson observed that the uniqueness of celebrities at that time was that they were unlike the audience. One of the celebrity watchers explained: "They are not ordinary, and I don't want them to be ordinary. . . . If they were like me, they wouldn't be interesting."[69]

Wood, Corbett, and Flinders identify "a shift away from the glamour of the red carpet and film star friends towards something more akin to the medium of reality TV where an individual's ability to appear ordinary, imperfect, 'everyday' and 'normal' is celebrated."[70] This shift can be connected to the third age of political communication, to the dissemination of reality shows, and to the further proliferation of social media and internet platforms. In reality

---

[66] Archer et al., "Celebrity, Democracy, and Epistemic Power," 30.

[67] Paula Diehl, "Populist Twist. The Relationship between the Leader and the People in Populism," in *Creating Political Presence: The New Politics of Democratic Representation*, ed. Dario Castiglione and Johannes Pollak (Chicago; London: University of Chicago Press, 2019), 131.

[68] Matthew Wood, Jack Corbett, and Matthew Flinders, "Just like Us: Everyday Celebrity Politicians and the Pursuit of Popularity in an Age of Anti-Politics," *The British Journal of Politics and International Relations* 18, no. 3 (2016): 581–98.

[69] Gamson, *Claims to Fame*, 160.

[70] Wood et al., "Just like Us: Everyday Celebrity Politicians and the Pursuit of Popularity in an Age of Anti-Politics," 582.

shows, ordinary people become celebrities only because they are exposed by mass media, and the same can be observed concerning influencers on social media. Here, private life and public staging are intermingled, and the distinction between reality and fiction has become fuzzy. The novelty is that their "celebrification" is less a matter of their "exceptional" qualities "but more because of the 'rags to riches' story of otherwise unexceptional individuals achieving success"[71] and can be articulated as anti-politics or protest against the establishment. "Everyday" celebrity politics fits perfectly with populist modes of communication and makes politicians look more "human." In politics, "appearing as 'special,' 'exceptional' or 'unique' is increasingly coming to be framed as more 'everyday' and 'normal' " and is explored by populists[72] in order to construct nearness to the people.

Empirically, "superstar" and "everyday celebrities" are more closely connected than they appear. Evita, Berlusconi, and Trump combine both, but they do it in different ways. A brief comparison can elucidate how "superstar celebrity politics" and "everyday politics" affect populist communication in the different ages of political communication. In Evita's case (the first age of political communication), her biography was a populist tool, which enabled her to demonstrate resemblance to the people's experiences. As an "everyday celebrity politician," suffering and vulnerability were constitutive elements of her image and were embedded in the populist narrative of the oppressed people. At the same time, she often presented herself in luxurious dresses and wore ostentatious jewelry, an element of "superstar" celebrity. Yet, this is different from Trump. Although Trump is a product of reality shows, suffering and emotional vulnerability are missing from his communication. Trump stages "everyday blue-collar tastes" but performs the billionaire (Ostiguy and Roberts 2016, 44), presenting himself as a winner, in contrast to the "losers." The same is valid for Berlusconi. Identification operates here in two ways: The leader demonstrates nearness through his similarity to the ordinary people by using popular taste and "bad manners,"[73] but at the same time, Trump and Berlusconi stress their structural distance from the popular classes by presenting almost unachievable objects of desire: success and luxury. Identifying with the leader's personal life, as in the case of Trump or Berlusconi, gives the followers the chance to symbolically

---

[71] Ibid., 584.
[72] Ibid., 585.
[73] Diehl, "Populist Twist."

participate in the desired objects that the leader possesses. It is not a coincidence that more and more billionaires like Andrej Babiš in the Czech Republic, Thaksin Shinawatra in Thailand, and Sebastián Piñera in Chile have become populist leaders using celebrity politics in the style of Trump and Berlusconi. This is a different identification than the one promoted by Evita's or Chávez's "everyday celebrity" performances of vulnerability and suffering. In contrast, populist performances of billionaires like Trump and Berlusconi lack "suffering" and vulnerability. They promote the "winner" ideology that is closely connected to the logic of "likes" disseminated in social media. Here, the popular element of their performances is reduced to staging "bad manners," but they are not able to mirror the experiences of the people in the way that Evita and Chávez did. A further difference between today's populist leaders adopting celebrity politics and those from the first age of political communication lies in hyperreality and the self-referentiality of mass media. Both are predominant features of politainment.

Politainment

The concept of politainment was developed by the German political scientist and media scholar Andreas Dörner in the early years of the new millenium. Building on the famous notion of infotainment originated by Postman, Dörner translates the idea of mixed genres of mass media to the field of politics. Like infotainment, politainment is a hybrid, but whereas infotainment mixes information and mass media entertainment, in politainment, entertainment is combined with political content and political communication, affecting the way politics is perceived. "Politainment refers to a certain form of public and mass-mediated communication in which political issues, actors, processes, patterns of interpretation, identities, and meanings are assembled in the logic of entertainment and rearranged in a new reality of the political."[74]

According to Dörner, politainment can occur on two levels: It can be performed as *entertaining politics* or *political entertainment*. In *entertaining*

---

[74] Author's translation. Original: "Politainment bezeichnet eine bestimmte Form der öffentlichen, massenmedial vermittelten Kommunikation, in der politische Themen, Akteure, Prozesse, Deutungsmuster, Identitäten und Sinnentwürfe im Modus der Unterhaltung, zu einer neuen Realität des Politischen montiert werden." Andreas Dörner, *Politainment. Politik in der medialen Erlebnisgesellschaft* (Frankfurt am Main: Suhrkamp, 2001), 31.

politics, political actors adopt elements of mass media entertainment to communicate with their constituencies. Berlusconi and Trump are very good examples of this. Berlusconi was famous for making fun of the institutions he was representing, for alluding to products of mass media entertainment in his speeches, and for performing as a comedian and singer.[75] Trump's celebrity performances and allusions to *The Apprentice* are also good illustrations of *entertaining politics*. The second level of politainment takes place as *political entertainment*. In this case, mass media entertainment takes on political topics, institutions, or actors to construct a fictional world and entertain the audience. Famous examples are the TV series *House of Cards* and the Danish production *Borgen*. Both are fictional mass media products that entertain by portraying and commenting on the way political institutions, actors, and procedures work. Their allusions to "real-world" political events and actors are easily recognized by the audience and become a source of entertainment.

It is not difficult to recognize the analogy with Street's two types of celebrity politics: politicians performing as celebrities, and celebrities advocating for political causes. The first type involves political actors, the second involves actors from the entertainment industry. But whereas Street addresses the type of actor, Dörner focuses on the structural frames[76] of political performance. Political actors performing entertainment mix two different frames: Because they occupy, or aim to occupy, a political office, they necessarily bring this institutional frame onto the stage. At the same time, their performative acts follow the codes and the scripts of entertainment, creating uncertainty about appropriate behavior,[77] meaning, and about the politician's representation role. This is important since it increases the fluidity of the borders not only between politics and entertainment, but also between reality and fiction.

The key element for understanding the effects of this fluidity in populist communication is performance. Politicians adopting politainment can switch between different frames, scripts, and codes, alternating between their role as politicians and their incarnation as entertaining fictional figures, and consequently confusing the expectations and perceptions of the audience. The populist Brazilian politician Fernando Afonso Collor de Mello was

---

[75] Paula Diehl, "Populismus, Antipolitik, Politainment. Neue Tendenzen der politischen Kommunikation," *Berliner Debatte Initial* 22, no.1 (2011): 27–38.

[76] Irving Goffman, *Encounters: Two Studies in the Sociology of Interaction* (New York: Bobbs-Merrill, 1961).

[77] Meyrowitz, *No Sense of Place*, 42.

probably the first politician to adopt such performances. In his presidential campaign and after his election in 1989, he intermingled the staging of his official role with telenovela's protagonists' performances, with quotations, and allusions to popular culture. During the presidential campaign he adopted the role of the "maharajah's hunter" against the corrupt elite, the title of a *political entertainment* telenovela at the time, and a character perfectly aligned with the populist narrative of the betrayed people. One of his most important campaign promises was "to hunt the corrupt elite." Berlusconi fits into the same category, but he added some irony and parody of his official role in his populist performances.[78] Having built himself up as a celebrity icon, Trump could refer to the public character he created and use it in his political performances. Like Berlusconi, Trump's appearance in Jimmy Fallon's "interview in the mirror" in 2016 deconstructs his own role as a politician and as a celebrity, adding irony to his performance. Distinguishing between the celebrity character "Donald Trump," the real man, and the presidential candidate is impossible. In the interview, Trump sits facing Fallon (who is dressed and wearing a wig with the same hair color as Trump's), as if a mirror separates them. The interview is started by Fallon: "Fallon's a lightweight. No way he deserves to interview me." Trump: "Me interviewing me, that's what I call a great idea."[79] The source of entertainment in this "mirroring" exercise is the deconstruction of the celebrity, which makes explicit the audience's tacit knowledge about the production of celebrity. At the same time, the ironic turn on Trump's political program deconstructs his own role. During the interview, Fallon asks Trump how he would get the Mexicans to build the wall. Trump: "Since I'm you, why don't you tell me how am I gonna get Mexico to build the wall?"

Faced with this phenomenon, the concept of politainment has a further advantage. It illuminates the interaction between *entertaining politics* and *political entertaining*. These two elements do not operate in isolation, but are rather interdependent and influence each other. They take advantage of mass media self-referentiality and, at the same time, help to increase self-referentiality. When Trump quotes his reality show *The Apprentice* during a political rally[80] or when Bolsonaro hires a comedian to answer journalists'

[78] Diehl, "Populismus, Antipolitik, Politainment"; Diehl, "Populist Twist."
[79] "Jimmy Fallon Donald Trump Interviews Himself in the Mirror," YouTube, April 24, 2017, www.youtube.com/watch?v=KwHuiWX18Dw].
[80] "'YOU'RE FIRED': President Trump Throws out Catchphrase during Rally," YouTube, June 28, 2018, www.youtube.com/watch?v=-JD9wHtzYGI.

questions in his place,[81] their performances refer to products of mass media entertainment and become themselves mass media entertainment, building a loop with new entertainment appropriation dynamics, as seen in the case of Trump's #FraudNewsCNN tweet. If celebrity politics is based on and creates hyperreality, politainment radicalizes it, contributing to the establishment of a new perception of and attitude toward mass-mediated reality, which is not necessarily committed to the truth. Politainment offers the audience the possibility to play with authenticity and to switch between reality and fiction, deeply affecting citizens' and representatives' relationship to the political.

Populism and Hyperreal Political Communication

The concept of hyperreality provides a better understanding of this process. The notion of hyperreality was discussed intensively in semiotics, media, and cultural studies in the 1980s and 1990s and was associated with postmodern popular culture. Authors interested in post-truth communication are now turning their attention to hyperreality in order to understand Trump's case.[82] In hyperreality, the distinction between reality and fake,[83] and between the real and the simulacrum,[84] has become unrecognizable. Umberto Eco's and Jean Baudrillard's seminal works are crucial for the understanding of this phenomenon. Eco first examined the obsession with reproducing reality through its representations, but he realized that in hyperreality, reality is not only preserved, but duplicated in more vivid colors. Moreover, such a duplication seems more real and authentic than the real objects it animates. Semiotically speaking, "The sign aims to be the thing, to abolish the distinction of the reference, the mechanism of replacement. Not the image of the thing, but its plaster cast. Its double, in other words."[85] Representation aims to replace its object, and it succeeds because it makes the experience of the object more intense. Hyperreality privileges exaggeration or, in Trump's

---

[81] "El Mundo: La Bochornosa 'Broma' de Bolsonaro Para Ningunear a la Prensa," YouTube, March 4, 2020, https://www.youtube.com/watch?v=PGHjmFmHG8c.
[82] Giovanni Maddalena and Guido Gili, *The History and Theory of Post-Truth Communication* (Cham: Palgrave Macmillan, 2020); Philip Pond, *Complexity, Digital Media and Post Truth Politics: A Theory of Interactive Systems* (New York: Palgrave/Macmillan, 2020).
[83] Umberto Eco, *Travels in Hyperreality* (New York: Harvest, 1986).
[84] Jean Baudrillard, *The Perfect Crime* (New York: Verso, 1996).
[85] Eco, *Travels in Hyperreality*, 7.

words "hyperbolic reality." Trump follows a logic of reality shows in which the audience experiences "not just the daily installments of new drama but also the bombastic, winking showmanship and frequent crossings into hyperbole and fakery."[86]

Yet hyperreality not only represents reality in a hyperbolic way, but also replaces the referent (real objects of representation) with signs. In the third age of political communication, consumers of mass media were confronted with a mass media environment which was "inundated with an overabundance of images and signs that no longer have referential value but, instead, interact solely with other signs."[87] Following Baudrillard, this can be described as the beginning of the process that replaces reality with simulacra. In his provocative book *The Perfect Crime*, he argues that reality has been "murdered," but unlike a common murder, there is no corpse.[88] The metaphor of the perfect crime describes the situation where representations do not refer to an existent referent in reality, but to other representations:

> Now, the image can no longer imagine the real, because it is the real. It can no longer dream it, since it is its virtual reality. It is as though things had swallowed their own mirrors and had become transparent to themselves, entirely present to themselves in a ruthless transcription, full in the light and in real time.[89]

That is the environment created by self-referential mass media based on hyperreality. Here the distinction between reality and fiction is suspended.

The consequences of hyperreality for political communication cannot be overestimated. Boydstun and Lawrence are right when they assert that today "presidentialness and electability may be shifting, perhaps shifting sharply, as politics becomes more influenced by celebrity and entertainment ... leaving the press in a more uncertain position vis-à-vis their winnowing power."[90] In the fourth age of political communication, the incapacity to determine the borders between private life and public appearance, between politics and

---

[86] Boydstun and Lawrence, "When Celebrity and Political Journalism Collide," 132.
[87] E. Deidre Pribram, "Seduction, Control, and the Search for Authenticity: Madonna's Truth or Dare," in *The Madonna Connection: Representational Politics, Subcultural Identities and Cultural Theory*, ed. Cathy Schwichtenberg (Boulder; San Francisco; Oxford, 1993), 189–212.
[88] Baudrillard, *The Perfect Crime*, 1.
[89] Ibid., 4.
[90] Boydstun and Lawrence, "When Celebrity and Political Journalism Collide," 133.

entertainment, and between reality and fiction has become ubiquitous and is aggravated by the dynamics of social media. In social media, everyone has the possibility to create content, consume and present politics as entertainment, to stage herself or himself as a celebrity, and to perform a semi-fictional character. Hyperreality becomes a characteristic of everyday social media interaction. Social media users perform in hyperreal mode and consume such performances, changing the perception and expectations of the audience. Anthropological research on celebrities provides a glimpse of attitudes generated by hyperreality. According to Gamson, by the 1980s, celebrity watchers could adopt various attitudes regarding celebrities. One of them anticipated the modes of perception in the fourth age of political communication: "the game player." For the game player, "The fact that 'most of it is not true,' that 'it can be interpreted in a million different ways,' is acknowledged but irrelevant."[91] Today, Gamson's findings seem to illuminate a mechanism that could explain the proliferation of "post-truth" political communication adopted by many populist leaders.

There is evidence "that digital interaction 'hollows out' signification, creating a hyperreal politics full of simulacra, just as Baudrillard described happening."[92] Therefore, it would be too simple to consider Trump a "liar," although he often tells falsehoods. Robin Lakoff is right when he argues that "it goes deeper," since Trump "is incapable of even imagining a distinction between truth and falsehood."[93] Moreover, this distinction does not matter anymore, and if it does, it is because it has become a source of entertainment, like the case of the "game player." Identification, too, seems to have changed. As the assault on the U.S. Capitol showed, identification with the populist leader/celebrity can be very personalized and politically articulated, but at the same time, the whole event entails a playful component. The violent performances of January 6, 2021, in some regards resembled wrestling shows[94] and connected to the impossibility of determining the line between reality and fiction. This is a crucial feature that distinguishes hyperreal politics from the traditional populism of figures such as Evita.

[91] Gamson, *Claims to Fame*, 173.
[92] Pond, *Complexity, Digital Media and Post Truth Politics*, 213.
[93] Robin T. Lakoff, "The Hollow Man: Donald Trump, Populism, and Post-Truth Politics," *Journal of Language and Politics* 16, no. 4 (2017): 600, 604.
[94] Sharon Mazer, "Donald Trump Shoots the Match," *The Drama Review* 62, no. 2 (2018): 175–200.

Conclusion

This chapter builds on a complex notion of populism that is able to grasp its fluidity and its capacity for creating hybrid combinations, including those with celebrity politics and politainment. However, ideologically, populism is heavily dependent on the distinction between reality and truth, since it assumes that the truth is with the people and needs to be spoken out by the leader. Although actors adopting populist ideology can use lies to construct the political, they would claim that these *are* true. As the case of Evita indicates, early populist arrangements with celebrity politics capitalized on the staging of the leader's private life and presented them as true experiences shared with the people. Her celebrity performances were connected to the populist narrative of the betrayed people. Their function was to "show" the "real" suffering of the people. Unlike Trump's performances, identification was not an egocentric or hyperreal exercise, but the vehicle for emotionally converting a political message and demonstrating the truth that had been obfuscated by the elite. If "Trump is the president who reveals that there is no president,"[95] Evita was the leader who revealed that leadership was connected to the real experiences of the people. This started to change in the third age of political communication, when politicians like Berlusconi and Collor de Mello adopted politainment, mixing frames, scripts, and roles and using mass media self-referentiality as an entertainment tool. The status of these performances concerning public speech, politics, and truth became uncertain.

Yet in the fourth age of political communication, populism's new arrangements with celebrity politics and politainment radicalize the hyperreal character of mass media, increasing the fictionality in its performances and detaching the content of communication from the notion of truth. This is an outcome of both celebrity politics and politainment, on the one hand, and digital and social media communication, on the other. Of course, this new arrangement of populism is not a ubiquitous phenomenon. Although politicians can lie, the majority of political communication seems to at least presume a distinction between truth and falsehood; cases like Trump's are not the rule. However, Trump points toward an arrangement of populism connected to a new perception and performance of politics operating predominantly in hyperreality. When populism meets

---

[95] Pond, *Complexity, Digital Media and Post Truth Politics*, 214.

celebrity politics and politainment and exacerbates hyperreality, the opportunity for detaching the content of political communication from the notion of truth increases.

The radicalization of hyperreality disrupts the very notion of the people's truth, making distinctions between the fictional or real status of performances, frames, and roles highly unstable. The turning point is not that politicians present lies as facts or as elements of reality, but that the notion of truth loses its relevance for political communication in a mass media democracy. At the same time, populists like Trump are still able to politically capitalize on the latent needs, dissatisfactions, and resentments of the heartland.[96] It seems that a double and contradictory logic has emerged from the new populists. On the one hand, truth is presented as irrelevant and "alternative facts" are possible; on the other hand, even though new populist performances have become playful, and violence can be enjoyed as in a wrestling show, these performances are associated with political messages and visions of the political. Such performances contribute to the establishment of a new perception of and attitude toward political communication, which is not necessarily committed to the truth.

How to make sense of the opposing populist and hyperreal approaches to truth present in the new arrangements of populism? Gamson asked a similar question: "How can stars be both true and false?"[97] Faced with the fourth age of political communication, scholars of populism should ask: How can populist leaders claim to speak the truth and at the same time declare truth irrelevant? I think the answer can be found in the different attitudes of early celebrity watchers detected by Gamson: the naïve attitude of the traditional believer; the second-order believer, who knows about the production of celebrity but searches for the truth behind it; the anti-believers adopting a skeptical attitude of disbelief; and the "game player." The game player operates in a semi-fictional perception despite her/his knowledge about the "fabrication system" of celebrities. Yet this does not prevent the game player from enjoying "the show." For the game player, reality and truth have become irrelevant or indistinguishable. Trump's performances target game players and transform the populist claim to truth. There is an apparent paradox here: the same game players are able to identify their political preferences with the right-wing populist content offered by Trump, to naïvely believe lies

---

[96] Maddalena and Gili, *The History and Theory of Post-Truth Communication*, 94.
[97] Gamson, *Claims to Fame*, 48.

about his opponents, and to follow a political agenda. This is also the case for Bolsonaro. My hypothesis here is that the new populist arrangement with celebrity politics and politainment stimulates alternation between the believer and the game player attitude. The examination of this hypothesis should be the object of future research.

14
Rhetorical Resonance
From Everyday Speech to Insurrection

Simon Lambek

Introduction

On January 6, 2021, a crowd[1] of Donald Trump supporters stormed the United States Capitol. Adorned with Trump paraphernalia and signs and garments proclaiming far-right ideologies, the crowd scaled walls and barricades and forced their way into the legislative building. Along the way, individuals destroyed public infrastructure and the belongings of members of Congress, killed and injured police officers, smeared feces, planted pipe bombs, and chanted for the murder of public officials. The crowd sought to delay or interrupt the peaceful transfer of power and instead secure the continued rule of someone who had lost a democratic election. The attempted putsch marked a suspension of the ritual of the peaceful transfer of power in the United States. For many, it was an explicit attack on the country's democracy.

Headlines in the days that followed emphasized the collective shock that many experienced seeing such an event take place. The *BBC* led with: "Capitol Riots: Panel of Americans 'Shocked' and 'Disgusted.'" *Reuters* emphasized: "World Shocked by Trump Supporters' Attack on U.S. Democracy." The *Associated Press* documented the reaction of world leaders "Express[ing] Shock at the Storming of the U.S. Capitol."[2] Indeed, in the emergency session

---

[1] There is no consensus on estimates concerning the size of the crowd. See Steve Doig, "It Is Difficult, if Not Impossible, to Estimate the Size of the Crowd That Stormed Capitol Hill," *The Conversation*, January 8, 2021, https://theconversation.com/it-is-difficult-if-not-impossible-to-estimate-the-size-of-the-crowd-that-stormed-capitol-hill-152889.

[2] Sam Cabral, "Capitol Riots: Panel of Americans 'Shocked' and 'Disgusted,'" *BBC News*, January 7, 2021, https://www.bbc.com/news/world-us-canada-55582166; Reuters Staff, "World Shocked by Trump Supporters' Attack on U.S. democracy," *Reuters*, January 6, 2021, https://www.reuters.com/article/us-usa-election-international-reaction-f-idUSKBN29B2VS; Christopher Torchia, Associated

Simon Lambek, *Rhetorical Resonance* In: *Populism, Demagoguery, and Rhetoric in Historical Perspective*.
Edited by: Giuseppe Ballacci and Rob Goodman, Oxford University Press. © Oxford University Press 2024.
DOI: 10.1093/oso/9780197650974.003.0015

of Congress held the evening of January 6, members of Congress on both sides of the aisle expressed extreme dismay, shock, and outrage.[3]

And yet, this assault on American democracy did not emerge from nowhere. In the weeks and months preceding the election, and with polls indicating a likely loss for then-president Trump, public figures on America's right began to give speeches and addresses which placed the legitimacy of the eventual election results in doubt.[4] These efforts escalated in the days following the election, starting with then-President Trump announcing at 2:30 a.m. on November 4 (just hours after votes were cast) that, contrary to ongoing vote tabulations, he had won the presidency. In the two months that followed, Trump and his allies attempted to interrupt vote certification processes, launched at least sixty-two lawsuits, solicited fake electors, and campaigned to have election results overturned.[5] Many with megaphones on America's right echoed these sentiments and, correspondingly, much of the Republican base followed suit on social media, in protests, and at rallies.

Beliefs about an election "stolen" from the American people remain widespread and commonplace on America's right. According to a *Reuters Ipsos* poll released on April 5, 2021 (several months after both the election and the storming of the Capitol), only 27% of Republicans viewed the 2020 presidential election as "legitimate and accurate." Further, according to the same poll, more than that 60% of Republicans answered either "strongly agree" or "somewhat agree" to the prompt: "The 2020 election was stolen from Donald Trump."[6] Likewise, a December 2021 poll from UMass Amherst found that only 21% of Republicans believed the Biden presidency to be legitimate.[7]

Press, "World Leaders Express Shock at Storming of U.S. Capitol," *PBS News Hour*, January 6, 2021, https://www.pbs.org/newshour/politics/world-leaders-express-shock-at-storming-of-u-s-capitol.

[3] See: Nicholas Fandos and Emily Cochrane, "After Pro-Trump Mob Storms Capitol, Congress Confirms Biden's Win," *New York Times*, January 6, 2021, https://www.nytimes.com/2021/01/06/us/politics/congress-gop-subvert-election.html.

[4] As I argue below, the election-denying movement actually began well before the 2020 election cycle.

[5] William Cummings, Joey Garrison and Jim Sergent, "By the Numbers: President Donald Trump's Failed Efforts to Overturn the Election," *USA Today*, January 6, 2021, https://www.usatoday.com/in-depth/news/politics/elections/2021/01/06/trumps-failed-efforts-overturn-election-numbers/4130307001/.

[6] See Reuters/Ipsos, "Trump's Coattails," April 5, 2021, https://fingfx.thomsonreuters.com/gfx/mkt/oakvelbwlpr/Topline%20Reuters%20Ipsos%20Trump%20Coattails%20Poll%20-%20April%2005%202021.pdf.

[7] See Tatishe M. Nteta, Jesse Rhodes, Ray la Raja, Alex Theodoridis and Jared Sharpe, "Toplines and Crosstabs December 2021 National Poll: Presidential Election & Jan 6th Insurrection at the US Capitol," December 28, 2021, https://polsci.umass.edu/toplines-and-crosstabs-december-2021-national-poll-presidential-election-jan-6th-insurrection-us.

And, despite the initial condemnation from many prominent Republicans, in early 2022 the Republican National Committee moved to label the events of January 6th as "legitimate political discourse."[8] To this day, the majority of Republicans believe the 2020 election to be fraudulent and the January 6th putsch legitimate. Those few prominent Republicans who remain critical of Trump and of the attempted putsch have faced censure, condemnation, and primary election defeats. And, during the 2022 midterm elections, a large percentage of Republican nominees ran (and ran successfully)[9] on claims of a stolen or fraudulent 2020 election.[10]

In this chapter, I ask: How did this widespread belief in a fraudulent election take hold? What was the means of persuasion that instilled such belief and identification? My intention is not so much to consider the motivation of those who sought to overturn the election,[11] though of course this is an important topic, but rather to theorize the nature of political persuasion that brought so many Americans to the side of the insurrectionists. My claim is that a new theorization of political rhetoric is needed to capture the form of persuasion at work in the "big lie" of election fraud—one that captures the gradual and iterative effects of everyday speech.

These effects are not well captured by the "rhetoric revival" literature, which tends to focus on exceptional speech—speech that triggers judgment and

---

[8] See: Jonathan Weisman and Reid J. Epstein, "G.O.P. Declares Jan. 6 Attack 'Legitimate Political Discourse,'" *New York Times*, February 4, 2022, https://www.nytimes.com/2022/02/04/us/politics/republicans-jan-6-cheney-censure.html

[9] While many election-denying candidates won, non-incumbent election-denying Republican candidates performed poorly in comparison to their non-incumbent Republican peers who did not make election denial central to their campaigns.

[10] As of July 18, 2022, 54% of Republican nominees for the House of Representatives had either explicitly called the election a fraud or suggested a possible or likely fraud. This is in comparison to the 18% of Republican nominees who had acknowledged publicly that Biden's win was legitimate. See Nathaniel Rakich and Kaleigh Rogers, "At Least 120 Republican Nominees Deny the Results of the 2020 Election, *FiveThirtyEight*, July 18, 2022, https://fivethirtyeight.com/features/at-least-120-republicans-who-deny-the-2020-election-results-will-be-on-the-ballot-in-november/. Trump appears to have been instrumental in elevating election-denying candidates, with public proclamations of belief in 2020 election fraud seemingly being a main criteria for soliciting a Trump endorsement. See Michael C. Bender, Rebecca Lieberman, Eden Weingart, Alyce McFadden, and Nick Corsaniti, "How Trump's Endorsements Elevate Election Lies and Inflate His Political Power," *New York Times*, August 21, 2022, https://www.nytimes.com/interactive/2022/08/22/us/trump-endorsements.html.

[11] There are likely many motivating causes, not least racial and gendered resentment. Indeed, as has been argued by several commentators, white identity politics in particular stands out as a motivating factor for contemporary U.S. politics: see, e.g., Kevin B. Anderson, "The January 6 Insurrection: Historical and Global Contexts," *Critical Sociology* 48, no. 6 (2021): 901–7; and Casey Ryan Kelly, "Donald J. Trump and the Rhetoric of *Ressentiment*," *Quarterly Journal of Speech* 106, no. 1 (2020): 2–24. More generally, the literature on "white ignorance" is helpful in understanding how white resentment operates as a political force. See Charles Mills, "White Ignorance," and Linda Martín Alcoff, "Epistemologies of Ignorance: Three Types," in *Race and Epistemologies of Ignorance*, ed. Shannon Sullivan and Nancy Tuana (Albany: State University of New York Press, 2007), 13–38 and 39–57.

imaginative thinking or, conversely, affectively charged speech that is strategically manipulative and that rapidly persuades or hoodwinks an audience.[12] What is missing from this literature, which would aid in our understanding of the lead-up to the insurrection and the rhetorical success of those on the right who sought to sow distrust in election institutions, is a framework that captures the political effects of far more mundane and commonplace forms of rhetoric—speech acts that are received in stride and that do not stand out as exceptional at the moment of their delivery, but which nonetheless have significant cumulative political effects. To this end, I propose the concept of "rhetorical resonance" and make a case for attending to the iterative constitutive effects of otherwise unremarkable everyday rhetorical encounters. Building from the hermeneutic theory of Hans-Georg Gadamer, I argue that rhetoric which "resonates" with our discursive horizons can nevertheless transform those horizons, ushering in new conditions of political possibility. My contention is that "resonant rhetoric" helps to explain the lead-up to the 2021 storming of the U.S. Capitol and its after-effects. Accounts which focus exclusively on exceptional rhetorical performances are likely to miss the way in which everyday political rhetoric shapes and re-shapes the horizons of political possibility.

The Rhetoric Revival

Recent years have seen what Brian Garsten calls a "rhetoric revival" in political theory.[13] There has been a renewed interest in persuasive, passionate, affective, and creative speech and communication, with scholars seeing rhetoric as both necessary for and beneficial to democracy and political freedom. In this literature, "good" rhetoric is celebrated when it generates judgment or critical reflection,[14] fosters deliberation,[15] resolves motivation

---

[12] See Bryan Garsten, "The Rhetoric Revival in Political Theory," *Annual Review of Political Science* 14 (2011): 159–80.
[13] Ibid.
[14] Rob Goodman, "The Deliberative Sublime: Edmund Burke on Disruptive Speech and Imaginative Judgment," *American Political Science Review* 112, no. 2 (2018): 267–79; Linda M. G. Zerilli, *A Democratic Theory of Judgment* (Chicago: University of Chicago Press, 2016); Melvin L. Rogers, "The People, Rhetoric, and Affect: On the Political Force of Du Bois's *The Souls of Black Folk*," *American Political Science Review* 106, no. 1 (2012): 188–203; Simon Lambek, "Nietzsche's Rhetoric: Dissonance and Reception," *Epoché: A Journal for the History of Philosophy* 25, no. 1 (Fall 2020): 57–80.
[15] Simone Chambers, "Rhetoric and the Public Sphere: Has Deliberative Democracy Abandoned Mass Democracy?," *Political Theory* 37, no. 3 (June 2009): 232–350; Bryan Garsten, *Saving Persuasion: A Defense of Rhetoric and Judgment* (Cambridge, MA: Harvard University Press, 2006); John S. Dryzek, "Rhetoric in Democracy: A Systemic Appreciation," *Political Theory* 38, no. 3

problems,[16] produces friendship across difference,[17] features mutual risk-taking on the part of speaker and audience,[18] or enables creative rearticulation of concepts.[19] "Bad" rhetoric, in contrast, is those speech acts that trade in manipulation or pandering, what Garsten calls the "twin evils" of rhetoric.[20] Bad rhetoric is disingenuous, treats the audience as mere object, or tricks, hoodwinks, or dupes audiences into acts they otherwise would not commit.

Whether good or bad rhetoric is highlighted, the object of analysis in this literature is generally speeches which stand out from everyday political talk. Often (though not always) ancient Greek or Roman oratory is taken as a launching point.[21] Paradigmatic rhetoric tends to be speeches made by significant and influential figures, during important occasions, often in rarified spaces, to large or influential audiences, particularly in times of uncertainty. For example, theorists focus on lauded presidential addresses, like those by Lyndon B. Johnson concerning civil rights legislation,[22] or famous passionate oratory from influential speakers like Frederick Douglass.[23] These speeches are weighty, forceful, and exceptional; their political effects stand out and are noteworthy.

This emphasis arose for good reason—as a response to the dominance of the "language of public reason," which, prioritizes neutral, sober, non-stylized, and unemotional (i.e., non-rhetorical) speech. The rhetoric revival literature has critiqued the language of public reason for being potentially exclusionary, politically impotent, or antidemocratic, and has persuasively contrasted such language with more exceptional (and inclusive) forms of speech. However, this emphasis on exceptional speech is also importantly one-sided. What is missing from the rhetoric revival literature is an analysis of other forms of political speech—speech that may be seen as unremarkable,

---

(2010): 319–39; Adam Adatto Sandel, *The Place of Prejudice: A Case for Reasoning within the World* (Cambridge, MA: Harvard University Press, 2014).

[16] Arash Abizadeh, "On the Philosophy/Rhetoric Binaries: Or Is Habermasian Discourse Motivationally Impotent?," *Philosophy & Social Criticism* 33, no. 4 (2007): 445–72.
[17] Danielle S. Allen, *Talking to Strangers: Anxieties of Citizenship since Brown v. Board of Education* (Chicago: University of Chicago Press, 2009).
[18] Rob Goodman, *Words on Fire: Eloquence and Its Conditions* (Cambridge, UK: Cambridge University Press, 2021).
[19] Torrey Shanks, "The Rhetoric of Self Ownership," *Political Theory* 47, no. 3 (2019): 311–37.
[20] Garsten, *Saving Persuasion*, 7.
[21] See, e.g., Goodman, *Words on Fire*.
[22] Garsten, *Saving Persuasion*; Sandel, *The Place of Prejudice*.
[23] Zerilli, *A Democratic Theory*.

perfunctory, or mundane at the time it is delivered, but which nonetheless is transformative. For the rhetoric revival literature, routine, everyday, and ordinary speech is generally seen as either non-motivating, politically insignificant, or, as is persuasively argued by Iris Marion Young, a tool for maintaining existing power arrangements.[24]

In this chapter, I propose an alternative rhetorical framework that centers more common or everyday rhetoric. Specifically, I focus on speech that is received by audiences as uneventful; that neither solicits sustained judgment or reflection, nor stands out as a specific or discrete moment of manipulation but is, instead, received in stride. This is not to say that such rhetoric is boring—to the contrary, it may contain emotion or rhetorical flourish. What matters for my purposes is less the content of rhetoric, than the way it is received by audiences. The kind of rhetoric I am interested in here is ordinary; it is experienced more in the sense of the German *erfahrung* than *erlebnis*. Receiving this rhetoric does not constitute an "event." Rather, the rhetoric is experienced in such a way that it flows without disruption into the other goings-on in one's life. Resonant speech, in other words, is received as but a moment within a *longue durée*; a nearly undifferentiable occurrence in a long progression of such occurrences. Yet, for the reasons I explore below, this type of speech can be profoundly transformative, with substantive persuasive effects.

Resonant Rhetoric and Horizons of Understanding

I propose that the rhetoric of election illegitimacy and theft that led up to the insurrection is best understood as "resonant" rhetoric. That is, it "resonated" with the discursive world and interpretive horizon of its audience, with effects that continue to reverberate over time. Consider the over 150 times (according to the *Washington Post*) that Trump gave false or misleading claims about 2020 election fraud *prior* to the election even occurring.[25] Through tweets, offhand remarks, and misleading statements, Trump built a world where unsubstantiated claims of election fraud became an expected and regular feature of political discourse. This phenomenon accelerated after

---

[24] Iris Marion Young, *Inclusion and Democracy* (New York: Oxford University Press, 2000).
[25] Glenn Kessler Salvador Rizzo, "President Trump's False Claims of Vote Fraud: A Chronology," *Washington Post*, November 5, 2020, https://www.washingtonpost.com/politics/2020/11/05/president-trumps-false-claims-vote-fraud-chronology/.

voting occurred, with continual claims of election fraud pouring in following the November 3, 2020, election, and has, of course, continued long after January 6, 2021.[26] Resonant rhetoric works in this way. It is simultaneously world-confirming and world-building. Rhetoric is resonant when it is predictable and received in stride; when it maps onto the interpretive horizons of those who receive it. Rather than clash with audience expectations, resonant rhetoric fits within the audience's expectations for what is intelligible, appropriate, or otherwise anticipatable speech.[27] What is more, the effects of resonant rhetoric are diachronic, shifting the interpretive horizons and discursive worlds of audiences over time.

The reason for this is the fundamentally open nature of what Gadamer calls our "horizons." Some depth is warranted here. In his magnum opus, *Truth and Method*, Gadamer posits in most concrete terms his philosophical hermeneutics, which universalizes the hermeneutic experience and equates interpretation with understanding. Central to his theory is Gadamer's claim concerning the universality of what he calls peoples' *historically effected consciousness* [*wirkungsgeschichtliches Bewußtsein*]. That is, our understanding of any given phenomenon, our very consciousness, is conditioned by our living within a historically given context.

For Gadamer, this context is social, but it is also fundamentally linguistic; it is tied to our belonging to a language or languages that evolve and develop over time. One's context is defined, in part, by the languages that they speak, where they live, how they live, their gender, their race, their ethnicity, their class, the groups to which they belong, their various other forms of identification, and so on. Our belonging to a linguistic and social context both enables and fundamentally shapes (and thereby also constrains) understanding. Language and contextual situatedness enable understanding because they bestow us with the fore-understandings that allow us to make sense of those phenomena we confront. Thus,

---

[26] The *New York Times* compiled a thirty-eight-minute video of "lie after lie" from Trump concerning a "stolen" election in the two months following election day. See Larry Buchanan, Karen Yourish, Ainara Tiefenthäler, Jon Huang and Blacki Migliozzi, "Lie after Lie: Listen to How Trump Built His Alternative Reality," *New York Times*, February 9, 2021, https://www.nytimes.com/interactive/2021/02/09/us/trump-voter-fraud-election.html.

[27] While there are similarities, I do not use "resonance" in quite the same way as Deva Woodly. For Woodly, resonance is primarily a retrospective concept (the rhetoric resonates with citizens given their preexisting opinions), whereas resonance for me is largely a future-oriented phenomenon. While resonant rhetoric resonates with a preexisting horizon of understanding, the rhetoric also resonates with an audience moving forward in time such that an audience's horizon comes to further incorporate that rhetoric. See Deva Woodly, "The Importance of Public Meaning for Political Persuasion," *Perspective on Politics* 16, no. 1 (2018): 22–35.

I understand what someone says because I understand the terms used, how they fit together, how they relate to other concepts, and how they relate to a broader context. Without this prior knowledge, or "prejudice" to use Gadamer's term, I would lack the necessary resources to make sense of that which I confront. Language and context shape (and constrain) understanding because one cannot step outside of one's historically effected consciousness when understanding. There is no view from nowhere, but always only a view from somewhere, with that "somewhere" providing the contours of what is knowable.

However, consciousness is neither rigid nor unchanging, but rather is something that is forever being altered with each new experience. Our ideas and understandings transform and shift continuously over time. Gadamer writes, "If we stick to what takes place in speech and, above all, in every dialogue with tradition carried on by the human sciences, we cannot fail to see that here concepts are constantly in the process of being formed."[28] While concepts are historically and linguistically given, they are never settled. As etymology shows us, meanings change. With each use and application of a concept, meanings are shifted.

Gadamer uses the visual metaphor of a "horizon" to help explore this phenomenon—a key concept for what I call resonant rhetoric. For Gadamer, a "horizon" represents what is knowable within one's place within a broad linguistic and historical (as well as political, cultural, social, and spatial) context. Gadamer writes, "The horizon is the range of vision that includes everything that can be seen from a particular vantage point."[29] That is, our horizon represents a vantage point from which we can see and beyond which we cannot see. Our horizon provides a view of the world, supplying a range of interpretive possibilities. When we interpret something, we do so from within our horizon, but as we interpret, our horizon shifts as well. As Gadamer writes, "The historical movement of human life consists in the fact that it is never absolutely bound to any one stand-point, and hence can never have a truly closed horizon. The horizon is, rather, something into which we move and that moves with us."[30] Every interpretation, act, thought, and every change in our context result in a shift in our horizons.

---

[28] Hans-Georg Gadamer, *Truth and Method*, trans. Joel Weinsheimer and Donald G. Marshall (New York: Bloomsbury Academic, 2013), 421.
[29] Ibid, 313.
[30] Ibid, 315.

Thus, horizons are open, because, for Gadamer, language is historical; language changes and evolves over time and we change along with it. People are born into a linguistic world and become who they are by situating themselves in that world using the language into which they are thrown. And, as people use and receive language, their world is continuously altered.

This means that as the language into which we are thrown shifts, changes, develops, or evolves, our horizons of understanding change as well. As we hear rhetoric, in other words, our horizons shift. This is the case even if what is said is *not* particularly noteworthy. Gadamer writes, "Inasmuch as the tradition is newly expressed in language, something comes into being that had not existed before and that exists from now on."[31] Every speech act contributes to a never-ending process of becoming, as each speech act is a case of concepts being applied anew. Even if a claim is felicitous to an already held opinion or belief, its assertion can work to entrench that opinion or belief, or shift where it fits within a system of beliefs. Conversely, even if an audience does not agree with the propositional content of a given speech act, the reception of the speech nonetheless has an effect on the horizon of the audience. This is because one's horizon extends beyond one's own opinions to cover those that are representable to them. Included within my interpretive horizon are not merely opinions that I hold, but ones that I know others hold and to which I have a view. Thus, the more an opinion or position is expressed, the more I may come to see it as acceptable or appropriate, the more it seeps into my discursive world.

Here then is the often-overlooked link between rhetoric and hermeneutics for Gadamer. It is precisely rhetoric that shifts horizons. This is because rhetoric, for Gadamer, is the inverse of interpretation. Gadamer writes, "Rhetoric and hermeneutics are intimately related: being able to speak, like being able to understand, is a natural human capacity that develops to the full without the conscious application of rules, although natural talents, along with the proper cultivation and practice, come into play."[32] Communication and interpretation presuppose each other. Insofar as politics is frequently about contestations over interpretive possibilities, the political consequences of rhetoric are immense. Gadamer writes, "all social and political manifestations of the will are dependent upon rhetoric's

---

[31] Ibid., 478.
[32] Hans-Georg Gadamer, "Rhetoric and Hermeneutics," trans. Joel Weinscheimer, in *Rhetoric and Hermeneutics in Our Time: A Reader*, ed. Walter Jost and Michael J. Hyde (New Haven, CT: Yale University Press, 1997), 49.

construction of public convictions."[33] What is politically possible is contingent on what rhetoric discloses.

This is obviously the case with singular speeches that win hearts and minds and which cause substantial and swift opinion change—those speeches that are usually covered in the rhetoric revival literature, and which Adam Sandel discusses specifically with reference to Gadamer.[34] These kinds of speeches might cause opinion change by clashing with horizons, causing audiences to stop and re-evaluate, or by passionately moving an audience through affectively charged imagery.[35] As I have argued elsewhere, by instilling "dissonance" in audiences, rhetors may alter opinions in audiences by way of inducing critical reflection and judgment.[36] But, these sorts of performances are rare. And, given the constant iterative process of horizon shifting, the political impact of rhetoric extends beyond these kinds of exceptional speeches. All speech, insofar as it is received, has transformative effects. When we listen to speech, our horizon shifts along with it, even if such shifting is minimal with regard to each specific speech act. However, the iterative effects of repeated similar speech can be profound.

Herein lies the power of what I call resonant rhetoric.[37] Over time, continual resonant speech can have profound effects by shifting the way ideas fit together, by centering ideas within horizons, or by expanding the spectrum of what people consider reasonable or appropriate speech. For example, when we hear something with which we obviously agree or disagree and that message is presented in a predictable manner, it is likely that we will receive the rhetoric as resonant. We do not stop and reflect because what is uttered does not stand out as surprising; it resonates with our pre-understandings. However, repeated exposure to the claim can slowly shift how it fits into our understanding of our world.

My claim is that the rhetoric of election fraud and illegitimacy functioned in this way. The "stickiness" of the rhetoric of election fraud, to use Maxime Lepoutre's terminology, is attributable to its resonant reception.[38] Claims

---

[33] Hans-Georg Gadamer, "Reply to My Critics," trans. George H Leiner, in *The Hermeneutic Tradition: From Ast to Ricoeur*, ed. Gayle L. Ormiston and Alan D. Schrift (Albany: State University of New York Press, 1990), 294.
[34] Sandel, *The Place of Prejudice*.
[35] Lambek, "Nietzsche's Rhetoric."
[36] Ibid.; and Simon Lambek, "Comedy as Dissonant Rhetoric," *Philosophy & Social Criticism* 49, no. 9 (2023): 1107–27.
[37] Resonance is my term, not Gadamer's.
[38] When discussing the "stickiness" of misinformation, Maxime Lepoutre writes, "The salience of politically relevant misinformation is problematic quite simply because it increases the

of election fraud were repeated so many times in such predictable and uneventful ways that audiences became habituated to them—they were unsurprising. And yet, their repeated invocation cemented the idea of fraud and illegitimacy in the eyes of Trump's supporters. These followers were not persuaded by any single speech. Rather, it was the iterative and cumulative effects of the speech of election fraud—its resonant reception—that created the conditions for the January 6th insurrection. To attribute these effects simply to one speech, such as the one Trump gave on January 6 immediately prior to the storming of the Capitol (or to a few significant speeches in particular), is misleading because it misses the resonant rhetoric that brought his supporters together in the first place and gave them a shared purpose—a united horizon of understanding.

The Resonant Rhetoric of Election Theft

Donald Trump's rhetoric has been a point of interest (and concern) since his initial foray into politics. One reason for this—as often noted by critics and fans alike, and as Trump himself has acknowledged[39]—is that Trump does not speak (or tweet) like most of his predecessors. Indeed, Trump's style is dissimilar to that of even most current high-ranking officials within his own party, although this is changing. This rhetorical peculiarity has led to descriptive investigations into why his rhetoric is successful and normative analyses concerning the effects of Trump's speech. Mary Stucky, for example, highlights Trump's lack of "educative" rhetoric and his substantial use of "vituperative" rhetoric as being distinctive and, more importantly, destructive to the institution of the presidency and American democracy more generally.[40] Kira Hall et al. highlight Trump's use of comedic, spectacle-driven, and entertaining rhetoric as crucial to his political success in a time of late

---

likelihood that people will accept the misinformation." Increasing the presence of misinformation, in other words, increases its acceptance. See Maxime Lepoutre, *Democratic Speech in Divided Times* (New York: Oxford University Press, 2021), 116.

[39] See Rebecca Morin, "Trump: My Social Media Use Is 'Modern Day Presidential,'" *Politico*, July 1, 2017, https://www.politico.com/story/2017/07/01/trump-tweets-modern-day-presidential-240170.
[40] Mary E. Stuckey, "'The Power of the Presidency to Hurt': The Indecorous Rhetoric of Donald J. Trump and the Rhetorical Norms of Democracy," *Presidential Studies Quarterly* 50, no. 2 (2020): 366–91.

capitalism,[41] something also considered by Giuseppina Scotto di Carlo in her comparison of Trump's rhetoric to that of Silvio Berlusconi.[42] With regard to the racial features of Trump's rhetoric, Rogers Smith and Desmond King detail Trump's use of what they call the rhetoric of "white protectionism,"[43] whereas Casey Ryan Kelly discusses Trump's use of ressentiment-fueled rhetoric to appeal to angry white voters as being particularly remarkable,[44] a claim that is akin to one made by Jeff Maskovsky, who describes Trump's use of "white nationalist postracial" rhetoric as key to his success.[45] William Connolly goes further, suggesting that Trump's rhetoric is similar to fascistic rhetoric,[46] something that is also entertained by Bonnie Honig.[47] And, indeed, Ayal Feinberg et al. argue that Trump's rhetoric at rallies led to a rise in "hate-motivated events," which were caused by fear induced in predominately white audiences.[48]

Following the storming of the Capitol, new scholarship on Trump's rhetoric and its relation to the attempted putsch has begun to emerge. Thus far, analyses have focused on the possibly distinctive features of Trump's speech on January 6 relative to his other speeches, the connections between the events of January 6 and historical precedents (both domestic and international), and the significance of broader social phenomena such as the global rise of far-right populism and the increased political viability of white supremacist movements.[49] In social psychology, work is being produced on the relatability of Trump's rhetoric, as well as the silo-ing effects of social media,

---

[41] Kira Hall, Donna M. Goldstein, and Matthew Bruce Ingram, "The Hands of Donald Trump: Entertainment, Gesture, and Spectacle," *HAU: Journal of Ethnographic Theory* 6, no. 2 (2016): 71–100.

[42] Giuseppina Scotto di Carlo, "The 'Trumpusconi' Phenomenon: A Comparative Discourse Analysis of US President Trump's and Former Italian Prime Minister Berlusconi's Political Speeches," *International Journal of Language Studies* 14, no. 2 (2020): 43–72.

[43] Rogers M. Smith and Desmond King, "White Protectionism in America," *Perspectives on Politics* 19, no. 2 (2021): 460–78.

[44] Casey Ryan Kelly, "Donald J. Trump and the Rhetoric of *Ressentiment*," *Quarterly Journal of Speech* 106, no. 1 (2020): 2–24.

[45] Jeff Maskovsky, "Toward the Anthropology of White Nationalist Postracialism: Comments Inspired by Hall, Goldstein, and Ingram's, 'The Hands of Donald Trump,'" *HAU: Journal of Ethnographic Theory* 7, no. 1 (2017): 433–40.

[46] William E. Connolly, "Trump, the Working Class, and Fascist Rhetoric," *Theory & Event* 20, no. 1 (2017): 23–37.

[47] Bonnie Honig, "Trump's Presidency Is Not So 'Unprecedented' after All," *ABC Religion & Ethics*, September 12, 2018, updated September 14, 2018, https://www.abc.net.au/religion/american-politics-hasnt-changed-under-trump/10235820.

[48] Ayal Feinberg, Regina Branton, and Valerie Martinez-Ebers, "The Trump Effect: How 2016 Campaign Rallies Explain Spikes in Hate," *PS: Political Science and Politics* 55, no. 2 (2022): 257–65.

[49] One of the first prominent academic engagements concerning the attempted putsch was a "forum" in the journal *Terrorism and Political Violence*. See Jeffrey Kaplan, "Introduction to the 6 January Forum," *Terrorism and Political Violence* 33, no. 5 (2021): 901–2.

which may have combined on January 6 to produce a crowd primed to storm the Capitol.[50]

Yet, in terms of both content and style, the speeches on January 6 from Trump and his backers were notably like those that had been given in the weeks and months leading up to (and following) the insurrection.[51] Trump and other prominent Republicans—including congresspeople, media personalities, and Trump's personal lawyers—alleged voter fraud daily in the weeks and months leading up to and then following the insurrection. From the Rose Garden, to Four Seasons Total Landscaping, to the *Fox News* airways, claims of a conspiracy against Trump and his supporters have been repeated persistently. According to reports, in the twenty-four days after the election alone, Trump tweeted or re-tweeted at least 200 posts containing misinformation or falsities.[52] And, as Hayley Miller writes, in the roughly two months between election day and January 6, Trump personally "lied that the election was rigged at least 68 times and that it was stolen or in the process of being stolen at least 35 times." She goes on, "He made claims of voter fraud and ballot-counting irregularities more than 250 times, specifically making baseless claims that voting machines tossed or changed votes at least 45 times."[53] In their repetition, claims supporting the "big lie" became commonplace.

It is in the repetition of the claims of election fraud that their perlocutionary force is most prominently located. That is, it is in the telling and retelling of claims, and the corresponding associated resonant effects, that the cumulative force of the rhetoric of the "big lie" becomes discernible. Through multiple repetitions of claims of massive fraud, a horizon of understanding which sees election denial as not only possible, but permissible and even central to many people's worldview, became entrenched.

Repetition, most glaringly of falsehoods, has been a key rhetorical technique of Trump's for years. For example, the *New York Times*, reporting on

---

[50] Helen C. Harton, Matthew Gunderson, and Martin J. Bourgeois, "'I'll Be There with You': Social Influence and Cultural Emergence at the Capitol on January 6," *Group Dynamics: Theory, Research, and Practice* 26, no. 3 (2022): 220–38.

[51] See Max Taylor, "Some Preliminary Thoughts Prompted by President Trump's 6 January Speech: Words, Enemies, Affordances," *Terrorism and Political Violence* 33, no. 5 (2021): 907–11.

[52] Todd Spangler, "Twitter Has Flagged 200 of Trump's Posts as 'Disputed' or Misleading since Election Day. Does It Make a Difference?," *Variety*, November 27, 2020, https://variety.com/2020/digital/news/twitter-trump-200-disputed-misleading-claims-election-1234841137/.

[53] Haley Miller, "Trump Claimed Election 'Rigged' or 'Stolen' over 100 Times Ahead of Capitol Riot, *Huffington Post*, February 8, 20221, updated February 9, 2021, https://www.huffpost.com/entry/trump-rigged-stolen-capitol-riot_n_602188e2c5b6173dd2f88c4f.

Trump's falsehoods over his first year in office, remarks at their incredible pace and commonplace quality,[54] noting that within only ten months of being in office, Trump had already accumulated as many as six times the total number of public lies as did Barack Obama over his full eight years in office.[55] A *Washington Post* tracker of Trump falsehoods lists 30,573 individual public instances made over his four years as president (or 21 public falsehoods per day), with escalating daily totals reaching a crescendo during the final days of his presidency.[56] Indeed, on the day prior to the 2020 election, the *Post* noted 503 public falsehoods—a capstone on a trend of increased falsehoods throughout his presidency. While these falsehoods cover many themes, many of the same claims were repeated persistently, most significantly the "big lie" of a stolen election.[57]

One possible effect of the broadcasting of persistent falsehoods is a withering away of the ground upon which true and false claims regarding phenomena like election fraud can be differentiated. Chambers and Kopstein discuss this in conjunction with what they perceive as elite-driven "wrecking" of the public sphere. The authors claim that incessant lying wreaks havoc on the public's ability to generate, discuss, defend, and challenge opinions—something also discussed in detail by Lisa Wedeen within the Syrian context.[58] This rendering "fuzzy the line between reality and unreality," the authors claim, makes "uncertain what is truth to begin with."[59] All told,

---

[54] David Leonhardt and Stuart A. Thompson, "Trump's Lies," *New York Times*, December 14, 2017, https://www.nytimes.com/interactive/2017/06/23/opinion/trumps-lies.html.

[55] David Leonhardt, Ian Prasad Philbrick, and Stuart A. Thompson, "Trump's Lies vs. Obama's," *New York Times*, December 14, 2017, https://www.nytimes.com/interactive/2017/12/14/opinion/sunday/trump-lies-obama-who-is-worse.html.

[56] Glenn Kessler, Salvador Rizzo, and Meg Kelly, "Trump's False or Misleading Claims Total 30,573 over 4 Years," *Washington Post*, January 24, 2021, https://www.washingtonpost.com/politics/2021/01/24/trumps-false-or-misleading-claims-total-30573-over-four-years/.

[57] Hawkman and Diem argue that characterizing the lie of election fraud specifically as the "big lie" can function to render all other lies as truths, thereby erasing the presence of systemic white supremacy, which is defended, they argue, by many of Trump's (and others') lies. Indeed, the attack on the Capitol, they argue, is inextricably linked to white supremacy. See Andrea M. Hawkman and Sarah Diem, "The Big Lie(s): Situating the January 6th Coup Attempt within White Supremacist Lies," *Cultural Studies← → Critical Methodologies* 22, no. 5 (2022): 490–504.

[58] Simone Chambers and Jeffrey Kopstein, "Wrecking the Public Sphere: The New Authoritarians' Digital Attack on Pluralism and Truth," *Constellations* 30, no. 3 (2023): 225–40; and Lisa Wedeen, *Authoritarian Apprehensions: Ideology, Judgment, and Mourning in Syria* (Chicago: University of Chicago Press, 2019).

[59] Chambers and Kopstein, "Wrecking the Public Sphere," 10. One mechanism that helps to produce this epistemic occlusion is the act of turning the "fake news" phenomenon on its head, with elites claiming that legitimate news which they dislike (such as claims that the election was *not* fraudulent) is itself "fake news." The authors refer to this as "fake fake news," which is also discussed in Simone Chambers, "Truth, Deliberative Democracy, and the Virtues of Accuracy: Is Fake News Destroying the Public Sphere?," *Political Studies* 69, no. 1 (2021): 147–63.

the effect is to "hollow out the conventional mechanisms by which public opinion takes shape," enabling the mass spread of problematic and pernicious worldviews.[60] Rather than being something which is accomplished by singular acts, by epistemic haymakers so to speak, it is the repeated jabs directed toward a society's epistemic ecosystem that cause massive epistemic damage.[61] In such an environment, falsehoods flourish.

With regard to the argument of this chapter, however, what is most significant is not necessarily the falsehoods themselves, nor even the *general* systemic epistemic damage done to the public sphere, but that audiences ceased to find the falsehoods the least bit surprising, with many, over time, echoing claims of election fraud themselves. In their influential 2019 book, *A Lot of People Are Saying*, Muirhead and Rosenblum write, "what mattered was not evidence but the number of retweets the president's post would enjoy: the more retweets, the more credible the charge."[62] For Muirhead and Rosenblum, repetition, rather than reasons or the rhetorical force of a singular piece of oratory, appeared to matter most for Trump influencing his "followers."[63] Corroborating Muirhead and Rosenblum's claim, Trump's eventual de-platforming from Twitter (and a corresponding silencing of his echoing claims of election fraud from the platform) in early 2021 allegedly produced a 73% decrease in election misinformation on the highly popular platform in the week following Trump's ban.[64] Hearing unsurprising falsehoods over and over again enabled the centering of those untruths in the horizons of audiences. When the resonant river of misinformation was

---

[60] Chambers and Kopstein, "Wrecking the Public Sphere," 10–11. The authors discuss how former Trump advisor Steve Bannon has explicitly acknowledged this strategy of epistemic destruction for political gain.

[61] Hannah Arendt famously also discusses this phenomenon. See Hannah Arendt, "Truth and Politics," in Arendt, *Between Past and Future* (New York: Penguin, 2006), 223–59.

[62] Russell Muirhead and Nancy L Rosenblum, *A Lot of People Are Saying: The New Conspiracism and the Assault on Democracy* (Princeton, NJ: Princeton University Press, 2019), 3

[63] Muirhead and Rosenblum refer to the then-president as the "Conspiracist in Chief." See ibid., xiii.

[64] Elizabeth Dwoskin and Craig Timberg, "Misinformation Dropped Dramatically the Week after Twitter Banned Trump and Some Allies: Zignal Labs Charts 73 Percent Decline on Twitter and Beyond Following Historic Action against the President," *Washington Post*, January 16, 2021, https://www.washingtonpost.com/technology/2021/01/16/misinformation-trump-twitter/. Chambers and Kopstein highlight this decrease in election misinformation when they argue that "bad actors" harm democracy by "wrecking" the public sphere. These bad actors, they argue, are far more dangerous than the technology they use (such as social media). A Berkman Klein Center for Internet & Society at Harvard University study arguably corroborates this argument. See Chambers and Kopstein, "Wrecking the Public Sphere"; and Carolyn Schmitt, Yochai Benkler, Casey Tilton, Bruce Etling, Hal Roberts, Justin Clark, Robert Faris and Jonas Kaiser, "Mail-in Voter Fraud: Anatomy of a Disinformation Campaign," *Berkman Klein Center for Internet & Society at Harvard University*, published October 1, 2020, https://cyber.harvard.edu/publication/2020/Mail-in-Voter-Fraud-Disinformation-2020.

blocked (with Trump's ban), so too did the associated flood of misinformation recede.

Of course, Trump was not alone in repeatedly claiming that the election was fraudulent, nor was Twitter (now "X") the only platform where such claims existed or continue to exist. In fact, it is notable just how widespread the rhetoric of election fraud is on the right, where the increasingly far-right Republican Party[65] has largely taken on the rhetoric of the "big lie."[66] Indeed, in both "legacy media" such as conservative talk radio and broadcast networks like *Fox News*, as well as in social media, there exists a right-wing media ecosystem that has regularly promoted the "big lie." Unsurprisingly, consumption of such media has been shown to be a predictor for belief in conspiracies, including the "big lie."[67]

The roots of this associated embrace of dubious claims pre-date Trump,[68] but it has accelerated, transformed, and increasingly radicalized,[69] under and now following Trump's political rise. And, while similar events to the January 6th insurrection spurred by far-right specious rhetoric have occurred in the past both within the United States and globally,[70] the current far-right and ethnonationalist turn in U.S. politics has gained new energy during Trump's political tenure, as has an associated increase in politicians and media members providing "alternative facts."[71]

---

[65] According to the *Washington Post*, as of 2021–2022, 22% of Republican state legislators were members of far-right Facebook groups. See Dana Milbank, "Not-So-Great Replacement: Extremists Become GOP Mainstream," *Washington Post*, May 16, 2022, https://www.washingtonpost.com/opinions/2022/05/16/republicans-far-right-group-statistics/. Relatedly, one criticism of Muirhead and Rosenblum (2019) is that the authors fail to appreciate the seemingly far-right character of the Republican Party and the party's centrality to "new conspiracism" in the United States. Similarly, critics highlight the book's lack of engagement with white supremacy as a guiding objective for new conspiracism. See James A. Morone, Judith Grant, Cristóbal Rovira Kaltwasser, Lawrie Balfour, Steven Smallpage, and Lida Maxwell, "A Discussion of Russell Muirhead and Nancy L. Rosenblum's *A Lot of People Are Saying: The New Conspiracism and the Assault on Democracy*," *Perspectives on Politics* 18, no. 4 (2020): 1150–61.

[66] See Anderson, "The January 6 Insurrection."

[67] Anthony R. DiMaggio, "Conspiracy Theories and the Manufacture of Dissent: QAnon, the 'Big Lie,' COVID-19, and the Rise of Rightwing Propaganda," *Critical Sociology* 48, no. 6 (2022): 1025–48.

[68] David T. Canon and Owen Sherman, "Debunking the 'Big Lie': Election Administration in the 2020 Presidential Election," *Presidential Studies Quarterly* 51, no. 3 (2021): 546–81, 547.

[69] Chambers and Kopstein argue that there is an asymmetry regarding the stickiness of misinformation in the U.S. public sphere, which is partly the product of an elite-driven radicalization of the Republican base. Radicalization in this instance is contrasted with polarization, with the former being associated with a willingness to "bend the rules" to keep power away from one's political opponents. See Chambers and Kopstein, "Wrecking the Public Sphere."

[70] See ibid.

[71] Then Trump advisor, Kellyanne Conway, coined the term "alternative facts" in 2017 when responding to a question concerning then-press secretary, Sean Spicer, appearing to have lied about the size of the crowd at Trump's inauguration. Rather than telling a falsehood, Spicer, claimed

This turn, and a corresponding embrace of election denial, developed throughout the Trump presidency. As far back as 2016, Trump publicly stated he would not concede an election loss, a promise which was repeated multiple times over the next four years.[72] And, holding true to these promises, Trump denied primary election defeats in 2016 and then later denied that he had lost the popular vote in that year's presidential election. What is more, the domain name "stopthesteal" was registered in 2016 by Trump ally Roger Stone in response to Trump's claims of fraud after losing to Ted Cruz in a Republican statewide primary contest. Indeed, following primary losses in 2016, small groups of Trump supporters gathered and chanted "stop the steal," a prelude for what was to come four years later. Populist claims of a shadowy, evil "deep state" working against "the people" had also been peddled for years, as had attacks on the media, with the press regularly being called "fake news" or, more severely, "enemies of the people." These features combined to produce a deep suspicion of any source contradicting the Trumpist line.

For Trump supporters, claims of elections "stolen" were, thus, old-hat by January 2021—something that they had been primed to expect for a long time. By the time of the attack on the Capitol, they had already been told that there was a conspiracy against their chosen candidate for years, cementing belief in a rigged system. This was coupled with long-standing claims that the Democrats were radical and corrupt, with Democratic leaders regularly being characterized as part of a nefarious "deep state" or, worse, members of secret pedophilia rings.[73] Supporters of the then-president were, thus, conditioned to believe the fix was in. They were also primed to view as suspicious any claim that was critical of this belief. Indeed, a large percentage of Republicans were committed to challenging the election result if it appeared that Trump had lost or was losing even *prior* to the 2020 election occurring.[74]

Conway, provided "alternative facts." See Jim Rutenberg, "'Alternative Facts' and the Costs of Trump-Branded Reality," *New York Times*, January 22, 2017, https://www.nytimes.com/2017/01/22/business/media/alternative-facts-trump-brand.html. The term marked an evolution from the infamous "not intended to be a factual statement" line from then-senator John Kyl (R-Ariz.), which he delivered after he was called out for providing a falsehood about Planned Parenthood in 2011.

[72] Brendan Hartnett and Alexandra Haver, "Unconditional Support for Trump's Resistance Prior to Election Day," *PS: Political Science & Politics* 55, no. 4 (2022): 661–7.
[73] The latter claim is central to the QAnon conspiracy theory.
[74] See Hartnett and Haver, "Unconditional Support." Hartnett and Haver argue that support for resisting the election was a matter of partisanship, rather than belief in misinformation about election fraud. However, the extent to which these reasoning frameworks can be separated can be questioned.

As Lane Crothers writes, "The insurrectionists thus claimed that they needed to support Trump not just out of a sense of personal loyalty, but also because he had won the election legitimately and they needed to work to 'stop the steal.'"[75]

Given the widespread, oft-repeated, and long-standing nature of claims of a stolen election(s), it is unlikely that specific speech acts were taken as especially noteworthy or exceptional, particularly those that occurred relatively late in a long progression of similar claims. Indeed, many of the vehicles of communication through which election falsehoods were disseminated do not especially lend themselves to a momentous reception. Twitter posts (now "X" posts) are a prime example. Tweets are limited to only 280 characters, are consumed daily and perfunctorily, and are read wherever the reader happens to be at the moment they look at their phone, computer, or tablet. Tweets are mundane and ordinary rhetorical performances, not exceptional ones. Likewise, the rhetoric one hears on the radio and on television is also likely to be taken in stride, for the simple reason that people regularly turn to the same news and media sources, which turn out characteristic coverage. And, while a Trump or "My Pillow Guy" rally might make for a rarified occasion, thereby putting an audience member in an altered state of reception, the rhetoric of election fraud itself is likely highly predictable for audience members, as it reinforces rather than challenges expectations. Such rhetoric is akin to playing the "old hits" rather than new music.

Thus, a different theory of persuasion is required to account for the persuasive effects of the rhetoric of election fraud from that which is offered by much of the rhetoric revival literature. I argue that the metaphor of "resonance" captures this form of persuasion. It is the added effects of repeated claims of election fraud that construct a new discursive possibility, that shift interpretive horizons. Individual claims of fraud resonated with preexisting claims and thus were received in stride. The more these claims were repeated, the more central they became to the audience's interpretive horizon; they resonated moving forward in time. Indeed, when tweets were coupled with other social media posts, podcast commentaries, radio broadcasts, internet articles, videos, and so on, a world of election fraud was reinforced. This iterative horizonal shifting over time created the conditions of possibility that enabled the storming of the Capitol. The continual rhetoric of a

---

[75] Lane Crothers, "Insurrectionary Populism? Assessing the January 6 Attack on the U.S. Capitol," *Populism* 4 (2021): 129–45.

stolen election and a mass conspiracy created a world where that position became central to the interpretive horizon of audience members. Thus, the attempted putsch should not be understood as surprising, or as an act made possible because a crowd was whipped up into a frenzy by singular speeches moments before it occurred. Rather, the attempted putsch was the product of the cumulative effects of resonant rhetoric, which has the power to transform ordinary speech into extraordinary politics.

The Normative Effects of Resonant Rhetoric

While my argument is that it is the resonant nature of the "big lie" that persuaded so many to believe the election to be rigged and fraudulent, resonant rhetoric is not itself a negative phenomenon. Indeed, most rhetoric, insofar as it is not jarring, disruptive, momentous, and so on, is resonant. Resonant rhetoric is as much a feature of liberal discourse as it is of populist discourse; it is as democratic as it is authoritarian. Indeed, it is a feature of the rhetoric of the orator who seeks to appeal to an audience's reason, as much as it is of the rhetoric of the demagogue. Our interpretive horizons generally provide us with the means to make sense of that which we confront. Resonance, thus, is our ordinary mode of reception. And, while resonance may not be conducive to the kinds of critical reflection or reflective judgment associated with the good forms of rhetoric celebrated by the rhetoric revival literature, if the message being delivered by resonant rhetoric is positive, so too will be the effects, as they will reverberate over time. Repeated claims that promote anti-oppressive praxis can have profound transformative effects of normalizing those anti-oppressive modes of being, cementing those practices in the horizons of audience members. Indeed, while he does not use the language of resonance, it is for this reason that Maxime Lepoutre advocates for what he calls "diachronic positive counterspeech" when combating misinformation.[76] Flooding the public sphere with the truth,[77] or with just and equitable claims, can have positive epistemic effects. Conversely, negatively valanced rhetoric, rhetoric that supports white supremacy for example, when received resonantly is almost certainly going to be highly damaging.

---

[76] Lepoutre, "Democratic Speech," 106–28.
[77] It is beyond the scope of this chapter to provide, defend, or discuss rival accounts of "truth."

The implication here is that rhetoric is never "mere" rhetoric. A politician saying something while failing to act on it, still has a political effect which should not be dismissed. Simply making a claim to an audience can have the transformative effect of centering that claim within that audience's horizon of possible or permissible opinion. Repeated similar claims can have a sedimenting effect, building over time. The kinds of speech that we promote in our society matter for shaping discursive futures, regardless of whether there is action that corresponds to such speech.[78] Indeed, as the constructivist turn in political theory reminds us, claims that "mobilize" populations (into, for example, a constituency of election deniers) can have massive political ramifications, shaping political communities moving forward in time.[79] Speech is a powerful thing.

This is why a recent Democratic Party strategy of backing far-right, election-denying Republican candidates during the primary stages of elections, for example, may be counterproductive to Democratic Party ends. Some high-ranking Democrats pursued this policy because they believed extremist candidates would perform poorly in the general election. However, providing a podium for these candidates to spout such rhetoric may push the electorate further to the right. While they may not win general elections (though this is by no means a certainty), such candidates lay the rhetorical groundwork for entrenched far-right politics. In much the same way that the Tea Party previously paved the way for Trump by normalizing particular forms of far-right politics in the United States, the gamble of providing a bigger microphone for far-right candidates may simply pave the way for a more entrenched far-right politics in the years to come. Electoral defeat does not mean ideational defeat, and a bigger microphone can reify far-right horizons. Insofar as the rhetoric of election denialism is received as resonant—increasingly likely the more it is uttered—the more those ideas seem plausible, possible, and permissible moving forward. After all, who would have thought in 2011 that the majority of the Republican Party ten years later would view an attack on the U.S. Capitol and a corresponding effort to overturn a democratic election as "legitimate political discourse"?

---

[78] This, of course, does not imply that political action is unimportant.
[79] See, e.g., Lisa Disch, *Making Constituencies: Representation as Mobilization in Mass Democracy* (Chicago: University of Chicago Press, 2021).

Conclusion

Giuseppe Ballacci and Rob Goodman

As we observed in the Introduction, our approach to the study of populism draws in important ways from the tradition of rhetorical analysis. Much more than a shared definition or evaluation of populism, rhetoric as a method of analysis is a unifying theme of this collection. While this volume does not posit a transhistorical ideology of capital-p Populism, it does presume the value of rhetorical analysis across a wide range of historical contexts, many of them quite distant from the contexts in which classical rhetoric developed. Despite its origins in classical antiquity, the rhetorical tradition has turned out to be highly relevant to the contemporary analysis of populism. In this Conclusion, we briefly note three key ways in which the rhetorical tradition remains valuable, and even essential, to the study of populism.

First, the classical tradition of rhetoric has long maintained an interest in the non-discursive elements of political persuasion—that is, those elements that cannot be directly reduced to argumentation. Of the five traditional "canons" of rhetoric, only the first two, *inventio* and *dispositio*, are strictly concerned with arguments and their arrangement. *Elocutio* could be said to lie at the intersection of argumentation and verbal style, while *memoria* and *actio* are canons of performance and delivery.[1] So while the tradition's foundational texts are explicitly dedicated to questions of verbal discourse, rhetoric's interest in the non-discursive has also made it suitable to much broader adaptation. Rhetoric is the study of persuasion, but it also includes the study of symbols, aesthetics, and performances—and this enlarged notion of rhetoric is very much on display in this volume's contributions. A speech can be analyzed from the standpoint of rhetoric, but—as the contributors to this volume show—so can architecture or the construction of political celebrity. As we have argued, this approach is especially essential

---

[1] Cicero, *De Inventione, De Optimo Genere Oratorum, Topica*. With an English translation by H. M. Hubbell. (Loeb Classical Library) (London: Heinemann, 1949).

to the study of populism, given the way in which populist arguments are implicit in and bound to distinctively populist styles and forms.

Second, then, our approach to the study of populism is rhetorical because it stresses the integration of content and form. Rhetoric, as both discipline and practice, has long been intimately concerned with the interrelation of *res* and *verba*: things and words, or content and form.[2] This concern is one of the essential through-lines of the rhetorical tradition, from classical antiquity to the present.[3] Take, for instance, Cicero's dialogue *De oratore*, his most important work of rhetorical theory. A participant in the dialogue suggests that one interlocutor should discuss the substance of speeches, while another discusses their style. Cicero has his mentor Crassus vehemently object to the idea:

> [It] divided two things that cannot exist separately. For since all discourse is made up of content and words [*omnis ex re atque verbis constet oratio*], the words cannot have any basis if you withdraw the content, and the content will remain in the dark if you remove the words.... Discovering words for a distinguished style is impossible without having produced and shaped the thoughts, and ... no thought can shine clearly without the enlightening power of words.[4]

The idea that content and form cannot be considered separately was, in fact, at the core of Cicero's rhetorical and philosophical view. In the same *De oratore*, he makes Crassus call for an end to the long quarrel between philosophy and rhetoric—the former concerned with the content and the latter with form—and emphatically defend their necessary union. According to Crassus's argument, if originally "knowledge of the most important things as well as practical involvement in them was, as a whole, called 'philosophy,'" the propagation of Socrates's idea that "the knowledge of forming wise opinions and of speaking with distinction" were two different enterprises led to their fatal separation.[5]

---

[2] See A. C. Howell, "*Res et Verba*: Words and Things," *ELH* 13, no. 2 (1946): 131–42.

[3] Giuseppe Ballacci, *Political Theory between Philosophy and Rhetoric: Politics as Transcendence and Contingency* (London: Palgrave Macmillan, 2018); Rob Goodman, *Words on Fire: Eloquence and Its Conditions* (Cambridge, UK: Cambridge University Press, 2022), 31–41.

[4] Cicero, *On the Ideal Orator [De oratore]*, trans. James M. May and Jakob Wisse (New York: Oxford University Press, 2001), 3.19, 24.

[5] Ibid., 3.60. On the union between philosophy and rhetoric in ancient rhetoric, see Ballacci, *Political Theory between Philosophy and Rhetoric*.

Quintilian, following this line of thought, offered similar advice to his students when he wrote: "Let care in words be solicitude for things [*curam ergo verborum rerum volo esse sollicitudine*]. For generally the best words are inseparable from their things and are discovered by their light." In contrast to those who viewed rhetoric as a mere ornament to pre-given and separate content, Quintilian insisted that "every utterance through which someone manifests a will necessarily has content and word" (*Inst. or.* 3.1.5). That is, the production and communication of meaning are part of the same endeavor.

In the humanistic tradition of rhetoric that grew from the work of Cicero and Quintilian, *ornatus* (the use of tropes and figures of speech to adorn a discourse) is understood not as an *a posteriori* embellishment of preexisting content, but as an essential contribution to that content. For instance, as Quentin Skinner explains in his analysis of the figure of *paradiastole*, or redescription, the figure does not simply allow an orator to express the same content in a range of ways.[6] Rather, it implies an essential alteration of the way in which we represent and thus understand the same facts: it is not a substitution of *verbum pro verbo*, but of *res pro re*. In fact, the great scholar of humanism Ernesto Grassi has argued that this attention to the constitutive interrelation of *res* and *verba*, subject-matter and its discursive articulation, is *the* distinctive trait of ancient rhetoric, particularly of the Roman and humanistic tradition.[7]

To study populism through its integration of *res* and *verba*—of what it has to say, and how it chooses to say it—is precisely to study it rhetorically, in the full sense of rhetoric. Even as the rhetorical tradition emphasizes the interrelation of form and content, it also assumes that this relationship can assume different configurations in different temporal and social contexts. Unlike an approach more sharply limited to populist discourse or style, a rhetorical perspective on populism thus enables us to recognize the mutually constitutive relationship of its form and content, and to treat this relationship as a problem to be explored and understood, rather than flattened out. Thus, while not all of the chapters in this volume have focused specifically on populist rhetoric, and while some have defended a "materialist" reading of populism, rhetoric—in the broad sense of the integration of form and content—has been a motivating impulse of this volume.

---

[6] Quentin Skinner, *Reason and Rhetoric in the Philosophy of Hobbes* (Cambridge, UK: Cambridge University Press, 1997), 144.
[7] Ernesto Grassi, *Rhetoric as Philosophy: The Humanist Tradition* (University Park: Pennsylvania State University Press, 1980).

Third and finally, rhetorical analysis, as we understand it, is committed to the investigation of controversial questions through argumentation *in utramque partem*, or on either side of the question. A classical statement of this commitment comes in Cicero's *De oratore*, and is again attributed to Crassus:

> [C]opiously arguing both sides of a general issue . . . is considered to be characteristic of the two philosophical schools that I discussed earlier [the Academic and the Peripatetic]. But among the ancients, it belonged to those who furnished the entire method and the whole fullness necessary for speaking about matters arising in public life. And rightly so, for we orators, too, should possess both the power and the art of speaking on both sides of an issue on the topics of virtue, moral duty, the fair and the good, the honorable and the expedient, honor, disgrace, rewards, punishments, and similar subjects.[8]

The alleged injustice that troubles Cicero's orators in this case—that philosophers have "invaded our inherited property" by passing off argumentation *in utramque partem* as their own invention—need not concern us here.[9] But the broader claim is worth pausing over: a method initially developed for the resolution of discrete political controversies can be applied to questions of much greater scope and breadth. For Skinner, this is "the central contention of rhetorical theory, the contention that there are two sides to every question, and thus that one can always argue *in utramque partem*."[10]

This book has also been informed by that contention—its spirit, at least, if not its letter. We can hardly reduce the questions raised by this volume's authors to two sides in direct conflict. Yet this book has not offered a "party line" on populism, its value, or its relationship with democracy. Instead, it has offered a wide range of contexts and comparisons—as well as a wide range of evaluations, in which populism appears as everything from a political pathology to a potential saving grace. We made this choice not from an absence of conviction, but from the presence of a very strong one: that the best way to get at the nature of populism is through a commitment to "copiously arguing." And in keeping with the rhetorical tradition, we leave the last word on all of these arguments to our audience—that is, to you.

---

[8] Cicero, *De or.*, 3.107–8.
[9] Ibid., 3.108.
[10] Skinner, *Reason and Rhetoric in the Philosophy of Hobbes*, 10.

Index

For the benefit of digital users, indexed terms that span two pages (e.g., 52–53) may, on occasion, appear on only one of those pages.

Acciaiuoli, Niccola, 131–32, 153
Acharnians (Aristophanes), 50–54
Adams, John, 180
Adams, John Quincy, 180, 244–45, 244n.12, 246, 254, 255–56
Adenauer, Konrad, 259
Aeschylus, 29, 48, 59–60
Albert the Great, 131–32
Alcibiades
    demagoguery and, 13, 56, 60, 183–85, 305–6
    flattery and, 184–85
    on his own superiority, 41–42
    parrhêsia and, 41–42
    Plutarch's account of, 176, 183–85
    Sicily expedition and, 39–40, 41, 42
alêthê (truth), 45–46
Alternative for Germany party (AfD), 217
The American Democrat (Cooper)
    anti-pluralism and, 175–76
    candor and, 193–94, 198–99
    demagoguery and, 21–22, 173–74, 175–76, 178–79, 181, 185–86, 188–89, 195–200
    on "the gentleman" and American political life, 194–95, 197–98, 199
    liberty and, 189, 191
    Menken's introduction to, 175
    pedagogical aims of, 175–76, 178–79, 185–87
    populism and, 175–76, 199–200
    proposed remedies for demagoguery in, 189–95, 196–97
    on public duties of private citizens, 192–94
    public opinion and, 187–89
    tyranny of the majority and, 174
Ankersmi, Frank, 218
anti-intellectualism, 8–9, 178
anti-parliamentarism
    anarchism and, 205–6
    anti-plutocracy and, 224
    anti-proceduralism and, 213–15

direct democracy and, 201–2, 206–8, 214–15, 218
    expert commissions and, 211
    monarchy and, 22, 205
    nationalist movements and, 210
    Pareto and, 223, 224–25
    populism and, 201–2, 204, 206–7, 208–9, 212–13, 215, 218–19, 220
    presidentialism and, 205, 206–7, 208, 214–15, 218
    professional politicians as target of criticism in, 207–9
    reduction of parliamentary powers and, 208
    temporal dynamics of politics and, 215–18
    topoi of, 22, 204, 209–13, 220
    See also parliamentarism
Antonius, Marcus (the elder), 90–93
Antonius, Marcus (the younger), 80–81, 89–93, 97–99
Apology of Socrates (Plato), 31, 45–47, 52, 76–77
Aquinas, Thomas, 106–7, 131–32, 133–34
Arditi, Benjamin, 10
Aristides, Aelius, 165–66
Aristophanes
    Cleon and, 51–52, 60–61
    demagoguery and, 13, 56, 60–61
    isêgoria and, 31–32
    parrhêsia and, 18, 30, 31, 50–54
    See also specific works
Aristotle
    demagoguery and, 13–14, 182–83, 278–80
    democracy and, 13–14, 20–21, 56, 61–62, 124–34, 131n.29, 135–36, 137–38, 140, 141–42, 144–45, 276–77, 309–10
    Machiavelli and, 125, 136–38, 144
    oligarchy and, 127, 130–31
    the poor and, 20–21, 124–34, 131n.29, 135–36, 137–38, 140, 141–42, 144–45
    republicanism and, 123, 125–26, 142–43
    rhetoric and, 148–50
    on the wisdom of the multitude, 134, 143

Asianist rhetorical style, 91
The Assembly (Athens)
  Alcibiades and, 60
  Archanians and, 50–52
  Cleon and, 35, 36–37, 60
  Diodotus and, 36, 43–44, 54
  isêgoria and, 31–32
  parrhêsia and, 18, 31, 33, 36, 43–44, 54
Athens
  Aristides on the virtues of, 166
  classical architecture and, 246
  demagoguery and, 13, 70
  democracy and, 13–14, 29, 31–32, 37, 41–42, 44–45, 48–49, 55–62, 66, 132–33, 304–5
  empire and, 34–35, 37
  Mytilenians and, 34–36, 38–39, 42–43
  Peloponnesian War defeat of, 44–45
  Persian War and, 35
  plague (430 BCE) in, 59
  populism and, 19
  Sicily expedition and, 39–44, 60–61
  Socrates's exclusion from, 44–45
  Thirty Tyrants' rule (404 BCE) in, 44–45, 56
Atticists
  Asianist rhetorical style and, 91
  Cicero and, 80–83, 84–86, 87–89, 91
  Demonsthenes, 84–86
  Julius Caesar and, 86, 87
  plainness of style and, 84, 87, 88–89
  republicanism and, 84
Augustine, 116–17

Babiš, Andrej, 331–32
Bachrach, Peter, 291
Bagehot, Walter, 203, 212
Baratz, Morton, 291
Baron, Hans, 123, 165–66, 167–68
Bartolus of Sassoferrato, 131–32, 153–54
Baudrillard, Jean, 335–36, 337
Bebel, August, 205–6
Behrens, Peter, 256
Benjamin, Walter, 261
Bentley, Arthur, 295–96
Berlin (Germany), 250–51, 253, 257–58, 277–78
Berlin, Isaiah, 270–71, 281–82
Berlin Reichstag attack (2020), 242–43, 265–66
Berlusconi, Silvio
  celebrity politics and, 327, 328, 331–32
  comedic rhetoric and, 351–52
  media empire of, 323
  "politainment" and, 315–16, 323, 338
  popular sovereignty calls by, 318
  populism and, 318, 327

"big lie" (election denialism in United States after 2020)
  erosion of democratic norms and, 292
  January 6 insurrection and, 342
  public opinion regarding, 342–43
  repetition of, 350–51, 360
  Republican Party and, 360
  as "resonant rhetoric," 346–47, 350–51, 359–60
  right-wing media ecosystem and, 356
Bismarck, Otto von, 205
Blackstone, William, 265
Boccaccio, 141–42, 154–55
Bolshevism, 306, 308
Bolsonaro, Jair
  celebrity politics and, 25, 315, 316, 339–40
  demagoguery and, 12
  "politainment" and, 315, 316, 334–35
  populism and, 12, 273–74, 316, 320
  social media and, 324–25
Bonn (Germany), 248
Borgen (Danish television program), 332–33
Boulanger, Georges, 206–7
Bracciolini, Poggio, 123, 146–47
Brandolini, Aurelio Lippo, 131–32, 141
Brasília (Brazil), architecture in, 254
Brasília parliament attack (2023), 242–43, 265–66
Brexit vote (United Kingdom, 2016), 312–13
Briguglia, Gianluca, 106–7, 121–22
Bruni, Leonardo
  Aristotle and, 164–65, 169–70
  Cicero and, 166–68
  democracy and, 131–33
  Florence celebrated by, 164–69
  humanism and, 147–48, 150–51, 157, 163
  republicanism and, 123, 141, 157, 163–65, 168
  rhetoric and, 157, 167–68
  virtuous rule and, 164–65, 168–70
  wealth and, 141
Brutus (Cicero), 83–84, 85, 86–87, 167–68
Brutus, Marcus Junius, 84–85
Buchanan, James, 259
Bucharest (Romania), 249
Burnham, James, 224–25

Caesar, Julius
  Antonius and, 91
  assassination of, 89
  Atticists and, 86, 87
  Catilinarian conspiracy (63 BCE) and, 110, 112–13

Cicero and, 80–83, 86–88, 90–91
Clodius and, 94
demagoguery and, 112–13
dictatorship consolidated (46 BCE) by, 83–84
imperialism and, 106–7, 121–22
public works and, 243
rhetorical style of, 86–87, 88–89, 90–91
Calmy-Rey, Micheline, 316
Calvus, Gaius Licinius, 84, 91, 96
Cambridge School, 123–24
Camillus, 153–54
Canovan, Margaret, 9–10, 319
Carafa, Diomede, 141
Carlyle, Thomas, 209–11
Carnegie, Andrew, 266
Casa del Fascio (Como, Italy), 252, 253
Catiline
  Catilinarian conspiracy (63 BCE) and, 106–7, 110, 112–13, 117–18, 119–20, 121–22, 159
  Cicero's evaluation of the rhetoric of, 80, 92–93
  death in battle of, 92–93
Cato, 106–7, 112–13
Ceaușescu, Nikolai, 249
celebrity politics
  digital media and, 324–26, 327
  epistemic power of celebrities and, 329–30
  hyperreality and, 25, 331–32, 334–37, 338–39
  illusion of intimacy and, 327–30
  media entertainment and, 25, 315, 326
  Perón (Eva) and, 315–16, 322, 327–28, 338
  "politainment" and, 25, 315–17, 332–35, 338–39
  populism and, 25, 315–16, 317–18, 321–22, 326, 328–29, 339–40
  reality television and, 330–31
  self-branding and, 324–25
  television and, 322–23
Charles I (king of Anjou), 118–19
Charles VIII (king of France), 134–35
Chartist Movement (Great Britain), 306
Chávez, Hugo, 269–70, 273–74, 275–76, 306, 327, 331–32
Churchill, Winston, 258–59, 260
Cicero, Marcus Tullius
  Antonius the elder and, 92
  Antonius the younger and, 89–93, 97–98
  Atticists and, 80–83, 84–86, 87–89, 91
  Catilinarian conspiracy (63 BCE) and, 112–13, 159
  decorum and, 88–89
  Demosthenes and, 89
  on difficulty of oratory, 97, 101
  doctrine of the three styles and, 85
  eloquence and, 88
  friendship and, 154
  humanism and, 146–47
  on inseparability of content and form, 362
  Julius Caesar and, 80–83, 86–88, 90–91
  Latini and, 20, 104–5, 106–7, 109–11, 112–13, 114–15, 116–18, 121–22
  on orators' relationship with an audience, 93–94, 96
  on oratory and social order, 110–11
  popularis rhetoric criticized by, 19–20, 82–83, 89–94, 96, 97–102
  republicanism and, 103–4, 108–9, 114–15, 116–17
  res publica identification of, 82, 97–99, 101
  rhetorical republicanism *versus* rationalist republicanism and, 20
  rhetoric and, 146–47, 148–50, 157–58, 159, 167–68
  on speeches to the senate *versus* speeches to the people, 99–100
  withdrawal from politics (46 BCE) by, 83–84
  See also specific works
civic humanism. *See* humanism
Cleisthenes, 58
Cleon
  Aristophanes and, 51–52, 60–61
  The Assembly and, 35, 36–37, 60
  Athenians described as "slaves" by, 35
  demagoguery and, 13, 56, 60–61, 305–6
  democracy and, 34–35
  Mytilenians and, 34–35, 36
  parrhêsia and, 34–35, 38
Clinton, Hillary, 313
Clodius, 80, 82–83, 92–94, 97, 99, 101–2
Code Napoleon, 265
Cola di Rienzo, 156–57
Cold War, 248, 271–72, 310
Cole, G. D. H., 284
Collor de Mello, Fernando Afonso, 316, 323, 333–34, 338
Communist Party (Soviet Union), 306, 309
Connolly, Joy, 108–9
Connolly, William, 296–97, 351–52
Cooper, James Fenimore
  biographical background of, 179–80
  demagoguery and, 21–22, 173–74
  education of, 179–80
  Plutarch and, 178–79, 181, 183–84, 185–86
  See also The American Democrat (Cooper)
Cooper, Susan Fenimore, 179

Coriolanus, 185, 313
Correa, Rafael, 269–70
Council of Five Hundred (Athens), 58
Crothers, Lane, 357–58
Cruz, Ted, 261, 357

Dahl, Robert
  checks and balances and, 271, 295–96
  on constitutional arrangements' inability to prevent tyranny, 295–96
  institutional reforms proposed by, 297
  New Haven studies of, 286–88
  on pluralism and oligarchy, 288–89
  on pluralism's normative goals, 293–94
  polyarchy and, 280, 285, 287–88, 289–92
  Rousseau and, 285–86
Davis, Charles Til, 105–6
De analogia (Julius Caesar), 86, 87
decisionism, 4–5, 8
decorum, 88–89, 96
De Gaulle, Charles, 208, 214–15
De inventione (Cicero), 103–5, 109, 111, 114–15, 146–47, 162
De legibus (Cicero), 103–4, 160–61, 165–66
demagoguery
  Alcibiades and, 13, 56, 60, 183–85, 305–6
  The American Democrat and, 21–22, 173–74, 175–76, 178–79, 181, 185–86, 188–89, 195–200
  Aristotle on, 13–14, 182–83, 278–80
  Athens and, 13, 70
  Cleon and, 13, 56, 60–61
  definition of, 173, 182
  democracy and, 15, 19, 62, 68, 185–89, 192–93, 196–97, 305–6
  etymology of, 13–14
  The Federalist Papers and, 173–74, 181–82
  flattery and, 14, 73–74, 76, 183–86, 188, 189–90, 195
  ideology and, 14
  in-group/out-group dynamics and, 176–77, 178, 190
  manipulation of crowds and, 67
  moralistic accounts of, 21–22, 175–76, 178–79, 181, 182–83, 195–97
  Plato and, 13–14, 19, 54, 64–65, 66–68, 70, 182–83
  populism and, 12, 14–15, 16–17, 55–56, 173, 176–78, 197, 199, 305–6
  rhetoric and, 10–11, 177, 195–200
  Roberts-Miller's analysis of, 173, 175–78, 198–200
  true belief and, 182
  "tyranny of the majority" and, 188–89, 199

  US constitutional design and attempts to prevent, 173–74, 181–82
De Mille, James, 203–4
democracy
  architecture and monuments in, 23, 243–44, 245–46, 248–50, 267
  Aristotle and, 13–14, 20–21, 56, 61–62, 124–34, 131n.29, 135–36, 137–38, 140, 141–42, 144–45, 276–77, 309–10
  Athens and, 13–14, 29, 31–32, 37, 41–42, 44–45, 48–49, 55–62, 66, 132–33, 304–5
  checks and balances and, 276–80
  demagoguery and, 15, 19, 62, 68, 185–89, 192–93, 196–97, 305–6
  democratic elitism and, 224, 240
  Eumenides and, 59–60
  iconography and, 23, 244–45, 246, 254–56
  illiberalism and, 275–76
  legislative referenda and, 312
  liberty and, 128
  lottery procedures for appointments to office in, 301, 304, 305
  "Machiavellian Democracy" and, 300–1, 312
  majoritarian legislative rules and, 304
  medieval and early modern critics of, 131–36, 144
  monumentality and, 23
  neoliberalism and, 299–300
  parliamentarism and, 201–2
  Plato and, 13–14, 19, 48–49, 54, 57–58, 62–68, 77, 276–77
  plutocracy and, 24–25, 299–300, 306–7, 310, 313
  the poor and, 20–21, 61–62, 124–34, 131n.29, 135–36, 137–38, 140, 141–42, 144–45
  populism and, 55–56, 201, 275–80, 293, 299–300, 301–4, 305, 306–10, 312
  public opinion and, 187–88
Democratic Centralism (Lenin), 309
Democratic Party (United States), 360
Demosthenes, 83–86, 89, 132–33, 184–85
De officiis (Cicero), 103–4, 120, 160–61, 166–67
De oratore (Cicero), 92, 99–100, 103–4, 147, 362, 364
De re publica (Cicero), 98, 116–17
De Senectute (Cicero), 161
De Tyranno (Bruni), 153–54, 165–66
De vita solitaria (Petrarch), 166–67
Diodotus
  The Assembly and, 36, 43–44, 54
  Mytilenians and, 35–36, 38, 42–43
  parrhêsia and, 35–37, 38, 40, 42–44, 47, 54
Disch, Lisa, 100–1
Discourses (Machiavelli), 136–39

dispositio (canon of rhetoric), 146–47, 361–62
Donation of Constantine, 107–8
Dörner, Andreas, 332–33
Douglass, Frederick, 345
Du Bois, W. E. B., 264–65
Dugan, John, 84
Duma building (Moscow), 259
Durkheim, Emile, 301–2
Duterte, Rodrigo, 12

East Germany, 249, 266
Eco, Umberto, 335–36
Egestaeans, 39–40, 41
electoral democracies, 303–4, 306–7, 308–9
elites
  corrupt elite tropes and, 3, 272–74, 277–78, 288–89, 293
  elite circulation and, 22–23, 228–29, 237–38, 239–40
  populism's condemning of, 8–10, 14–15, 16–17, 55–56, 78, 95, 177–78, 199, 272–73, 288–89, 293, 319, 333–34
Ellison, Thomas, 179–80
elocutio (canon of rhetoric), 146–47, 362
eloquence, 21, 84–85, 86, 87, 88, 89–90, 110, 147, 150–51
eloquentia (speaking out), 21, 150
Erdoğan, Recep Tayyip, 12, 255
Eumenides (Aeschylus), 59–60
Euripides, 30. *See also specific works*
European Union, 202–3, 206–7, 217–18
everyday speech, 343–46

Fallon, Jimmy, 333–34
fascism
  architecture and, 250–52, 267
  elitism and, 223, 224
  iconography and, 254
  Pareto and, 22–23, 223, 224–25
  populism and, 290
  as "thick ideology," 3
The Federalist Papers, 173–74, 181–82
Federal Reserve Building (Washington DC), 250–51
Feinberg, Ayal, 351–52
Filelfo, Francesco, 141–42
Finland, 206–7, 217
Five Star Movement, 206–7
Flavio, Biondo, 141
Florence (Italy)
  Bruni's praise of, 164–69
  Great Council and, 20–21, 125, 134–35, 143
  Guelf faction in, 104–5, 107–8, 120
  humanism and, 146–47
  Italian city-state rivalries and, 157–58, 164–65, 166–67
  Loschi's criticisms of, 157–61
  medieval discussions of democracy in, 134
  republicanism and, 20–21, 105–7, 134–36, 138, 142–43, 157–58, 163–66
  Salutati's literary defense of, 160–62
Florentine Histories (Machiavelli), 136, 169–70
France
  anti-parliamentarism in, 205–7, 210
  Fifth Republic in, 202
  Fourth Republic in, 202
  monarchy in, 116
  Napoleonic regime in, 210
  National Assembly in, 242–43, 261–62
  parliamentarism and, CROSS
  revolution (1789) in, 238–39, 254–55, 261–63
Franklin, Benjamin, 180
Franklin, Wayne, 179–80
Fraser, Nancy, 268, 274–75
Freeden, Michael, 8
Freedom Pary (FPÖ, Austria), 217
Front National (France), 219
Funeral Oration (Pericles), 48–49, 58–59

Gadamer, Hans-Georg, 25–26, 343–44, 347–50
Galeazzo II Visconti, 153–54, 157–58, 164–65, 166–67
Gamson, Joshua, 327, 330, 336–37, 339–40
Garsten, Bryan, 148–50, 344–45
George II (king of England), 205
George of Trebizond, 146–47
Germany
  anti-parliamentarism in, 205–6, 211
  East German regime (1949–89) in, 249, 266
  Nazi era in, 250–52, 308
  Weimar Republic Era in, 277–78
  West German regime (1949–89) in, 242–43, 248, 251, 252
Ghibelline faction (Florence), 104–5
Giannotti, Donato, 141, 143
Giles of Rome, 131–32
Gorgias (Plato)
  constructive engagement with the masses and, 57–58, 69–77
  demagoguery and, 14, 66–67, 68, 69, 73–74, 76, 182–83
  on *dēmos* and the rhetorician, 67–68, 74–75
  on music and collective discipline in Athens, 71, 73–74
  on Socrates' philosophical discussions and audiences, 74–77
Göring, Hermann, 207, 214
grandi, 139

Grassi, Ernesto, 363
Great Britain. *See* United Kingdom
Great Council (Florence), 20–21, 125, 134–35, 143
Great Depression, 310
Grillo, Beppe, 320–21
Guarino of Verona, 141
Guelf faction (Florence), 104–5, 107–8, 120

Haake, Hans, 256
Habermas, Jürgen, 243–44, 280–81, 282–83
Hall, Kira, 351–52
Hall of the People (India), 262, 263–64
Hamilton, Alexander, 180–82
Hankins, James, 141, 151–52, 153–54, 164–68, 169–70
Herwegh, Georg, 210–11
Hippolytus (Euripides), 30
Hirtius, Aulus, 87
History (Thucydides)
  demagoguery and, 13, 56
  early modern translations into Latin of, 132–33
  Egestaeans and, 39–40, 41
  Mytilenians and, 34–36, 38–39, 42–43
  Nicias and, 39–46
  parrhêsia and, 18, 34–44
  Sicilian expedition and, 39–44, 60–61
History of the Florentine People (Bruni), 166–67, 169–70
Hitler, Adolf, 260, 309, 351–52
Hitz, Zena, 65n.24
Homer, 32–33
Honig, Bonnie, 351–52
House of Cards (television show), 332–33
House of Commons, 258–59
How to Found a Republic (Patrizi), 169–70
How to Tell a Flatterer from a Friend (Plutarch), 176, 183–85
humanism
  education and, 147–48, 151, 155, 163
  republicanism and, 104–5, 123, 136, 141
  rhetoric and, 21, 146–51, 157–58, 159, 167–68, 169–70
  virtuous rule and, 152–53, 164–65, 168–70
  wealth and, 141
  See also The Renaissance
Hungary, 157, 206, 212, 275–76
hyperreality, 25, 315–17, 331–32, 334–37, 338–39

The Iliad (Homer), 32–33
India, 242–43, 262

inventio (canon of rhetoric), 361–62
Ion (Euripides), 30
isêgoria (equality in public speaking), 18, 31–33, 51
Italy
  anti-parliamentarism in, 206–7
  Bolshevism in, 306
  fascist era in, 250–51, 252
  French invasion (1494) of, 134–35
  "politainment" in, 315–16
  populism in medieval era in, 20
  urban expansion during medieval era in, 20
  See also specific cities

Jacobinism, 230–31, 306, 308
James, William, 283
January 6th insurrection (United States, 2021)
  "big lie" of election denialism and, 342
  gendered analysis of, 265
  legitimacy of Congressional representatives denied in, 261
  "legitimate political discourse" framing of, 25–26, 342–43, 360
  peaceful transfer of power targeted by, 341
  personalized identification with Trump's leadership and, 337
  police officers attacked in, 341
  Republican Party and, 360
  rhetorical resonance and, 25–26, 343–44
  Trump and, 337, 341, 350–51
  US Capitol seized and damaged in, 242, 263–64, 265–66, 341
Jefferson, Thomas, 245, 259
John of Jandun, 131–32
John of Paris, 131–32
John of Viterbo, 113–14
Johnson, Lyndon B., 345

Karlsruhe (Germany), 248
Kelly, Casey Ryan, 351–52
Kepes, György, 253–54, 256
King, Desmond, 351–52
Knott, Stephen F., 173

Laclau, Ernesto
  authoritarian tendency in populism and, 274–75
  concentration of power and, 284
  discursive practices and, 4
  on populism and "authenticity of the people," 273–74
  on populism as "empty signifier," 8
  populism as political logic and, 2–3, 5, 225

INDEX   371

rejection of mainstream democratic
  institutions by, 278–80
Lakoff, Robin, 337
Lamachus, 39–40, 53–54
Lane, Melissa, 13, 182–83
La rettorica (Latini), 104–5, 116–17, 120
La Revelliere-Lepeaux, Louis-Marie, 263
Laski, Harold, 284
Latham, Earl, 271
Latini, Brunetto
  on Catilinarian conspiracy, 110, 112–13,
    117–18, 120, 121–22
  Cicero and, 20, 104–5, 106–7, 109–11, 112–
    13, 114–15, 116–18, 121–22
  on civic lords' qualifications, 118–21
  on connection between eloquence and public
    affairs, 109
  constitutional government typology of,
    115–17, 118
  on counsel and oratory, 111
  demagoguery and, 112–13
  on eloquence and wisdom, 110
  exile from Florence of, 120
  factionalism opposed by, 120–21
  Florentine politics and government and,
    20, 104–5
  Guelf faction and, 104–5, 107–8, 120
  liberty and, 113–14
  on oratory and social order, 110–11
  Pocock on, 107–8
  populism and, 20, 105–6
  republicanism and, 20, 104–9, 112, 113–15,
    118–20, 121–22, 123
  on rhetoric and governance, 109–10
  Roman Republic in the works of, 112, 114–
    15, 116, 117–18, 121–22
  on the study of politics, 116
Latter-Day Pamphlets (Carlyle), 210
Laudatio Florentinae Urbis (*Panegyric of the
  City of Florence,* Bruni), 157, 163, 165–66
Laws (Plato), 57–58, 69–73
Le Bon, Gustave, 223
Lee, Alexander, 105–6
Lefort, Claude, 278–80
Lenin, Vladimir Ilyich, 219, 305–6, 309
Lepoutre, Maxime, 350–51, 359
Lesbos, 34
Levitsky, Steven, 296–97
liberalism
  as anti-political doctrine, 270–71
  checks and balances and, 271
  constraints on power and, 280
  deliberation and justification in, 8–9, 14–15

democracy and, 280
ethical pluralism and, 282
pluralism and, 24, 269–70
populism and, 280
representative government and, 15
Liebknecht, Wilhelm, 210–11
Life of Alcibiades (Plutarch), 176, 183–85
Li livres dou tresor (Latini). *See* Latini, Brunetto
Lind, Michael, 12
Lindblom, Charles, 271, 285–86, 289–93, 294–
  95, 297
Livy, 153–54, 165–66
Löbe Haus (Berlin), 258, 262
Lomas, Charles W., 182
Loschi, Antonio, 157–61
Louis Bonaparte, 214–15
Louis I (king of Naples), 153
Lucchese, Filippo del, 124–25
Lutyens, Edwin, 262

Machiavelli, Niccolò
  Aristotle and, 125, 136–38, 144
  elitism and, 224–25
  on empowered populations' correct
    judgments, 308–9, 312–13
  in Florentine government, 134–35, 169–70
  humanism and, 147–48
  on need for institutional arrangements
    securing economic equality, 310–11
  Pareto and, 231–32, 239
  political punishments and, 314
  Polybius and, 136–37
  the poor and, 20–21, 138–43, 144–45
  regime typology of, 136–38, 144–45
  republicanism and, 20–21, 106–7, 123–25,
    136, 137–43, 144–45, 309–10
  Savonarola and, 136
  Sparta and, 141–42
Madison, James, 181–82, 293–96, 308–9
Maduro, Nicolás, 12
Mar-a-Lago Club (Florida), 266
Marius, 95–96
Marquis of Monferrato, 153
Marsilius of Padua, 104–5, 123, 131–32, 133–35
Marx, Karl, 138–39, 205–6, 217, 285–86
Mason, George, 181–82
McCarthyism, 260, 271, 289–90
McCormick, John, 124–25, 138–39
Medici, Pietro de', 134–35
memoria (canon of rhetoric), 146–47, 361–62
Mencken, H. L., 175
Michels, Robert, 22–23, 201, 222–23, 289–90
Middle Ages, 104–7, 121–22

Mill, John Stuart, 174, 278–80
Miller, Hayley, 353
Mills, C. Wright, 289–90
Modi, Narendra, 12, 242–43, 262
Moffitt, Benjamin, 2–3, 7, 269–70, 281–82, 297–98
Monoson, Sara, 63, 71–72
Moonves, Leslie, 320–21
Morales, Evo, 269–70, 273–74, 275–76
Morgan, Kathryn, 70–71
Morstein-Marx, Robert, 79–80
Mosca, Gaetano, 22–23, 222n.1, 222–25, 289–90
Mouffe, Chantal
   discursive practices and, 4
   left populism endorsed by, 274–75, 293
   on neoliberalism's decline, 268
   on populism and democracy, 275–76
   on "the populist moment" and "the return of the political," 219–20
   on "the spiritualisation of enmity," 296–97
Mudde, Cas
   on populism and anti-pluralism, 199, 269, 271–72, 281
   on populism and democracy, 275–77
   on populism and elite theory, 289–90
   on populism and "general will," 272–73
   on populism and ideology, 178n.22, 319
   on populism and issues excluded from the political agenda, 291, 293
   populism typology of, 2–3
   on "the populist Zeitgeist," 320–21
Müller, Jan-Werner
   on alternative ways to articulate populist aims, 296–97
   on anti-democratic nature of populism, 275–76
   on checks and balances, 271, 276–81, 282–83
   on populism and anti-pluralism, 175–76, 199–200, 269–70, 272–73, 281–82
   on populism and the "general will," 272–73
   on populism as "moralistic imagination of politics," 177–78
   "single authentic people" concept rejected by, 273–74
Mumford, Lewis, 248
Münkler, Herfried, 249–50
Murdoch, Rupert, 323
Mussolini, Benito, 251–52, 305–6
Mytilenians, 34–36, 38–39, 42–43

narodniki, 16–17
Nazism, 250–52, 308
neoliberalism, 268, 299–300

Netanyahu, Benjamin, 12
New Haven (Connecticut), 286–88
Nicias, 39–46
Nicomachean Ethics (Aristotle), 153–54, 161
Nietzsche, Friedrich, 241
Novara (Italy), 153–54
nudus speaking style, 19–20, 80–83, 88–93, 96

Oakley, Francis, 105–6
Obama, Barack, 328, 353–54
Ober, Josiah, 56, 129–30
Ochoa Espejo, Paulina, 296–97
On Friendship (Cicero), 154
Oration for Nanni Strozzi (Bruni), 168–69
Orator (Cicero), 83–85, 88
Orbán, Victor, 212, 214, 275–76
Oresme, Nicole, 131–32
ornatus (use of tropes to adorn a discourse), 81–82, 363
Ostrogorski, Moises, 223

Palast der Republik (East Berlin, East Germany), 249, 266
Palatine Hill (Rome), 243
Palatul Parlamentului (Bucharest, Romania), 249
Panathenaicus (Aelius Aristides), 165–66
Pandolfini, Pier Filippo, 142–43
Pareto, Vilfredo
   anti-parliamentarism and, 223, 224–25
   biographical background of, 222
   demagoguery and, 236–38, 240
   democracy and, 22–23, 223
   derivations and, 227–28, 232–36, 240
   elite circulation and, 228–29, 237–38, 239–40
   emotions in politics and, 232–36
   enthymemes and, 235–36
   fascism and, 22–23, 223, 224–25
   French Revolution and, 238–39
   Machiavelli and, 231–32, 239
   plutocracy and economic inequality criticized by, 22–23, 224, 225–26, 230, 239
   residues and, 227–30, 233, 236–39
   social heterogeneity and, 227–28
   speculators and, 225–26, 229, 233, 236–37, 240
   theory of argumentation and, 234
Paris Commune (1871), 205–6
parliamentarism
   debate and deliberation in, 201–2, 203–4, 209, 212, 214, 215, 257–58
   European Union and, 202–3
   France and, 202
   procedural style of politics and, 201–2, 203–4, 209, 213–14, 216, 258

professional politicians and, 203, 207
temporal dynamics and, 204, 215–16, 217–18
transparency and, 253
United Kingdom and, 202–3, 204
See also anti-parliamentarism
Parnell, Charles, 210
parrhêsia (frank speech)
Aeschylus and, 29
Alcibiades and, 41–42
Aristophanes and, 18, 30, 31, 50–54
The Assembly and, 18, 31, 33, 36, 43–44, 54
Cleon and, 34–35, 38
definition of, 29
democracy and, 49, 54
Diodotus and, 35–37, 38, 40, 42–44, 47, 54
Euripides and, 30
History and, 18, 34–44
isêgoria and, 31–33, 50
Nicias and, 40–41, 42–44
Plato and, 18, 31, 44–49, 54
political benefits of, 36–37
Sicily expedition and, 39–40
Socrates's practice of, 33
stability potentially threatened by, 18, 30, 33, 44–45
subterfuge and, 36, 40, 42–43, 44–45, 47, 53–54
true belief and, 18, 42–43
trust and, 37
Patrizi, Francesco, 131–32, 134–35, 150, 169–70
Pedullà, Gabriele, 124–25, 132–33
Peloponnesian War, 34, 44–45. See also *History* (Thucydides)
People's Party (United States), 16–17, 306, 309
Pericles, 48–49, 58–59, 127–28, 132–33, 165–66, 305–6
Perón, Eva, 315–16, 317, 318, 322, 327–28, 331–32, 338
Perón, Juan Domingo, 315–16, 318, 322
The Persians (Aeschylus), 29
Persian Wars, 35
Peter of Auvergne, 131–32, 134
Petrarch (Francesco Petrarca)
Cicero and, 146–47, 153–55
Cola di Rienzo and, 156–57
friendship and, 153–55
humanism and, 147–48, 151–52, 155, 163
poetry and, 154–55
republicanism and, 151–52
virtuous rule and, 152–57, 169–70
Philippics (Cicero), 83–84, 89–90, 92–93, 97–98, 159–60
Philips, Anne, 269

Phoenician Women (Euripides), 30
Piano, Natasha, 224–26, 230
The Pilot (Cooper), 180
Piñera, Sebastián, 331–32
Plato
on collective gatherings, 69, 70–72, 77
demagoguery and, 13–14, 19, 54, 64–65, 66–68, 70, 182–83
democracy and, 13–14, 19, 48–49, 54, 57–58, 62–68, 77, 276–77
isêgoria and, 31–32
parrhêsia and, 18, 31, 44–49, 54
populism and, 19, 55, 57
See also specific works
pluralism
checks and balances and, 271, 276–77, 281, 285, 294–96
Cold War and, 271–72
community-power debates and, 286–88
diversity and, 269–70
ethical pluralism and, 269–70, 281–83
identity politics and, 269
interest groups and, 285–86
liberalism and, 24, 269–70
lifestyle pluralism and, 282
metaphysical pluralism and, 283–84
oligarchy and, 288–89
political pluralism, 284–90, 294–95
polyarchy and, 285
populism and, 16–17, 24, 177–78, 199–200, 209, 268–72, 281–82, 288–89, 293–98
subcultural pluralism and, 292–93
Plutarch
Asianist rhetorical style and, 91
Cooper and, 178–79, 181, 183–84, 185–86
demagoguery and, 13, 21–22, 175–77, 178–79, 181, 182–85, 189–90, 195
early modern translations into Latin of, 132–33
nineteenth-century US readers of, 180
Pocock, John, 107–9, 112
"politainment," 25, 315–17, 332–35, 338–39
Politics (Aristotle), 126–34, 144, 153–54, 182–83
Polsby, Nelson, 271
polyarchy
conditions of, 292
dispersion of power and, 290
institutional reforms to preserve, 297–98
oligarchy and, 289–90
political pluralism and, 285
populism and, 290–93
precariousness of, 289–93, 297
Polybius, 136–37

popularis rhetoric in the Roman Republic
  Cicero's criticism of, 19–20, 82–83, 89–94, 96, 97–102
  identification with the audience and, 96–97, 101–2
  nudus (naked) speaking style and, 19–20, 80–83, 88–93, 96
  Sallust and, 95–96
  social antagonisms and, 101–2
populism
  anti-parliamentarism and, 201–2, 204, 206–7, 208–9, 212–13, 215, 218–19, 220
  authoritarian tendency in, 272–75, 280, 285, 290
  "bad manners" and, 4, 7, 10, 14–15, 320, 325–26, 331–32
  charismatic leadership and, 4–5
  communicative dimensions of, 319–24
  concentration of power and, 274–75, 288–89
  content approach to, 2–3, 4–7
  decisionism and, 8
  demaguery and, 12, 14–15, 16–17, 55–56, 173, 176–78, 197, 199, 305–6
  democracy and, 55–56, 201, 275–80, 293, 299–300, 301–4, 305, 306–10, 312
  discourse and, 2–3, 4, 8–9
  elites condemned in, 6–7, 8–10, 14–15, 16–17, 55–56, 78, 95, 177–78, 199, 272–73, 288–89, 293, 319, 333–34
  "fake news" and, 316–17
  form approach to, 2–3, 4–7
  Global Financial Crisis of 2008 and, 268
  identity politics and, 177–78
  ideological dimensions of, 319, 320–21, 334–37, 338–39
  ideology and, 2–3, 6, 7, 8–9
  liberalism and, 280
  national identity and, 307
  nostalgia and, 217
  oligarchy and, 288–89
  "the people" valorized in, 8–10, 14–15, 16–17, 55–56, 78, 177–78, 212–13, 272–73, 277–78, 288–89, 293, 319–20
  pluralism and, 16–17, 24, 177–78, 199–200, 209, 268–72, 281–82, 288–89, 293–98
  plutocracy and, 24–25, 299
  political enmity and, 308
  as political logic, 2–3, 5, 25
  polyarchy and, 290–93
  popular sovereignty and, 3, 7, 14–15, 212
  "populist mood" and, 9–10
  representative government and, 15–16
  rhetorical approaches to studying, 2, 10, 361–62, 363–64
  rhetorical strategies and, 78–79
  social media and, 215, 274–75, 321–22
  taboo breaking and, 320–21
  technocracy and, 212–13
  as "thin" ideology, 3, 8–9, 14–15, 178n.22, 319
  xenophobia and, 24–25, 274–75
Postman, Neil, 322–23, 332
Praça dos Três Poderes (Brasília, Brazil), 254
The Prince (Machiavelli), 228–29, 239
Pro Archia (Cicero), 154–55, 157
Pro Plancio (Cicero), 93–94
Pro Sestio (Cicero), 93, 98–99, 103–4
Protagoras (Plato), 31–32, 75–76
Ptolemy of Lucca
  democracy and, 131–32, 133–35, 138
  liberty and, 113–14
  papal superiority doctrine and, 107–8
  republicanism and, 104–5, 106–7, 123, 135–36
Putin, Vladimir, 12

Quintilian, 146–47, 363
Quirini, Lauro, 131–32, 164–65

Rancière, Jacques, 276–77, 278–80
Rasmussen, Steen Eiler, 246
Rawls, John, 281–82
Reagan, Ronald, 322–23, 327
Redecker, Eva von, 264
Reichstag building (Berlin), 247–48, 253, 256, 261–62
The Renaissance, 21, 104–5, 146–51, 252
The Republic (Plato)
  on collective behavior in Athens, 70–72
  demaguery and, 54, 64–65, 67, 68, 69
  democracy and, 19, 48–49, 54, 57–58, 62–67, 68
  on *dēmos* and power, 68, 69
  parrhêsia and, 48–49, 54
  on relations between women and men, 48
republicanism
  Cambridge School and, 123–24
  constitutional government and, 119–20
  exclusivist idea of, 123–24
  humanism and, 104–5, 123, 136, 141
  liberty and, 113–14
  the poor and, 20–21, 138–43, 144–45
  populism and, 20–21, 124–25
  "radical republicanism" and, 124–25, 136, 142–43
  rationalist republicanism and, 20, 103–4, 108–9
  respublica and, 124

rhetorical republicanism and, 20, 103–4, 108–9, 111, 114–15
Roman Republic and, 105–8, 112, 113–14, 118, 121–22
voluntary agreement and, 114–15
wealth and, 138–39, 141–42
Republican Party (United States), 342–43, 360
Re regimine civitatum (John of Viterbo), 113–14
rhetoric
anti-parliamentarism and, 22, 204, 209–13, 220
canons of, 146–47, 361–62
demagoguery and, 10–11, 177, 195–200
disruptive rhetoric and, 10
everyday speech and, 343–46
humanism and, 21, 146–51, 157–58, 159, 167–68, 169–70
populism studied through examination of, 2, 10, 361–62, 363–64
The Renaissance, 21, 146, 147–50
rhetoric revival scholarship, 10–11, 159, 344–46, 350, 358–59
Rhetoric (Aristotle), 129–30, 146–47, 168
rhetorical resonance
"big lie" of US election denialism and, 346–47, 350–51, 359–60
everyday speech and, 343–46
horizons of understanding and, 346–51
January 6 insurrection and, 25–26, 343–44
repetition and, 360
Richard, Carl J., 180
Ripa, Cesare, 255
Rittinghausen, Moritz, 205–6
Robert of Naples, 152
Roberts-Miller, Patricia, 173, 175–78, 198–200
Robespierre, Maximilen, 261–62
Roe v. Wade, 295–96
Roman Republic
classical architecture and, 246
constitutional government of, 117–18, 121–22
demagoguery and, 14
Latini on, 112, 114–15, 116, 117–18, 121–22
liberty and, 113–14
medieval republicanism and, 105–8, 112, 113–14, 118, 121–22
See also *popularis* rhetoric in the Roman Republic
Rome, medieval era in, 118–19, 156–57
Rosanvallon, Pierre, 15
Rosenblitt, J. A., 79–80, 95
Rousseau, Jean-Jacques
on enlightened agreement, 282–83

popular festivals and, 262–63
popular sovereignty championed over representation by, 207–8, 213–14
rhetoric and, 148–50
Rovira Kaltwasser, Cristóbal
on populism and anti-pluralism, 269, 271–72, 281
on populism and democracy, 275–77
on populism and elite theory, 289–90
on populism and "general will," 272–73
on populism and issues excluded from the political agenda, 291, 293
Rummens, Stefan, 280
"Rumors of War" (Wiley), 256

Sallust, 79–80, 82–83, 95–96, 97, 112, 153–54
Salutati, Coluccio, 123, 146–47, 157–58, 160–63
Salvini, Matteo, 12, 25, 315, 316, 324–25, 327
Sandel, Adam, 350
Sanders, Bernie, 313
Sartre, Jean-Paul, 213
Savonarola, 134–36, 138, 141–43
Saward, Michael, 100–1
Scala, 135–36, 138
Schmidt, Helmut, 248
Schmitt, Carl, 9–10, 207–8, 220, 257–58, 277–80, 309
Scholasticism, 123–24, 147–48
Schröder, Gerhard, 316
Schumpeter, Joseph, 285–86
Scotto di Carlo, Giuseppina, 351–52
Senate (Rome), 98, 99–100, 117–18, 140, 210, 310–11
Senate (United States), 259
Seneca, 153–54
Shinawatra, Thaksin, 331–32
Sicilian expedition (Peloponnesian War), 10, 39–44, 60–61
Sighele, Scipio, 223
Sipilä, Juha, 213
Skinner, Quentin, 105–6, 108–9, 123, 151–52, 363, 364
Smith, Rogers, 351–52
socialism, 3, 214, 238–39, 266, 301–2
Socrates. See *Apology of Socrates* (Plato)
Soini, Timo, 209, 211
Solon, 58, 127–28, 132–33
Sparta
Acharnians and, 50, 52–53
citizen warriors in, 141
Peloponnesian War victory by, 44–45
republicanism and, 141–42
Sicily expedition and, 40–41

Speer, Albert, 250–51, 262
Stacey, Peter, 151–52
Stone, Roger, 357
Strache, Hans-Christian, 327
Straumann, Benjamin, 108–9
Street, John, 327, 333
Stücklen, Richard, 242–43
Stucky, Mary, 351–52
Suetonius, 91, 154–55

Taine, Hippolyte, 230–31, 238–39
Táíwò, Olúfémi O., 245
Tan, James, 94, 96
Tarde, Gabriel, 223
Tatum, W. Jeffrey, 93
Taylor, John Orville, 174
Tea Party, 307–8, 356, 360
Terragni, Giuseppe, 252
Thesmophoriazusae (Aristophanes), 30, 31–32
Thirty Tyrants (Athens), 44–45, 56
Thucydides. *See History* (Thucydides)
Tiberius Gracchus, 306, 310–11
Tocqueville, Alexis de, 174, 278–80, 293–95
Trattato di Sociologia Generale (*The Mind and Society,* Pareto). *See* Pareto, Vilfredo
True Finns, 206–7, 212–13, 217
Truman, David, 271
Trump, Donald
  anti-parliamentarism and, 206
  The Apprentice television show and, 328–29, 332–33, 334–35
  "big lie" of election denialism and, 292, 342–43, 346–47, 353–54, 356, 359, 360
  celebrity politics and, 25, 315, 316, 327–29, 331–34, 338–39
  comedic rhetoric and, 351–52
  demagoguery and, 12, 14
  democratic norms attacked by, 296–97
  federal civic architecture executive order (2020) by, 241–42
  hyperreality and, 335–36
  inaugural speech (2017) by, 320–21
  January 6 insurrection and, 337, 341, 350–51
  Mar-a-Lago as site of government work for, 266
  "politainment" and, 315, 316
  political enmity among the supporters of, 308
  populism and, 212–13, 273–74, 316, 320–21, 327, 338–39
  social media and, 324–26, 334–35
Twitter, 355–56, 358

Ulbricht, Walter, 249
United Kingdom
  anti-parliamentarism in, 205, 209–10
  Brexit vote (2016) in, 312–13
  parliamentarism in, 202–3, 204
  Westminster parliamentary building in, 242–43, 250, 258–59
Urbinati, Nadia, 78n.1, 240, 290
US Capitol attack (2021). *See* January 6th insurrection (United States, 2021)
US Capitol building, architecture of, 262, 263–64

Vatter, Miguel, 124–25
Vennamo, Veikko, 208–9, 211
Vergerio, Paolo, 141
Vettori, Piero, 131–32
Visconti, Filippo Maria, 166–67
Visconti, Giangaleazzo, 157–58, 166–67
Voltaire, 254–55

Walpole, Robert, 205
Washington DC, architecture in, 245, 250–51, 262, 263–64, 265–66
Wasps (Aristophanes), 60–61
Weber, Max, 211
Wedeen, Lisa, 354–55
Weimar Republic, 277–78
West Germany, 242–43, 248, 251, 252
Westminster parliamentary building (London), 242–43, 250, 258–59
White, Steven K., 281
Who Governs? (Dahl), 286–89
Wiley, Kehinde, 256
Wilhelm II (kaiser of Germany), 247–48, 256
Witt, Ronald, 105–6
Wolf, Martin, 12
Wolin, Sheldon, 276–77
World War II, 310

Young, Iris Marion, 345–46

Ziblatt, Daniel, 296–97